algeria:
the politics of a socialist revolution

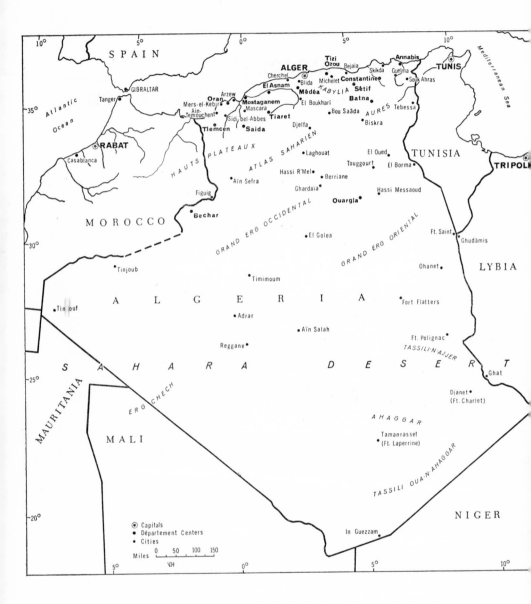

SPAIN

10°   5°   0°

Mediterranean Sea

Atlantic Ocean

GIBRALTAR

Tanger

Tizi Ozou
ALGER   Bejaia   Annabis
Cherchel   Blida Michelet Constantine   TUNIS
El Asnam   KABYLIA   Sétif   Guelma
Arzew   Médéa   Batna   Souk Ahras
Oran Mostaganem El Boukhari
Mers-el-Kebir Mascara   Bou Saâda   AURES   Tebessa
Sidi bel-Abbes Tiaret   Biskra
Aïn-Temouchent
Tlemcen   Saïda   Djelfa

RABAT   TUNISIA

Casablanca

35°

HAUTS PLATEAUX   Laghouat   El Oued
                                 Touggourt   El Borma
ATLAS SAHARIEN   Hassi R'Mel   Berriane
Aïn Sefra   Ghardaia   Hassi Messaoud
Figuig   Ouargla   Ft. Saint
MOROCCO   Ghudàmis
Bechar   GRAND ERG OCCIDENTAL   GRAND ERG ORIENTAL   LYBIA

30°   El Golea

Tinjoub   Ohanet
                Timimoum
TRIPOLI

ALGERIA   Fort Flatters
Tin Jouf
Adrar
Aïn Salah   Ft. Polignac
Reggane   TASSILI·N·AJJER

SAHARA   DESERT   Ghat
25°
ERG CHECH   Djanet
                                        (Ft. Charlet)
MAURITANIA
MALI   AHAGGAR
                    Tamanrasset
                    (Ft. Laperrine)

TASSILI OUA·N·AHAGGAR

20°
NIGER

⊛ Capitals
● Département Centers
• Cities
        0   50   100 150
Miles ⊢──┴──┴──┴──┤

In Guezzam

5°   0°   5°   10°

ALGERIA
the politics of a socialist revolution

david and marina ottaway

UNIVERSITY OF CALIFORNIA PRESS
BERKELEY AND LOS ANGELES · 1970

UNIVERSITY OF CALIFORNIA PRESS
BERKELEY AND LOS ANGELES, CALIFORNIA
UNIVERSITY OF CALIFORNIA PRESS, LTD.
LONDON, ENGLAND
COPYRIGHT © 1970 BY
THE REGENTS OF THE UNIVERSITY OF CALIFORNIA
LIBRARY OF CONGRESS CATALOG CARD NUMBER: 70–83210
PRINTED IN THE UNITED STATES OF AMERICA

to nicholas

preface

We intend this book to be a political history of Algeria and an analysis of the political behavior of the men who played a prominent role in that history. It is our contention that it is this political behavior, a reflection of the spirit of politics of the country that has given to the Algerian socialist revolution its peculiar character, while ideologies and foreign models have played only a secondary role. Some will take issue with the use of the term "socialist revolution" in reference to events in Algeria since 1962. It is our feeling, however, that such an objection is the consequence more of an abstract notion of socialism than of a comparison with the realities in other countries generally accepted as socialist. In our study we have chosen to emphasize those elements that are peculiar to Algerian politics rather than the problems the country shares with other new nations. For this reason the book is not organized altogether according to what might be considered classical areas of inquiry. Rather, we followed the time sequence of the major events during the period under study, using each event to discuss the broader issue involved.

The material for this book was gathered during a three-year stay in the country, much of it through conversations and interviews with Algerian politicians and laymen. To all those who, wittingly or unwittingly, helped us to understand the complexities of Algerian politics, we extend sincere thanks. We also owe a large debt of gratitude to Professor Immanuel Wallerstein of Columbia University, who kindly agreed to read the manuscript, offering perceptive criticism and much needed encouragement. Our close friend John McKenzie devoted long hours to a close reading of the text, waging an unrelenting battle in behalf of clarity of expression. If the book is easily readable, it is largely due to his persistent efforts.

The map was drawn by Mrs. Virginia Herrick.

D. and M. O.

contents

Glossary

AAPSO	Afro-Asian Peoples' Solidarity Organization	An organization of African and Asian political groups, often but not always government sponsored, and of nationalist movements
ALN	Armée de Libération Nationale	The Algerian nationalist army; the military arm of the FLN
ANP	Armée Nationale Populaire	The post-independence Algerian army
APS	Algérie Presse Service	The Algerian government press agency
BNASS	Bureau National d'Animation du Secteur Socialiste	The organization put in charge of the self-managed sector in 1963
CCE	Comité de Coordination et d'Exécution	The executive body of the FLN between 1956 and 1958
CCRA	Coopératives de Commercialisation de la Réforme Agraire	The organization in charge of commercializing produce of the self-managed farms
CCSA	Caisse Centrale des Sociétés Agricoles	The government credit and loan bank for the socialist farm sector
CGT	Confédération Générale du Travail	A French Communist-dominated labor union
CNDR	Comité National pour la Défense de la Révolution	A coalition of opposition groups established in July 1964
CNRA	Conseil National de la Revolution Algerienne	Legislative body of the FLN between 1956 and 1962
CNS	Compagnie Nationale de Sécurité	National Security Corps
CRUA	Comité Révolutionaire d'Unité et d'Action	A revolutionary organization founded in April 1954, soon replaced by the FLN

FEMP	Fédération des Etudiants Militants du Parti	A party-sponsored student organization formed in 1968
FFS	Front des Forces Socialistes	An opposition party led by Hocine Ait Ahmed
FLN	Front de Libération Nationale	The Algerian nationalist organization, which became the country's official party after independence
FNLA	Frente Nacional para Libertação de Angola	An Angolan nationalist movement led by Holden Roberto
FNTT	Fédération Nationale des Travailleurs de la Terre	The Algerian farm workers union
FTEC	Fédération des Travailleurs de l'Enseignement et de la Culture	The Algerian teachers union
GPRA	Gouvernement Provisoire de la République Algérienne	The provisional wartime government of the Algerian nationalists
ICFTU	International Confederation of Free Trade Unions	An organization of non-Communist trade unions
JFLN	Jeunesse du Front de Libération Nationale	The FLN youth organization
MDRA	Mouvement Démocratique du Renouveau Algérien	An opposition party founded by Belkacem Krim in 1967
MNA	Mouvement National Algérien	A wartime nationalist movement led by Messali Hadj and opposed to the FLN
MPLA	Movimento Popular para Libertação de Angola	An Angolan nationalist movement led by Dr. Agosthino Neto
MTLD	Mouvement pour le Triomphe des Libertés Démocratiques	A nationalist movement led by Messali Hadj before the war of independence
OAS	Organisation de l'Armée Secrète	The French terrorist organization formed in 1961
OAU	Organization of African Unity	An organization of African states based in Addis Ababa, Ethiopia
OCAM	Organisation Commune Africaine et Malgache	An organization of moderate French-speaking African states

OCRA	Organisation Clandestine de la Révolution Algérienne	An opposition group formed in 1966 by Mohamed Lebjaoui
ONRA	Office National de la Réforme Agraire	The government office in charge of the socialist farm sector from 1963 to 1967
ORP	Organisation de la Résistance Populaire	A clandestine opposition party formed by Mohamed Harbi and Hocine Zahouane in 1965; it became PAGS in 1967
PAGS	Parti d'Avant Garde Socialiste	The opposition party that replaced the ORP in 1967
PCA	Parti Communiste Algérien	The Algerian Communist Party, clandestine since December 1962
PLO	Palestine Liberation Organization	The leading Palestinian nationalist organization
PPA	Parti du Peuple Algérien	An Algerian nationalist party led by Messali Hadj, replaced by the MTLD in 1946
PRS	Parti de la Révolution Socialiste	An opposition party founded by Mohamed Boudiaf in 1962
SAP	Sociétés Agricoles de Prévoyance	A subsidiary of the ONRA in charge of provisioning self-managed farms
UDMA	Union Démocratique du Manifeste Algérien	An Algerian nationalist party founded by Ferhat Abbas in 1946
UDRS	Union pour la Défense de la Révolution Socialiste	An opposition party founded by Mohamed Boudiaf, Mohand ou el-Hadj, and Belkacem Krim in 1963
UGEMA	Union Générale des Etudiants Musulmans Algériens	The wartime nationalist student organization
UGTA	Union Générale des Travailleurs Algériens	The Algerian labor federation
UNCAC	Union Nationale des Coopératives Agricoles de Commercialisation	A union of cooperatives set up in 1966 to commercialize produce of self-managed farms; it replaced the CCRA
UNEA	Union Nationale des Etudiants Algériens	The post-independence Algerian student organization

| UNFA | Union Nationale des Femmes Algériennes | The Algerian women's organization |
| UPA | Union Populaire Algérienne | An Algerian nationalist party formed by Ferhat Abbas in 1938 |

introduction

T he outbreak of the Algerian Revolution in November 1954 her-
alded the beginning of a new era of revolution and guerrilla
warfare throughout Africa. Although Algeria was not the first
African territory to demand its independence, it was the first to launch
a full-scale war of national liberation and thus the first to make an international issue out of the "internal affair" of a colonial power. The
war in Algeria startled the Western world and provoked in France a
long series of political crises which finally destroyed the Fourth Republic and brought General Charles de Gaulle to power. It persuaded
France to grant independence to Tunisia and Morocco as well as to its
fifteen sub-Saharan colonies before other such costly wars could break
out. Britain and Belgium found in the Algerian Revolution one more
sign that the tide of colonial history had turned, and they made no attempt to hold on to their African colonies by force of arms.

In addition, Algeria's attainment of independence in July 1962 was
an event of great importance to the Third World, where it was seen
as eloquent proof of the ability and determination of colonized peoples
to take their fate into their own hands. To liberation movements
throughout Africa, Algerian independence seemed to promise that
their struggle would not be in vain. In the Arab world, it was interpreted as a victory of the entire Arab nation over the Western powers.

Under the leadership of President Ahmed Ben Bella, Algeria immediately embarked upon a second revolution, aimed at destroying the
social and economic order of the colonial era and at making Algeria
into a socialist country. Thousands of rich French farms, small factories,
hotels, cafés, and movie houses were nationalized and put under the
management of workers' committees. But the "socialist revolution" did
not go much further—except in Ben Bella's speeches and on the socialist
banners that bedecked the country. Communist diplomats and Marxist
intellectuals in Algiers seriously doubted that the measures taken
amounted to a socialist revolution, and Eastern bloc observers joked

in private that it was impossible to build socialism without socialists. Fidel Castro, despite his warm friendship with Ben Bella, repeatedly postponed an announced visit to Algeria, reportedly because he too doubted that the country was really a "socialist sister." Even Ben Bella's rather idealistic Marxist advisors began to wonder whether Algeria's helter-skelter course was the road to socialism.

Many in Algeria and abroad, however, believed in the Algerian "socialist revolution and hoped that it would spread from its North African stronghold over the entire continent. Algeria became a standard-bearer of the "African revolution," and Ben Bella set out to rally progressive forces throughout Africa against the "imperialist" Western nations, which he saw as striving to trap the weak and newly independent countries of Africa in the web of neocolonialism. He turned Algeria into a major training center for African revolutionaries and a haven for political exiles from all over the world.

Within a few months after independence, Algeria was being courted by the major powers of the world, and the country's course was being watched with interest or concern in many capitals. President Charles de Gaulle considered Algeria France's "narrow door into the Third World," and he was determined not to make Algeria into a new Cuba by turning his back on this former colony. Soviet Premier Nikita Khrushchev welcomed Ben Bella to Moscow as "Comrade President" and bestowed upon him the Lenin Peace Prize and the Hero of the Soviet Union Medal, the highest honors ever accorded to a leader of the Third World. The Chinese Communists also chose Algeria as a prime target for their efforts in Africa and did their best to befriend its revolutionary leaders. Interpreting Algeria's course as a steady drift into the Communist sphere of influence, Washington marked a new danger point on the map of the cold war.

The Third World also took note of the course of events in Algeria. Fidel Castro hailed Algeria's new socialist revolution and called Ben Bella his brother, joining him in ranting against the trinity of "colonialism, neocolonialism, and imperialism." Egypt's President Gamal Abdel Nasser joined forces with Ben Bella to wage a *jihad* (holy war) against the "reactionary" Arab regimes and to export the socialist revolution to other parts of Africa. Together they fought Algeria's border war against "feudal" Morocco, shipped Soviet arms to the Congolese rebels, and worked to build the movement for Afro-Asian solidarity into an organized force. By 1964, when the African chiefs of state were called upon to select a site for the forthcoming second Afro-Asian Conference, it seemed only natural for the choice to fall upon Algiers.

The Afro-Asian Conference never took place. On June 19, 1965, ten days before sixty African and Asian heads of state were to gather in Algeria, Ben Bella was ousted by Colonel Houari Boumediene, his minister of defense, in a military *coup d'état*. The conference was cancelled, but the repercussions of Ben Bella's overthrow did not stop there. A shattering blow was dealt to the Afro-Asian solidarity movement and to the "African revolution." Ben Bella, like Lumumba before him, lived on in the hagiography of revolutionary Africa, but the revolution had been badly weakened, its forces thrown into disarray. The winds of reaction began to blow across the continent, and within a year half a dozen other leaders were overthrown in military *coups d'état*, among them another pillar of the "African revolution," Kwame Nkrumah.

The *coup d'état* in Algiers brought to light the fragile basis of Algeria's socialist revolution. Not that the country had previously been considered a model of stability: Western diplomats had long pointed to the three million unemployed, the diminishing returns in the socialist sector, and the fantastic waste of capital on prestige projects; Communist diplomats had noted the highly unscientific nature of Algeria's socialism, the lack of planning and organization, the "bourgeois mentality" of the majority of the country's civil servants, and the sharp competition from the remaining private industrial sector. Both viewed with concern the acute shortage of trained civil servants, the chaos in the administration, and the increasing unrest of Algerians, who had been promised much but given little.

Despite these apparent weaknesses of the Algerian government, Algerians and foreigners alike were totally surprised by the *coup d'état*. The army had kept its secret well, and no one suspected that Ben Bella, then near the pinnacle of success, was about to fall to an uncertain fate. Ben Bella was not a hated dictator, maintaining himself in power through police-state methods. The majority of the population, especially the peasants, still supported him. Only a small minority was really set against him, and at the time of the *coup* he had just reached an agreement with the strongest of the opposition groups, the Kabylia-based Front des Forces Socialistes. The more dynamic political groups in the country were on his side, in some instances pushing him faster than he wanted to go. The peasants, the workers of the nationalized farms and factories, the youth, and the women of the cities were over-whelmingly for him. So were the intellectuals, less because they ad-mired him as a man than because he gave them a role in politics. Yet when Ben Bella was suddenly arrested in the early hours of the morn-ing on June 19, only a handful of people, students for the most part, openly protested. The party and the labor union did not act; the crowds that only a few weeks before had turned out to shout "Yaya Ben Bella" stayed at home; the intellectuals in the party and government, usually so verbose, were also silent. But if few came to Ben Bella's defense, very few apart from the new figures in power hailed the end of the "diabolic dictator," and literally nobody was heard to shout "Yaya Boumediene." Were Ben Bella's erstwhile supporters intimidated by the army? In 1954, fear of the powerful French army had not been enough to stop Algerians from taking up arms. The army of Colonel Boumediene was much weaker, and there was a good chance that it would split in the event of a civil war. Still, there was no reaction.

The apparent public indifference to the *coup* seemed surprising, since Ben Bella had been popular with the masses. Popularity had not brought him political strength, however, because no institutions had been created to transform this enthusiasm into political support. Al-gerians had seldom been called upon to express their political opinion, although the vast majority had followed closely and passionately the politics of the country. Although the country had a national assembly, the deputies had been chosen by the party's leaders and not by the people. The regime was not representative in the Western sense of the word: it had not been designated in a free election by a people faced with a choice of candidates and programs. Nor was it representative in the Marxist sense of the word: it had not issued from a specific social class or economic interest group.

Since independence, politics in Algeria had been almost exclusively a question of personal relations, alliances, and rivalries among a rela-tively small group of wartime leaders. The country had all the trappings of a modern socialist state—a constitution, a national assembly, a single party with its political bureau, central committee, and ideological pro-gram. But the institutions were only a facade behind which a struggle among political clans and personalities went on undisturbed. Ideologi-cal conflicts played a remarkably small role in the politics of the coun-try, despite constant references to socialism, democracy, and Islam on the part of Algerian politicians. Slogans and principles were the slings and arrows used to attack rival factions in public, but convictions were rarely so strong that persons professing opposing ideologies could not come together in surprising alliances. Ferhat Abbas, president of the National Assembly, condemned Ben Bella's "Marxist-Leninist scientific socialism," opposing to it his own brand of "democratic and humanistic socialism"; however, he did not hesitate to back Ben Bella as the latter rose to power. Hocine Ait Ahmed, the principal Kabyle opposition leader, denounced Ben Bella as a "fascist dictator" and then maneuvered for a post in the Ben Bella regime. Ben Bella's Marxist advisors regarded the army as a reactionary force, but some of them tried to negotiate for positions in the Boumediene regime before passing to the opposition and branding Boumediene an "enemy of the workers."

Despite what Algerian politicians like to think, the force behind politics in Algeria since independence has not been a conflict of ideologies or the struggle between the bourgeoisie on the one hand and the workers and peasants on the other. Rather, it has been the contest for power among dozens of groups and clans. This continuing struggle of clans has also been the source of the country's political instability. The importance of clans in the politics of North Africa is not a new phenomenon. The medieval Arab historian Ibn Khaldun singled out the pronounced clannishness of North Africa's predominantly Berber society as a primary cause of the instability of North African empires. His work contains some ideas that, *mutatis mutandis*, help to explain contemporary Algerian politics.[1]

Ibn Khaldun asserted that all North African dynasties contained the seeds of their decay and destruction in the very force that initially brought them to power. He referred to this force as *asabiya*, a term that can best be translated as "clannishness" or "esprit de corps."[2] Asabiya

1. Abd ar-Rahman Ibn Khaldun was born in Tunis in 1332 of a wealthy and influential family that occupied a prominent place in the political and cultural life of the city. Like Machiavelli, to whom he has often been compared, Ibn Khaldun was not only a witness of the politics of his time, but also an actor in them. He held high positions under several sultans in North Africa and Spain until he finally abandoned politics in 1378. From that time on, he dedicated himself to a life of study and teaching in Tunis and later in Cairo, where he died in 1406. His theories on the rise and fall of North African empires are set forth in *The Muqaddimah*, which is the introduction to his economic, social, and political history of medieval North Africa. Ibn Khaldun is considered by many scholars to be a scientific historian and one of the greatest philosophers of history the world has known.

2. The Arab word *asabiya* is generally used in a pejorative sense. The word appears in one verse of the Koran which says, "Is it asabiya to love one's people? No, answered the Prophet, but it is asabiya to help one's people in an unjust action." It is only in Ibn Khaldun's work that the word is used in a technical sense without mak-

was the force that bound together the members of each tribe and gave some chiefs the power to impose their rule on other tribes and to found empires. Asabiya was also the tie between the tribal chiefs and the sultan that gave the empire its cohesion. The allegiance of the tribal chiefs to the sultan, however, was menaced by the strength of asabiya within the tribes, since each tribe remained a distinct political entity resisting incorporation into a larger state. In order to survive, the sultan needed to free himself from dependence on the tribal chiefs by finding a more solid and lasting foundation for his rule; but the tenacious clannishness of the innumerable Berber tribes of North Africa inevitably prevailed, and the empires fell apart. This cyclical process of the rise and fall of empires that Ibn Khaldun describes amounts essentially to the failure of North African dynasties to pass from the feudal state to a more stable and modern form of political organization—a failure, in short, to find a substitute for asabiya in less personal and more formal institutions of government.[3]

The nature of politics in Algeria today remains much the same as it was in the time of Ibn Khaldun.[4] However, asabiya is no longer based

---

ing any value judgment. For a long and detailed discussion of the various meanings of the term, see Yves Lacoste, *Ibn Khaldoun*, (Paris: Maspero, 1966), pp. 133–155.

3. The French historian Yves Lacoste has summed up in the following terms Ibn Khaldun's theory on the decline of North African empires: "It is not so much [the end of] this asabiya that Ibn Khaldoun regrets. Ibn Khaldoun describes without hostility how the sultan destroys this asabiya the tribal structures of which have become an obstacle to the organization of the state. Why then is the state condemned? Because it cannot find a force capable of supplanting asabiya. The state is hardly in place when the reasons for its growth are replaced by the germs of its decline. This vicious circle, that prevents the real consolidation of the dynasty could be slowed up or even broken if in the struggle against the tribal aristocracy the sultan could lean on a new political force. The state, whose structures are the very negation of those of the tribe, must bolster itself with forces that are not of a tribal nature." Lacoste, p. 161.

4. There is debate among scholars whether Ibn Khaldun considered asabiya to be a universal form of political behavior or a specifically North African phenomenon. Ibn Khaldun used the term only in his analysis of the political instability of North Africa. He saw asabiya as a characteristic of the small nomadic Berber tribes, whose members depended on the solidarity of the group to survive the difficult conditions of nomadic life and attacks by other tribes. Although he pointed out that conditions in North Africa were basically different from those in the rest of the Arab world, he never maintained that asabiya was exclusively a North African characteristic. The authors believe that the concept of asabiya as a political force offers a useful tool in the analysis of situations distinguished by the existence of numerous, closely knit political clans composed of individuals bound together essentially by personal ties and not by common ideals. In Algeria asabiya is a particularly important feature of political life, partly because of the strong influence of the Berbers and partly because the revolution divided political power among a large number of groups.

on family or tribal structures; these have been destroyed by 132 years of French colonialism and by the revolution. The "clans" of which Algerians constantly talk today are not composed of individuals tied together by blood relations, but rather of persons brought together by the struggle for independence. Perhaps these persons were in the same political party before the outbreak of the revolution, or fought in the *maquis* (underground) together, or spent years together in prison. Some may have risen together in the ranks of the National Liberation Army or worked together in the exiled Provisional Government.

The system of alliances that brought Ben Bella to power was very similar to that on which the sultans founded their empires. Around Ben Bella gathered a small group of well-known national figures, army officers, and guerrilla commanders, each man the leader of his own clan. The members of the alliance were held together by strictly personal ties and shared no community of ideals or common political program. There was not even the beginning of a political consensus between Ben Bella, a romantic revolutionary, and Ferhat Abbas, an exponent of classical democracy, or between Colonel Boumediene, a fervent advocate of a "return to the sources" of Islam, and Mohamed Khider, a would-be dictator of no particular faith. The composition of the opposition groups was identical to that of the group in power. Thus politicians could, and did, switch from one alliance to another with amazing agility. Today's heroes could be tomorrow's traitors, and vice versa.

Relations between Ben Bella and his viziers began to deteriorate very soon after independence. Khider, secretary-general of the party, and Abbas, president of the National Assembly, were forced to resign within a year, and they removed from the grand alliance the clans under their control. It became essential for Ben Bella to find new supporters. The Front de Libération Nationale (FLN), the only legal party and in theory the supreme power, was too faction-ridden and poorly organized to be the new political force he was looking for. Ben Bella was compelled to turn to the other national organizations, in particular to the Union Générale des Travailleurs Algériens (UGTA), the militant labor federation. At first he tried to assure himself of the support of these organizations by appointing his men to their top posts. This gave him new allies, but it was still a system of personal allegiances that held the regime together.

Ben Bella's effort was successful for a limited time only. The UGTA was a socialist labor federation seeking political power for the workers, and it refused to be subjected to the control of Ben Bella's vassals. The politically active student union, the FLN youth organization, and Ben Bella's own camarilla of Marxist advisors were also pressing their demands that Algeria be made into a socialist country; they were unwilling to support Ben Bella unless he carried out the socialist policies he so vocally professed. An alliance based on a political program rather than personal ties slowly began to develop, and this alliance was a step toward the creation of a more stable political system in Algeria. The change became noticeable at the UGTA's second congress in March 1965, when Ben Bella accepted a new leadership that was not of his choosing but that was nonetheless willing to support him. Ben Bella appeared to have found a new political force to replace the allies tied to him only by asabiya, but this force was not yet institutionalized and had not found its place in Algeria's single-party state. Ben Bella therefore continued until the time of his ouster to depend primarily upon asabiya to keep himself in power.

In early June 1965, Ben Bella decided to eliminate Foreign Minister Abdelaziz Bouteflika, one of Colonel Boumediene's closest allies, and take over the ministry himself. In order to gain support for this move against his former allies, Ben Bella offered freedom and a post in the Cabinet to one of his imprisoned enemies, Hocine Ait Ahmed, in return for the latter's support. But Boumediene, whose own position was indirectly threatened, acted first and deposed Ben Bella. The arrest of the Algerian president and of a few of his key aides and ministers was enough to throw into disarray the disparate forces that had provided the basis for his power. Ben Bella was the keystone of the alliance, and without him the regime collapsed. The socialist groups to which Ben Bella had recently turned were not organized into a political machine capable of going into action by itself. With the downfall of Ben Bella, the evolution of the political system in Algeria was arrested. A new clan, gathered around the enigmatic figure of Boumediene, took over the reins of power. More than ever before, asabiya was the cement that held the regime together. A new sultan reigned, and rumors of palace conspiracies and of rebellions of feudal lords ran wild through the country. Algerian politics remained the politics of clans and personalities.

chapter one
the crisis of independence

Nationalism, that magnificent song that made the people rise against their oppressors, stops short, falters and dies away on the day that independence is proclaimed. Nationalism is not a political doctrine, nor a program. If you really wish your country to avoid regression, or at best halts and uncertainties, a rapid step must be taken from national consciousness to political and social consciousness.[1]

Frantz Fanon

In the spring of 1962, Algeria appeared to be emerging from a dark era of its history. After more than a century of colonial domination and eight years of a bloody war, in March France and the Algerian nationalists reached an agreement that ended hostilities and provided for an orderly process leading to Algeria's independence. Although France respected the agreement, the transition of Algeria from a French "department" to an independent nation was scarcely orderly. In fact, the darkest period of Algeria's colonial history was to come at the dawn of independence. As Algerian authorities later recalled:

> July 1962 was a black month in Algeria. Not enough doctors for the mutilated victims of the last bombs. Not enough typists, civil servants, or secretaries; one lone telephone operator lost in the vast Oran exchange to answer calls and replace, if possible, her two hundred European colleagues who had fled. A single preciously-guarded typist in the cabinet of President Ben Bella. In the office of the newly-appointed minister of education, not a file, not a folder, not even a telephone was left. The departing French officials had left nothing but emptiness behind them. There would be no bread, perhaps no water. . . . Alarming rumors spread through the back streets.[2]

1. Frantz Fanon, *The Wretched of the Earth*, trans. Constance Farrington, (New York: Grove Press, 1966), p. 161.
2. *Algeria on the Move* (Algerian National Center of Documentation and Information, 1965). The brochure was prepared expressly for the Afro-Asian Conference.

In Ben Bella's own words, the country was a "desert" and an immense "vacuum" at the dawn of independence.

> Everyone remembers the situation we inherited. Everything was deserted—communication centers, prefectures, and even the administration so vital to the country. When I entered the prefecture in Oran, I personally found just seven employees instead of the five hundred who had previously worked there. The departure of the French attained a proportion of 80 per cent, even 90 to 98 per cent in some technical services such as the highway department. And to that you must add the loss of all statistical records burned or stolen . . .[3]

These statements of the situation are not exaggerated, nor do they present a false picture of Algeria in the summer of 1962. They convey the reality, the way the French *pieds noirs* (colonists) wanted it to be. The last months of "Algérie Française" saw carloads of French terrorists of the Organisation de l'Armée Sécrète (OAS) race through the streets of Algiers and Oran gunning down innocent Moslems of both sexes and all ages. By some strange quirk of fate and history, the worst single disaster of the war came two days after Algeria was officially declared independent, when a Moslem demonstration in Oran touched off a three-hour gun battle that took 95 Algerian and European lives and left 163 other persons wounded.[4] The last defenders of France's *mission civilisatrice* made primary targets of hospitals, schools, telephone exchanges, power plants, statistical centers, and government buildings. The University of Algiers library was burned in the *Götterdämmerung* of the OAS. Tons of explosives were set off in these strategic centers and used against factories and stores until the country was totally paralyzed.

The OAS failed in its major objective, however. It did not succeed in unnerving the Moslem Algerians to the point where they would lose control of themselves and attempt a massacre of Europeans. The OAS hoped that such a massacre would force the French army to fire upon the infuriated Algerian crowds and thus to side openly with the French right-wing extremists. But the massacre the OAS sought to provoke

---

It was never put on sale, and most copies were burned after the *coup d'état* of June 19.

3. Ben Bella's speech to youth leaders at El-Riath, April 4, 1963. Quotations from Ben Bella's speeches have been taken from collections published by the Ministry of Information. His speeches can usually also be found in *Le Peuple* and *Alger Républicain*. Henceforth, only the date of a particular speech will be given.

4. UPI dispatch, July 7, 1962.

did not take place, largely as a result of the incredible self-control shown by the Algerians and their leaders. In the cities agents of the Front de Libération Nationale encouraged this self-control by stationing their own gunmen around the edge of the Arab quarters and making it clear that they would shoot down anyone who lost his temper. Nonetheless, fear of what might happen in independent Algeria forced most of the one million French, Spanish, Italian, and Maltese pieds noirs to leave. During the summer of 1962, the twelve-mile road from Algiers to the Maison Blanche Airport was lined with the abandoned cars and belongings of panic-stricken Europeans whose only concern was to escape the nightmare they had helped to create. Emigrés crowded the airports and harbors, sometimes spending days in search of a passage on the packed planes and boats. By October, over 800,000 had fled the country.

Only a small minority of those who left had been actively involved with the OAS. French terrorists had operated only in the cities and not even in all of them. Constantine and Bone, the largest cities in eastern Algeria, were the scene of only a few bomb explosions and killings. It was mainly in Algiers and Oran that the OAS waged its hideous war in defense of the West and French civilization. Many Europeans fled not because they had compromised themselves in the OAS, but because security was almost totally lacking in Algeria. Throughout the summer and well into the fall, there were more guns in the hands of ex-guerrilla fighters than in the hands of policemen. Guerrilla bands were in control of many areas in the interior, even running the town halls in some cases. They raided the isolated farms of Europeans, looting and often killing. At Medea, fifty miles south of Algiers, such bands were still terrorizing the population in January 1963, when the army was finally called in to re-establish order. Many a European saw his house occupied before his eyes or was frightened by his neighbor's fate into leaving. By October, the French Embassy had a list of 1,900 Europeans missing and supposed dead.

In the European community, or what was left of it, stories circulated of houses and apartments being stripped of furniture and belongings while the owners were away at work. Some left at eight to come back at five and find the locks of their apartments changed and an Algerian family installed. Thousands of cars were stolen, some driven until their gas tanks were empty and then abandoned along the road. Algerian officials, where they existed, were seldom willing to take the side of a Frenchman—an understandable attitude after eight years of war against France; in any case, they had more serious problems on their hands in that hectic period than the fate of the home of a pied noir, or of an Algerian for that matter. The wheels of the administration were barely turning because the great majority of French civil servants and technicians had left and there were few competent Algerians to replace them. But the lack of trained civil servants, the absence of statistics and records, the destruction of school buildings, hospitals, and vital centers were only the beginning of the war-weary country's plight.

From May 1962, when the nationalist leaders met at Tripoli, until September of that same fateful year, Algeria was the scene of a bloody struggle for power among contending clans. The Front de Libération National (FLN), the political organization that had led the country in the war for independence, had never been monolithic. During the war, however, the front's leaders had done their best to maintain the appearance of unity before the eyes of the French and the outside world. With the conclusion of the Evian Peace Agreements in March 1962,[5] each of the numerous factions within the front began to jockey for a position in the future leadership of independent Algeria.

The roots of the struggle for power that marked the first months of Algeria's independence go far back into the history of the Algerian nationalist movement. The movement, which got under way in the 1920s,[6] was never dominated by one party or a single personality, as were similar movements in many other African countries. Until the

5. The Cease-fire and Peace Agreements were concluded at Evian, Switzerland, on March 19, 1962, after nearly two years of periodic contacts and negotiations. The first round of talks between the FLN and the French government was held at Melun, Switzerland, in June 1960. Negotiations began more seriously at Evian on May 20, 1961, and continued with numerous interruptions until March 1962. The agreements were never actually signed by either party because the French refused to give formal recognition to the FLN. The French did not hand over control of the country directly to the FLN but to a mixed French-Algerian "provisional executive" that was to supervise a referendum for independence on July 1, 1962, and run the country until elections for a national assembly could be held.

6. Algeria's nationalist movement got under way in 1926 in France with the creation of the left-wing Etoile Nord-Africaine led by Messali Hadj, a semi-religious agitator working in Paris who appealed entirely to Algerian workers in France. The only other group advocating independence at this time was the Association des Oulémas Réformistes d'Algérie, set up in 1931 by Cheikh 'Abd el-Hamid Ben Badis in Algiers. For the best short history of the nationalist movement, see Roger le Tourneau, *Evolution Politique de l'Afrique du Nord Musulmane* (Paris: Armand Colin, 1962), pp. 312–354.

outbreak of the revolution, two principal figures contended for leadership, Messali Hadj and Ferhat Abbas.[7] The former advocated direct revolutionary action to gain Algerian independence, while the latter waged a legal battle for equality of rights and for the eventual assimilation of Algeria into France. As the hope of assimilation gradually proved illusory, Hadj's party became the dominant force in the nationalist movement. However, the authority of Hadj himself was increasingly challenged, until finally, in April 1953, a faction of his Mouvement pour le Triomphe des Libertés Démocratiques (MTLD) revolted against his dictatorial rule. It was this dissident faction of Messali Hadj's party that, with no more than 2,400 followers, began guerrilla warfare against the French on November 1, 1954,[8] issuing on that day a proclamation that announced the creation of the Front de Libération Nationale and called for Algeria's independence.[9] By 1956, most Algerian nationalists, including Abbas, had joined the FLN. Only Messali Hadj had refused to rally and had founded a new party, the Mouvement National Algérien (MNA), which discredited itself by waging war as much against the FLN as against the French.

The experience of dictatorship under Messali Hadj convinced the founders of the FLN to adopt a system of collegial leadership. "Is it our intention to create an independent Algeria especially for one person or for an oligarchy?" asked the dissident members of the MTLD in 1953.[10] This question was to be raised again and again during the revolution and has remained to this day a leitmotiv of Algerian politics. The founding members of the FLN, the "historic nine" of the Algerian Revolution, made a pact promising one another to make all decisions

7. In 1937, Messali Hadj created the Parti du Peuple Algérien (PPA), his first party in Algeria. The following year, Ferhat Abbas organized the Union Populaire Algérienne (UPA), which called for the integration of Algeria into France and equality of rights for Moslems and Frenchmen. Both parties were soon outlawed but were later resurrected under different names. In 1954, Messali Hadj headed the Mouvement pour le Triomphe des Libertés Démocratiques (MTLD), formed in 1946. Ferhat Abbas led the Union Democratique du Manifeste Algérien (UDMA), also created in 1946. Abbas was a deputy in the second (all Moslem) college of the Algerian Assembly.

8. For personal accounts of the launching of the revolution, see an interview with Mohamed Boudiaf in *Le Monde*, November 2, 1962. See also *Révolution et Travail*, No. 100, October 29, 1965.

9. The FLN proclamation of November 1, 1954, can be found in le Tourneau, pp. 386–388.

10. From the documents of the second clandestine congress of the MTLD, held in Algiers April 4–6, 1953; quoted in le Tourneau, p. 377.

collectively in order to prevent the rise of another dictator.[11] Although the vicissitudes of the war removed from the active leadership of the FLN all but one of the nine men, the principle of collegial leadership was maintained and embodied in the Conseil National de la Révolution Algérienne (CNRA), created in 1956 as the FLN's supreme body.[12] The system of collegial leadership effectively prevented any one man from dominating the FLN, but it greatly encouraged the rise of personal rivalries and factional disputes among the Algerian nationalists.

The extremely decentralized organization of the FLN that was necessitated by the war also contributed to the formation of factions within the CNRA. By the end of the war, the leadership of the FLN was divided among a multitude of groups that were more or less independent of each other. In September 1958, a provisional government, the Gouvernement Provisoire de la République Algérienne (GPRA), had been created to represent the Algerian "state" abroad.[13] From its base in Tunis, the GPRA waged an intensive campaign to win diplomatic recognition and to gain support for Algeria's independence; indeed, it was largely because of this diplomatic offensive that Algeria obtained its independence after the French had won the war militarily.

11. In March 1954, dissident members of the MTLD set up the Comité Révolutionaire d'Unité et d'Action. The CRUA had twenty-two members and a five-man directorate composed of Mohamed Boudiaf, Mustapha Ben Boulaid, Larbi Ben M'Hidi, Mourad Didouche, and Rabah Bitat. During the summer of 1954, the directorate was expanded to include Belkacem Krim, who brought the support of the Kabylia to the CRUA, as well as Hocine Ait Ahmed, Ahmed Ben Bella, and Mohamed Khider, all living in exile in Cairo. The members of the directorate became known as the "historic nine" of the Algerian Revolution.

12. The CNRA was created at a meeting of top FLN leaders held inside Algeria in the Soummam Valley, August 20, 1956. It had a membership of thirty-four, which was later expanded to fifty-four and then to seventy-two. It was headed by the five-man Committee of Coordination and Execution (CCE), which in September 1958 was replaced by the GPRA. The FLN statutes defined the CNRA as "the supreme body of the FLN," and the provisional constitution declared that it was "the depository of the national sovereignty" and the country's legislative body. Thus the CNRA acted both as a sort of central committee and as a parliament. Because of the difficulty involved in bringing its members together, the CNRA did not meet often. The Tripoli meeting from May 25 to June 6, 1962, was the sixth gathering of the CNRA.

13. The Provisional Government was established September 19, 1958. It was created in response to President de Gaulle's speech of June 4, 1958, in which he promised equality of political rights to Moslem Algerians. The FLN rushed to set up the GPRA in order to make clear that it would not accept any solution other than total independence. All tendencies were represented in the GPRA. Ferhat Abbas, one of the most moderate FLN leaders, was made the first president; however, he and some of the other moderate ministers were ousted from the GPRA in August 1961. The new president, Benyoucef Ben Khedda, was considered much more radical.

Also based in Tunisia, at Gardimaou near the Algerian border, was the General Staff of the Armée de Libération Nationale (ALN), the military arm of the FLN.[14] The General Staff, which had direct control over the major force of the ALN, some 40,000 soldiers stationed in Tunisia and Morocco, was almost completely independent of the GPRA. Both the GPRA and the General Staff were cut off from the theatre of the battle by formidable defense lines of electrified barbed wire and mine fields, which the French built in 1957 along Algeria's borders with Morocco and Tunisia.

Algeria itself had been divided by the FLN into six military regions called *wilayas*.[15] As the wilayas became increasingly isolated from the General Staff, their chiefs became powerful warlords, enjoying a large degree of autonomy and deciding by themselves political and military strategy. The wilaya leaders, who had taken the brunt of the French army operations and suffered heavy losses, commanded only small forces by the end of the war, perhaps 6,000 men in the entire country. They regarded with disdain the "outside army," which had sat out half the war in Tunisia, and resented any encroachment of the General Staff on their local fiefdoms. The war thus divided political power and authority among the wilaya leaders, the General Staff, and the GPRA, while personal rivalries created additional divisions. The infighting among the FLN leaders was bitter and not limited solely to political intrigues. Some of the wilaya commanders died under unclear circumstances, probably victims of jealous rivals rather than of the French army. A group of ALN officers even attempted a *"coup d'état"* against the GPRA in 1956.[16]

14. The ALN General Staff was set up February 9, 1960, with Colonel Houari Boumediene as chief of staff, and Major Slimane (Ahmed Kaid) and Major Ali Mendjli as his assistants. The General Staff commanded the ALN forces stationed in Tunisia and Morocco, and in theory the guerrilla forces inside Algeria.

15. The FLN adopted the divisions originally set up by Messali Hadj's PPA: Wilaya One, Aurès Mountains in eastern Algeria; Wilaya Two, North Constantine in eastern Algeria; Wilaya Three, the Kabylia; Wilaya Four, the Algiers region; Wilaya Five, western Algeria; and Wilaya Six, the Sahara Desert. The cities of Algiers and Oran were organized as "autonomous zones" under separate commands.

16. The "conspiracy of the colonels" involved seven officers of the General Staff-East (Tunisia). It was an episode in the conflict that opposed military and civilian leaders throughout the war, and it was particularly directed against the ministers who controlled military operations—Belkacem Krim, Lakhdari Ben Tobbal, and Abdelhafid Boussouf. The officers involved were arrested in November 1958 and sentenced to death by a military court presided over by Colonel Boumediene; however, not all of them were executed. Three of the officers involved in the plot, Major Abdellah Belhouchet, Major Abid Said, and Major Ahmed Draia, became members of the Revolutionary Council.

Five of the founding members of the FLN did not participate in the struggle for power, having been imprisoned by the French early in the war.[17] These "historic leaders"—Ahmed Ben Bella, Mohamed Boudiaf, Hocine Ait Ahmed, Mohamed Khider, and Rabah Bitat—had thus earned the reputation of being "the pures" among the nationalist leaders. If imprisonment had won them fame and an image of purity, it had not put an end to their political ambitions. In March 1962, they came out of prison determined to play once again a prominent role in the history of Algeria.

The meeting of the CNRA at Tripoli in May 1962 brought together for the first time all the principal nationalist leaders in a confrontation that had momentous consequences. The purpose of the Tripoli meeting was essentially twofold: to elect a political bureau that would assume the control of the FLN and to draw up a political and economic program for independent Algeria. The Political Bureau was destined to become the most powerful political body in the country. Not only was it to head Algeria's only party, it was also to draw up the list of candidates for the National Assembly, which would in turn select a prime minister. Control of the Political Bureau thus became all-important to the warring factions, each afraid of being excluded from the future leadership of the country. Consequently, all basic questions concerning the future organization of the Algerian state, already sadly neglected during the war, were left undiscussed at Tripoli.

The fate of many groups and individuals depended upon the outcome of the Tripoli meeting. The leaders of the Provisional Government were fighting to stay in control but were hard pressed to justify their actions since 1958. The officers of the ALN General Staff feared they would be ousted if the GPRA leaders remained in power, since relations between the two factions had been extremely tense for over a year.[18]

17. Ben Bella, Boudiaf, Ait Ahmed, and Khider were captured by the French in October 1956, while flying from Rabat, Morocco, to Tunis in a Moroccan plane. The pilot, a Frenchman, obeyed orders radioed by the French Army Command in Algiers and landed the plane at the Algiers Airport, where the four were arrested. Rabah Bitat was captured in Algeria in February 1955. Only one other "historic leader" survived, Belkacem Krim, minister of the Interior in the GPRA.

18. In September, 1961, President Ben Khedda ordered that the ALN General Staff be dissolved and replaced by two separate staffs, one to be in charge of the troops stationed in Tunisia and one of those in Morocco. The wilayas were to go directly under the control of the GPRA. This was the system used before the creation of the General Staff in 1960. Colonel Boumediene refused to accept the reorganization and forced the project to be dropped. Thereafter, the GPRA and the General Staff were at loggerheads.

The wilaya commanders were in a particularly difficult position; both the GPRA and the General Staff were interested in gaining their support for the coming showdown but were bound to deprive them in the long run of the power they had gained during the war. For the five historic leaders it was an excellent moment to make their bid for power by playing on divisions within the CNRA.

During the Tripoli meeting, the outside world became aware for the first time of another storm brewing in Algeria, but not until months later did it become possible to understand the meaning and nature of the conflict that shook the country to its very foundations. The elaboration of the FLN's future program was the first task of the twelve-day meeting. The Tripoli Program,[19] as the document produced at the conference was later called, began with a general analysis of Algeria's colonial heritage and the situation facing the country at independence. It dealt at length with the two issues that seemed most important at the time: the liquidation of the OAS and the problems posed by the presence of a large French population. It also outlined in vague terms an economic program that indicated that Algeria would be a socialist country. The most controversial section of the Tripoli Program was a violent attack on the Provisional Government for its mismanagement of the FLN during the war years. Here was the real bone of contention between the "pures" and the "impures." The GPRA leaders,[20] the "impures," were accused of "anti-revolutionary deviations," of "paternalistic and petit bourgeois attitudes," and of a total lack of ideological drive. They were castigated for having failed to root out "the feudal spirit that has impregnated the whole life of the Maghreb since the Middle Ages."

> Although the FLN has been the relentless enemy of feudalism, combatting it in its everyday social manifestations, [the party] has done nothing to keep [feudalism] out of certain levels of its own organization; in particular, it has forgotten that it is precisely the abusive conception

19. The Tripoli Program was drafted before the meeting by a seven-man committee headed by Ben Bella and composed of M'hamed Yazid, Mohamed Ben Yahia, Reda Malek, Mohamed Harbi, Mostepha Lacheraf, and Abdelmalek Temmam.

20. The Tripoli Program mentioned no names, but it was no secret that those under attack were above all President Ben Khedda, Vice-President and Minister of the Interior Belkacem Krim, Minister of Arms and Liaisons Abdelhafid Boussouf, and Minister of State Lakhdari Ben Tobbal. The last three composed the Interministerial Committee of War set up in January 1960 and were considered to be the most powerful members of the GPRA.

of authority, the absence of rigorous standards, and the lack of political education that favor the birth and rebirth of the feudal spirit.

.   .   .   .

Just as there were in the past territorial fiefs, so there can also be political fiefs . . . the formation of which is made possible by the complete absence of democratic education among the militants and the people.[21]

Although intended as a criticism of the GPRA, the above passage was an accurate analysis of the power structure of the entire FLN. The heaviest legacy of the war for independence was indeed the "political feudalization" of the country.

After what must have been an acrimonious debate, the Tripoli Program was reportedly adopted unanimously. No agreement, however, was reached on the composition of the Political Bureau. The nominating committee, which was controlled by Ben Bella and his supporters, proposed a list of seven men: Ahmed Ben Bella, Mohamed Khider, Hocine Ait Ahmed, Mohamed Boudiaf, Hadj Ben Alla, Rabah Bitat, and Mohammedi Saïd.[22] None of the prominent GPRA members were included. An initial sounding taken by the nominating committee showed that over half the members of the CNRA supported the list but that the required majority of two-thirds was not certain. The list, however, never came to a vote.[23] In an effort to postpone the election, CNRA President Benyoucef Ben Khedda took advantage of a gross insult by Ben Bella to storm out of the conference.[24] He was immediately followed by his allies, who were equally anxious to block the voting, and then by his enemies, who feared he might plot behind their backs. In the end, a slim majority of CNRA members remained at Tripoli, and they adjourned the meeting.

21. See Front de Libération Nationale, *Projet de Programme pour la Réalisation de la Révolution Démocratique Populaire* (undated), pp. 16–20. Henceforth, this publication will be referred to as *Projet de Programme*.

22. The bureau was thus made up of five historic leaders plus two lesser figures. Ben Alla had fought inside the country until his capture in November 1956, but he had never held a prominent post. He was a faithful follower of Ben Bella and made himself known at Tripoli, where he launched a violent attack against Ben Khedda. Mohammedi Saïd was a Kabyle leader bitterly opposed to Belkacem Krim and was a minister of state in the GPRA.

23. This version comes from a member of the nominating committee and appears the most probable. The Political Bureau's version was that a formal vote took place and that the list was approved by a majority. French sources give still a third version: there was a formal vote, but neither this list nor another composed of Ben Khedda, Belkacem Krim, Ben Bella, Boudiaf, and Abbas received a majority of votes.

24. Ben Khedda left Tripoli on June 7, 1962. French sources claim that an attempt was made to force his resignation as GPRA president but that the vote fell short of the necessary two-thirds majority.

For a few weeks neither side acted. Then on June 30, the eve of the referendum for independence, the Provisional Government moved to break up the coalition of its opponents by dismissing the three top officers of the ALN General Staff—Colonel Houari Boumediene, Major Slimane (Ahmed Kaid), and Major Ali Mendjli. This action immediately consolidated the alliance between the General Staff and Ben Bella, who denounced the GPRA decision within twenty-four hours. Within a few days, two rival blocs formed. On one side were the nominees to the Political Bureau (except Boudiaf and Ait Ahmed), the ALN General Staff, and a group of moderates led by Ferhat Abbas who were bitterly opposed to those who had ousted him as GPRA president in 1961. On the other side were most members of the GPRA, notably President Ben Khedda, Belkacem Krim, and Abdelhafid Boussouf. Boudiaf and Ait Ahmed did not formally join either group but were closer to the latter faction.

On July 11, Ben Bella triumphantly entered Algeria from Morocco and moved to establish his hold over the western part of the country. He and his allies set up their headquarters at Tlemcen and were thereafter known as the Tlemcen group. In a speech given shortly afterwards in Oran, Ben Bella gave a fairly good summation of the position of both sides: "I am for unity but not at any price."[25] Undoubtedly each side would have preferred to avoid a showdown but not if the price was its own defeat. President Ben Khedda and the GPRA ministers had also returned to Algeria, establishing their headquarters at Tizi Ouzou, capital of the Kabylia, the stronghold of the country's Berber minority. From there, the "Tizi Ouzou group," as the GPRA faction was now called, conducted its campaign.

As the situation steadily deteriorated, the outside world sought in vain to discover ideological or political differences that might explain the division. Some observers believed that the Tlemcen group was opposed to the Evian Agreements and to close cooperation with France and that the Tizi Ouzou group, which included several top negotiators at Evian, were in favor of them. Others considered the politicians around Ben Khedda partisans of Western democratic institutions and those around Ben Bella proponents of either a radical socialist state or a military dictatorship. The location of the two factions' headquarters and to some extent even the composition of the two factions gave rise to speculation about a conflict between Berbers and Arabs. The exis-

25. UPI dispatch, July 12, 1962.

tence of ideological differences between the two sides was denied in
the July 13 editorial of the FLN party organ *El-Moudjahid*, which
stated that "this crisis is based on no opposition of an ideological nature
whatsoever, since the CNRA, at the time of its last meeting, adopted
unanimously the project for the orientation of the FLN program
[Tripoli Program]." Three days later, M'hammed Yazid, for many
years information minister of the Provisional Government, admitted in
an interview that the crisis was essentially one of leadership and that
it was based on conflicting opinions of "what ought to be the leadership
and above all which men must compose it."[26]

For a while the struggle was limited to a barrage of speeches and
press communiqués. Then on July 22, the Tlemcen group made a dramatic announcement:

> In keeping with the majority decision of the CNRA, which called upon
> each member of the Political Bureau to assume his responsibilities be-
> fore history in the application of the political program adopted unani-
> mously on June 4, 1962, the Political Bureau of the Front of National
> Liberation has decided to assume its responsibility within the legal
> framework of the Algerian republic's institutions as of today and until
> a sovereign national congress [of the FLN] can be held.[27]

At the same time, the outright condemnation of the GPRA voted at
the Tripoli meeting was made public in an effort to discredit the Tizi
Ouzou group.[28] Strictly speaking, "the legal framework of the Algerian
republic's institutions" did not give power to the Political Bureau, since
the CNRA had not officially voted it into office. However, the Tizi
Ouzou group had nothing with which to oppose this self-investiture.
Under the strain of the conflict, its solidarity was giving out; more
important, the troops of Colonel Boumediene were advancing slowly
but steadily from Tunisia and Morocco towards Algiers. On July 28,
President Ben Khedda finally announced that the GPRA had agreed

26. Interview with Radio Station Europe I, July 16, 1962.
27. UPI dispatches, July 22, 1962. The declaration was read by Ali Boumendjel
at a press conference in Tlemcen. Almost the entire Tlemcen group was present for
the occasion: Ben Bella; Khider; Abbas; Boumediene; Ben Alla; Ahmed Francis,
ally of Abbas and former GPRA finance minister; Colonel Chaabani, Wilaya Six
commander; Colonel Si Othmane, Wilaya Five commander; Colonel Tahar Zbiri,
Wilaya One commander; and Major Slimane of the ALN General Staff.
28. This condemnation was voted at Tripoli on June 9, 1962, after a number of
delegates had stormed out. It singled out President Ben Khedda, Krim, Ben Tobbal,
Boussouf, Yazid, and Saad Dahlab.

to accept the composition of the Political Bureau proposed at the Tripoli meeting.[29]

The fate of Algeria was, however, no longer entirely in the hands of the Tlemcen and Tizi Ouzou groups. For reasons beyond the control of either faction, fighting had broken out near Constantine on July 25 between the political commissary of Wilaya Two, Major Si Larbi, and the commander-in-chief of the same wilaya, Colonel Saout el-Arab. Si Larbi had acted mostly out of personal ambition, but since he was siding with the Tlemcen group and Saout el-Arab with the Tizi Ouzou group the fighting assumed national importance. On the same day, Colonel Mohand ou el-Hadj, commander of Wilaya Three (Kabylia), declared publicly that he would not recognize the authority of the Political Bureau and asked for an immediate meeting of the CNRA to resolve the crisis.

The actions of Si Larbi and Mohand ou el-Hadj brought the wilaya forces into the struggle. During the Tripoli meeting and later in July, the wilaya leaders had met repeatedly in an effort to work out a common position, but they had failed. The commanders of Wilaya Five (Oran), Wilaya One (Aurès Mountains), and Wilaya Six (Sahara) had given their support to the ALN General Staff and the Tlemcen group. This was not by chance. During the war, these three wilayas, closest to the frontiers, had remained in contact with the outside army and had been kept best supplied with arms after the borders were closed by the French army. On the other hand, Wilaya Two (North Constantine), Wilaya Three (Kabylia), and Wilaya Four (Algiers) were isolated and their leaders embittered by the lack of directives, arms, and provisions coming from the outside. Their leaders therefore lined up with the Tizi Ouzou group against the General Staff. The positions taken by the wilaya leaders cannot, however, be entirely attributed to wartime grievances and hardships. There is no doubt that some leaders, namely Si Larbi, Saout el-Arab, and Mohand ou el-Hadj, were motivated primarily by the desire to maintain their own fiefdoms in independent Algeria.

After the capitulation of the GPRA, talks opened in Algiers between representatives of the Tizi-Ouzou and Tlemcen groups, and on August

29. At this time, neither Boudiaf nor Ait Ahmed had agreed to sit in the Political Bureau. Boudiaf announced on August 2 that he would participate, but he resigned three weeks later. Ait Ahmed never accepted a seat in the bureau.

2 three points of agreement were announced: (1) the Political Bureau would remain as it was; (2) elections for a national assembly would be held on August 27; and (3) the CNRA would meet one week after the elections. But the agreement could not be carried out because many of the wilaya leaders were not ready to accept the authority of the Political Bureau, which was backed by the ALN General Staff. They were particularly wary of the planned "reconversion" of the ALN into the new Armée Nationale Populaire (ANP). The plan involved the merger of the wilaya military forces with the troops previously stationed outside Algeria. The Political Bureau also demanded that the wilaya commanders choose between a career in the ANP and one in the party, refusing to allow them to remain at the same time officers and politicians. The principle of the army's reconversion had been clearly spelled out in the Tripoli Program: "The accession of Algeria to independence requires that one part of the ALN return to civilian life, giving its cadres to the party, and that the other part form the core of the national army."[30] However, the wilaya leaders saw reconversion primarily as a means of eliminating them from the political scene and consequently resisted it.

"Pacification" of the wilaya commanders became the principal preoccupation of the Political Bureau. The offensive was conducted on two fronts: Ben Bella and Khider tried on the one hand to work out with the wilaya leaders a list of candidates for the National Assembly and on the other to win over to their side some of the most recalcitrant commanders by promising them top posts in the new ANP or the party. For instance, Saout el-Arab was offered the military command of Wilaya Two (Constantine) in return for his support of the Political Bureau.[31] But Mohand ou el-Hadj and Si Hassan, commanders of Wilayas Three and Four respectively, could not be won over to the Political Bureau. In a joint communiqué on August 24, they declared their willingness to accept the principle of reconversion, but not the Political Bureau's interpretation of the term:

> To consider the ALN an army that must go back to its barracks is to forget the real sense of the struggle that it has carried on alongside the

30. *Project de Programme*, p. 59.
31. Saout el-Arab accepted the offer. As a result, fighting broke out once again on August 17 between troops faithful to him and those under Si Larbi, who coveted the command for himself. It was Si Larbi who finally won out.

people. To attack the problem of reconversion from the top, that is to dissolve the wilaya commands, means to push aside the militants, thus leaving the door open to opportunists and those who collaborated with the colonial regime. The wilaya commands will remain in power until the formation of an Algerian government legally approved by the people.[32]

In reply, Khider first threatened that the Political Bureau might resign, asserting it was "no longer able to assume its responsibilities." This menace, designed to intimidate the dissident wilayas, was never carried out. Instead, the bureau decided to replace the political authority it lacked with the military force it had on its side. On August 30, Khider appealed from Algiers to the troops led by the General Staff and to those of Wilays One, Two, Five, and Six, which now supported the Political Bureau "unconditionally."[33] Once again fighting broke out, this time on a large scale. The Algerian people were appalled. In Algiers on the night of September 1, a crowd of twenty thousand people invaded the Palais d'Eté, the French governor general's former summer residence, shouting *"Baraket es-Senin!"*—"Seven years of war are enough!" In the backcountry, around Aumale, Boghari, and Tiaret, peasants threw themselves in the line of fire to stop the fighting, crying *"Baraket Dirigeants!"*—"Enough, leaders!" For a few days, the absence of authority in the country was complete. Then on September 4, Ben Bella appeared in Algiers for the first time and declared confidently that the crisis was over. This time the crisis was indeed nearly over. The troops of Colonel Boumediene were advancing steadily toward the capital through Wilaya Four, at the expense of several hundred ALN "brothers" who had fought eight years for independence, only to die in a civil war. On September 9, Colonel Boumediene entered Algiers, and the victory of the Political Bureau was assured.

On September 20, nationwide elections for the National Assembly, first scheduled for August 27 and seven times postponed, were finally held.[34] Six days later, the assembly empowered Ben Bella to form a

32. UPI dispatch, August 24, 1962.
33. The leaders of these four wilayas promised their support to the Political Bureau in a joint declaration of August 28, 1962.
34. The National Assembly was composed of 196 deputies, representing the Tizi Ouzou group as well as the Tlemcen group. Of the 196 deputies, 59 were former guerrilla officers or members of the ANP. In addition, there were 16 Europeans and 9 women. Eighty-one per cent of the 6.5 million registered voters participated in the election.

government, and on September 28 the first Ben Bella Cabinet was approved by an overwhelming majority.[35] Abbas was elected president of the Assembly; Khider became secretary-general of the party; and Boumediene remained entrenched at the head of his army. There was no longer any talk of holding a meeting of the CNRA. The Tizi Ouzou group had lost the battle for Algiers, but the new regime did not have complete control over the country. The Kabylia was still in the hands of the wilaya forces; Si Larbi had not yet given up his "fief" in the Constantine region; and guerrilla bands were roaming the countryside unchecked.

The pacification of the country was only the first step. The Ben Bella regime also had to organize the state, and for this task it was ill-prepared. The Political Bureau was a head without a body, the rank and file having been disillusioned and scattered during the summer crisis. The National Assembly was new, inexperienced, and more a debating society than a legislative body. The army, to which Ben Bella owed his victory, could not take an active role in politics until the delicate problem of reconversion—integration of the wilaya forces into the ANP—had been solved. As things stood, the moment army officers were named to political positions, wilaya leaders would also demand posts. This demand the Ben Bella government could not satisfy without undermining its own authority because the wilaya leaders had too much local power. The forced withdrawal of the army from politics weakened Boumediene's role in the regime and considerably strengthened Ben Bella's, but it also prevented the president from making use of the only organized force in the country. The major weakness of the regime was pointed out in a fiery accusation by one of its arch enemies, Belkacem Krim: "In truth, the plan of the Ben Bella group is clear: destroy all the structures of the revolution in order to clear the way for personal power on the road toward dictatorship."[36] Whatever Ben Bella's intentions may have been then, it was all too true that the "structures of the revolution" had been destroyed. The problem Ben Bella faced was how to create new political institutions by means of which the ties between the people and the government could be re-established.

For a time, such problems were forgotten in the euphoria of indepen-

35. The Ben Bella Cabinet was approved 158 to 1, with 19 abstentions and 14 unexcused absences. See Appendix I for the composition of the Cabinet. The GPRA and the Provisional Executive officially ceased to exist the day the National Assembly held its first session.

36. UPI dispatch, August 27, 1962.

dence and in the sense of relief that followed the end of the summer crisis. Enthusiastic crowds turned out to hear the president and his ministers wax rhapsodic over the future of Algeria and the socialist revolution: unemployment would end in a matter of months; all children would soon be in schools; French farm lands would be given to the peasant and French factories to the workers. In the speeches of the nation's leaders and in the imaginations of those who listened, the dream of the Algerian Revolution was alive. In essence it was mankind's eternal dream of a life of plenty and happiness for all, a dream that seems particularly close to reality just after a country becomes independent.

Not only the people of Algeria were caught up in the overweening enthusiasm of the first months of independence. Algeria's independence aroused great expectations in the leftist intellectual circles of Europe, where the Algerian Revolution had long been portrayed as the fight of political good against political evil. In the writings of Frantz Fanon, the Haitian-born prophet of a new man that was to arise out of colonized peoples' struggle for freedom, many in Europe and the Third World found eloquent justification for their almost mystical enthusiasm about the new Algeria.[37]

In the first months after independence, political exiles, French Communists, Marxists of all nationalities, revolutionaries from other African countries, engagé intellectuals, and do-gooders of all kinds flocked to Algeria as if to the promised land. Young Eastern bloc volunteers came to help their Algerian counterparts in the reconstruction of villages destroyed by the war. Frenchmen burdened with a guilty conscience over the ravages of the futile eight-year war came to atone for the sins

---

37. Frantz Fanon, a Haitian-born psychiatrist, came to Algeria in 1952 to work at a hospital in Blida. After the outbreak of the revolution, he sided with the FLN, and in 1957, after participating in a strike of doctors sympathetic to the FLN cause, he was forced to flee to Tunisia. There he began working for GPRA and became its ambassador to Ghana, Guinea, and Mali. He died in 1961 in Washington, D.C., where he had been sent in extremis for treatment of leukemia. From his experience with the Algerian Revolution, he drew inspiration for two works, L'An V de la Révolution Algérienne and the more famous Les Damnés de la Terre. For Fanon, the nationalist revolutions under way in the Third World were preparing the way for a social and cultural revolution that would allow the colonized peoples "to begin anew the history of mankind." He believed that the countries of the Third World could avoid repeating the sins of the Western world only if the peasants, not the bourgeoisie or the urban workers, seized power. He considered urban labor to be a privileged class and therefore a conservative force in the underdeveloped countries. Fanon's work has become the bible of revolutionaries throughout Africa and Latin America, and more recently has become popular in leftist circles in the United States.

of France by establishing a new French-Algerian cooperation. Left-wing intellectuals of all persuasions arrived in droves, seeking to make a dream come true in Algeria that they had been unable to realize in their own countries. After the realistic and tragic interlude of the summer crisis, Algerian independence began under the spell of a collective dream. Algeria seemed destined to become a utopia.

chapter two
the algerian people

When you have read all the books available, studied the statistics, taken the economic machinery apart and analyzed the political situation, can you be said to understand Algeria? Not at all. For knowledge does not imply understanding. An understanding of the country depends upon the experience of its moral climate. To abstract studies an essential human dimension must be added. . . . Yes, Algeria is above all a little known people passionately gripped in an anguished search for its destiny.

Algeria on the Move

During the summer and fall of 1962, one actor was noticeably absent from the scene, although to judge from the speeches of Algeria's leaders it was all the time on center stage: the People. The word was pronounced like a magic formula that could grant morality and legality to actions and maneuvers hardly motivated by either. The People, hailed throughout the country on placards and banners as "the only hero" of the revolution, appeared to be a united body, whose only concern was the common good. As is most often the case, there was little truth in the official "revolutionary" rhetoric. The people were not a united body animated by a single will and purpose, but a war-weary population of uprooted peasants much more concerned about their own immediate fate than about the destiny of the country. Moreover, the people were never allowed to choose their leaders, and consequently their opinion of the various contending factions was totally irrelevant to the outcome of the summer struggle. The fall elections were held after the Political Bureau had imposed itself upon the nation.

While Algeria's leaders were busy fighting one another in the name of the people, Algerians began building new lives. A new social order began to take shape in the country at the dawn of independence. After more than a hundred years of French colonization and eight years of war, there was not much left of the old order. Since the invasion of the French expeditionary forces in 1830,[1] Algerian society had undergone a steady process of disintegration. The political and social structure of the country began to crumble as the inhabitants fled from the path of the French army, which slowly advanced inland burning towns, wheat fields, and forests, and ruthlessly crushing the resistance of the tribes. It took the French army just twenty-one days to force the dey of Algiers to surrender and thus bring to an end 314 years of Turkish suzerainty over Algeria.[2] The dey had never really ruled over more than the city of Algiers itself. Under his nominal authority, the country was a veritable mosaic of fiefs, autonomous towns, and independent tribes, subjected to periodic taxation, but not to direct political control. Still, the French conquest eventually required an expeditionary force of 100,000 soldiers and seventeen years of warfare before the country was finally pacified. The emir Abdelkader, a fierce warrior and religious leader from western Algeria, rallied many of the indigenous tribes in a strenuous resistance to the French penetration.[3]

The surrender of the emir in 1847 marked the end of the military conquest and the beginning of colonization.[4] The population, having already been forced to flee the French army, was now permanently driven off the land by the invasion of land-hungry pioneers—the original

1. A 37,000-man expeditionary force landed at Sidi Ferruch, twenty miles west of Algiers, on June 14, 1830. The dey of Algiers, Hussein, surrendered after the city's fort was bombarded on July 5, 1830.

2. Turkish rule began in 1516, when the people of Algiers called upon the brothers Aroudj and Khair ed-Dinn, better known as Barbarossa, to drive out the Spanish installed in the Fort of Peñon, situated on an island in front of the city. The Barbarossa brothers drove out the Spanish with the help of Turkish janissaries and thereafter made Algiers a province of the Ottoman Empire, over which they ruled. In 1830, Algiers was nominally part of the empire and was ruled by a dey in Algiers and beys in Constantine, Medea, and Oran.

3. Abdelkader came from an influential family of religious leaders in the region of Mascara. He became emir at the age of twenty-four. Having fought and defeated the French several times, in 1837 he signed with them the Treaty of Tafna, which recognized his sovereignty over western Algeria. The treaty was soon broken, and in 1839 Abdelkader launched a holy war against the French, which lasted eight years. He was first exiled in France and then allowed to leave for Damascus, where he died in 1883. His remains were brought back to Algeria with great ceremony on July 5, 1966.

4. Despite the surrender of Abdelkader, fighting continued in the Kabylia until 1857. There were revolts in 1863 and 1864 among the Ouled Sidi Cheikh of southwestern Algeria and again in the Kabylia in 1871. But these local revolts did not prevent the penetration of the French colons, who numbered close to 500,000 by the 1880s.

pieds noirs. In 1863, a French *senatus consultum* made compulsory the division of tribal lands, clearing the way for the purchase and plunder of individual plots by the French *colons* (colonists). It also divided Algeria into new administrative units, splitting many tribes. These measures irreversibly upset the tribal structures, and Algerian society, "thrown off balance and in a complete state of disorder, [was] swept down a dizzy path leading to the abyss."[5] As one of Algeria's early nationalists remarked, the *senatus consultum* brought about an "agrarian revolution"—at the expense of the peasants.[6]

As the French settled in the fertile valleys along the coast and later on the high plains further inland, thousands of Algerians retreated into the mountains or fled to Tunisia and Morocco. But most remained, to be forced into the new world created by the French presence. The men became wage workers on the land that had once been theirs but now belonged to the French, or else they emigrated to the French-built towns and later to France in search of jobs. In the cities as well as in the countryside, Moslem women entered French homes to work as servants. The large Algerian landowners became rare and the landless peasants more and more numerous. The craftsmen of the towns disappeared as goods made in France or in local French factories invaded the markets. In fact, Algerian handicrafts survived mainly as an art practiced by young Moslem girls in centers run by the French Catholic Pères Blancs. To be sure, there were vast regions of barren inhospitable land where few colons settled, but even there Algerians could not escape the French, who were the law and the economic power. If there were no French civil servants or colons, there were French-appointed *caids* (Moslem municipal officials), *bachagas* (high-ranking military or civil officials), and *aghas* (army officers) to enforce French law and order. And even in the forgotten Saharan oases and the mountains of the Kabylia, the people became dependent on French merchants to market locally grown dates and figs.

Algerians, whether they liked it or not, were thus brought into the world of the French, but most were allowed in only to serve the pieds noirs. They entered French society as farm laborers, unskilled workers, street cleaners, doormen, and at best typists and clerks. Of the two thousand civil servants who worked in the General Government Build-

5. Pierre Bourdieu, *The Algerians* (Boston: Beacon Press, 1962), p. 129.
6. Abdelaziz Khaldi, *Le Problème Algérien* (Algiers: En-Nahdha, 1946), p. 13.

ing in Algiers in 1957, only eight were Moslems.[7] The pieds noirs did not want to have an Algerian middle class competing with them for jobs and status. Nonetheless, a small Algerian elite survived within the social system created and controlled by the French. Perhaps fifty-thousand Algerians belonged to this elite—the few remaining big land-owners, the caids, some wealthy merchants, and a small number of professional men.[8]

The Algerian elite became in time very French. It could not have done otherwise, since the colons had done everything to eradicate Islam and impose French culture. Most of the Koranic schools and *medersas* (high schools) were shut down. Mosques were turned into churches, or else the *imams* (priests) were appointed by the French administration, which made sure they would not spread the seeds of an Islamic revival. French was the official language of the land; Arabic was considered a foreign tongue. Those who wanted an education had to turn to the French, and the French opened their schools only to a small number of Algerian children, who thus learned about "their" cultural heritage—their ancestors the Gauls, Racine and Corneille, and the French Revolution.[9] The day came, in the period between the two world wars, when the French-educated Algerians began to demand assimilation, complete equality of civil and political rights with the French. But efforts to obtain these rights were systematically blocked by the pieds noirs who, like the white trash of America's South, were determined to preserve their own status and not to allow a bridge between the two societies. By 1946, about forty-six thousand Algerians out of a total population of seven and a half million had full French citizenship. For the vast majority of Algerians—98 per cent of them—assimilation was an ideal too far removed from the everyday reality to be taken seriously. Those who did not resign themselves to French domination did not ask for a place in the world of the French, but for the total destruction of that world. Finally, in 1954 the assault came.

7. Thomas Opperman, *Le Problème Algérien* (Paris: Maspero, 1961), p. 38n.

8. This is the figure cited by the Algiers Charter, the party's ideological program. It appears to be based on a French estimate given in the Constantine Plan, a program for Algeria's industrial development drawn up by the French in 1958.

9. Before World War Two, the number of Moslem children in French schools was negligible. Ferhat Abbas recalls that there were just fifty Algerians at Algiers University in 1930. After the war, the French liberalized their education policy, and by 1954 15 per cent of Algerian children of school age were attending primary schools. However, there were still only 6,200 Algerians in French high schools and only 600 at Algiers University.

The revolution meant another violent upheaval in Algerian society. It took nearly eight years of guerrilla warfare, of massive destruction in the countryside, of bloody demonstrations in the city, of terrorism and repression all over the country before Algeria became independent. In all, about 8,000 hamlets were destroyed; more than 2,000,000 peasants were uprooted and herded helter-skelter into "regroupment villages"; 300,000 victims fled to Tunisia and Morocco; and at least 250,000 Algerians, and possibly close to 1,000,000, were killed.[10] With 500,000 French troops and 200,000 Algerian auxiliaries—the largest colonial army ever assembled—the French won most of the battles, gained control over most of the land, but lost Algeria in the end.

For the first time in a century, Algerians were forced to look beyond the daily quest for bread. No one could remain indifferent: the FLN and the French compelled Algerians to take sides, often infringing on established values and mores. In the face of the choices Algerians had to make, paternal authority and tradition lost much of their weight, and family ties weakened and often broke. In some cases, brother fought against brother and son against father. There were women who threw away the veil for the first time in their lives to carry arms or run messages. Women who had never dared to talk to men outside the family found they were called upon to hide unknown guerrillas in their homes or care for wounded soldiers. Most Algerians learned to challenge the established authority, and many were forced to accept orders from guerrillas who had no legal power but had guns. In any case, they learned to respect or fear a person for his role in the revolution and not because of his French-given title.[11]

During the war, a remarkable degree of unity was achieved among the various strata of Algerian society, which the French had long believed divided and acquiescent. The goal of the Front of National Liberation was to make "the liberation of Algeria . . . the work of all

10. Estimates of the number of Algerians killed during the war vary widely. President de Gaulle declared in November 1959 that 150,000 Algerians had already been killed. At the end of the war, French officials put the total number of Algerian deaths at around 250,000. The Algerians first claimed they had lost 1,000,000, but later they upped the figure to 1,500,000 without any explanation. In addition to the 2,000,000 peasants put in regroupment villages and to the 300,000 refugees, perhaps another 1,000,000 peasants moved into the cities. Bourdieu estimates that fully one-third of the Algerian population was displaced during the war. See Bourdieu, p. 163.

11. For a more detailed, if somewhat romanticized, analysis of the wartime experiences Algerians underwent, see Frantz Fanon, *L'An V de la Révolution Algérienne* (Paris: Maspero, 1960).

Algerians and not of just a fraction of the people."[12] The FLN was successful, at least in the sense that people from all social classes joined the ranks of the nationalists; but people from all classes also stayed on the side of the French. The Algerian Revolution began and remained strictly a movement for national liberation and never took on the character of a social revolution setting one class against another within Algerian Moslem society. Despite the predominance of peasants among the guerrillas, it never became the peasant revolution that Frantz Fanon portrayed. The peasants, in fact, were fighting more a holy war against the French infidels than a revolution against the big landowners.

The program of the FLN reflected this character of the war. Although nationalist propaganda insisted upon expropriating the land of the French colons and handing it over to the peasants, talk of social and economic reforms was left purposely vague for fear of frightening the Algerian bourgeoisie into siding with the French:

> The total liberation of the national territory, power to the people, the land to the peasants, the elimination of the colonial economy, the destruction of the remains of the medieval and feudal period, these are some of the goals Algerians already favor; the attainment [of these goals] will constitute the democratic revolution. In the present phase, [the democratic revolution] is limited to the war of national liberation.[13]

The hiatus between the war of national liberation and the democratic revolution was much longer than the FLN anticipated. With independence, everything fell apart. The summer of 1962 saw the massive departure of the French, who for 132 years had held Algerian society together. The Provisional Government, which had held the nationalist forces together, disappeared in the summer struggle. There was no longer a common enemy all could agree to fight or a leadership all could agree to obey.

For eight years, independence had been a magic word that promised all things. Suddenly independence was there, and there was nothing magic about it. The nation for which hundreds of thousands of Algerians had rallied and fought so long became a concern of second-rate importance. Although they still turned out en masse to acclaim their leaders coming back after years of exile and imprisonment, Algerians

12. Laroussi Khalifa, *Manuel du Militant Algérien* (Lausanne: Edition de Minuit, 1962), p. 121.
13. Andre Mandouze, *La Révolution Algérienne par les Textes* (Paris: Maspero, 1961), pp. 33–34. The quotation comes from *El-Moudjahid*, the wartime FLN organ.

were no longer inspired to work for the commonweal. Moreover, the bitter struggle for power among Algerian leaders was enough to dishearten and disgust even the most militant nationalists.

Thus Algerians turned to their private affairs, going back to pick up the broken pieces of their former lives or seeking to make new lives for themselves in the enormous vacuum created by the flight of 800,000 Frenchmen. In the words of one prominent Algerian scholar:

> The individual was reduced by the colonial system to living for himself. . . . Algerian society was resuscitated by the revolution. Individuals . . . re-established their social ties to serve the national cause. . . . But with the cease-fire, individualism seemed to revive: in numerous cases, the individual again broke his ties with society in order to grab an attractive job or a vacant [French] property. The race for personal profit severed the ties that the pact of the national revolution had created.[14]

In the scramble for positions and personal well-being, an Algerian middle class began to develop. At the same time, however, Algeria's new leaders pledged to carry out a socialist revolution, countering the spontaneous development of a new bourgeoisie. As a result, considerable tension was created within Algerian society. The formation of a sizeable middle class seriously impeded the launching of a socialist revolution, while the few socialist measures taken prevented the consolidation of the new middle class.

Algiers, the capital city of nearly one million inhabitants, illustrates with particular vividness the contrasts and paradoxes that characterize Algerian society in the present period of transition. In the streets, which have lost none of their bustling activity despite the French exodus, Moslem men and women impeccably dressed in European clothes mingle with those still cloaked in burnoose and turban or hidden behind the *haik* (traditional garment) and veil. Downtown Algiers is tied up in traffic jams twice a day, just as it was when the French were there, as Algerians in late model French cars make their way home from work. The city has its Bon Marché of Paris fame and its state-run department store, Les Galeries Algériennes, formerly Les Galeries Françaises. It has its chain of state-operated Magasins Pilotes stocked with canned goods from the Eastern bloc countries and its privately owned Mozabite corner grocery stores crammed with French, German, Italian, Scandinavian, and American goods as well as an incredible array of local products ranging from oil lamps to hand-

14. Malek Bennabi, *Perspectives Algériennes* (Algiers: En-Nahdha, 1964), p. 67.

woven rugs. There are ten- and twenty-story apartment buildings and *bidonvilles* (shantytowns) at the edge of the city. There are colorful open-air markets where one haggles for plastic shoes and second-hand clothing, and Parisian *haute couture* shops where one pays fancy prices for trade names.

Algiers is much more like Marseilles than Fez or Rabat. It is a French-built city where only the picturesque Casbah, squeezed in between the business district and the former French working-class quarters of Bab el-Oued, reminds the visitor he is really in North Africa. Otherwise the city, with its sidewalk cafés and tree-lined streets, its port and fish markets, its yacht club and luxurious hillside villas, its carefully trimmed gardens and early twentieth century architecture resembles the cities of the French Riviera. This modern city was left to the Algerians by the 350,000 French who lived there. The few remaining pieds noirs complain that life has drastically changed with "*les événements*,"[15] that the city is dead, and that the elegant sensual women who were the pride of Algiers are gone.

Something has definitely changed, but the city is far from dead. In the beautiful villas and modern apartment buildings overlooking the bay, in the expensive shops and restaurants downtown, Algerians have taken the place of the departed French. They have cars, television sets, and refrigerators. They speak French as often as Arabic even among themselves or else a mixture of Algerian dialect and French. This is Algeria's bourgeoisie, composed of the elite that kept its wealth and position during the French occupation and the nouveaux riches who made their fortunes overnight in the chaos of independence. But the rich, old and new, try not to show off their wealth in "socialist" Algeria. On the contrary, wealthy Algerians and civil servants drive the same model Peugeots and Citröens, while army officers, a new class of their own, ride in German BMW's. The number of private cars, about 90,000 in all Algeria, or three-fifths the number before independence, is mystifying, considering that the top salary paid by the government is 2,000 dinars ($400) a month.

The Algerian bourgeoisie faces many problems today. Its position and function in "socialist" and "revolutionary" Algeria is far from clear. The party and the labor union consider the bourgeoisie "retrograde

15. The French pieds noirs used this expression, which means "events," when referring to the war. It reflected their unwillingness to admit that a full-scale war was in fact under way.

and re[...]
to date, [...]
sonnel, h[...]
the top po[...] [...]e administration, paying only lip service to demands
for purges. The government has also periodically wooed the businessmen, trying to get them to invest their capital in the depressed economy.
In the first four years of independence, only one fairly large private
factory—a textile plant near Sétif—was built, and it proved a financial
failure. The government's erratic economic policy, on the other hand,
has cost many businessmen their factories, farms, hotels, shops, and
restaurants, seized in waves of nationalizations in 1963 and 1964.
Courted one day and vilified the next, the bourgeoisie has preferred to
keep a large part of its capital (250 million dinars [$50 million]) in
France and has played a cautious hand with both the Ben Bella and
Boumediene regimes. Socialist slogans and speeches constantly remind
the bourgeoisie just how precarious its situation is even today.

These slogans and speeches mean something entirely different to
another relatively privileged class: the urban workers. In independent
Algeria, where only one man in four is regularly employed, the 300,000
urban workers are indeed a privileged class. In the cities they have
taken the place of the European workers, just as the Algerian bourgeoise
has supplanted its European counterpart. They live in the abandoned
apartments of the former French working-class districts, patronize the
cafés that were once OAS hangouts, and affect many of the French
workers' habits. After work they stroll up and down the main streets
or sit drinking and talking in the cafés. On Saturday night they crowd
the movie houses and on Sunday the soccer stadiums and the beaches.

If those with a steady job are a privileged minority, they are not
necessarily content with their lot. Strikes are common even in the
state-owned enterprises. Some want better working conditions and
higher salaries to meet the ever rising cost of living in the cities; others
want to take over the remaining private industries. If a factory is run
by the state, the workers are often clamoring to take over management
themselves, and if it is already run by the workers, more often than not
the workers have just as many grievances against the government over
lack of credits and contracts for their enterprises or over holdups in
the payment of salaries. Yet it is only the urban workers and a small
number of state-farm workers, about 220,000 who have benefited from
socialism after five years of independence. For the country's three

million unemployed who spend their days endlessly sipping tea in cafés, basking in the warm sun, scavenging the garbage pails at night, or lining up for handouts, "socialism" is a meaningless word. The signs and banners that bedeck the country carry no message for them. The slogans do not incite the have-nots to revolt against the haves, but exhort all Algerians to join hands in the building of a socialist Algeria. Just how the mass of unemployed should contribute to, or benefit from, the socialist revolution has yet to be made clear.

Consequently, hundreds of thousands of Algerian workers take the overnight boat trip to Marseilles or the two-hour flight to Paris in search of jobs. By 1964, there were over 500,000 Algerians in France alone and about 700,000 in all of Europe, or close to three-quarters the number of full-time jobholders in Algeria. Emigration has served as a safety valve for potential social unrest at home and has also greatly helped the economy of Algeria. In 1965, Algerian workers in France sent back a billion French francs ($200 million) to their families, nearly twice the sum the Algerian government received from oil and gas royalties that year. Meanwhile, the number of unemployed in the country continues to rise as 50,000 Algerians join the labor force every year, as thousands of peasants abandon the countryside and come to the cities, and as private industries, faced with shrinking markets, lay off more workers or close down for good.

After independence, the influx of job-seeking peasants doubled the population of many towns and cities. The larger towns of eastern Algeria, notably Constantine, Annaba, and Sétif, were particularly affected by the migration because tens of thousands of refugees returning from Tunisia moved to the urban centers. Many of the peasants took shelter in half-finished housing developments, begun in the last years of French Algeria. The fact that these apartment buildings had no plumbing or electricity, sometimes not even doors and windows, did not stop them. They settled in with their families, and often their sheep and chickens, obstinately resisting all efforts to evict them. Later other immigrants crowded into the bidonvilles, which had been vacated by former inhabitants who had become squatters in abandoned French dwellings. The sudden increase of population, coupled with the disorganization of the administration, caused enormous problems that city authorities are still working to solve today. Most of the Algerians who moved into the "biens vacants," the former French apartments, could not, or would not, pay rent or water and electricity bills. It took au-

thorities four years to even make an inventory of the thousands of
"biens vacants" and even longer to get the new occupants to pay
their bills. In the meantime, buildings began to deteriorate, as no one
was in charge of making repairs. Broken-down elevators, filth in the
hallways and staircases, and leaking pipes became distinctive marks
of buildings in the cities.

Despite hard times, there is no actual starvation in independent
Algeria, primarily because the salary of many a jobholder goes to support the extended family, from children to distant relatives. But the
solidarity that tied Algerians together during the revolution is rapidly
fading, even if everyone from the president down to the street sweeper
is addressed as *khoya* (my brother). In fact, it is only among the
women that one still finds a remarkable degree of solidarity bridging
social barriers. In Algeria, unlike Tunisia, the great majority of Moslem
women still wear the veil today. Only in the cities are there some signs
that emancipation is underway. There, many more young girls are
going to school today than ever before, and many more are working
in offices and shops. But Algeria is still a man's world. Five years after
independence, there is no modern civil code, and the government
seems to be in no hurry to promulgate one. A project for a new family
code drawn up by the government in 1966 was extremely conservative,
so much so that it finally had to be dropped because of vigorous pro-
tests from Algeria's feminists. As a result, Algerian women are still
subjected to the dictates of seventh century Koranic law, with few
modifications. Although poligamy is rare, repudiation of wives and
desertion of families have greatly increased in Algeria's unsettled
society.

In theory the government favors the emancipation of women, but in
practice very little has been done to encourage it. The few women who
have tried to join the FLN have met with stiff opposition and mostly
outright refusal,[16] and at the entrance to City Hall in Algiers, as in
many other public buildings, there are still two windows marked respectively "Information for Men" and "Information for Women."
Fadela M'Rabet, one of the most militant Algerian feminists, has vividly
summed up the situation of women in Algeria:

16. See Fadela M'Rabet, *La Femme Algérienne* (Paris: Maspero, 1964) for a
highly interesting but partisan account of the difficulties of Algerian women in independent Algeria.

Most marriages are still forced unions; fathers are still all-powerful and can interrupt at will the studies of their daughters [in order to marry off or cloister them], and husbands are completely free to repudiate their wives or to marry four. There are innumerable abandoned wives with children to support. . . . If one must be able to earn a living in order to be free, how can Algerian women be free? There are less than a thousand salaried women employed in agriculture, and even fewer in industry; they are just as scarce in the administration. . . . In the PTT [the post office department], which employs by far the greatest number of women, female personnel account for only one-eighth of the total, or about 1,400; 110 women work in the Ministry of Education, 68 in the Ministry of Foreign Affairs, 26 in the Ministry of Youth, and 20 in the Ministry of Tourism. And most of these are cleaning women or typists.[17]

Algerian men are not the only obstacle on the road to emancipation. The women themselves have many complexes to overcome, as Fadela M'Rabet has frankly admitted:

We must state this very clearly right at the beginning: most Algerian women are slightly "touched" and unbalanced; they have some manufacturing [built-in] defects, and the judgments of men about them are generally well founded. It is for them as it is for a colonized people: they are what their masters have made them.[18]

The Union Nationale des Femmes Algériennes (UNFA) was unable even to hold a congress during the first four years of independence because of its incapacity to organize. Its members, although determined to break the bonds of tradition, were often afraid to behave in an untraditional manner. At one UNFA meeting, embarrassed officials asked male journalists present to leave the hall, explaining that the women attending were too shy to speak in front of men. In addition, there is considerable opposition to emancipation among the older women, who see in it only the loss of their traditional grasp over the daughter-in-law. When, for example, a man axed his wife to death in Algiers because she tried to attend a Women's Day rally, the old women of the Casbah blamed Ben Bella, seeing in his speeches about emancipation the real cause of her death. Despite these obstacles, the movement for emancipation is slowly gaining strength in the cities. In the rural areas, however, tradition is stronger than ever today, and the prospects for emancipation are dim.

17. Letter to the French newspaper *Le Monde*, August 15, 1965.
18. M'Rabet, p. 87.

The principal cause of social change in post-independence Algeria was, as we have seen, the exodus of the European population. Three-quarters of the French lived in the cities, and most of the others were concentrated in the rich coastal plains, where they had developed a modern agricultural sector. In these parts of the country, their departure provoked an upheaval; but in the vast hinterland, where 70 percent of the country's twelve million people live, there were few colons and therefore little change took place. On the contrary, tradition regained the strength it had temporarily lost during the war. The differences between the modern and traditional sectors are as great today as they were during the French occupation. In the fertile valleys along the coast, everything is French, from the towns, all alike in their layout and architecture, to the huge plantations, orchards, and vine-yards. The colonial towns, built on the ruins of the *medinas* destroyed in the French conquest, bear little trace of Algeria's Arab past. They are characterized by regular blocks of individual white or dun-colored houses, red tile roofs, geranium-covered balconies, the straight tree-lined main street, and the central square with its trinity of church, town hall, and schoolhouse.

The rich land of the coastal plains, particularly in the Mitidja and Cheliff valleys, is covered with sprawling plantations up to 3,000 hectares in size, which the French bragged were the equal of California's best. The colons used the most modern techniques to grow wine grapes and citrus fruits, which together accounted for 65 per cent of farm revenue and were Algeria's two principal exports. These plantations, some 22,000 throughout the country, now belong to "the people" and have been regrouped into 2,300 enormous state farms theoretically run by the workers themselves. Where before independence these farms realized over one billion French francs ($200 million) in net profits, today they bring to the Algerian government less than one-tenth of this sum.[19] The state farms employ 220,000 full-time workers, mostly the ones who worked there under the French colons. During the war, these workers proved to be the least revolutionary of Algeria's peasants, preferring to keep their jobs rather than to join the maquis. Ironically,

19. See Colonel Houari Boumediene's interview with the Cairo newspaper *Al-Ahram*, October 8–10, 1965. The text of the interview can be found in *Révolution Africaine*, No. 143, October 23, 1965. For further information on the farm sector before independence, see *Tableaux de l'Economie Algérienne* (Algiers, 1960), pp. 128–153.

they are among the few who have profited from Algeria's socialism. They participate in the management of the farms, earn a regular salary, and are assured a minimum eight dinar ($1.60) daily wage, a third more than they earned under the French. The state-farm workers today have much more responsibility and authority than they ever previously had, more in fact than they are prepared to handle, as we shall see later.

The state farms occupy about 18 per cent of all cultivated land in northern Algeria, but they account for over half of the total farm production in the country. In fact, it is only the state farms and some of the largest properties owned by Algerians that are cultivated with modern, high-yield methods. There are about 8,500 Algerians who own more than one hundred hectares. They constitute Algeria's small "landed aristocracy," which will lose much of its land if the oft-postponed agrarian reform ever takes place. So far, only a few Algerian landholders, accused of collaborating with the French, have had their lands expropriated.[20]

The vast majority of private farms are very small and belong to the traditional sector. There are about 450,000 Algerian families that eke out a living on plots of ten hectares or less of arid land, mostly located in the mountainous regions and on the high plains. The annual per capita income of the small peasant farmers is estimated to be between 300 and 500 dinars ($60–$100). The two main activities in the traditional sector are the growing of wheat and the raising of sheep, and both are highly dependent on the irregular rainfall. A dry winter—generally one out of every three—decimates the herds and cuts the wheat harvest in half. Even in a normal year, the exhausted and poorly cultivated land seldom produces the twenty million quintals of wheat necessary to feed the entire population. The tools used to till the land are often very primitive. It is common to see peasants scratching the

20. French and Algerian statistics on the agricultural sector vary considerably. For example, the French indicate that there are about 10 million hectares of cultivated land in northern Algeria, while the Algerian figure is 13 million hectares. The French figure for French-owned land was 2.7 million hectares; yet the Algerians indicate that the socialist sector, which in theory includes all former French-owned land, occupies 2.29 million hectares. It is an Algerian estimate that the state farms occupy 17.6 per cent of all cultivated land. There are no post-independence statistics for the number of private farms. The French figures for farms owned by Algerians were: 8,500 farms over one hundred hectares; 16,580 between fifty and one hundred hectares; 167,170 between ten and fifty hectares; 332,529 between one and ten hectares; and 105,954 less than one hectare. See *Tableaux de l'Economie Algérienne* (Algiers, 1960) and *L'Algérie Agricole*, No. 1, May 1966.

earth with wooden ploughs drawn by mules or camels, and in the last few years it has become even more common because of an acute shortage of tractors. The traditional sector has received scarcely any attention since independence, although Algeria's leaders always under-line the imperative necessity to put an end to the disequilibrium be-tween the traditional and the modern sectors. The government has promised an agrarian reform since 1962 but has yet to carry out its promises. The government has also talked of rebuilding the villages destroyed during the war, of constructing dams to irrigate more land, and of providing technical assistance, loans, and machinery to the small farmers, but has done little that is tangible with respect to these projects.

The peasants, for their part, have not proven to be as revolutionary as they were during the war of independence. They have not agitated to obtain an agrarian reform or to force the government to give more at-tention to their problems. Nor have they responded to appeals for "the mobilization of the masses," at least not in a revolutionary manner. When they have offered voluntary work and pooled their meager re-sources, it has most often been to build a mosque rather than a school or public fountain. Since independence, over four hundred mosques have been built or restored by this means. The number of new mosques is just one indication that the peasants, after the interlude of the war, have returned to their old ways and values. A renewed interest in the re-ligious brotherhoods, which were discredited as centers of reaction by the FLN during the war, is another indication. Indeed, in the absence of any leadership from the party or government, the peasants have fallen once again under the influence of the traditional authorities—*marabouts* (holy men), imams, and village chiefs and elders.[21]

Among the Algerian peasants, the peoples of Berber origin stand out as a group apart. The Berbers, the descendants of North Africa's first inhabitants, have maintained thier individuality, if not their racial purity, through successive invasions of Phoenicians, Romans, Vandals, Arabs, Turks, and French. The Berbers, about a quarter of the Algerian population, are today still fiercely jealous of their independence, and as Ibn Khaldun noted as long ago as the fourteenth century, they are

---

21. A survey conducted in 1965 by a group of American Quakers in the Collo Peninsula, west of Skikda, showed that in nearly 90 per cent of the hamlets there was no party official or representative of the administration. Often the only repre-sentative of the government was the *garde champêtre*, or rural constable.

characterized by a particularly strong spirit of clan. Undoubtedly the clannishness that permeates Algerian politics today is due in part to the influence of the Berbers.

There are four peoples of Berber stock in the country: the Kabyles, the Shawia, the Tuaregs, and the Mozabites. The Kabyles, who number more than two million, are by far the most important. They speak their own language, and despite their early conversion to Islam, they have maintained their own customs. Each small Kabyle village—and there are hundreds of them—is practically a separate political entity, and the village council, or *djemaa*, still functions informally alongside the administration. The Kabylia, 6,500 square miles of steep mountains where little more than fig and olive trees grow, cannot feed all its inhabitants. Consequently, thousands of young Kabyles leave their villages on the mountaintops every year to go to Algiers or France in search of work. It is, in fact, the Kabyles who make up the bulk of Algerian immigrants in Europe. Kabyles also hold the majority of posts in the present Algerian administration as the result of a French policy that sought to play Berbers against Arabs, favoring the former and in particular providing them with more education. Despite its natural poverty, the Kabylia was the only region of Algeria to see a building boom after independence, with stone, tile-roofed homes going up everywhere amidst the ruins of villages destroyed during the war. It is on the money sent back by the Kabyle workers in France that the Kabylia lives and builds today.

Fully nine-tenths of Algerian territory is the Sahara Desert, a wasteland the size of Western Europe inhabited by only 720,000 nomads and oasis-dwellers. There is as much diversity in the desert as in the north, and considerably more wealth, thanks to numerous oil and gas fields. Algeria's gas reserves are second only to those of the United States and are the equal of Russia's.[22] But the wealth of the Sahara does not belong to its inhabitants and has not brought any revolution, socialist or other, to the people. Their lives go on at the same slow sleepy pace in the sun-baked mud huts and in the small desert gardens of the oases, where some wheat and vegetables are painfully cultivated in the shade of the palm trees to complement the basic diet of dates. Since independence,

22. Algeria's gas reserves are estimated at 80 million cubic feet. The country's oil production in 1966 was about 33 million tons and production is expected to increase to 42 million tons in 1967. Oil revenues in 1966 amounted to 700 million dinars ($140 million).

there has only been one major change in the Sahara: the French Foreign Legion and the Camel Corps, which ruled supreme over the desert for fifty years, have left. Most of the oases have been hard hit by the departure of the French army, which provided thousands of jobs. Until early 1966, for example, the Tuaregs of Tamanrasset and Djanet in the deep south got a major part of their income by digging tunnels for French underground atomic tests. Now the only jobs to be found are in the oil and gas fields, which employ about 6,000 local inhabitants. Tourism, to which local authorities hopefully look for economic relief, is just beginning. The Air Algérie plane that makes a swing through the biggest oases once or twice a week attracts big crowds of curious local inhabitants to the airport but still brings only a few hardy tourists.

There is a "rich" Sahara in the north, where a network of good roads connects the oases to the coast, bringing in tourists and allowing the export of dates to the northern cities and abroad. But where the macadam ends and the sand *pistes* begin, communications become slow and expensive and the oases exceedingly poor even by Sahara standards. Dates grown in the deep south are of poor quality and cannot be sold in the north. Only the neighboring countries to the south, Mali and Niger, provide a market for these dates which are bartered for live sheep, wheat, butter, and wood. The other principal export of this area is salt, which the Tuaregs still transport south once a year as they have done for centuries. In fact, the entire southern half of the Sahara is oriented more toward the "Sudan" than toward Algiers.[23] The nomadic tribes disregard frontiers, and the caravan traffic between the Sahara oases and northern Mali and Niger still follows age-old routes, although the truck now often takes the place of the camel.

The Sahara is oriented toward the south but ruled by the north; most of the top officials—prefects, gendarmes, and army officers—come from northern Algeria. They feel out of place and isolated in the desert and in turn are often considered as much foreigners as were the French. These officials have only limited control over the vast expanses under their jurisdiction. There are nomadic tribes whose size and wherabouts are only vaguely known. In the far south, the blue-veiled Tuaregs, a proud race of distant Berber origin, still recognize their king, the ammenokal, as the supreme authority. In 1962, the ammenokal was named second vice president of the National Assembly in an effort to integrate

23. The inhabitants of the Sahara still refer to Mali and Niger as the Sudan, the ancient name of the area.

the Tuaregs into independent Algeria. But this did not prevent the tribes of the Adrar Iforhas and the Hoggar from staging a rebellion in late 1963, which was finally crushed by the combined forces of Mali and Algeria.

There is another people in the Sahara whose attachment to independent Algeria is questionable—the Mozabites of Ghardaia. Ibadite Moslem puritans who sought refuge from persecution deep in the Sahara in the eleventh century, they have kept their cohesion and puritanism to this day. The relative prosperity of the M'Zab, a complex of five oases with a total population of about 80,000, is due to the money sent back by the men who traditionally migrate to the northern cities, where they have cornered the grocery business. The Mozabites are not popular in the country; other Algerians reproach them for their attachment to money and their religious heterodoxy. The Mozabites, for their part, scorn Algeria's experiment with socialism, claiming that they have been the only true socialists for centuries because all Mozabites are taken care of by the community. Independence brought only one major change in the life of the M'Zab: the 6,000 Jews who lived in a veritable ghetto in Ghardaia left practically overnight, as did nearly all of the 140,000 Jews in Algeria. Officially, the Mozabites have given up their traditional form of city government, the assembly of the elders, but there is no dobut that the M'Zab is still governed by its inhabitants.

After 132 years of colonization, there is little in Algeria today that the people can regard as specifically Algerian. The economic structures and towns and cities are part of the French legacy, as is in some areas even the landscape. The education Algerians receive, the authors they know best and admire, the language they most often read and write are also French. The revolution and independence have given educated Algerians a new consciousness of their "depersonalization" and of the Islamic culture from which they have been severed by the French domination. Some of them hope that independence will eventually bring a revival of Islamic culture, a "return to the sources"; but others oppose a renaissance of Islam, seeing in it a return to the dead past, and look instead to French culture as the link to the modern world and its technology. Most Algerians are confused by the choice facing them, often seeing in the culture they know least the fulfillment of needs left unsatisfied by their education. There are Algerians brought up in the

Islamic schools who refuse to be traditionalists, just as there are Algerians brought up in French schools who refuse to be Cartesian thinkers. There is, for example, the wealthy owner of a transportation company, educated in a Koranic school, who left his Sahara oasis for the first time only a few years ago. He has received little French education, but now that he has money he spends his vacations in France, buys his clothes there, and loves French popular songs. In conversation with a foreigner he can even go so far as to refer coyly to France as the "metropole," and he is very anxious to let it be known he was in Paris on business only last week. And there are many like him. On the other hand, there is the young pharmacist educated in Paris who strips off his white gown at closing time and joins his fellow members of the Aissaouia Brotherhood to dance into a religious trance, lick red hot knife blades, and pierce his skin with needles. And there are many like him, even among the highest government officials.

French culture is still far from being supplanted in Algeria, and French remains by necessity the language used in the administration and in most schools. Four years after independence, only the first grade was taught entirely in Arabic because of the lack of Arabic-speaking teachers. Algerian students show remarkably little interest in pursuing Arabic studies. The minister of education announced in 1966 that some of the country's five Arabic-language high schools might have to be closed down for lack of students.[24] French remains the language of the majority of literate Algerians. The official French-language daily El-Moudjahid regularly outsells the official Arabic daily by nearly three to one.[25] Even the few fervent supporters of Islam and its renaissance in Algeria who are promoting a campaign against the domination of French culture must rely principally on French to spread their mes-

24. According to the Ministry of Education, only 1,468 out of 120,416 high school students were pursuing Arabic studies in the 1965–66 scholastic year. See Ministère de l'Education Nationale, *Bulletin Intérieur*, No. 13–14, April 4, 1966.

25. In 1966, the circulation of the French-language daily *El-Moudjahid* was between 40,000 and 50,000, while *Al-Chaab*, the Arabic-language daily, had a circulation of about 15,000. The French-language daily *El-Moudjahid* should not be confused with either the FLN wartime publication *El-Moudjahid* or with the Arabic weekly of the same name appearing after independence. Unless otherwise indicated, references to *El-Moudjahid* are to the French-language daily. Similarly, there were two publications after independence that bore the name *Al-Chaab*: one is the Arabic daily that still exists today, and the other is a French-language daily that appeared from September 1962 until February 1963, when it became *Le Peuple*. References to *Al-Chaab* are to the French-language daily.

sage.[26] Undoubtedly independence has brought a renewed interest in Islam, expressed in the building of mosques, learning to read and write Arabic, or joining the religious brotherhoods. But most Algerians still discuss Islam and its culture with the detachment of an anthropologist lecturing on some remote civilization. Many are reluctant, even embarrassed, to talk about their traditions and customs and are quick to point out that the war has wiped out much of the old world and its ways.

It is particularly to Algeria's restless youth, more than 50 per cent of today's population of twelve million, that tradition appears a loathsome burden from which they are determined to escape. Social life, for one thing, is full of frustrations for them. Dreams and desires stirred by the example of the French and fed by Parisian magazines shatter constantly against the walls of tradition, which keeps teenage girls as home and prevents young Algerians from marrying freely.[27] For many, the first step toward liberation is the escape from the countryside and the smaller towns, where customs weigh heavily on daily life. Except for rare individuals motivated by idealistic fervor, few educated young Algerians want to return to the *bled* (countryside). The failure of half a dozen voluntary projects promoted by youth organizations and the refusal of most students to aid in literacy campaigns or help the understaffed administration during the summer indicated just how few "militants" there were among the Algerian youth. Whether they reject the old world entirely or work to promote its change, young Algerians do not look to the past for their ideals. However, like their elders, they do not know where to look.

In many Algerians there is something of the Ferhat Abbas who in 1936 wrote the famous essay "France is Myself," in which he denied the very existence of an Algerian nation: "I interrogated history, the living and the dead; I even visited the cemeteries: nobody answered me."[28]

26. The association Al-Qiyam Al-Islamiyah, a highly conservative group of traditionalist Algerians, publishes irregularly a magazine called *Humanisme Musulman* in both French and Arabic. The French edition has the largest circulation.

27. The number of sensational weekly magazines sold in Algeria is considerable. According to a study made by *El-Moudjahid* in April 1966, the circulation of the *"presse du coeur"* was given as 48,500. The two most widely read weeklies were *France-Dimanche* and *Ici Paris*, with a combined circulation of 20,000. See *El-Moudjahid*, April 12, 1966. These weeklies were banned from the country in early 1967.

28. Ferhat Abbas, "La France C'est Moi," published in *L'Entente*, February 23, 1936. See also le Tourneau, p. 314.

The answer at that time came only from the ulama, the reformist religious leaders, who claimed they had studied the past and present history of Algeria and found the nation Abbas could not discover. For them, Algeria was part of the great Islamic nation stretching from the Red Sea to the Atlantic. Yet even the ulama's explanation did not geographically distinguish Algeria from neighboring Tunisia and Morocco or give it a personality distinct from that of the other Arab states.

In any case, most French-educated Algerians feel that the arguments of Islamic culture had little importance then and have little now. Their adherence to the nationalist movement in 1954 did not imply a sudden discovery of the Algerian nation. It meant that, like Abbas, they had come to realize that assimilation was impossible and that revolution was the only way out of an intolerable condition of political and social inferiority. Independence has not automatically brought the answer to the agonizing question of what it means to be Algerian after more than a century of "depersonalization" under the French. The question will probably cease to be a burning one when Algerians can read and write their own language better than French and know the history of North Africa and the Arab world better than that of France. Today Algerian intellectuals are just beginning to "decolonize history"[29] and to rediscover their heroes of the resistance to the French invasion like the emir Abdelkader, and their spiritual leaders of the past like Cheikh Ben Badis and Cheikh Ibrahimi.[30]

Algeria, like most other newly independent African countries, is today faced with the problem of welding together into a nation the different groups that make up its population. The problem is not dramatic:

29. Décoloniser l'Histoire (Paris: Maspero, 1965) is the title of a book by Mohammed Sahli, an Algerian historian. The book attempts to correct myths about Algeria's past propagated by the French to justify their conquest of Algeria. Sahli was named ambassador to Peking in 1966.

30. Cheikh 'Abd El-Hamid Ben Badis, born in Constantine in 1892, founded the Association des Ouléma Réformistes d'Algérie in 1931. The ulama were deeply influenced by the Salafi reform movement underway in Egypt, which preached the necessity for a renaissance of Islam through a return to its original purity. The ulama hoped that a cultural renaissance would give the Arab countries the strength to free themselves from colonial domination. Cheikh Mohamed Bachir Ibrahimi was another leader of the association, particularly active in setting up Koranic schools and medersas (grade and high schools). He openly called for Algeria's independence in 1953. When Cheikh Ibrahimi died in Algiers in May 1965, his funeral was attended by an enormous crowd. Many foreign observers interpreted the funeral procession as a veiled demonstration by the more conservative elements against Ben Bella's socialist policies.

the country's unity is not menaced by the revolt of tribes or the secession of regions. But Algeria does not have a strong tradition of political unity. Unlike Tunisia and Morocco, which both enjoyed the rule of a single dynasty for centuries, Algeria was never subjected to the control of a central government until the French conquest. The French imposed unity and established the country's present-day boundaries but gave the Algerians no role in the running of the country. They set up an administration staffed almost entirely by Frenchmen, while in Tunisia and Morocco, which both became protectorates, they ruled through indigeneous administrations.

The different groups in the country—Arabs, Kabyles, Shawia, Mozabites, and Tuaregs—still think of one another as quite different people. The Kabyles are hypersensitive to their lack of representation in the government, while the Arabs appear all too aware of the grasp the better educated Kabyles have on the wheels of the administration. Rare is the Kabyle, however, who talks seriously of secession or regional autonomy for his homeland. The differences among the various peoples are not so strong as to necessitate the establishment of a federal political system; yet they are strong enough to force the local administration to find an informal *modus vivendi* with the leaders of each group, be it the Kabyle djemaa or the Tuareg ammenokal.

Algerians have other characteristics that render difficult the consolidation of the new state. Their extreme individualism and distaste for regimentation border on anarchy and make "the mobilization of the masses," for which Ben Bella constantly called, a laughable slogan. Clannishness pervades Algerian politics, tending to turn the République Algérienne Démocratique et Populaire into a "république des camarades," while the constant disputes among personalities have made the history of independent Algeria largely one of "quarrels among enemy brothers."[31] Algerians have a deep distrust for the official thesis, a distrust that dates back to the war years when the FLN and the French were both trying to indoctrinate the people. In independent Algeria, people still scorn the government-controlled press and radio. Rumors run rampant, and the Algerians, officials and public alike, read the Parisian dailies and listen to Radio Montecarlo for "straight" infor-

31. Both expressions come from Ferhat Abbas's letter of resignation delivered to the National Assembly on August 12, 1963, and have since become part of Algerian political jargon.

mation on Algeria. French dailies, when they are not seized,[32] still sell nearly as many copies as Algerian ones.

Suspicion and distrust also mark the Algerians' attitude toward one another and toward all foreigners. Two Algerians meeting for the first time are likely to give each other a polite but thorough questioning before deciding whether to talk freely or not to talk at all. Under both the Ben Bella and Boumediene regimes, "parallel" secret services have thrived, making people very leery of informers. The government, for its part, operates like a secret society. Biographies of ministers and basic statistics are handled like classified material, and "intoxication campaigns," the deliberate spreading of rumors by both the government and the opposition, take the place of factual information. In many ways, Algeria is still living in the revolution's atmosphere of secrecy.

Independence has not provided the stability Algerian society badly needs; on the contrary, it has brought into the open the conflicting aspirations of different groups. The Algerian bourgeois, including many civil servants, are satisfied to have replaced the French and are against any radical social or economic reforms. The left-wing intellectuals and the urban workers regard independence as only the first step toward the complete liberation of Algeria, which will not be achieved until a socialist revolution has taken place, and the conservative and religious elements seek a renaissance of Islam that will counter Western culture and atheistic socialism. These divisions within Algerian society have not been in themselves the cause of instability. It is the country's leaders who are primarily responsible, because in their struggle for power they have exploited the latent social tensions to further their personal aims. In so doing, they have exacerbated the conflicts and perpetuated instability.

32. In 1966, the circulation of the three principal dailies sold in Algeria was as follows: Le Monde, 10,000; France Soir, 20,000; and Le Figaro, 3,000. In addition, French news weeklies have a very large circulation: Paris-Match sells 12,000 copies; Le Journal du Dimanche, 22,400; Le Canard Enchaîné, 7,000; Nouvel Observateur, 2,500; L'Express, 3,000; and Candide, 2,000.

chapter three
the march decrees

Speeches are enough to make the peasants want the land, speeches won't be enough to make them stop wanting it.[1]

André Malraux

Self-management, which became the keystone of Algeria's "democratic revolution" in March 1963, was no child of scientific socialism. Begotten in the chaos and anarchy reigning in Algeria at independence, born in a period of strife within the Ben Bella regime, it soon became a problem child many Algerian officials secretly wished had never been born. During the summer civil war, the economic situation in Algeria became catastrophic. Activity all but came to a halt following the exodus of the French. Even the few who courageously stayed on through the summer closed down their factories and boarded up their shops. In the countryside, where guerrilla bands were in control, the remaining 4,500 French farmers were not investing a penny in their future.[2] Unemployment, chronically high in the country, had reached alarming proportions.

The Provisional Executive,[3] a mixed Algerian-French caretaker government set up by the Evian Agreements to run the country until an Algerian government could be formed, was hardly qualified to cope

1. André Malraux, *Man's Fate* (New York: Modern Library, 1934), p. 148.
2. The exact number of French farmers who remained in Algeria in the fall of 1962 was never known. In October 1963, however, at the time of the nationalization of remaining French lands, the French Embassy in Algiers estimated that there were between 4,000 and 5,000 farms, covering one million hectares, still in French hands.
3. The Provisional Executive was to take charge of administration, maintain law and order, and prepare the referendum for independence. It was to have its own police force, which in practice never functioned. The Algerian delegation to the executive was headed by Abderrahmane Farès, one-time president of the Algerian Assembly under the French. The executive was dissolved September 24, 1962, the same day on which the GPRA officially ceased to exist.

with such a critical situation. It had no real hold over the country, since the Algerians considered it a puppet in the hands of the French. The administration, a mixture of Algerians who had served under the French and of men appointed by the wilaya leaders, barely held together. It was not until the end of August that the Provisional Executive finally arrived at some decision about what to do with the abandoned French properties, which were steadily growing in number. A decree published on August 24 put all vacant farms, factories, houses, and shops under the protection of the state.[4] The French owners were given thirty days from the publication of the decree (September 7) to come back and resume management of their farms and factories. If the owners failed to return by the end of this period, the prefects were authorized to appoint managers to run the enterprises. The decree was an emergency measure aimed at reviving economic activity in the country. There was no threat of nationalization. Indeed, the Provisional Executive was by its very nature pledged to French-Algerian cooperation and looked to the French to save Algeria from chaos. Numerous appeals for the return of French civil servants, technicians, factory owners, and farmers appeared throughout the summer in both the Algerian and French press. But the French were in no hurry to return. Algeria was still deep in civil war, and the French newspapers reported that Europeans were being kidnapped and assassinated. In asking the French to return, the Provisional Executive was inviting them to play a singularly dangerous game—physically dangerous since the executive could not ensure their safety, economically dangerous since it could not guarantee that their properties would not be nationalized after its demise.

Not all Algerians were as anxious as the Provisional Executive to see the French return. Many of them, "that fauna of war profiteers and speculators" as Ben Bella called them,[5] had rushed to seize whatever abandoned properties they could and had no desire to hand back what they had taken. During the summer, hundreds of villas, apartments, shops, restaurants, and cafés were bought up at ridiculously low prices, or simply taken over without further formalities. In the cities Algerians were busy selling to each other property they did not own; more than a few made their fortune by this means. It was more difficult to speculate with farms and factories, however, because the workers knew well who was the owner and were not ready to accept orders from just

4. *Journal Officiel de l'Etat Algérien*, September 7, 1962, Ordonnance 62,020.
5. Ben Bella's speech to the first UTGA congress, January 17, 1963.

anybody. It took some authority to seize a farm—some sort of official title or a gun. Nevertheless, in many regions there was a great deal of trafficking in vacant farms. Guerrilla leaders, army officers, labor union and FLN officials all wanted their share of the war booty. There was less wheeling and dealing over abandoned French factories because it took considerable know-how to exploit them; besides, the owners had often destroyed or shipped to France much of the machinery, so that most factories could not be reopened without a sizable investment.

Those who seized French farms were mostly acting on their own initiative. For instance, Major Si Larbi, commander of Wilaya Two (Constantine), got hold of at least a dozen farms, which he ran by sending his aides around to give orders and take away the harvest. In the Cheliff Valley, officers of Wilaya Four tried to divide the French lands among their men but finally had to give up because of opposition from the workers. At the edge of the Sahara, Colonel Chaabani, head of Wilaya Six, was "renting" out to his friends the French lands he had seized in the Bou Saâda area and the date-palm plantations around Biskra.

The only organized effort to take in hand the abandoned farms and factories was made by the UGTA, which resumed its activities inside Algeria shortly after the cease-fire.[6] The federation's leaders were pursuing two objectives in the summer of 1962. First, they wanted to reopen the factories and organize the work on the vacant farms—in short, to get people back on the job. Second, by providing leadership to the workers of the abandoned enterprises, they hoped to attract new members to the union and at the same time establish the UGTA as a strong, autonomous organization. The UGTA leaders were aware that the union risked becoming a subdivision of the party, as is the case in most single-party states.

The federation went into action even before the referendum for independence was held, and on June 20 it issued an appeal calling upon the workers to go back to their jobs. Explaining that the UGTA had repeatedly requested the Provisional Executive to reopen the factories and protect the workers from OAS terrorist attacks, and that the

6. The Union Générale des Travailleurs Algériens was founded on February 24, 1956, partly to counter a rival union organized by Messali Hadj earlier the same month. By June 1957, many of the first UGTA leaders were in prison, where the first secretary-general, Aissat Idir, died. The other leaders fled to Tunis, where the UGTA was based until the end of the war. As a consequence, the federation had hardly any organization inside Algeria at the time of the cease-fire in March 1962.

executive had either been unable or unwilling to act, the appeal concluded: ". . . our battle is soon going to take a new form. . . . The
resumption of economic activity will allow the workers to take the
initiative, to be present everywhere, to participate, to direct and control
the economy of our country."[7] The meaning of this vague declaration
was made clear in the following weeks, when the UGTA began to
organize the workers to take over management of the abandoned enterprises. Although the federation was better organized in the factories,
it was on the farms that it achieved the most significant results. In the
Mitidja and Cheliff valleys, UGTA officials set up workers' committees
to run the huge French farms they had wrested from the hands of
guerrilla officers and even financed some of these committees out of
union funds.[8] The idea and practice of self-management were thus
introduced in Algeria; however, the number of farms organized in this
manner was comparatively small, and the UGTA was taking as active
a role in the management as the workers themselves.

The UGTA had neither the men, the funds, nor the power to organize
workers' committees on a nationwide scale. There were simply too
many closed factories and abandoned farms and too much competition
from guerrilla bands, the party, and the army. Recognizing that the
economic situation continued to deteriorate, on August 18 the UGTA
appealed again to the Provisional Executive, asking it to persuade or
force the French owners to reopen their factories and return to their
farms: "If there is a negative answer, the government must organize
a system of management by the workers. . . . This is an emergency
measure imposed by necessity and not inspired by doctrinal principles."[9] The UGTA's appeal was still extremely moderate, since it did
not call for the nationalization of the abandoned farms and factories.
But the Provisional Executive turned a deaf ear to the UGTA proposal
for management by the workers and in its decree of August 24 ordered
instead that the prefects take charge of the abandoned enterprises. The
idea of setting up workers' management committees nevertheless continued to gain ground in Algeria and was given official status when

7. *Le Monde,* June 21, 1962.
8. See *L'Ouvrier Algérien,* No. 2, October 19, 1962, and No. 3, November 1, 1962.
The UGTA claimed in July and August that it had organized forty-three farms
with 2,300 workers around Boufarik and an unspecified number of farms around
Orleansville. It also claimed to have advanced 500,000 dinars ($100,000) to help
the farms near Boufarik.
9. *L'Ouvrier Algérien,* No. 1, August 18, 1962.

Ben Bella, in his inaugural speech of September 28, announced to the National Assembly that he had already named a commission to study the creation of such committees.

Actually, the influence of the UGTA probably had relatively little to do with the turn events were taking.[10] During the war years, many GPRA members had visited Yugoslavia, one of the first countries to recognize the exiled Provisional Government, and were therefore familiar with that country's experiment with workers' self-management. Other nationalist leaders, among them Ben Bella, had studied during long years in prison the Russian, Chinese, Cuban, and Yugoslav revolutions. To the vast majority of these leaders, the Yugoslav type of socialism was the most appealing because it was the most democratic and the best suited to the Algerian mentality. But the decisive influence on the form socialism was to take in Algeria was undoubtedly that of the coterie of foreign intellectuals who acted as Ben Bella's personal "brain trust" during his first two years in power. Many of these advisors called themselves Trotskyites and were connected with the Fourth International. Their basic conviction was that the only true socialist system was one that put the power directly in the hands of the workers and not under the control of an oppressive state bureaucracy. A system of self-management was for them the only desirable form of economic organization.

The Trotskyites had a long history of involvement in the Algerian Revolution, having been one of the first groups in Europe to support the cause of the FLN. Michel Raptis, alias Pablo, one-time head of the Fourth International, had worked for the FLN since the beginning of the war and in early 1962 had been commissioned to draw up a project for a land reform in Algeria. In the fall of 1962, Ben Bella named Raptis to the special commission set up to study the institution of a self-management system in Algeria. Also appointed were Luftallah Solliman, an exiled Egyptian Trotskyite, and Mohamed Tahiri, a Moroccan land reform expert sympathetic to the Trotskyite philosophy. The Algerian members of the commission, among them Mohamed Harbi, later director of the weekly Révolution Africaine, and Abdelkader Maachou, director of the newly created Bureau National des Biens Vacants, were intellectuals of a similar persuasion. Algeria thus became

10. Several UGTA leaders and Trotskyite advisors of Ben Bella interviewed by the authors were of this opinion. In fact, UGTA leaders were rather bitter because they had not been consulted.

the first testing ground for the revolutionary theories of the Trotskyites, who had never before had the influence they were to enjoy for eighteen months in Algeria. In the Trotskyite publication *Sous le Drapeau du Socialisme*, Algeria became the *enfant chéri*, in turn praised, cajoled, warned, and criticized, but never considered quite able to walk on its own two feet.

The commission worked quickly. Its first two decrees were signed on October 22 and 23, and appeared in the very first issue of the government's *Journal Officiel* along with the publication of the list of members in the first Ben Bella Cabinet.[11] One of the decrees, aimed at stopping rampant speculation, forbad all further transactions of abandoned French properties and nullified all those that had taken place since July 1, 1962. The other decree instituted management committees on the abandoned farms. These committees were to be elected by the workers, who in turn were to choose a president to act as farm manager. The property rights of the French owner were not put in question, since the decree gave the prefects the power to return the farm to the legitimate owner if he came back. But the decree also stated that the committees would in any case continue to participate in the management of the farms. No role was indicated for the state in the running of the farms or in the election of the committees. A month later, a similar decree set up management committees in the vacant factories,[12] and in early November government officials inaugurated the first committees with great fanfare. The revolution was again under way.

If socialism had come to Algeria, few seemed aware of it. The UGTA weekly *L'Ouvrier Algérien* almost ignored the decrees, although they enacted the measures the federation had been asking the government to take for months. The Algerian newspapers devoted a few articles to the decrees and to the inauguration of the first management committees, and then forgot about the whole business. In the National Assembly, the newly elected deputies were busy arguing over the rules of procedure to be adopted and paid no attention to the promulgation of the decrees. Even during the first debate on government policy in early December, deputies talked of the biens vacants as if management

11. *Journal Officiel de la République Algérienne Démocratique et Populaire*, No. 1, October 26, 1962, Décrets 62–02 and 62–03. Henceforth, this publication will be referred to as *Journal Officiel*.

12. *Journal Officiel*, No. 5, November 23, 1962, Décret 62–38.

committees had not been created. As Ben Bella declared at that time: "Some brothers do not appear to understand the importance of that act."[13]

However, the decrees were a turning point for the country and for the workers. Self-management, which had begun through the initiative of the UGTA and the workers, became a creature of the government and particularly of Ben Bella. The expression "self-management" entered the official language, but so did the expression "state farm," raising considerable doubt about what the government meant by self-management.[14] Another important consequence of the decrees that received little attention, was that the decrees greatly reduced the probability of the return of the French, since they obliged owners to accept co-management with the workers. But the French farmers had few illusions about their future in Algeria. As one of them wrote:

> Our role should be that of a buffer aimed at softening for some time the shock of a too brutal transition between two opposed economic systems. Our relatively high output should help to make up for the drop in production that will undoubtedly result from the creation of a new system not yet in good running order.

He also noted that

> in the eyes of some Algerian leaders, ideological principles now outweigh economic considerations. But it is only in economic terms that we can judge our interest in staying on in this country.[15]

Indeed, the government was giving top priority to political goals and appeared oblivious to economic difficulties. "Almost all committees are now in place," wrote the party weekly *El-Moudjahid* in early December, "but few are really managing. Without credits, what can they do? They guard the farms."[16] The situation had not changed much by the beginning of March 1963, when *El-Moudjahid* denounced the lack of rule or method in the financing of the state farms.[17] Some of the farms were receiving funds from the Sociétés Agricoles de Prévoyance (SAP), a system of government-run farm banks created by the French; others

13. Ben Bella's speech before the National Assembly, December 12, 1962.

14. *Al-Chaab*, the government-run daily, appeared on November 14, 1962, with a banner headline on the front page: "Inauguration of the First State Farm." The ceremony took place at the Abbo farm at the edge of the Kabylia.

15. Letter from a farmer living in the Constantine area, *Le Monde*, November 6, 1962.

16. French-language weekly *El-Moudjahid*, No. 104, December 1, 1962.

17. French-language weekly *El-Moudjahid*, No. 118, March 9, 1963. Interview with the director of the Bureau National des Biens Vacants.

received aid from the Ministry of Agriculture or the Ministry of Labor and still others from the prefectures. Many, however, got no money at all from the state, and the private banks were extremely reluctant to extend credit to the worker-run farms, despite a government guarantee on such loans.[18]

By the end of January, even the UGTA was no longer of any help to the workers' committees because it had lost its fight for autonomy and had been put under the control of undynamic party-appointed leaders. Tensions between the UGTA and party had existed since Ben Bella had come to power. The federation wanted to remain an autonomous organization and resented any interference in its affairs from the party or the government. The FLN was determined to gain control of the UGTA, appealing to the Tripoli Program to justify its position. In fact, the program gave some weight to both sides in the dispute; it stated that "the party must see to it that the orientation of the national organizations is coherent with its general program," but also that "the party respects the autonomy of the union, the essential role of which is to defend the material and cultural interest of the workers."[19]

The conflict between the federation and Ben Bella came into the open in early November, when the prime minister declared at a press conference that total autonomy was against the principles set forth in the Tripoli Program and that the UGTA could only be "autonomous within the party."[20] Undoubtedly Ben Bella could ill afford to allow the federation, with over 200,000 members,[21] to remain an independent force at a time when the ruling party was still weak and poorly organized. Nonetheless, an agreement was reached in mid-December that gave the UGTA a large degree of autonomy.[22] The party recognized the federation's right to organize meetings, hold a congress, and elect its officials without outside interference. In exchange, the UGTA pledged to respect the Tripoli Program and to toe the party line. However, the agreement was never respected.

18. *Journal Officiel*, No. 6, November 30, 1962, Décret 62–98.
19. *Projet de Programme*, p. 58.
20. Press conference of November 3, 1962. See *Al-Chaab*, November 4–5, 1962.
21. *Rapport d'Orientation*, document of the first UGTA congress. The union claimed its membership was "coming close to 300,000," but other estimates put the figure closer to 200,000.
22. See *Al-Chaab*, December 21, 1962. The UGTA regarded the agreement of December 19 as its "birth certificate," since the party appeared to have officially recognized the UGTA as an independent organization. See the *Rapport d'Orientation*, first UGTA congress.

The UGTA congress that began on January 17, 1963, was the scene of a bitter, underhanded struggle between party-appointed and union-elected delegates. Ben Bella presided at the opening ceremonies and told the delegates that in a socialist state a labor union must not just fight for higher salaries and better working conditions, but must also take an active role in the running of the economy. He cited the management of the vacant farms and factories as the area in which the federation had an important role to play and called upon the federation to organize the workers of the farms as well as those of the factories. Ben Bella's speech suggested that he was willing to give the UGTA the leading role it asked for, but the outcome of the congress proved just the contrary. On the very next day, Party Secretary-General Khider rounded up several hundred goons and packed the congress hall, even taking over the seats reserved for invited foreign observers. From that point on, UGTA delegates were booed off the podium every time they tried to speak, while the very mention of Ben Bella's name by party delegates triggered off uncontrollable applause from the goons. Finally, in the midst of pandemonium, union leaders were forced to abandon the podium to the pro-party factions. When the congress ended on January 20, the UGTA had lost all its autonomy and gained a leadership subservient to the party and totally discredited by union members.[23] Thereafter, the UGTA made little effort to give the workers' committees the guidance and aid they so badly needed.

Even as Ben Bella was shackling the federation, the commission he had appointed was preparing legislation aimed at making Algeria into a workers' state. At the end of March, three decrees were published unexpectedly in the midst of a political storm. Relations between Ben Bella and Khider had become very tense by that time, ostensibly because of a difference of opinion over the role of the party. Actually, the point at issue between the two former allies was control of the FLN. Ben Bella feared that Khider was using the party to build himself a power base, and he was therefore determined to oust Khider from the post of secretary-general. Adding to Ben Bella's difficulties, the French exploded an atomic bomb at their Sahara nuclear test site on the eve of the first anniversary of the Evian Peace Agreements; this became known to

23. The new leadership was composed of Rabah Djermane, first secretary; Areski Ziani, responsible for organization; Mohamed Tahar Chafai, finances; Cheikh Benghazi (former head of Messali Hadj's Union), foreign relations; Mohamed Flissi, press and information, Safi Boudissa, agriculture; Ali Remli, education.

the public, creating much embarrassment for the Algerian government and triggering off a crisis in French-Algerian relations. It was the right moment for announcing a popular measure that would turn the attention of the Algerians from the dark to the bright side of independence.

On March 29, Ben Bella went before the nation on television and radio to announce that the government had decided to entrust the workers once and for all with the management of all vacant farms and factories. He dramatically called upon the workers "to prove to the world that the Algerian Revolution wants to, and can, be in the vanguard of modern-day socialist experiences." He told them:

> Close up your ranks. Show the world that you are the masters of your destiny, [that you are] united, vigilant, and conscious of your duties and rights. Organize yourselves so that everywhere throughout Algeria the workers' assemblies can meet and so that everywhere . . . the management committees, democratically elected, can undertake the exalting task of the socialist edification of our country.[24]

In order to dramatize the beginning of the reign of socialism in Algeria, Ben Bella had the army take over—with an impressive display of force —the huge La Trappe farm belonging to the Borgeaud family, one of the most prominent families in the history of French colonization.[25]

The document that was to put Algeria in the vanguard of socialism was composed of three decrees which became known as the March Decrees. None of the decrees had been discussed by the party or submitted to the National Assembly for its approval. Ben Bella, who was using the decrees for his own purposes, wanted to take all the credit for them. The first decree defined the meaning of vacancy as applied to French properties in the country: any enterprise that ceased regular production and any house or apartment left unoccupied by the owner or his legal tenant for more than two months was to be declared vacant and put under the protection of the presidency.[26] The narrow door left open for the return of the French owners by the decrees of the previous October was thus closed for good. In effect, several hundred thousand French properties were nationalized by this decree, although the word "nationalization" was carefully avoided in the text and in all speeches in order to prevent subsequent demands for indemnities.

24. Ben Bella's speech of March 29, 1963.
25. The 1,800 hectares farm belonging to Henry Borgeaud was taken over on March 31, 1962. In the following weeks, 150,000 hectares of French land were seized from other well-known colons.
26. *Journal Officiel*, No. 15, March 22, 1963, Décret 63–88.

The second decree established that the vacant enterprises would be run by the workers and spelled out in detail the system of management as follows:[27]

1. A general assembly, composed of all permanent workers of an enterprise, to adopt the enterprise's annual plans for production, procurement of new equipment, and marketing, to check the accounting, and to decide the distribution of tasks among the workers. The assembly was to meet at least once every three months, and if the enterprise had over thirty workers it was to elect:

2. a workers' council, numbering from ten to one hundred members, which duplicated many of the functions of the general assembly but had more direct control over management, since it met monthly. The council also hired and fired workers and elected:

3. a management committee, composed of three to eleven members, which was to draw up the budget and all plans to be submitted to the vote of the assembly and council. The committee was also empowered to make decisions concerning short-term loans, marketing, and buying of equipment and materials without consulting the general assembly or the workers' council. It elected:

4. a president, who called and presided over all meetings of the assembly, council, and committee, and countersigned all financial and legal documents of the enterprise (these documents were also signed by the director). The president was to be elected annually, while the members of the management committee and of the workers' council were elected for three-year terms, one-third being re-elected every year.

5. A director represented the state in every enterprise. He acted as treasurer and chief accountant; in addition, he was responsible for the day-to-day operations of the enterprise. The director was a member of the management committee, although he was named by the state and was responsible not to the workers but rather to:

6. a communal council. This council was composed of the presidents of self-managed enterprises in each *commune* (township) and of representatives from the party, the UGTA, the army, and the local administration. It was supposed to help set up, organize, and coordinate the self-management system. It also approved the nomination of the directors, whom it could also dismiss.

The third decree established the principle that the profits of the enterprise should be shared among the workers, except for unspecified per-

27. *Journal Officiel*, No. 17, March 29, 1963, Décret 63–95.

centages that were to be given to a national employment fund and a national investment fund.[28] Thus the workers became directly interested in the productivity of the enterprise.

The decrees affected approximately 200,000 apartments and houses;[29] over 16,000 farms,[30] covering about eight hundred thousand hectares of the most fertile land and employing perhaps seventy thousand workers;[31] and 450 industrial enterprises, only 5 per cent of which were large factories.[32] In addition, they affected hundreds of hotels, restaurants, cafés, shops, and other commercial enterprises.

The highly complex and sophisticated system of management set up by the March Decrees required for its successful functioning a degree of education and experience that far exceeded that of the Algerian peasantry, of which only 5 per cent were even literate. Furthermore, the organization of the system had not been carefully studied in all its aspects, and many provisions of the decrees created conflicts within the enterprise and between it and the state. In the first place, the role of the assembly and that of the workers' council so overlapped that there was hardly any point in having both; indeed, the councils were seldom set up. Second, the decrees led to strife between the permanent workers, who were members of the assembly and shared in the profits, and the seasonal laborers, twice as numerous (440,000), who did not participate in either the management or the sharing of profits.[33] Third, a sharp

28. *Journal Officiel*, No. 17, March 29, 1963, Décret 63–98.
29. The number of abandoned French apartments and houses was estimated to be between 200,000 and 250,000. A nationwide census was undertaken twice but was neither time completed with any degree of accuracy.
30. The number of farms that had been taken over by March 1963 was never determined. By October 1963, however, only 4,000 to 5,000 farms were still in French hands. The total number of French farms in Algeria was 22,037. Since numerous farms were seized between March and October, there were probably around 16,000 abandoned farms in March 1963.
31. According to the Algerian government, there were about 1.2 million hectares in the socialist sector in May 1963. This figure included about 220,000 hectares that the French government had set aside for an agrarian reform and about 150,000 hectares seized immediately after the publication of the March Decrees. By October 1963, all French land, 2.29 million hectares (Algerian estimate), had been taken over.
32. Estimates of the number of abandoned factories and shops varied between 450 and 500. The only large factories in the socialist sector were ACILOR, a metallurgic plant; Verrerie d'Afrique du Nord, a glass works; Filatures de Fort de l'Eau, a textile plant; and Minoterie Narbonne, a flour mill. About half the enterprises employed ten workers or less.
33. The decree of March 28, 1963, stated that only permanent workers could receive bonuses and that only permanent workers could share in the profits. The number of permanent farmhands is estimated today at around 220,000 and the number of seasonal laborers at around 440,000.

conflict developed between the elected management committee and the state-appointed director. Although the system was supposed to give power to the workers, it had in fact given the greatest authority to the director, over whose activities the workers had no control. Only the communal councils were empowered to remove the directors, and these councils very seldom existed.

In addition to fathering all these problems, the decrees failed to spell out the role of the government agency in charge of the socialist sector. From the text of the decrees, it appeared that this agency was charged only with naming the directors and with making sure that the plan of each enterprise would fit into the national plan. The self-managed enterprises had no representation in the government agency and thus no way of preventing it from imposing other limits on their autonomy. This arrangement gave Ben Bella a free hand to do whatever he liked with the socialist sector, and he very soon made use of this power.

The three decrees so much ballyhooed in the press and in speeches were not the only ones concerning the nascent socialist sector that Ben Bella signed at this time. A decree of March 18 set up the Office National de la Réforme Agraire (ONRA) to carry out an agrarian reform and organize the management of the state farms.[34] The ONRA was the new government agency for the state farms. It was not under the presidency, which was supposed to supervise the socialist sector, but under the Ministry of Agriculture and Agrarian Reform. From the point of view of a rational organization of the farm sector, it was only natural that the self-managed farms should come under this ministry, especially since the March Decrees were said to be the first step of an agrarian reform. But the creation of the ONRA was a serious blow to the self-managed farms. Ali Mahsas, the office's first director and later minister of agrarian reform, believed in state control and not in self-management, and he soon deprived the farms of all but nominal autonomy.[35] Ironically, the authors of the March Decrees, who had no regard for practical problems, made Mahsas's efforts to undermine self-management easier by failing to establish a system of financing and marketing geared to

34. *Journal Officiel*, No. 15, March 22, 1963, Décrets 63–89 and 63–90.
35. Ali Mahsas was one of Ben Bella's oldest and closest friends. The two men had escaped together from the Blida Prison in 1950, after their arrest for organizing a holdup of the Oran post office in April 1949 to get funds for the MTLD. During the escape, Ben Bella apparently saved Mahsas's life. Later Mahsas was credited with saving Ben Bella from assassination in Tripoli, Libya. Ironically, it was Mahsas who did the most to undermine the self-management system and thus Ben Bella's popularity.

the needs of the socialist sector. These problems were thus left to Mahsas to resolve.

On April 18, Ben Bella signed another decree, which obliged the self-managed farms to market their produce through the same organization that was financing them and recommended that these farms no longer use private channels for marketing but only the state-run SAP and the Caisse Centrale des Sociétés Agricoles (CCSA).[36] This decree was a flagrant violation of the March Decrees, which explicitly stated that the management committee "chooses the channel for the marketing of the produce." This decree was followed a week later by still another one, which put the SAP and the CCSA directly under the control of the ONRA and established that only the ONRA could grant loans and credits to the socialist farms.[37] Thus just one month after the publication of the March Decrees, the so-called self-managed farms had lost all right of decision over two crucial matters—financing and the marketing of their produce.

Ben Bella had in effect taken away from the farm workers with one hand what he had just given them with the other. But this sleight of hand passed unnoticed as the country plunged into a new euphoria. In early April, Ben Bella left on a triumphal tour of the country, waving the March Decrees as the banner of Algeria's socialism. Then on May 15, the government launched a nationwide campaign for the "democratic reorganization" of the self-managed enterprises. Ben Bella opened the campaign, declaring that the government was determined to put an end for good to all practices contrary to the letter and spirit of the March Decrees. Elections for the workers' councils and management committees took place across the country, and an effort was even made to set up the communal councils. Ben Bella's popularity was greatly enhanced by the establishment of the self-management system, which strengthened his hand against his ally-turned-enemy, Khider. Moreover, he now had a socialist system "specifically Algerian" to hold up as an example for other Arab and African countries to follow.

Self-management was largely a myth, however, and the reality gave little ground for enthusiasm. While the farms had been deprived of much of their autonomy, the factories of the socialist sector were left totally to themselves and were hardly able to keep afloat. At first they were left under the control of the presidency and of the Bureau National

36. *Journal Officiel*, No. 23, April 19, 1963, Décret 63–123.
37. *Journal Officiel*, No. 26, April 30, 1963, Décret 63–161.

d'Animation du Secteur Socialiste (BNASS), which was primarily concerned with propaganda and the explanation of the decrees to the workers;[38] then, during the summer of 1963 they were put under the authority of the prefects; finally, in January 1964 they were placed under the control of the Ministry of National Economy. As a result of these constant changes, the factories were given little help. Most of them did not even have a state-appointed director. The government did not favor the worker-run enterprises in awarding its contracts, and it often failed to pay its bills for months or years when it did do business with them. At the same time, the state held them liable for taxes and debts left unpaid by the departed French owners.

The management committees were thus left on their own to work out solutions to a multitude of problems; however, problems proved overwhelming. The worker-run factories were forced to turn for loans and credits to private banks, which were naturally hostile to the socialist sector. They also had to compete with private companies, which had the necessary capital, the know-how, and the business contacts that public companies lacked. What is more, the 450 enterprises of the socialist sector were simply outnumbered by the some 2,500 enterprises of the private sector. Competition from private industry was thus seen as the major problem by the workers of the state factories. As one angry delegate to the 1964 congress of industrial workers declared:

> The private sector . . . is organized into a chamber of commerce and a chamber of industry. In short, it is organized, has the means, and knows the markets. Moreover, it does not hesitate to enter into an alliance with world capitalism to maintain its privileges. The private sector is very strong. It tries to sabotage us, to steal our markets, to find out our professional secrets even through underhanded means. . . . But our experience of a year and a half of self-management shows that after [the publication of] the March Decrees the self-managed enterprises were left to take care of themselves.[39]

The socialist sector had other problems besides government interference, lack of government aid, and competition from private enterprise. The authors of the March Decrees, intellectuals with a blind faith

38. On April 4, 1963, the Bureau National des Biens Vacants became the Bureau National d'Animation du Secteur Socialiste (BNASS).

39. See *Le Peuple*, March 30, 1964. *Al-Chaab* became *Le Peuple* on March 21, 1963. Since December 11, 1962, the government has also published an Arabic-language daily called *Al-Chaab*, which still exists today.

in the revolutionary spirit of the working class, had assumed that Algeria's workers and peasants would be capable of understanding the principles of self-management and of putting them into practice. This was simply not true. The political education of the peasants was minimal. The war of national liberation had taught them mainly about nationalism and independence, and the FLN wartime slogan "the land to the peasants" had been widely interpreted to mean that the French lands would be distributed to individuals and not organized into collective farms. The workers of the industrial sector, some of whom had been members of the French Communist-dominated labor union, the Confédération Générale du Travail (CGT), and of the French Communist party, were somewhat better prepared to understand the March Decrees. But most of the workers had been kept unskilled under the French and did not have the training or technical knowledge to run an enterprise. Consequently, there was a considerable need for the technical and political education of the workers.

A major effort was made to train cadres after independence, but the shortage of trained workers was too great to be filled quickly, and the problem grew steadily worse as more farms and factories were either abandoned or nationalized. By the end of 1964, almost one-third of the 2,284 state farms still had no accountants, and most of the existing farm accountants were graduates of a six-month accelerated training course.[40] Half of the farms still had no directors and had only untrained substitute managers with nothing but an eight-week training course behind them. Agronomists and mechanics were rare throughout the country.[41] The industrial sector was no better off. By the end of 1963, only about twenty-five directors had been named by the government, although there were about 450 enterprises. Bachir Boumaza, then minister of industry, announced as late as July 1965 that only 80 per cent of the 500 self-managed enterprises then in the socialist sector could give some

40. The 22,000 French farms were regrouped into 2,284 huge state farms because of the shortage of cadres and state directors.

41. These figures are derived from a Ministry of Agrarian Reform report presented to the farm workers' congress in December 1964. In May 1966, it was estimated that the farm sector (socialist and private) needed 3,000 agronomists, 6,000 agricultural technicians, 10,000 instructors, 500 accountants, 4,500 bookkeepers, 2,500 trained farm directors, and 20,000 specialized workers. See *L'Algérie Agricole*, No. 1, May 1966. The shortage of agronomists and technicians was somewhat relieved by the presence of foreign assistants. By the end of 1964, there were just four Algerian agronomists.

account of their financial situation.[42] But at least efforts were being made
to train cadres and technicians.

The political education of the workers, on the other hand, was sadly
neglected after independence. The UGTA, scarcely able to cope with
its own internal problems after its first congress, was unable to undertake such a task. Furthermore, it had never organized outside the cities,
a failing for which Ben Bella had criticized its leaders at the congress.
Yet the party provided no help in educating the workers. It was seldom
represented on the farms or in the factories, and when party cells were
in fact set up, they were established more to counteract the influence of
the UGTA than to educate the workers. Instructors of the BNASS,
mostly teenage graduates of crash indoctrination courses, made swift
appearances on farms and in factories, gave brief pep talks, and then
disappeared for months. The communal councils, which were supposed
to "interest the workers in the problems of self-management," atrophied
after a few weeks of nominal existence, if they were established at all.

Left to itself, the elaborate system of self-management soon deteriorated. Elections took place in the spring of 1963 and only seldom thereafter. The workers' councils, in the words of one Algerian official, "died
in the effort to give birth to a management committee,"[43] and meetings
of the general assemblies rarely took place. Power was soon concentrated in the hands of a few members of the management committee.
On many farms, the president or the director took over the vacant house,
and with it the way of life, of the French colon. Some directors managed
to make small fortunes by getting on the payrolls of half a dozen farms.
With few accountants available to keep the books, members of the
management committees and ONRA officials found it easy enough to
help themselves to the farms' funds; embezzlement and corruption became widespread. Many workers on the farms were helping themselves
to the produce, sometimes to feed their families and sometimes to sell
it on the side. The workers could not always be blamed: payment of
salaries was often delayed, in some cases as long as three months. Some
farms had far more permanent laborers than were needed because the

42. Boumaza's speech to the presidents of industrial management committees.
See *El-Moudjahid*, July 8, 1965. *Le Peuple* became *El-Moudjahid* on June 20, 1965,
the day after the ouster of Ben Bella in a military *coup d'état*.

43. Hamid Temmar, *Les Problèmes Organiques de l'Autogestion* (unpublished
study made for the Ministry of Agriculture in 1964). Extracts have been published
under the title "Le Choix des Organes de l'Autogestion dans l'Algérie de l'Ouest" in
Revue Algérienne des Sciences Juridiques, Politiques, et Economiques, No. 4, December 1964, pp. 7–36.

president and other members of the management committee were hiring relatives and friends; other farms had far too few workers because the committee was anxious to divide up hypothetical profits among as few persons as possible. The industrial sector fared no better than the agricultural, and it was just as ridden with scandals. In some cases, state officials opposed to the principle of self-management took advantage of these scandals and scrapped the management committees altogether. Such was the case of ACILOR, a metallurgy plant in Oran and one of the country's largest enterprises, where the Ministry of Industry finally dismissed the management committee and appointed a director with full powers.

The adoption of the self-management system in Algeria was largely the outcome of the chaos that reigned in the country at independence. In the confusion, a small group of intellectuals dominated by foreign Trotskyites was able to impose its ideas. Unfortunately, these intellectuals were only interested in promoting the takeover of power by the workers in order to prevent bureaucracy from choking the revolution, as they believed had happened in the Soviet Union and other Communist countries. They were oblivious to economic problems. Indeed, one of the originators of the March Decrees told the authors that he had categorically refused to discuss the economics of self-management at meetings of the special commission appointed by Ben Bella. For him, self-management was the means by which to wrest power away from the Algerian bourgeois, who had gained control of the new administration, and to establish a true workers' state. The economics of self-management were a practical problem of secondary importance, not worth considering until the workers had gained power.

Ben Bella, who was also more concerned with politics than with economics, saw that the institution of self-management would be a popular move and would therefore strengthen his own position. Thus the immediate interests of Ben Bella and the Trotskyites converged, though their ultimate goals were different. Algeria was in any case bound to institute some form of socialism, since thousands of farms and factories had been abandoned by their French owners. The point at issue was who would run the farms and factories—the state or the workers. There were pressures for both solutions, and it was the special interests of Ben Bella and his foreign advisors that proved decisive. Once the decision had been made, there was no turning back. The workers would not give up without a fight the power the March Decrees had promised them. Moreover, Algeria's international prestige as a revolutionary country was tied to maintaining the self-management system. Nevertheless, the opponents of self-management were numerous even among Ben Bella's closest allies, and they worked steadily and quietly to make "self-management" a state-run affair. The effective application of the March Decrees thus became a key issue in the politics of independent Algeria, the rallying cry of the workers, and the indispensable slogan of two successive regimes. Algeria had become a prisoner of the myth of self-management.

chapter four
the constitution
and the state

In the second phase, the sovereign usurps all authority; he deprives the people of it and fights off all attempts by those who would like to share power with him. As long as this phase lasts, he makes an effort, by his good deeds, to win support and to gain a clientele and a great number of followers in order to repress the members of his own clan and family who have the same origin and the same right to power.[1]

Ibn Khaldun

The March Decrees established Ben Bella as the champion of the workers and peasants, providing his regime with a popular basis. But his newly acquired popularity did not put an end to "the quarrel of enemy brothers" or solve the problem of giving the young republic institutions that would ensure its political stability. According to the FLN provisional constitution,[2] the CNRA was to remain the supreme body of the state until the holding of a party congress, at which time the FLN would give the country new institutions. However, the CNRA vanished during the summer civil war, and with it the device designed to provide for an orderly organization of the new state. By September 1962, the supreme body was *de facto* the Political Bureau, a five-man committee that had seized power with the backing of the army. The bureau had subsequently organized elections for the National Assembly, which in turn chose Ben Bella to form a government. In this

1. Ibn Khaldoun, *La Muqaddima*, extracts ed. Georges Labica (Algiers: Hachette, 1965), p. 114.
2. The provisional constitution can be found in Laroussi Khelifa, *Manuel du Militant Algérien* (Lausanne: La Cité, 1962), pp. 15–21. The document called *Institutions Provisoires de L'Etat Algérien* was adopted by the CNRA in 1958, at the time of the formation of the GPRA.

manner, Algeria had gained its first institutions, but it still had no constitution to establish the respective roles of the party, the government, and the assembly. Moreover, there was no consensus among Ben Bella and his allies about the form of government Algeria should have, since each leader favored a political system that would enhance his own power. Mohamed Khider, secretary-general of the FLN, wanted a single-party system in which the government and assembly played subordinate roles. Ben Bella also favored a single-party system but viewed the party as an instrument in the service of the government. Ferhat Abbas, president of the National Assembly, sought to establish a parliamentary regime with a multi-party system, thus making the assembly the most important institution.

No leader of the stature of a Lenin or a Mao Tse-Tung or even of a Castro had emerged from the war to dictate the theory and practice of the Algerian socialist revolution. Algerian politicians lacked the capacity to elaborate a coherent doctrine. Even in Ben Bella's brain trust, no one showed a propensity toward concrete political analysis. Algerian leaders appealed simultaneously to the principles of Western democracy and Communist doctrine, adding to this mixture a specifically Algerian attachment to collegiality.[3] For instance, in the FLN provisional constitution and in the wartime party statutes, division of powers, single-party rule, democracy within the single party,[4] and collegial leadership were all declared to be fundamental precepts. In practice it would have been almost impossible to give Algeria effective institutions while respecting all these principles at the same time. The resulting system— a collegial executive checked by a national assembly, both in turn controlled by a party inside which democracy allowed all political

3. The principle of collegial leadership, first expressed in the pact among the "historic nine," was reaffirmed at the Soummam Valley Conference in August 1956. Ben Bella, who was unable to attend this conference, later denounced it as a breach of the pact binding the historic leaders. Abbane Ramdane, who emerged from the Soummam Conference as the strongest FLN leader, in turn accused Ben Bella of attempting to become the sole leader of the FLN. Ramdane insisted that the principle of collegiality be maintained, and the five-man Committee of Coordination and Execution was set up to be the executive body of the front. The principle was reaffirmed in the provisional constitution of 1958, but interestingly enough it was absent from both the Tripoli Program and the Algiers Charter, both of which were written under Ben Bella's leadership.

4. On this point, the Tripoli Program stated: "The party must function on a democratic basis. This means an active political life inside the party and a constant dialogue between the base and the summit. . . . Freedom of discussion and criticism within the party is a fundamental right of every militant." *Projet de Programme*, p. 56.

tendencies to coexist—would have been forever deadlocked in debate and incapable of taking action.

The problem of giving the country political institutions and an ideological charter was complicated from the beginning by the assumption that these issues could only be settled at a party congress. The wartime provisional constitution stated that such a congress should be held immediately after independence. But the FLN was in no condition to organize a congress at that time, as the nationalist leaders recognized at Tripoli:

> The amalgamation of state institutions and FLN structures [during the war] has reduced the party to nothing more than an administrative apparatus. Inside the country the effect of this amalgamation was that the FLN was stripped of all its responsibilities and consequently . . . annihilated.[5]

The Tripoli Program also stated:

> The reconversion of the FLN into a political party has become indispensable to the country's progress. . . . The ideological unity that should tie party members together must be based upon their revolutionary conviction and their voluntary and conscious adherence to the doctrine and program of the party.[6]

This doctrine and program were supposed to be hammered out at the party congress, but the party had to be totally reorganized before the congress could take place. Yet it was not clear how the party could be reorganized before its program and doctrine had been spelled out. This was the first dilemma Ben Bella and his allies should have faced and tried to resolve. But such theoretical questions were of minor concern to Algeria's leaders, each of whom was taking advantage of the existing confusion to try to impose the political system of his choice. From September 1962 until the following September when the constitution was approved, the politics of Algeria were marked not by ideological debate but by a power struggle among Ben Bella, Khider, and Abbas that ended by solving many of the internal contradictions of the group in power but did little to give the country workable institutions of government.

The struggle centered around the writing of the constitution. In the fall of 1963, the National Assembly was charged to write this document, in flagrant contradiction to the assumption that only a party congress could debate such an important issue. It was an aberration to decide

5. *Ibid.*, p. 20.
6. *Ibid.*, p. 55.

that the constitution would be written independently of and prior to the promised political charter; logically, the constitution should have been part of the charter or at least should have stemmed from it. As it was, the process was reversed. The National Assembly started its work in the best tradition of parliamentary democracy. Even Ben Bella treated the assembly with deference in his inaugural speech:

> So far as the constitution of the republic is concerned, your assembly is entirely sovereign. . . . At the same time, the life of the nation and the management of its affairs will be carried on within the framework of the laws for which you yourselves and the government have the initiative.[7]

The National Assembly, however, was scarcely prepared to play such an important role. About one-third of its 196 members were former guerrilla leaders, many of whom could neither read nor write, and only a few of the deputies had had some previous experience in the French-dominated Algerian Assembly before independence.[8] After naming Ben Bella prime minister and approving his government, the National Assembly became bogged down for two months in debate over its own rules of procedure and over the electing of committees, including one committee to be devoted to the examination of projects for the constitution. The selection of committee members took place for the most part not in the assembly, but at the Villa Joly, Ben Bella's private residence. This irregularity was the first covert infringement of the sovereignty of the assembly.

By early December, the assembly had not yet voted a single law. In the meantime, Ben Bella and his ministers had been more active than the deputies in exercising legislative power. Decree after decree appeared in the *Journal Officiel*, from which the word law was absent until December 13.[9] The deputies did not protest against a practice that clearly exceeded the powers of the government and usurped their own prerogative. However, the assembly was not totally composed of *Beni-oui-oui*, of yes-men ready to praise every move made by the Ben Bella

7. Ben Bella's speech to the National Assembly, September 28, 1962.
8. For the most complete breakdown of the deputies' background, see *Le Monde,* September 15, 1962.
9. The first law voted by the assembly concerned the creation of the Central Bank. The bill was presented by the government on December 10, discussed in commission, and voted without amendment. See *Journal Officiel,* No. 10, December 28, 1962, Loi 62–144.

government.[10] During a debate on the government's general policy that began on December 5, fifty-nine deputies freely expressed their criticism, reminding the government of all the urgent problems it had not yet faced; but only one speaker raised the fundamental question of the government's right to issue decrees.[11] Moreover, the deputies seemed content simply to criticize, for few introduced bills to press the government into taking action on the issues they deemed crucial. The only two bills of importance, which concerned the establishment of a self-management system and the formation of peasants' cooperatives, were presented on December 10 by Ait Ahmed, one of the two historic leaders who had refused to sit in the Political Bureau.[12] Interestingly enough, these bills were "lost" and only reappeared in July, by which time the March Decrees had made them obsolete.

Ben Bella, for his part, did nothing to help the assembly fulfill its task. If the deputies themselves presented few bills, the government proposed even fewer. It mainly submitted highly technical bills such as the budget or the bylaws of the new Central Bank, which were beyond the comprehension of most deputies and were invariably approved after short debate and with few modifications. The only controversial bill presented to the assembly was one concerning the granting of Algerian citizenship to foreigners, which was the object of passionate debate for two weeks in March 1963.[13] Ben Bella made all major political decisions by decree, without consulting the assembly, which consequently exercised no control over the government. Indeed, Ben Bella warned the deputies in December that it was not their prerogative to establish policy:

> I think it is necessary to define the relations between the assembly, the government, and the party. These relations are based on a clear prin-

10. Deputies selected by the French to represent the Moslem population at the Algerian Assembly before independence were called "*Beni-oui-oui*," literally "sons of yes, yes" or "the yes, yes tribe."

11. See the speech of Mohamed Ghersi, *Journal Officiel*, Débats Parlementaires, December 8, 1962.

12. The bills, which were not published, were numbered 05 and 06, which shows just how many bills had been presented to the assembly by that time. They were brought before the assembly on July 2, 1963.

13. The bill was discussed in the assembly from March 1 to 13, 1963. The new law submitted all foreigners to the same naturalization procedures, and the French charged that it violated the Evian Agreements, which gave the French residents the right to choose freely between French or Algerian citizenship during a three-year period.

ciple: the government and the assembly have a role of execution; but the elaboration of the political thought of the nation is reserved for the party.[14]

His position was amply justified by the Tripoli Program, which stated that "the party decides the over-all policy of the nation and inspires the activity of the government."[15] But it was a sharp change from the deferential attitude he had shown in his inaugural speech, in which he declared that the assembly was "entirely sovereign."

In his warning to the deputies, Ben Bella had recognized the supremacy of the party not only over the assembly, but also over the government. On the latter point, however, his true opinion was not the one he had expressed. Even if he accepted the theory of the party's pre-eminence, Ben Bella was not in fact willing to accept the practical implications of the theory, namely that he himself, the prime minister, was subordinate to Khider, the party's secretary-general. A rivalry between the two allies had been latent since the defeat of their common enemy, the GPRA. Ben Bella and Khider were divided by their ambitions rather than by any deep-seated ideological convictions. They were both men of action, equally skilled in the art of politics. They even agreed on many issues such as outlawing the Algerian Communist party and curbing the independence of the UGTA. But both of them had been preparing for a confrontation. Each was building himself a personal base of power, Khider by means of the party and Ben Bella through the March Decrees.

The confrontation came in early April. Ben Bella had set out on a triumphant tour of the country to reap the fruits of the March Decrees. Khider remained in the capital but did not sit by idly. On April 3, he called a three-day conference of 250 top party cadres, his own appointees, and had them approve a resolution demanding that a party congress be held before the end of the term of the National Assembly in order to draw up the constitution. On April 9, he held a press conference to announce that this resolution had been "unanimously adopted" by the party cadres. He admitted, however, that the Political Bureau had not been consulted because it could not be convoked in Ben Bella's absence. The maneuver was a blatant bid by Khider to bypass Ben Bella and hold a congress that he himself would control.

Khider's press conference convinced many of Ben Bella's advisors

14. Ben Bella's speech to the National Assembly, December 12, 1962.
15. *Projet de Programme*, p. 56.

that the time had come to move against the secretary-general. To intimidate Khider, some of them proposed staging a gigantic demonstration to welcome Ben Bella on his return to the capital. However, on
April 11, while this proposal was still under discussion, news that Mohamed Khemisti, the youthful foreign minister, had been shot in broad
daylight reached Ben Bella, then in Philippeville (Skikda) in eastern
Algeria. Ben Bella immediately flew back to the capital, fearing that the
attack on Khemisti might be part of a larger plot. As it turned out, the
crime was not political, and consequently there was no need for Ben
Bella to maintain a pretense of solidarity with Khider.[16] On April 18,
the official daily *Al-Chaab* carried on the front page, between Khemisti's
daily medical bulletin and the announcement of a tree-planting campaign, an item that reported that Khider had resigned from his post
as party secretary-general but was still a member of the Political Bureau.
Ben Bella was immediately elected to replace him. Khider later claimed
that only three of the Political Bureau's five members—Ben Bella, Ben
Alla, and Mohammedi Saïd—had been present for the election.[17] Ben
Bella never denied it.

In an interview given to the French daily *Le Monde* a few days after
his resignation, Khider explained that the Political Bureau had been
divided over his proposal to hold a party congress before the end of the
summer and that he had stepped down "to save the country the risk
of a catastrophe."[18] Undoubtedly he also calculated that he did not
have the power to displace Ben Bella, whose popularity had greatly
increased with the publication of the March Decrees. The disagreement between Khider and Ben Bella actually went much further than
the timing of the congress. The two leaders were at odds over whether
the party should be an African-style mass organization as Khider would
have it or a Soviet-style elite corps as Ben Bella proposed; whether
party officials could also be government officials as Khider argued; and
whether the party should be the principal policy-making body as Khider
intended to make it. The former secretary-general spoke of democracy
and the division of powers to justify his position:

16. Khemisti was the victim of a crime of passion. He was shot by a former suitor
of his wife, who was immediately arrested, later condemned to death, and then
pardoned because of insanity. Khemisti remained in a coma until May 7, when he
died inopportunely during the visit of President Gamal Abdel Nasser. Ben Bella took
over the post of foreign minister until September 1963.
17. See *Le Monde*, April 21–22, 1963.
18. *Ibid.*

> Our suffering people must make their voices heard through the party
> cadres and certainly not through the representatives of the govern-
> ment. . . . That is why I believe that the separation of powers is the *sine
> qua non* of the success of our efforts.[19]

For his part, Ben Bella claimed that only Khider was making himself
heard through the party cadres, who were not true representatives
of the people but the secretary-general's lackeys, the *racaille*, or scum,
as he tersely described them:

> This party has become a state within the state, with its civil servants,
> its secretaries, and its chauffeurs who are sometimes more numerous
> than in the administration. I know of some party members who col-
> laborated with the French during the revolution. How could our people
> have confidence in such persons? No, it is not in these conditions that
> we can envisage the holding of a party congress.[20]

There was much truth in Ben Bella's words, although probably his
major objection was that the party officials were Khider's men and not
his own. As for the separation of powers for which Khider appealed,
Ben Bella claimed that in fact it had become "duality of power," which
was leading not to democracy but to chaos. With Khider removed, Ben
Bella abruptly changed his mind about the representiveness of the
party's officials, although there was no purge or major overhaul of the
FLN. He adopted the former secretary-general's proposal that the constitution be written by the party rather than by the National Assembly.

The assembly had not yet begun to discuss the constitution. Two
projects had been presented to the assembly in April, one by Ferhat
Abbas, the other by a group of five deputies. But by July, neither
project had been brought to the floor, although the assembly was due
to be dissolved in September. The failure of the assembly to act was
crucial because it allowed the Political Bureau to draw up its own
project for a constitution, which was submitted to party officials in Algiers, Oran, and Constantine in July. The project naturally received
overwhelming approval, and it was then presented with great ceremony
to a gathering of two thousand top party and government officials at
the Majestic Theater in downtown Algiers.[21] With the final blessing of
this group, the project was duly submitted to the National Assembly in

19. See the interview of Khider and Ben Bella in the Tunisian weekly *Jeune
Afrique*, No. 131, April 28, 1963.
20. *Ibid.*
21. The meeting at the Majestic took place on July 31, 1963.

late August by five deputies: Ali Mendjli, Cherif Belkacem, Mohamed Kadi, Mohamed Zaouaoui, and M'Hammed Omar Benmahjoub.[22]

The official project, the only one to be discussed by the National Assembly, spelled out the goals of the "people's democratic revolution" and outlined what one deputy defined as a "constitutional regime of government by the party."[23] The Algerian Constitution, although it established a single-party system, borrowed liberally from the French Fifth Republic. The preamble affirmed Algeria's dedication to socialism, self-management, and the "anti-imperialist struggle," and it promised Algeria's support to all liberation movements. Arabic was proclaimed the national language and Islam the religion of the state, although freedom of religion was recognized as a fundamental right. Algeria subscribed to the Universal Declaration of Human Rights and specifically condemned the use of torture, a direct consequence of wartime experiences in the hands of the French army.

The constitution declared that the FLN was the only party allowed to exist in Algeria and that as such it was empowered to "establish the nation's policies" and to "control the activity of the National Assembly and the government." Candidates for the assembly and the presidency were selected by the party and were elected for five-year terms by all Algerian citizens over nineteen years of age. The system was a compromise between a presidential and parliamentary regime: the president was elected by the people, but he was responsible to the National Assembly. A vote of no-confidence by the majority of deputies forced the president's resignation and at the same time the dissolution of the assembly, a procedure copied from the French Fifth Republic. However, during the debates in the assembly it was made clear that the party alone would decide such a move. As one deputy put it, "the party asks the deputies, militants it has designated, to vote a motion of no-confidence in the president of the republic. Well disciplined, the assembly executes the party's orders."[24] In effect, all power was in the hands of the party. The party named the deputies and the president,

22. It is interesting to note that two of the five deputies were close associates of Colonel Boumediene. Ali Mendjli was a member of the wartime General Staff and Cherif Belkacem was an aide of Boumediene's during the war. This choice adds to the evidence that Ben Bella and Boumediene were still working together at this time.

23. Quoted in François Borella, "La Constitution Algérienne," Revue Algérienne des Sciences Juridiques, Politiques, et Economiques, No. 1, January 1965, p. 61.

24. Quoted in Borella, p. 75.

the party established the political line of the country, the party controlled the members of the assembly and the president, and the party
decided if and when they should resign.

In protest over the method by which the constitution had been
elaborated, Ferhat Abbas resigned on August 12 from the presidency
of the National Assembly. In a long self-righteous letter to the deputies,
he explained the reasons for his resignation, accusing Ben Bella of
having violated the sovereignty of the assembly by submitting "the
project for the constitution to the so-called cadres of a party that in fact
does not yet exist."[25] Abbas went much further, challenging the entire
political line of the Ben Bella regime. He declared that Ben Bella
had totally distorted the meaning of the Tripoli Program by turning the
"democratic and humanistic socialism" the nationalist leaders had voted
for into "Marxist-Leninist socialism." He maintained that the assembly
alone was sovereign because it alone had been elected by the people;
therefore, the assembly should have written the constitution and even
named the members of a party central committee to replace the defunct
CNRA. The Political Bureau, according to him, had no mandate from
the people, having usurped its power during the civil war. Abbas's
legalistic arguments had no real foundation: in no document was there
a basis to his claim that the assembly should name the Central Committee and thereby control the party. Moreover, as Abbas well knew,
even the legitimacy of the assembly was questionable because the deputies had been chosen by the Political Bureau and elected by voters who
had been presented with a single list.

Abbas also charged that the proposed constitution opened the way
to one-man rule, and he called instead for a parliamentary regime. He
later told the authors that he favored a two-party system, but he admitted that once the principle of a single party was abandoned there
would be at least three parties—the FLN, his own, and the Algerian
Communist party. Abbas's claim that there would be no more than
three parties appears to have been unrealistic, because other leaders
like Ait Ahmed, Boudiaf, and Khider would undoubtedly have tried to
organize their own parties, bringing on an unstable political situation
similar to the one that characterized the French Fourth Republic. In
any case, there was no constitution that could have saved Algeria from
a one-man regime in the summer of 1963, since Ben Bella and his allies

25. Abbas's letter of resignation, dated August 12, was widely circulated in
Algiers in mimeograph form but was not printed in the local press.

already controlled the government, the party, and even the assembly. More than a one-party system, more than a presidential regime, Algeria was, as Abbas declared, a "république des camarades." Abbas dramatically called upon all Algerians to speak out against this kind of republic, but few answered his appeal. Those who did, dissidents like Khider, Boudiaf, and Ait Ahmed, offered not an alternative political system but the replacement of Ben Bella's camarades by their own. Most of them took a head count of their supporters, sized up Ben Bella's forces, and then retreated without giving battle, like the condottieri of the Italian mercenary armies. In one case, however, it was the losing party that got away with the war booty. Mohamed Khider left the country in June for Switzerland, where he had transferred $12 million in Party funds from Lebanese banks, money collected during the war and never returned to Algeria.[26] Nonetheless, he was not expelled from the FLN until April 1964, and he was even permitted to return to Algeria several times in the fall of 1963.

The assembly discussed the party-written constitution for just one week, made a few minor changes, and adopted it on August 28 by a vote of 139 to 23, with 8 abstentions. Most of the negative votes came from Kabyle deputies and from moderates siding with Abbas, who were opposed to Ben Bella's policies in general rather than just to the constitution. On September 8, a nationwide referendum approved the constitution by a majority officially stated to be 96.8 per cent.[27] Ben Bella was elected president of the republic a week later, officially by 99.6 per cent of the vote.[28] However, in the Kabylia, where Ait Ahmed had called for a boycott of the referendum and of the presidential election, there were a large number of abstentions.

On September 18, Ben Bella formed a new cabinet from which most

26. Khider was able to transfer this money because in addition to being secretary-general, he acted as treasurer of the party. The FLN later filed suit against him in Swiss courts. The case dragged on for a long time and still had not come to trial when Ben Bella was ousted in June 1965. The Boumedienne government dropped the suit, for unexplained reasons, until Khider's death in January 1967.

27. Of the 6,391,818 registered voters, 5,287,229 voted: ayes, 5,166,195; noes, 104,861; blank or invalid, 16,173.

28. In the presidential election held September 15, 1963, 5,827,618 people voted: Ben Bella, 5,805,103; blank or invalid, 22,515. The number of registered voters who abstained in the presidential election was only half the number of those who abstained in the referendum. The lower number of abstentions in the presidential election gave some indication of Ben Bella's personal popularity. However, both elections were widely believed to have been rigged by the government, so that not too much importance should be attached to these figures.

of the moderates were excluded.[29] The ministries were divided up between the Ben Bella and Boumediene clans, the only two that still remained in the alliance formed during the summer civil war. Ben Bella's group took the Ministry of Agriculture (Ali Mahsas), the Ministry of National Economy (Bachir Boumaza), the Ministry of Justice (Hadj Smaïn), and the Ministry of Social Affairs (Mohamed Nekkache); in addition, three other allies of Ben Bella—Mohammedi Saïd, Amar Ouzegane, and Sadek Batel—were named respectively second vice-president, minister of state, and under-secretary of state for youth and sports. Boumediene's clan took the vice-presidency and the Ministry of Defense (Boumediene), the Ministry of the Interior (Ahmed Medeghri), the Ministry of Foreign Affairs (Abdelaziz Bouteflika), the Ministry of Education and Information (Cherif Belkacem), and the Ministry of Tourism (Ahmed Kaid). Rabah Bitat, a member of the Political Bureau close to Khider, was given the honorific title of third vice-president, but he resigned the next day and later left the country.[30]

Secretary-general of the party, head of government, president of the republic, master of the assembly, and backed by Colonel Boumediene's army—Ben Bella was by any standard running a one-man regime. The heterogeneous alliance of the first year, in which Ben Bella had shared the power with other historic leaders, was now dissolved. The former GPRA leaders who had once seemed a threat had either given up politics altogether, like former President Ben Khedda, were launching harmless salvoes against Ben Bella from abroad, like Belkacem Krim,[31] or had joined the regime, like M'hammed Yazid.[32] Of Ben Bella's declared opponents, Khider was abroad and Boudiaf was under arrest

29. Among those excluded were: Ahmed Francis, minister of finance, and Amar Bentoumi, minister of justice, both linked to Ferhat Abbas; Laroussi Khelifa, minister of industry and energy, linked to the army but excluded for incompetence; and Mohamed Khobzi, minister of commerce, a Mozabite who was later arrested for embezzlement. The only ally of Abbas who remained in the Cabinet was Ali Boumendjel, minister of reconstruction.

30. Bitat had been at odds with Ben Bella ever since the resignation of Khider. In May, he had lost the important post of coordinator between the party and the national organizations. The post was taken over by Hadj Ben Alla, Ben Bella's right-hand man.

31. Krim resigned from the National Assembly and left for Geneva in early September. In an open letter that appeared in Swiss newspapers on September 8, Krim said that the assembly no longer represented the nation and that he refused to be "a toy or an accomplice of a fascist dictatorship."

32. Yazid, minister of information in the GPRA, was elected to the assembly and became the head of its committee on foreign relations. He also served as Ben Bella's personal envoy and as Algeria's representative to the Afro-Asian Peoples' Solidarity Organization (AAPSO).

deep in the Sahara. Only Ait Ahmed, who had left the National Assembly in June 1963, was actively organizing an opposition group. Among his remaining allies, Ben Bella stood out as the undisputed leader. There was nobody to challenge him in the Political Bureau, now reduced to three men (Ben Bella, Ben Alla, and Saïd), or in the government, except Colonel Boumediene, who as yet showed no sign of political ambition, being absorbed in the task of organizing the new National People's Army (ANP).

Yet the Ben Bella regime was hardly a dictatorship, and Algeria was still a long way from being a police state. In the first place, the regime was not well enough organized to institute a reign of terror over the country. Second, Ben Bella could not use the army without taking the risk of provoking rebellions among the former wilaya commanders; moreover, he did not even control the ANP directly. Third, Ben Bella did not have the character of a dictator. He was an easy-going person with a great deal of personal charm and political acumen, who preferred to negotiate with his enemies rather than to fight them. A romantic revolutionary rather than a scientific socialist, Ben Bella never tried to impose upon Algerians a dogmatic doctrine or a rigid party line. Indeed, he was quite vague in his definitions of Algerian socialism, which he described variously as "Arabo-Islamic socialism," "scientific socialism," and "Castro-style socialism."[33] The Algerian president had little formal education—he had dropped out of high school—and could be easily influenced by persons he considered his intellectual superiors. However, he had acquired a great deal of political experience through his participation in the nationalist movement since the end of World War Two, and he had a gift for outmaneuvering his enemies.

Ben Bella's opponents accused him of making himself the object of a personality cult. Undoubtedly he loved to be cheered by large crowds and to be jostled by admiring peasants and workers. On the other hand, he never had statues erected in his honor, as Nkrumah did in Ghana, or streets named after him, as Bourguiba did in Tunisia. Nonetheless,

33. Cherif Belkacem, coordinator of the FLN after the overthrow of Ben Bella, talked of Ben Bella's five socialisms: "The first time we heard Ben Bella talking of socialism, it was 'Castro-style socialism.' We all applauded. At a second meeting, it was a 'specific socialism.' We again applauded. At a third meeting, [it was] a 'scientific socialism.' At a fourth meeting, [it was] an 'Arabo-Islamic socialism.' He invented still a fifth socialism when he said 'I accept the Marxist economic analysis, but I reject the analysis of scientific materialism,' and we applauded once again." See Belkacem's interview with a Tunisian journalist in the FLN weekly Révolution Africaine, No. 143, October 23, 1965.

being an ambitious man with a desire to write his name is history, he preferred being in the international limelight to staying at home to cope with day-to-day unglorious problems. He scoffed at accusations that he was becoming a dictator:

> If there is any people in the world that will not accept a dictatorship, it is [the people of] this country. Algerians have proved that they can be very much united in a struggle for freedom, but they won't follow anyone once peace has returned. Personally, I am convinced that dictatorship hasn't the slightest chance in this country. . . . A police state, which is one of the characteristics of a dictatorship, does not exist here. When poor Khemisti was assassinated, I could have used this absurd crime as a pretext to round up all my opponents and to assure myself of five years of peace and quiet. But I didn't, because I don't have the makings of a dictator.[34]

Indeed, his was no reign of terror, although the prisons were not empty, either. There were 2,500 political prisoners in the country by 1965, but most had been arrested for their participation in the armed rebellion in the Kabylia. Of the hundreds arrested for having carried arms against the state, only six were executed.[35] There were abuses of power, however. Several deputies were arrested merely for expressing opinions hostile to Ben Bella, and some of the political prisoners were tortured, although the president publicly condemned such practices. In numerous instances, Ben Bella showed a total disregard for legality, but he showed little interest in using force, except as a last resort. He never used the police or army to break up strikes, even in the socialist sector. The GPRA leaders, some of whom feared for their lives after the summer civil war, are all alive today, and not one was even arrested.

There was no attempt to impose a Communist-style regimentation of the masses. Ben Bella talked of "mobilization of the masses," and indeed he meant mobilization and not regimentation. People were not forced to "volunteer," a fact that goes a long way toward explaining the failure of many voluntary schemes. The Algerian president had essentially three instruments at his disposal to mobilize the war-weary

34. Interview with the Swiss Television Network, published in the *Tribune de Lausanne*, October 4, 1963.

35. Mohamed Chaabani, commander of the then Sixth Military Region (the Sahara), revolted against the regime in July 1964. He was caught on July 8, 1964, and executed after a military trial on September 3, 1964. Five members of the Kabylia-based Front of Socialist Forces who had participated in an attack on Ben Bella's private residence were executed on September 2, 1963.

country; the party, the administration, and propaganda. Speeches and slogans created a climate of expectation during the first year, but there was no follow-up effort to channel the people's enthusiasm into concrete action. The FLN, which was intended to act as the link between the government and the people, was poorly organized, particularly in the countryside. Party leaders were much more absorbed in fighting among themselves than in indoctrinating and organizing the masses.

The Algerian administration was the only institution that maintained some presence and control throughout the country. However, it was not the revolutionary administration that Ben Bella's Trotskyite advisors sought to establish, a system in which people's councils would run the townships just as the management committees were running the farms and factories. The administration was still the cumbersome and overcentralized one that the French had set up, except that it had become even less efficient because of the departure of most French civil servants. The French had divided the country into fifteen departments, each headed by a prefect named by the governor general in Algiers. Each department was subdivided into *arrondissements* (districts) headed by a subprefect, also named by the governor. The 100 *arrondissements* were divided into *communes* (townships), which numbered 1,590. The communes where there were a large number of colons were run by an elected mayor and council as in France. The others, about two-thirds of the total, were run by appointed officials. After independence, the French system was maintained with only two major changes: the number of communes was reduced to 630 (later 675), mainly because of cost and lack of trained civil servants; and all the communes were run by appointed "special delegations" pending the elections of communal assemblies. The delegations remained in power until February 1967, when the elections were finally held.

The administration had 70,000 employees on its payroll in April 1963, but the number soon reached 100,000. In 1959, the number had been 63,000. The sharp increase in the number of civil servants after independence did not mean better administration. The turnover was fantastic, and civil servants were hardly installed in one post before they started jockeying for another, often in a different ministry. The turnover of prefects reached such proportions that Ben Bella's critics called it the "waltz of the prefects." Many of the top posts were left vacant for want of competent cadres, while lower-echelon positions were often overstaffed, partly because of the government's effort to provide jobs for war veterans.[36] Ten per cent of employees in every ministry and service had to be veterans, who, being mostly illiterate, could only be employed as doormen, janitors, and chauffeurs.

A census taken in April 1963 gave some idea of the actual composition of the new administration: 13,729 employees were French technical assistants; 22,182 were Algerians of the wartime "colonial promotion";[37] and 34, 097 were Algerians recruited after independence. In Algeria administration employees are divided into four classes: (A) planning and decision-making positions; (B) managerial position; (C) clerical positions; and (D) subordinate jobs. According to one analysis of the census, 43 per cent of Class A and 77 per cent of Class B civil servants were French nationals or Algerians of the colonial promotion.[38] As Ben Bella's Marxist critics were quick to point out, the composition of the civil service was not one to promote a socialist revolution. The breakdown according to training and national origin, however, did not tell the whole story. Of the French technicians, some had come to help turn Algeria into a socialist country and others to take advantage of the higher pay and the Mediterranean climate. Yet there was considerable evidence to substantiate the charge that the administration was anti-socialist in its practices. For instance, in awarding contracts the administration very often favored private French and Algerian companies over the worker-managed ones. It was usually slow in applying government directives, and even emergency projects like Operation Plow of 1962 were invariably allowed to bog down in red tape.[39]

The apathetic and conservative attitude of the administration was such a critical problem that Ben Bella, prodded by deputies, the UGTA, and his left-wing advisors, promised again and again that a full-scale

36. The Algerian government stated in 1964 that there were 860 high-level posts vacant in the administration: 10 in the prefectural corps (prefects and subprefects); 100 in the central administration; and 750 in the departmental administration. At that time, 15,682 war veterans had jobs in the administration. See Ministère de l'Orientation Nationale, *Algérie An II*, 1964, pp. 33–34.

37. The expression refers to Algerians admitted into the French civil service beginning in 1956 as part of a series of measures adopted by the resident minister, Robert Lacoste, to win over the Moslem population.

38. Gerard Chaliand, *L'Algérie est-elle Socialiste?* (Paris: Maspero, 1964), p. 89.

39. Operation Plow (Opération Labours) was launched in the fall of 1962 to plow and sow the wheat fields on the abandoned French farms and on other lands abandoned during the war. The administration came in for sharp criticism because it had favored the private sector, had been slow to obey orders from Algiers, and had caused long delays in the distribution of seeds and fertilizer.

purge would be carried out. Such a purge never took place, however, partly because there were simply no replacements for the graduates of the colonial promotion and partly because Ben Bella was afraid of stirring up a political storm. The administration was a beehive of clans, each one controlling a ministry, a service, or a department, and consequently purging one official meant provoking the resentment of a large number. As one of Ben Bella's erstwhile Marxist supporters wrote:

> If the purges have remained a myth, it is because it would first be necessary to get rid of the clans that have implanted themselves in the administration. The minor purges carried out so far have been transformed into personal revenges among rival clans. Each ministry tries to eliminate those civil servants who don't belong to the clan. . . . The state has been taken over by clans that have their clientele, each using its influence in its particular domain. The administrative services have been swollen to give posts to one's friend, and the favoring of some clans [over others] has become a method of government.[40]

The rivalry among ministers was so great that each refused to share basic statistics with the others, and many had their own secret police. The Central Bank and the Customs Office were almost autonomous bodies within the administration, taking orders from nobody and moving at their own leisurely pace. Ben Bella was once forced to go down to the harbor in person in order to clear through customs a shipment of pipes that the government had ordered for the construction of its own oil line. This division of the administration into rival clans undermined Algeria's socialist revolution far more than the "bourgeois mentality" of the civil servants.

The administration was not only unwieldy, but also costly. The administrative budget alone amounted to roughly 2.9 billion dinars ($580 million) in 1963, while only 2.4 billion dinars ($490 million) were budgeted in this same year for economic development, and less than half this amount was actually spent. The administrative budget by far outstripped the revenues of the state, and it was only French aid, 1.63 billion francs ($326 million) in 1962 and 1.27 billion francs ($255 million) in 1963, that kept Algeria afloat in the first years after independence. Despite constant talk of austerity measures, administrative costs continued to rise, reaching 3.05 billion dinars ($610 million) in 1965, while outlays for economic development had declined by that year to roughly 1.4 billion dinars ($280 million) because the govern-

40. Chaliand, p. 95.

ment had not been able to make use of funds earmarked for that purpose in previous years. Moreover, funds budgeted for development often had to be transferred to the administration to take care of "unforeseen expenses"; these amounted to 900 million dinars ($180 million) in 1964. The government's problem was compounded by the difficulty of collecting taxes or even securing payment of water, gas, and electricity bills. In 1963, tax revenues were 630 million dinars ($126 million) below the estimated 2.7 billion dinars ($539 million). The socialist sector, which included the once highly profitable French farms, did not pay any taxes during the first three years of independence. Oil revenues, which Algerian officials at first viewed as a panacea for all financial woes, only amounted to 225 million dinars ($45 million) in 1963 and 700 million dinars ($140 million) in 1966.

The administration, far from being the government's badly needed link with the people, was the same oppressive, slow-moving bureaucracy that Algerians had already learned to distrust before independence. It was not an instrument in the hands of Ben Bella or anyone else. Ben Bella could issue decrees and get the assembly to put its stamp of approval on any laws he wanted, but he could not assume that the administration would apply these decrees and laws. Nonetheless, it was a highly centralized administration, which left no place for local initiative. All local projects had to be approved in Algiers, and the communes had no funds directly under their control. The building of a village fountain or of a bridge on a country road required months of paper work and a dozen stamps of approval, followed by months of waiting until the money arrived from Algiers. It was not this administration that could mobilize the masses, carry out crash programs, or help the crippled socialist sector. Yet this was the administration that was the backbone of the Algerian People's Republic.

chapter five
the opposition

The tragedy of the division of the Algerian elite, each person polarized and even vassalized by historical or incidental feudal ties, recalls the tragedy of the French left after World War Two. . . . It is this tragedy that we are living today. The avant-garde forces are divided not by ideas, but by men.[1]

Hocine Ait Ahmed

During his thirty-three months in power, Ben Bella was constantly accused by his opponents and critics of leading the nation on an uncharted course toward ever greater chaos. Yet the course he followed was repeatedly dictated by the pressures the opposition exerted on the government. This opposition came mainly from two sources: the historic leaders and the wartime guerrilla commanders.

Nine men had launched the revolution in 1954, and six of them—Ben Bella, Khider, Boudiaf, Ait Ahmed, Bitat, and Krim—had survived the liberation struggle. Each of the nine believed that he had a legitimate right to participate in the leadership of the country after independence. However, only three—Ben Bella, Khider, and Bitat—were still in power by the end of the summer crisis, and by the fall of 1963 Ben Bella had eliminated the other two. The historic leaders who had lost out in the struggle considered Ben Bella a usurper of the power that belonged to all of them collectively by virtue of their role in the revolution. They did not accept the 1962 elections for the National Assembly or the 1963 referendum for the constitution and the subsequent presidential election as the legitimation of Ben Bella's authority. The constitution might well state that "the national sovereignty resides in the people," but the historic leaders nonetheless believed that

1. Hocine Ait Ahmed, *La Guerre et l'Après-Guerre* (Paris: Minuit, 1964), p. 152.

they alone were the incarnation of Algeria's sovereignty. Only Ben Bella rejected the notion that those who had launched the revolution had an inherent right to leadership. Undoubtedly he would have felt differently had he not been in power.

The former wilaya commanders also believed that they had a legitimate right to a leading political role. A spokesman for the Wilaya Four command had made this clear during the civil war in the summer of 1962:

> Those who during seven and a half years of an atrocious war carried on alongside the people the struggle against the colonialist forces wish to point out that, having exercised the political, administrative, and military power, they have been, and still are, the real authority that issues from the people.[2]

Despite the victory of Colonel Boumediene's army over the wilaya forces during the civil war, some of the guerrilla leaders succeeded in entrenching themselves in their former wilayas by assuming the title of "regional military commanders" of the ANP. However, their positions were not secure because Boumediene was determined to make the ANP into a modern army, substituting progressively well-trained officers for the guerrilla commanders, who were for the most part illiterate. Realizing that they had little chance in competition with the Algerian officers who had previously served in the French army or with the cadets who were being sent abroad for training, the former guerrilla leaders were on the defensive and were ready to side with any faction that promised them some position of power. None of them was particularly interested in ideological issues or in the political orientation of the group he sided with as long as he was assured a role.

Indeed, it was a characteristic common to most of Ben Bella's opponents not to be fastidious about the political beliefs of their allies. Opposition groups were not bound internally by ideological convictions, nor were their differences with Ben Bella primarily ideological. The language of the opposition was usually couched in highly ideological terms, giving the impression that different political choices were at stake; yet a closer examination of the various programs proposed by opposition groups showed that they bore a startling similarity to each other and often to those of Ben Bella. For instance, both Boudiaf and Ait Ahmed, who led different groups, appealed to "scientific socialism"

2. UPI dispatch, August 5, 1962.

and advocated a system of self-management, but so did Ben Bella. The opposition to the president was not a single united movement, but rather a kaleidoscope of clans and personalities. Although they all had a common cause—the ouster of Ben Bella—the opposition leaders were so divided by petty quarrels and jealousies that only once in three years did they manage to form a loose alliance against their common enemy.

There was only one political group in Algeria that, while opposing Ben Bella on many issues, never became an outright opposition movement. This was the Parti Communiste Algérien (PCA), whose leaders sought to cooperate with Ben Bella in order to further their long-term aims. The PCA was very different from other Algerian political parties. It had a well-disciplined membership, tied together by allegiance to a definite ideology rather than to a personality, and a coherent program.

The Algerian Communist party had existed in Algeria since shortly after World War One, first as a section of the French Communist party and then, after 1935, as an autonomous organization. The PCA was open to Moslems as well as to Europeans, but few Moslems joined, partly because an atheistic doctrine had little appeal for them and partly because the Communists advocated assimilation of Algeria into France, opposing independence. Significantly, Messali Hadj, who started as a member of the Communist party in France, broke all ties with the Party in 1937 and founded the Parti du Peuple Algérien (PPA), which had as its declared goal Algeria's independence. In 1948, the Algerian first secretary of the PCA, Amar Ouzegane, was expelled for "nationalist deviations"; his expulsion underlined the Party's attachment to the European rather than to the Moslem community.[3] Not surprisingly, the PCA reacted very coolly to the outbreak of the revolution in 1954, and only in 1956 did it try to join the liberation struggle, setting up an independent maquis in the mountains near Algiers. This maquis was wiped out almost immediately by the French army, and the surviving Communist guerrillas joined the ALN, which agreed to accept them as individuals but not as members of the PCA. The Communist party thus played no major role in the war of independence, although some individual Communists participated fully. One of them was Henri Alleg, a Frenchman and codirector of the Communist daily *Alger Républicain*, who earned an international reputation by exposing

3. Ouzegane later wrote a book, *Le Meilleur Combat* (Paris: Julliard, 1962), which contains a bitter critique of PCA policies toward the nationalist movement.

the practice of torture by the French army in Algeria. In his book
La Question, Alleg described the horrors of torture he himself had
undergone at the hands of French paratroopers, shocking the French
public.

With independence, the PCA wasted no time in trying to reorganize.
Taking advantage of the confusion engendered by the civil war, it
resumed publication of *Alger Républicain,* which had been banned by
French authorities during the war. The daily, which was printed with
the help of funds and reporters sent from the French Communist newspaper *L'Humanité,* soon had a large circulation. During the summer
crisis, *Alger Républicain* avoided taking sides, but after the September
election it became a fairly outspoken critic of the regime, while carefully avoiding attacking Ben Bella personally. The daily tended to act
as the self-appointed conscience of the socialist revolution and soon
became a source of embarrassment to Ben Bella.

The existence of the Communist party also worried the president.
Although the PCA had less than 6,000 members after independence, it
was far better organized and disciplined than the FLN.[4] In early November, after the government banned a public meeting of the PCA in
Sétif and a press conference planned by the Party's first secretary,
Bachir Hadj Ali, in Algiers, relations between the PCA and Ben Bella
became tense. In order to avoid an open clash with the regime, the
PCA did not protest the measures and sought instead to initiate a
dialogue with the FLN. The Communist party weekly *El-Hourriya*
even declared that the Communists were willing to join forces with
the FLN to create a united party, citing as an example the merger of
the Cuban Communist party with Fidel Castro's July 26 Movement.[5]
But the FLN was not of the same mind, and on November 29 the Communist party was formally banned along with *El-Hourriya* on the
grounds that the Tripoli Program had established the principle of a
single party. *Alger Républicain,* however, was allowed to continue
publication. On the very next day, it carried a heavily censored editorial that protested the interdiction but also said:

> We want to avoid an emotional reaction that would counter our con-
> stant efforts to unite [with the FLN]. We will continue to work in the

4. According to a U.S. State Department report of January 1965, the Algerian
Communist party then had a membership of about 5,500. The PCA was said to be
the second largest Communist party in Africa after South Africa's. See *Maroc Infor-
mations,* January 21, 1965.

5. *El-Hourriya,* No. 4, November 23, 1962.

direction we have chosen: to support all positive measures taken by the government while maintaining our freedom to criticize constructively everything that seems to us to go against the real interests of our people.[6]

Alger Républicain continued openly to criticize the regime until early 1963, after a meeting between Henri Alleg and Ben Bella, when it began to tone down its commentaries. Nevertheless, it continued to expose the difficulties the workers were having with the government and to publish outspoken "letters to the editor." The daily sung the praise of Cuba, propagandized for the Soviet Union and other Eastern bloc countries, and kept up a steady attack against the United States and its policies in the Congo, Cuba, and Vietnam. With a circulation of about 80,000, more than twice that of the government-run daily *Al-Chaab*, the Communist newspaper became the most influential paper in the country.

The position the PCA took toward the Ben Bella regime was explained by Bachir Hadj Ali in a speech given in Paris in March 1963:

> There is *de facto* agreement . . . between us Communists and our FLN brothers on essential objectives and political orientation. In fact, the PCA program has in its present stage the same aims and the same orientation as the Tripoli Program.[7]

Despite the conciliatory attitude of the Communists, Ben Bella remained deaf to any suggestion of formal cooperation between the FLN and the PCA. Nevertheless, he went to great lengths to make it clear that Algeria was not anti-Communist and even invited the Communists to join the FLN as individuals. Ben Bella was apparently fearful that the banning of the PCA would tarnish his revolutionary image and impair Algeria's relations with the Soviet Union because as late as April 1963 he was still publicly offering explanations for his action:

> We have dissolved the Communist party. Some have interpreted this as an arbitrary measure, a sign of anti-Communism. I repeat, this is absolutely not the case. Haven't we made it clear . . . that it was not admissible, that there was no question of making of the Communist party a privileged organization, while we set forth as a principle the existence of a single party. We could not allow the Communists to hold meetings

---

6. *Alger Républicain*, November 30, 1962.
7. Bachir Hadj Ali, *Qu-est-ce Que c'est qu'un Révolutionnaire Algérien en 1963?* (Paris: Editions Sociales, 1963), p. 3. This is the reprint of a paper presented during the Week of Marxist Thought held in Paris March 13–20, 1963.

and to carry on legal activities and then tomorrow refuse the same to
the MNA, the PRS, and maybe even the UDMA, the MTLD, and
the *ulama*.[8]

Indeed, Ben Bella never persecuted the PCA, which continued to exist
clandestinely without causing the government any trouble. The policy
of the Communist leaders eventually paid off, for in 1964 Ben Bella
turned to them for support.

A much more serious problem with which Ben Bella had to deal immediately after coming to power was the wilaya commanders' challenge to the government and to the ANP General Staff. In January 1963,
Colonel Boumediene eliminated the six wilaya districts and set up in
their place seven new military regions as part of the process of recon-
verting the ALN. He also tried to move the wilaya commanders out of
their fiefs, but not all would leave. The Kabylia, now the Seventh Military Region, had to be left in the hands of Colonel Mohand ou el-Hadj;
the Biskra area, the new Fifth Military Region, remained under the
command of Colonel Chaabani; and Constantine, now the Sixth Military Region, was still headed by Major Si Larbi (Ben Redjem Larbi).

Si Larbi, who during the summer civil war had already fought his
private battle to seize control of Wilaya Two, continued to rule the
region with total disregard for any higher authority. He refused to bow
to his military superiors and meddled in civilian affairs, appointing his
men to important posts in the party and administration and even ex-
ploiting a good number of abandoned French farms. There was little
law and order in the area around Constantine, as the population was
constantly being subjected to the levies of Si Larbi's men. Ben Bella
initially avoided a direct confrontation with the unruly commander,
fearing to upset the fragile peace established at the end of the civil
war. On February 8, however, Si Larbi openly challenged Ben Bella.
In a press conference in Constantine, he accused government officials
of discriminating against the war veterans and demanded a purge of
the opportunists in the party and administration. Ben Bella immedi-

---

8. Ben Bella's speech of April 4, 1963. The MNA (Mouvement National Algérien) was the party founded by Messali Hadj after the outbreak of the revolution;
the PRS (Parti de la Révolution Socialiste) was a clandestine party organized by
Boudiaf in September 1962; the UDMA (Union Démocratique du Manifeste Algérien) and the MTLD (Mouvement pour la Triomphe des Libertés Démocratiques)
were pre-independence parties led by Ferhat Abbas and Messali Hadj respectively;
and the Association des Ouléma Réformistes d'Algérie was an organization of religious leaders.

ately stripped Si Larbi of his title and sent Colonel Boumediene and Bitat to Constantine to force the major to step down and to install a new commander. For reasons that remain unclear, Si Larbi yielded without a fight and retired from the army.

The ouster of Si Larbi did not altogether put an end to the insubordination of the former guerrillas in the Constantine area. There were still uncontrollable bands terrorizing the countryside, and discontent among the war veterans was rife, as Ben Bella found out during his tour of eastern Algeria just after the publication of the March Decrees. In Souk Ahras, Guelma, and Constantine, war veterans booed him and carried banners demanding the pensions that had been promised them. In mid-June, there were mutinies in army units stationed in Constantine and Skikda that, although crushed immediately, indicated the continued existence of a malaise in the army. The malaise, as events were later to prove, was not limited exclusively to eastern Algeria. However, until the fall of 1963, there were no more incidents involving the army. In the meantime, Ben Bella had to cope with the stiffening opposition of the historic leaders.

On June 21, Boudiaf and three of his associates were arrested by the army's secret police. The arrests caused considerable surprise, since Ben Bella had until that time chosen to ignore the clandestine Parti de la Révolution Socialiste (PRS), which Boudiaf had founded in September 1962 on the day of the elections for the National Assembly. The PRS was not considered a serious menace to Ben Bella. It had only a few hundred members, recruited mostly among Algerian workers in France and disgruntled labor union officials, and it did little more than periodically distribute tracts attacking the regime. Indeed, the PRS was so weak that it promptly collapsed after Boudiaf's arrest.

Boudiaf was considered a Marxist, but he did not collaborate with the Algerian Communists. He claimed to be a rigorous "scientific socialist" and advocated immediate nationalization of key sectors of the economy, state control of foreign commerce, the organization of a truly revolutionary party, and the creation of a powerful, autonomous labor union.[9] In effect, he echoed the Tripoli Program, to which Ben Bella also swore allegiance. But Boudiaf criticized the president for his slowness in applying the program, for his improvisations and lack of planning, for his failure to purge the party and civil service, and for his collaboration

9. For a summary of Boudiaf's views, see his book, *Où Va l'Algérie?* (Paris: Librairie de l'Etoile, 1964), pp. 157–208.

with persons like Ferhat Abbas and Teufik el-Madani, who were opposed to socialism. Ironically, Boudiaf had admitted the day before his arrest that the opposition, still poorly organized, offered no real alternative to the regime in power:

> It is not difficult to imagine a new crisis similar to the one that opposed the Tlemcen group to the old GPRA; you would see the formation . . . of a coalition made up initially of some of the present opponents, later joined by numerous opportunists, and finally by a great number of deserters [from the ranks of Ben Bella's supporters]. That would only lead to more disorder and confusion.[10]

Despite his incisive analysis of the state of the opposition, Boudiaf had apparently been involved in a plot to overthrow Ben Bella. A few days after Boudiaf's arrest, Ben Bella, while speaking in the National Assembly, accused Boudiaf of conspiring against the government but gave no details. It was later revealed that Boudiaf, along with Colonel Mohand ou el-Hadj, Belkacem Krim, other officers of former wilayas Three and Four, and some members of the FLN organization in France had founded a new clandestine party called the Union pour la Défense de la Révolution Socialiste (UDRS) and planned to launch an armed rebellion on July 10.[11] After Boudiaf's imprisonment, however, the party was dissolved.

Boudiaf's arrest provoked a violent quarrel between Ait Ahmed and Ben Bella in the National Assembly on June 25. After this clash, Ait Ahmed never returned to the assembly, withdrawing to his homeland, the Kabylia, in order to organize his own opposition. At a press conference on July 9, the Kabyle leader explained that he had only accepted his seat in the National Assembly in the hope of helping to bring about national reconciliation and that he had decided to leave because he no longer believed that such reconciliation was possible. Ben Bella, he claimed, had diverted the country from the goals of the revolution and had allowed the political life of the nation to be reduced to "politics of clans and *zaims* [chiefs]." Ait Ahmed's conception of the revolution's goals was fairly confused, but his program did not appear to differ

10. See Boudiaf's interview with *Le Monde*, June 25, 1963. The interview was given before his arrest.

11. The source of this information is Ait Ahmed, who during his trial in April 1964 confirmed that Boudiaf had been plotting an armed insurrection. He gave further details in FFS *Bulletin Intérieur*, No. 1, August 8, 1966, which was circulated shortly after his escape from prison. Ait Ahmed wrote that he had been asked to participate but had refused and even urged the others to postpone the planned insurrection.

substantially from those of Ben Bella and Boudiaf. Ait Ahmed considered himself a "scientific socialist," and he was particularly fond of discussing events in a "dialectical perspective." He was an enthusiastic exponent of self-management, priding himself on having submitted to the National Assembly the first bills for the organization of management committees, and he wanted to extend the system to other areas, particularly to local government. His views on the party were contradictory. Sometimes he called for the creation of the proverbial "revolutionary avant-garde party," while at other times he advocated a multi-party system.[12] His most immediate aim was to bring about the reconciliation of the country's revolutionary forces by holding a party congress in which all the historic leaders would participate.

A few days after Ait Ahmed's press conference, Belkacem Krim, another of the historic leaders, also violently attacked the Ben Bella regime in an interview with the French daily Le Monde.[13] The opposition was becoming more vociferous, but the government still brushed it off as inconsequential:

> Although there are opponents, there is no opposition. . . . They do not offer decisive arguments . . . capable of crystallizing the scattered elements of this opposition so vague in its program or of arousing Algerians from their serenity and making them forget that sebaa senin baraket [seven years of war are enough].[14]

The analysis was correct enough, but it overlooked the fact that scattered opponents could also be troublesome, as Boudiaf's abortive plot and several other incidents during the summer proved. In mid-July, Colonel Saout el-Arab, the former commander of Wilaya Two, was arrested for subversive activities. On August 20, the army discovered and destroyed a maquis that had been organized in the Kabylia by a group of thirty extreme left-wing Algerians and Frenchmen. Furthermore, the resignation of Ferhat Abbas from the presidency of the National Assembly in August brought into the open the opposition of the moderates, who until then had avoided publicly taking a stand against the regime. Despite the disaffection of both moderates and radicals, the Ben Bella government was not seriously threatened until an armed rebellion broke out in the Kabylia in the fall of 1963.

12. For a summary of Ait Ahmed's views, see his book La Guerre et l'Après-Guerre, pp. 165–204.
13. Le Monde, July 12, 1963.
14. Le Peuple, July 13, 1963.

The first sign of trouble in the region was the abstention of about half the Kabyle voters in the September 8 referendum for the Constitution. The call for a boycott had been issued by Ait Ahmed, who during the summer had organized a new clandestine party, the Front des Forces Socialistes (FFS).[15] Ait Ahmed had initially planned to launch his rebellion on the eve of the referendum but had been forced to postpone it when Colonel Mohand ou el-Hadj, military commander of the Kabylia, refused at the last moment to join him. The colonel's change of mind, the first of many, was the result of contacts with representatives of Ben Bella, who was already aware of the plot and had even tried—without success—to negotiate a settlement with Ait Ahmed. Finally, on September 29 Ait Ahmed publicly announced the formation of the FFS at a meeting held in Tizi Ouzou, capital of the Kabylia. Alongside him were Colonel el-Hadj and two deputies from the Algiers region.[16]

In the colorful language of Algerian politicians, Ait Ahmed described Ben Bella as an "unnatural mixture of Napoleon, Batista, and other fascists" and called upon Algerians to join the FFS in its struggle against the "fascist dictatorship." But he made it clear that his was not an uncompromising opposition by calling for the formation of a five-man directory, composed of Ben Bella, Khider, Boudiaf, Bitat, and himself, to discuss the problem of Algeria's leadership. Colonel el-Hadj, for his part, made a declaration accusing Ben Bella of shunting aside the former guerrilla leaders and appointing instead wartime "collaborators" to the top posts of the army. It was clear Colonel el-Hadj feared that Ben Bella and Boumediene would eventually oust him, just as they had ousted other wilaya commanders like Si Larbi, Tahar Zbiri, and Si Othmane.[17] On the same day as the Tizi Ouzou meeting, a group of former officers from Wilaya Four, who had organized a maquis in the

15. The first FFS tract appeared in Algiers on September 4, 1963, calling for a boycott of the referendum. The day before, Ait Ahmed had explained in an interview with *Le Monde* the reasons for the boycott: "Just as the elections of September 20, 1962, legalized the *coup de force* of the Tlemcem group, so the referendum scheduled for September 8 has no other aim than to legitimate the constitutional *coup de force*."

16. The two deputies were Mourad Oussedik and Areski Hermouche, alias Major Si Said, a former officer of the Wilaya Four Command.

17. Colonel Tahar Zbiri, the former commander of Wilaya One (Aurès Mountains), had been removed from his command in the reorganization of the military regions in January 1963. Colonel Si Othmane, the former head of Wilaya Five (Oran), had become a party official in Oran after being forced to resign from the army.

mountains south of Algiers, made similar declarations.

The presence of Mohand ou el-Hadj, who commanded 3,600 men in the Seventh Military Region, seemed to give some teeth to the opposition. Indeed, it appeared that Algeria was once again on the brink of civil war. However, Ait Ahmed denied that the FFS was dragging the country into another armed conflict: "There is no question of secession . . . . Colonel Mohand ou el-Hadj and his men have not mounted a putsch but taken a political position. In principle, we are not opposed to a dialogue with our adversaries. . . ."[18]

The government immediately relieved Colonel el-Hadj of his command but otherwise tried to play down the opposition in the hope of negotiating a peaceful settlement. Instead of moving a large number of troops into the Kabylia, Ben Bella launched a political counterattack aimed at discrediting and isolating the FFS. On September 30, he charged that the Kabyle opposition was backed by the king of Morocco and announced that Moroccan troops were poised on the Algerian frontier ready to attack. At the same time, he moved to appease the restive wilaya leaders, appointing Colonel Tahar Zbiri as chief of the ANP General Staff. On the following day, he nationalized the remaining French lands (about one million hectares), and began taking over Algerian properties belonging to wartime "traitors" and "profiteers."

Ben Bella's next move was to ask the assembly for exceptional powers to deal with the FFS, and these powers were immediately granted. He also met privately with eleven Kabyle deputies, asking them to act as intermediaries in the conflict. Although Ait Ahmed had numerous contacts with Ben Bella's envoys, he announced on October 4 that he would not accept mediation. Ben Bella then ordered the army into the Kabylia, and Boumediene's troops slowly closed in on Michelet, the stronghold of the resistance. There were a few minor clashes and endless palavers between the ANP and FFS forces but no major battles, and by October 12 the army had taken over Michelet, while the rebels retreated into the surrounding mountains.

In the meantime, the situation along the Algerian-Moroccan border had steadily deteriorated after an initial clash between Algerian and Moroccan soldiers on October 8. The conflict, which stemmed from Morocco's long-standing claims to a part of the Algerian Sahara along

18. Ait Ahmed made this statement at a press conference held in Michelet, the headquarters of the FFS, the night of the meeting in Tizi Ouzou. See *Le Monde*, October 1, 1963.

the ill-defined border, was not directly tied to the outbreak of the rebellion in the Kabylia, although the Moroccan government was obviously taking advantage of Algeria's internal difficulties to press its demands. Ben Bella, for his part, exploited the border conflict to rally his supporters, and even some of his opponents, in defense of the nation. On October 15, he mobilized the country for war, calling for volunteers and the re-enlistment of former guerrilla fighters. Ben Bella and many of his ministers donned military uniforms, and Algerians, seized by war fever, forgot their differences. The response to the president's call for volunteers was tremendous, with close to 100,000 Algerians signing up to go fight the war against invading Moroccan forces. Even the FFS offered its services in defense of the homeland, and indeed Colonel el-Hadj left for the Sahara frontier with a large contingent of Kabyle troops. Four of the six deputies who had originally sided with the FFS also rallied to the government. Ait Ahmed was thus forced to call a truce on October 24, promising, however, that the struggle would resume as soon as the war with Morocco was over.

Ait Ahmed had failed to rally widespread support for his cause. Neither Khider nor Krim formally joined him.[19] The FFS remained almost entirely a Kabyle movement and did not even have the backing of all the Kabyle leaders. The majority of Kabyle deputies remained neutral; at least four top officers of the Seventh Military Region Command refused to follow Colonel el-Hadj; and two of the nine batallions stationed in the Kabylia remained loyal to Ben Bella. Furthermore, the FFS did not have the support of all the Kabyles, as was shown by the fact that 50 per cent of the voters ignored the call for a boycott and approved the constitution. There were several reasons for the failure of the FFS to attract a large number of followers. First, being based in the Kabylia and led for the most part by Kabyles, the FFS aroused the suspicions of Algeria's predominantly Arab population. Second, the front, which claimed to be a socialist movement, did not appeal to the numerous Algerians who opposed Ben Bella because of his socialist policies. Third, Ait Ahmed's evident willingness to negotiate for a posi-

19. Khider returned to Algeria in the fall of 1963 to play the role of mediator between the FFS and Ben Bella. He arranged two secret meetings between Ait Ahmed and Ben Bella which took place in Algiers in early November; however, it appears that he later helped to finance the FFS. Krim was reported to be in Morocco and was publicly accused by Ben Bella of acting as a liaison agent between the FFS and the Moroccan government. However, as early as September 11, the FFS disassociated itself from Krim. See *Le Monde*, September 12, 1963.

tion in the regime alienated those who wanted to oust Ben Bella from power altogether. Finally, Ben Bella succeeded in splitting the ranks of the FFS by making skillful use of the border conflict.

After forcing the FFS into declaring a truce, Ben Bella negotiated with Mohand ou el-Hadj so that el-Hadj would not rejoin the FFS. On November 13, after the frontier war had subsided, Ben Bella concluded a formal agreement with the dissident colonel that provided for an amnesty for all army officers and civilians who wished to leave the FFS and return to legality; the release of all political prisoners, including Boudiaf; and a party congress within five months with the participation of all leaders of the revolution. The agreement was signed by many other Kabyle leaders, including Abdennour Ali Yahia, one of the most outspoken critics of the regime among the deputies, and Belkacem Krim. Several former officers of Wilaya Four also signed the agreement, weakening the opposition in the Algiers region.[20] On November 16, Boudiaf was released from prison as Ben Bella had promised, and on the same day the president announced that a party congress would soon be held.

Ait Ahmed did not accept the agreement negotiated by Colonel el-Hadj, since Ben Bella made it clear that he would not allow any of his opponents on the preparatory committee for the congress. After reorganizing the remnants of the FFS, Ait Ahmed declared an end to the truce on February 23. In the following months, guerrilla bands carried out hit-and-run attacks against police and party officials, and ambushed ANP troops stationed in the Kabylia. Although the FFS guerrilla force was not large after Colonel el-Hadj's defection—it consisted of perhaps 400 armed men—it made effective use of the same terrorist tactics that had been so successful during the war of independence. The FFS intensified its guerrilla warfare in the spring of 1964, at the time of the party congress. French sources estimated that about 100 persons were assassinated or killed in clashes between the army and the FFS in April and May. By mid-June, at least twenty party officials had been killed in the Kabylia, some of them hanged, others shot down in cold blood.

In April 1964, the long-awaited party congress was finally held, and

20. An official communiqué that appeared in *Le Peuple* on January 27, 1964, revealed that fifteen persons had signed the agreement of November 13. The communiqué was published in response to an FFS campaign aimed at discrediting Colonel el-Hadj.

Ben Bella was elected secretary-general. Thereafter, he felt that his position was much stronger, and his confidence was reflected in a new attitude toward the opposition. Upon returning from a three-week tour of Eastern bloc countries that followed the party congress, he took a much tougher stand against the FFS. On May 29, Ben Bella for the first time publicly branded Ait Ahmed a traitor and warned that members of the FFS could no longer expect clemency from the government. Two days later, the FFS answered by attempting to assassinate Ben Bella at his private residence; he narrowly escaped, and two guards were badly wounded.[21] The attack visibly shook Ben Bella, who immediately ordered the arrest of many suspected FFS sympathizers in the government and a step-up of the campaign against the "counterrevolution." On June 11, after a meeting of the newly created FLN Central Committee, it was announced that the party was organizing a "people's militia" in the Kabylia and other troubled areas to deal with the guerrilla bands and that the assembly would be called upon to vote a law instituting capital punishment.

In his campaign against the opposition, Ben Bella also decided to bring under heel another of Algeria's stubborn warlords, Colonel Chaabani, who was threatening to join forces with the FFS. The twenty-six-year-old officer had been a problem for Boumediene and Ben Bella since independence. Chaabani, like Si Larbi, was one of the guerrilla commanders who had sided with Ben Bella in the 1962 civil war but had thereafter refused to make any concession to the central government. As commander of the Fifth Military Region, Chaabani ruled with an iron hand over the northern edge of the Sahara, appointing his own men to all key positions in the area from Djelfa to Biskra. He openly condemned Ben Bella's socialism as contrary to the precepts of Islam and refused to let management committees be set up on the abandoned French farms and date plantations in his region. Instead, he took over the farms himself and then "rented" them out to his friends. He sympathized with the FFS, and only the outbreak of the war with Morocco prevented him from joining the front in the fall of 1963. Even while fighting at the Moroccan frontier, Chaabani kept his troops under a

---

21. The assassination attempt took place late at night. A carload of FFS terrorists opened fire on Ben Bella's car as it was entering the driveway leading to the Villa Joly. One of the terrorists threw a grenade, which exploded just behind the car. The five men who participated in the attack were captured shortly afterwards.

separate command, refusing to put them directly under the control of the General Staff.

In an effort to remove Chaabani from his fief, Boumediene abolished the Fifth Military Region in March 1964 and offered the troublesome colonel a post on the General Staff. But Chaabani refused to accept the promotion that would have severed him from his base of power. During the party congress, he delivered a fiery attack against both Boumediene and Ben Bella. He accused Boumediene of surrounding himself with French-trained officers who had been late in joining the liberation struggle; Ben Bella he attacked for listening to Marxist advisors who had imported doctrines foreign to Algeria's Arabo-Islamic tradition. The president nonetheless continued his attempts to placate Chaabani, and had him elected to the new seventeen-man Political Bureau. However, even a post in the country's highest ruling body could not entice the recalcitrant colonel away from his fief. At the end of June, Ben Bella and Boumediene formally ordered Chaabani to come to Algiers and take up his post on the General Staff and his seat in the Political Bureau. Chaabani again refused and on June 30 entered into open rebellion, joining Ait Ahmed in the armed struggle against the regime.[22] The next day, Colonel Boumediene moved his troops swiftly into Biskra, where Chaabani had his headquarters, but the dissident colonel had already retreated into the desert with about 1500 men.

At the same time, representatives of Ait Ahmed, Boudiaf, and Chaabani were meeting with Khider in Switzerland to discuss the formation of a united opposition movement. On July 6, the Comité National pour la Défense de la Révolution (CNDR) was formed. Its purpose was to organize armed resistance throughout the country with the intent of ousting Ben Bella and Boumediene. Ait Ahmed and his assistant, Colonel Si Sadok (Slimane Dehilès), were in command of the Kabylia; Boudiaf and Moussa Hassani, a former minister in the first Ben Bella Cabinet, where in charge of eastern Algeria; Chaabani was responsible

---

22. Colonel Boumediene gave a different version of the Chaabani affair after the June 19 *coup d'état*. He claimed that Ben Bella had deliberately incited Chaabani to revolt in an effort to divide the army and weaken the General Staff. He even maintained that Ben Bella was in constant contact with Chaabani during the short-lived rebellion. See Boumediene's interview with the Cairo newspaper *Al-Ahram*, October 8–10, 1965, the text of which is reprinted in *Révolution Africaine*, No. 143, October 23, 1965. See also Boumediene's speech to a conference of party officials on June 19, 1966.

for operations in the Sahara; and Major Si Moussa, a former ALN officer, was the leader of a maquis in western Algeria. The CNDR was partly financed by Khider, who declared on July 7 that he was putting the FLN funds in his possession at the disposal of the opposition. Ferhat Abbas was also reported to be in contact with the CNDR, although he never formally declared his support for the movement.

The CNDR was the result of an alliance of clans with conflicting tendencies, an alliance very similar to the one that had brought Ben Bella to power. The leaders of the CNDR had only one aim in common, that of overthrowing Ben Bella and seizing power. A bourgeois like Abbas, a warlord like Chaabani, and declared socialists like Boudiaf and Ait Ahmed undoubtedly could not agree on anything else. In any case, the CNDR did not last long enough to oblige its leaders to come to terms with their differences. On July 8, Colonel Chaabani was surprised by a detachment of the ANP in an oasis near Bou Saâda and surrendered with eighty of his men without firing a shot. Most of his troops rejoined the ANP. Major Si Moussa was captured on July 13, and the armed opposition was thus reduced to the FFS in the Kabylia and a small force led by Hassani in the Constantine region.

While the ANP was fighting guerrilla bands, Ben Bella began to purge the party and the assembly of his opponents. On July 4, the Central Committee expelled Chaabani, Khider, Ait Ahmed, and Moussa Hassani from the party. Five members of the Central Committee and eleven deputies were ousted from their posts for having collaborated with the opposition.[23] Shortly thereafter, Ben Bella had five deputies and two of his former ministers arrested.[24] Ferhat Abbas and Rabah Bitat were confined to their homes, and the former was later deported to an oasis deep in the Sahara, where he remained for almost a year. The time of the *"revolution sans prisons"* had definitely passed. After hesitating for months to use force and police-state methods, Ben Bella was now determined to wage an all-out war against his opponents. He

23. Excluded from the Central Committee were Mohamed Djerba, Tahar Ladjal, Hocine Saci, Said Abadou, and Mohamed Chenoufi. Expelled from the National Assembly were Colonel Si Sadok, Moussa Hassani, Amar Bentoumi, Abdelkader Bentoumi, Brahim Mezhoudi, Ali Cherif, Tahar Ladjal, Hocine Saci, Ahmed Ben Brahim, Cheikh Kheredine, and Amar Sekhri.

24. The five deputies arrested were Abderrahmane Farès, former head of the Provisional Executive and chairman of the assembly's finance committee: Boualem Oussedik; Abdelkader Bentoumi; Brahim Mezhoudi; and Hocine Saci. The two former ministers were Amar Bentoumi, minister of justice, and Mohamed Khobzi, minister of commerce, who was later charged with embezzling government funds.

had met their demand for the holding of a party congress and had invited them to participate. Most of them refused to attend, thereby forfeiting the only "legal" means they had for expressing their dissent. Ben Bella thus felt he had no obligation toward them and no reason to be lenient, as he made clear in his treatment of Chaabani, who was condemned to death by a military court in Oran and executed on September 3.[25] The day before, the five FFS terrorists who had carried out the assassination attempt against Ben Bella had also been executed.

By the fall of 1964, Colonel Boumediene had committed two-thirds of his army of 50,000 to fighting the guerrillas in the Kabylia and eastern Algeria. With the approach of the elections for the new National Assembly, which were set for September 20, the FFS once again stepped up the pace of its activities. As in the fall of 1963, Ait Ahmed ordered a boycott of the elections. Official returns showed that only 57 per cent of the Kabyles voted, and the actual participation was probably closer to 40 per cent.[26] The boycott was the last major success of the FFS. Ait Ahmed and several of his aides were captured on October 17, after an informer had betrayed their hiding place.

After Ait Ahmed's arrest, the opposition movement was on the wane. Several hundred FFS members either surrendered or were captured during the winter and were later sentenced to prison terms ranging from a few months to twenty years. The FFS ceased to be a threat to the regime, but it continued to present a danger for party and administration officials in Kabyle villages. There were still occasional assassinations of officials to remind the government that the FFS existed. After Ait Ahmed's capture, however, most of Ben Bella's remaining opponents were operating from outside the country. Khider was living in Madrid and wandering from capital to capital trying to make contact with other Algerian exiles. Boudiaf was also in Europe, trying to keep together the remnants of the CNDR and periodically launching fiery verbal

25. Chaabani is the only figure of national importance to have been executed since Algeria's independence. It is still unclear why he was not pardoned. Colonel Boumediene maintains that Ben Bella categorically refused to consider pardoning Chaabani after the latter was condemned by the military court. Ben Bella maintained that he had been forced against his will not to grant a pardon because of pressures from the army. After the June *coup d'état*, Boumediene repeatedly denied that he was responsible for Chaabani's death, throwing all the blame on Ben Bella. However, Ben Bella's version appears the most probable.

26. There was also a partial boycott in the Constantine region, where the turnout of voters dropped to 78 per cent as compared to 89 per cent in the presidential election of September 1963.

attacks on the Ben Bella regime. Belkacem Krim, after attending the party congress in April 1964, had flirted with the CNDR and then finally retired from politics, spending much of his time in Switzerland. Ben Bella's aides belittled the exiled opposition, which they appropriately titled the maquis des Champs Elysées.

In April 1965, Ben Bella finally put Ait Ahmed, Major Si Moussa, and four of their accomplices on trial.[27] Khider, Boudiaf, Colonel Si Sadok, and five other persons were judged in absentia.[28] The group appeared before a three-judge revolutionary criminal court in what a French lawyer for the defense called "a trial in the purest revolutionary style."[29] The trial took place behind closed doors, and Ait Ahmed ended by defending himself in a four-hour speech in which he covered the entire history of the nationalist movement in an effort to explain the necessity for the creation of the FFS. The trial ended on April 10, and the sentences were as expected: Ait Ahmed and Si Moussa were condemned to death and the four others were given prison sentences ranging from five to twenty years in prison. The eight leaders judged in absentia were also condemned to death. The next day, Ben Bella commuted the death sentences imposed on Ait Ahmed and Si Moussa to life imprisonment, as was also expected.

The trial attracted little attention. Algerians were tired of civil strife, especially the Kabyles, many of whom deeply resented the exactions of the FFS. Most Algerians had dismissed the movement as a purely Kabyle affair, and indeed the only areas outside the Kabylia where guerrilla bands had operated with some success were the mountainous regions north of Constantine, where extreme poverty and neglect by the central government had resulted in widespread discontent. For the most part, Algerians had had enough of political intrigues, of maquis, of assassinations, and above all of being used by politicians like Ait Ahmed, Boudiaf, and Chaabani.

Although the opposition failed in its major aim, it succeeded nonetheless in undermining the regime. Ben Bella spent a year negotiating

27. The four accomplices were Mohamed Chala, Ait Ahmed's personal assistant; Madjdid Achour, formerly a high official in the Ministry of Public Works; Ahmed Aiche, a pharmacist in Tizi Ouzou; and Father Jean de Falco, a Père Blanc who lived in a small village near Michelet and had acted as treasurer of the FFS.
28. The five others judged in absentia were Abdelkader Bentoumi, Hachemi Achour, Mohamed Ben Younès, Chala Achour, and Slimane Amirat.
29. The lawyer was Pierre July, former minister for North African affairs under Premier Mendès-France.

and compromising with his opponents. He agreed to hold a party congress under the sign of national reconciliation, even though doing so made impossible the creation of the homogeneous socialist party that he so badly needed as a basis for his regime. The reconciliation of the historic leaders did not take place, but a number of lesser opposition figures were admitted or permitted to remain in the party's leadership. Thus the FLN remained the unstable coalition of clans it had been ever since its foundation, and Ben Bella was left without a political instrument to enforce his policies. Furthermore, the existence of an armed opposition greatly increased the importance of the army, thereby strengthening Boumediene's position with respect to Ben Bella's.

chapter six
the congresses

A congress held without the presence of the authentic representatives of the people can only be an absurd sham; in order to open the road to socialism, the existing apparatus would have to be asked to commit suicide. This kind of suicide has no historical precedent.[1]

Gerard Chaliand

By September 1963, Ben Bella was president of Algeria, secretary-general of the party, and head of government. He had practically dissolved the alliance that had brought him to power. Ferhat Abbas, Mohamed Khider, and Rabah Bitat had been eliminated, and of his original principal allies only Colonel Houari Boumediene remained. The president had replaced his old associates with a group of trusted aides, among them Hadj Ben Alla, the new president of the National Assembly; Ali Mahsas, minister of agriculture; Bachir Boumaza, minister of national economy; and Mohamed Nekkache, minister of social affairs. In addition, he had his personal "brain trust" composed of men like Mohamed Harbi, editor of the weekly *Révolution Africaine*; Hocine Zahouane, head of the Algiers section of the FLN; Abdelaziz Zerdani, former editor of *Le Peuple*; and various foreign advisors. Ben Bella's new allies, while less troublesome than his old ones, did not bring large numbers of supporters to the regime. They drew their strength from the president, depended on him entirely for their authority and position, and therefore did not add anything to the power of the alliance. It was like a General Staff without an army. Ben Bella alone had a popular following, but he had as yet no organization backing him. Consequently, in October 1963 he set about channeling the popular support he had gained from the March Decrees into an orga-

1. Gérard Chaliand, *L'Algérie est-elle Socialiste?* (Paris: Maspero, 1964), p. 94.

nized force, trying to restructure the FLN into the mythical "revolutionary avant-garde party" and seeking to associate the peasants and workers in the decision-making process.

Ben Bella undertook this new step of the revolution in the exuberant style that had come to mark his rule. Already during the summer of 1963, he had launched a series of "campaigns" to popularize his policies and mobilize the nation. May had been the month of the Campaign of National Solidarity[2] and of the Democratic Reorganization of the Management Committees; July had seen the Campaign for the Explanation of the Tripoli Program; and August was the Month of the Constitution. In September, Algerians were twice called upon to go to the polls. After the elections, Ben Bella accelerated the pace of the revolution, nationalizing the remaining French farms and hundreds of commercial and industrial enterprises, launching the Campaign for the Restitution of Ill-gotten Properties, and organizing the congress of state-farm workers.[3] In mid-November, he announced the installation of the preparatory committee for the party congress, thereby initiating a long series of speeches, meetings, and articles in the official press about the forthcoming event. At the beginning of February 1964, there was a token distribution of profits to the workers on the self-managed farms. In March, the country celebrated the Fortnight of the March Decrees, which ended with the Day of the March Decrees, and immediately afterwards the workers of the socialist industrial sector held their congress. The grand finale came in April with the party congress.

This long series of campaigns and congresses was Ben Bella's method of involving the peasants and workers in the revolution and in the process of government. It was certainly not Western-style democracy, since the people only became involved after decisions had been made

2. The Campaign of National Solidarity, which began on April 30, 1963, was intended to raise funds for the construction of new factories and for the relief of unemployment. The equivalent of several million dollars, much of it in jewelry donated by women, was raised during this campaign. The money was never accounted for.

3. Ben Bella announced on October 1, 1963, that the government would nationalize properties belonging to Algerians who had sided with the French during the revolution and to those who had taken advantage of the post-independence chaos to enrich themselves. The nationalizations affected only some of the property that in theory should have been expropriated; nonetheless, some farms and several hundred hotels, cafes, shops, and movie houses were taken over in October. French interests were more seriously affected. In addition to one million hectares of French land, the government nationalized the three remaining French-owned newspapers, *L'Echo d'Oran*, *La Dépêche d'Algérie*, and *La Dépêche de Constantine* (September 15); bus companies (September 27); other French-owned transportation companies (October 4); and a variety of other enterprises.

by the government. Ben Bella once explained his style of democracy in this way:

> To those who speak of classical democracy, . . . I want to say that this event [the congress of farm workers] is an example of real democracy, . . . the democracy that we put in the service of those who need it the most and of those who have something to defend, namely the revolutionary gains made since independence.[4]

In practice "real democracy" meant that Ben Bella made decisions on his own and then offered participation in the political process to those who had gained something by his decisions and therefore had a stake in his regime. For example, he drew up the March Decrees without consulting the National Assembly or the UGTA and then convinced the peasants and workers that self-management was the system most beneficial to them. At this point only, did he invite the workers of the socialist sector to express their opinion on self-management and suggest improvements. This particular form of democracy nonetheless permitted Algeria's workers to participate in the political process more than they ever had before.

The first congress Ben Bella organized was that of the state-farm workers, held October 25–27 in Algiers. It was called suddenly, in the midst of the rebellion in the Kabylia and the war with Morocco, for the evident purpose of mobilizing support for the regime. It was hastily organized: only a week separated the announcement of the congress on October 8 from the regional preparatory meetings, and the main report to be discussed was not published or made available to the delegates until the opening day. Once the congress convened, it immediately became clear that party and government officials were running the show. The program was drafted entirely by the Political Bureau, and the regional meetings were run by prefects or party officials. Minister of Agriculture Ali Mahsas presented the principal report on the problems facing the management committees, while party officials worked behind the scenes supervising the work of the commissions charged with writing the final resolutions.

Nevertheless, the discussion was lively and not at all flattering to the government. The 2,500 delegates had long lists of grievances. They complained of insufficient funds to run the farms, bottlenecks in the state-run marketing system, a lack of farm machinery and repair ser-

4. Ben Bella's press conference of October 8, 1963.

vices, a shortage of agronomists and other trained personnel, constant delays in payment of salaries, the nonexistence of a social security program, and a shortage of decent housing and schools for the children. Many of the delegates complained that the government had not explained sufficiently how the self-management system was supposed to work and that consequently the March Decrees were not being applied correctly. The ONRA was accused of not respecting the autonomy of the management committees on the one hand and of not providing the committees with sufficient technical assistance on the other. The workers also complained that the war veterans whom the government had settled on the farms were behaving like masters, refusing to work or to take orders like the other workers. All these criticisms were fully reported in the government-controlled press, and no one intervened to stop the delegates from talking, as had been done at the UGTA congress in January 1963. At the closing of the congress, Ben Bella could truthfully say:

> You have all had the opportunity to speak, to give your opinion, and to make suggestions. Each delegate has been able to speak his mind freely, as can in Algeria today all those who earn their living by the sweat of their brow, . . . all those who are engaged in the building of the country.[5]

If freedom of speech had indeed prevailed, the voting of final resolutions was hardly democratic. Drafted by party-controlled commissions, the resolutions were quickly voted by a show of hands and applause. Nevertheless, they suggested remedies for most of the problems cited by the farm workers, calling specifically for the creation of marketing cooperatives and a state-run bank for the socialist farm sector, the training of hundreds of agricultural experts, and the setting up of state-run repair shops for farm machinery. They also demanded the distribution of farm profits as promised by the March Decrees and a new wage scale with a higher minimum wage.

The ONRA applied the resolutions voted by the farm workers as it deemed fit, meeting some demands in full, others only partially, and simply overlooking a few. The minimum wage was increased by 30 per cent to eight dinars ($1.60) a day and a new wage scale was established, but the ONRA continued to pay salaries only after long delays, causing considerable discontent among the farm workers. In February 1964, the

5. Ben Bella's speech of October 27, 1963.

government distributed for the first and only time a share of the farm profits. In reality this "share" was a bonus, granted even to the workers on deficit farms, which were the vast majority. The workers on profit-making farms received 230 dinars ($46.00), roughly the equivalent of one month's minimum salary, and the others were given 110 dinars ($22.00).

The ONRA also organized marketing cooperatives, the Coopératives de Commercialisation de la Réforme Agraire (CCRA), but they were cooperatives in name only since they were run entirely by the ONRA. Furthermore, the management committees complained that the CCRA took away their produce without issuing a receipt and later credited to the farm's accounts, which the ONRA kept, an arbitrary sum. Thus the committees never received any direct payment for the produce they sold and depended on eternal "advances" from the ONRA to pay the workers and operate the farms. The ONRA also set up the repair shops demanded by the farm workers, but the management committees complained that the shops charged much higher prices than the private shops did.[6] As for the state bank, it was not officially created until June 1966 and was still not operating in mid-1967. Since the UGTA was almost completely absent from the agricultural sector, the farm workers had no organization to defend them and to pressure the government into applying the resolutions voted at their congress;[7] consequently, the problems of the self-managed farm sector went largely unsolved.

In late March 1964, 1,000 workers from the socialist industrial sector met to discuss their problems. Their congress was far better organized than that of the farm workers, although it too was a party-run affair. The main report was again written by the Political Bureau, but it was published in the press well in advance of the congress, so that the workers knew what to expect. In addition, many of the delegates were militant UGTA members, politically aware and capable of arguing their points of view.

6. The workers complained that the ONRA repair shops, called Unions du Matériel Agricole, required the management committees to sign blank checks, which UMA employees filled out charging exorbitant prices.

7. There were numerous strikes on the state farms during the winter of 1964, mainly because of the long delays in the payment of salaries. The strikes were not part of an organized campaign, however. The farm workers were not included in the UGTA until December 1964, when the National Federation of Farm Workers was founded.

The three-day congress, which began on March 28, saw the government once again under heavy attack for its failure to give adequate aid
to the self-managed enterprises. The delegates spoke critically of those
"messieurs the civil servants who on the one hand approve President
Ben Bella and on the other do nothing but create problems for us."[8]
One of these problems was that the government rarely bought from the
worker-run enterprises, and when it did it failed to pay its bills for
months.[9] Nevertheless, the government was very strict in demanding
that these enterprises pay taxes, social security premiums, and even
debts left behind by the French owners. One delegate complained that
his factory had been penalized 5,000 dinars ($1,000) for delaying
payment of its social security tax, although the enterprise was facing
bankruptcy. He commented wryly: "Should we penalize in turn the
ministries that never pay their bills?"[10] Other delegates accused the
government of crippling the socialist sector by imposing high duties on
essential machinery and spare parts imported from abroad. Some demands echoed those made by the farm workers: creation of a state
bank to finance the socialist sector; reorganization of the marketing
system; and training of more accountants and technicians.

The delegates to the congress did not limit themselves to a discussion
of the technical problems dwelt upon by the party-prepared reports.
A good number of delegates appeared determined to exercise the right
of self-management promised them by the March Decrees, a right that
Ben Bella had dramatically reaffirmed at the opening of the congress:

> We believe that our socialist regime must be molded, moved, and in-
> spired to action by the rank and file, by the workers of the factories and
> of the land, the producers of all wealth, to whom we entrust the man-
> agement of the economy and progressively that of the entire state.[11]

Despite these eloquent words from Ben Bella, the party made every
effort to keep the congress under its control. The delegates reacted
energetically, however, and finally succeeded in obtaining more representation on the commissions set up to draft the final resolutions. The

8. See *Le Peuple*, March 30, 1964.
9. One delegate complained that the ONRA bought all its fertilizer from the
private sector. On the following day, March 31, the ONRA published a clarification
explaining that it had ceased buying from the socialist sector because of higher
prices and late deliveries.
10. See *Le Peuple*, March 30, 1964.
11. *Ibid.*

determination of the industrial workers to assert themselves was quite evident. One delegate declared:

> The party could explain and solve many problems if it organized cells in every enterprise. The presence of the UGTA would also be a guarantee that the interest of the workers would be defended. We ask all the delegates not to wait for orders from above to organize themselves. . . . Many workers and peasants are former members of the FLN. It is in the interest of self-management that they start immediately to organize party cells because we workers want to be present at the FLN congress next month. To do that, we have to organize without waiting for anybody to come and organize us.[12]

However, the government had no intention at that time of letting the workers organize independently. Indeed, the delegates did not even succeed in freeing their congress from the party's control. The final resolutions, presented by the commissions and voted as usual by a show of hands and applause, were those drawn up by officials of the FLN and the Ministry of National Economy. Suggestions for reviving the communal councils and for establishing regional councils with similar functions, repeatedly made by the workers, were not taken into consideration.[13] Nor was a proposal for the creation of a special ministry for the self-managed enterprises, the reason being that many top officials in the Ministry of National Economy, including Minister Bachir Boumaza, favored direct state control over the nationalized enterprises and did not want to see the self-management system strengthened or extended to other companies. Boumaza made this clear at the closing of the congress:

> Soon another decree will be published, which will force the private enterprises to follow certain rules. If they refuse to comply, a government commissary will be named in place of the present [private] management, and he will be assisted by a company committee elected by the workers.[14]

---

12. *Ibid.*

13. The March Decrees had provided for the creation of communal councils, of which the presidents of the management committees were members. The role of the councils was to help organize the self-managed sector and to educate the workers; in addition, the councils could dismiss the state directors upon the request of the management committees. These councils seldom functioned, however, leaving the workers without any means of recourse against the state directors.

14. See *Le Peuple*, March 31, 1964. The company committees (*comités d' entreprise*) were quite different from the management committees. They had existed even before independence in all private enterprises, in accordance with French law. They represented the workers in all labor disputes and cooperated with the company

Indeed, only a few of the private concerns nationalized after March 1963 and none of the dozen new textile, tannery, and clothing factories built by the government were given over to the workers to manage.

The issue of the distribution of profits is perhaps the best illustration of the conflict over self-management both within the government and between it and workers. The March Decrees had established that a part of the profits, roughly one-third, should be distributed among the workers of a particular enterprise. However, in early 1964 the UGTA executive committee urged that all profits be reinvested to accelerate the economic development of the country.[15] Most of Ben Bella's advisors insisted that the profits be distributed in order to prove to the workers that they were not simply wage earners, but managers with a direct interest in productivity. Ben Bella sympathized with this view, but he also desperately needed funds for economic development. The majority of delegates to the congress definitely favored the distribution of profits, but they lost out. Although the final resolution upheld the principle of profit-sharing, it also urged that the workers not receive more of the profits than would be equivalent to one month's salary. This was hardly profit-sharing, above all considering the fact that the workers in private enterprises had long been receiving an extra month's salary, known as the "thirteenth month bonus," at the end of each year.

The resolutions voted at the congress of industrial workers, like those passed at the congress of farm workers, were usually imperfectly applied or were not applied at all. The industrial workers called for the creation of a state bank to finance the socialist sector and asked the government to give priority to the self-managed enterprises in the awarding of its contracts, provided bids from these enterprises were no more than 20 per cent higher than those from private companies. Neither of these resolutions was heeded. It was also proposed that the 450 worker-run enterprises, most of which were small concerns, should be

---

in organizing training programs and social assistance projects, but had no role in management.

15. On January 5, 1964, the UGTA executive committee unanimously approved a resolution underlining the necessity for reinvesting profits in order to reopen abandoned French factories, still closed for lack of funds, and to build new factories. Workers of COBISCAL, a biscuit company, had already voted to reinvest profits in their company rather than distribute them. Both Mohamed Harbi, editor of *Révolution Africaine*, and Minister of National Economy Bachir Boumaza denounced the UGTA resolution as contrary to the letter and spirit of the March Decrees. Boumaza's position was determined less by conviction than by a desire to avoid a conflict with the workers.

regrouped by branch of activity into unions in order to enable them
to compete more successfully with the private sector.[16] This regroupment was partially carried out during the summer of 1964, but only in
a few cases did the unions help to make the self-managed factories more
competitive. The workers, moreover, were further removed from the
management, since the individual management committees were replaced by a single consolidated committee. An article in the UGTA
weekly *Révolution et Travail* depicted the consequences of one such
consolidation:

> The regroupment was carried out in a hurry. . . . About three hundred
> workers from eight enterprises have found themselves involved in a
> system that was supposed to help them, but that in reality has not
> solved any of their problems such as employment, marketing, buying
> materials, etc. Whereas before the workers in each enterprise had a
> director and a management committee responsible to them, now they
> are deprived of the possibility and means to make themselves heard be-
> cause of the creation of a general management committee with an in-
> visible director and a president always on the move.[17]

Of the new consolidated enterprises, only a few such as COBISCAL, a
biscuit company, and the *Huileries Modernes d'Alger*, a vegetable oil
concern, actually flourished.

The congresses of farm and industrial workers brought no significant
improvement in the functioning of the self-management system. Their
importance was above all political: they kept discontent with the running of the system from turning into discontent with Ben Bella, and
they gave the workers a sense of being an important political force in
the country. Indeed, Ben Bella was deliberately cultivating this feeling
of importance in the workers and peasants, hoping to assuage the tensions that had arisen between them and the government. Actually, as
we have seen, little attention was paid to the demands of the workers;
however, the illusion of "real democracy" was enough to gain Ben Bella
the workers' sympathy, and when he later needed support against the

16. A decree of June 8, 1964, provided for a complex organization of the socialist
industrial sector. Enterprises of "local importance" were to be grouped into "departmental unions" organized like cooperatives. Enterprises of "national importance"
were put directly under the Ministry of National Economy. All unions came under
the supervision of the ministry's Coordinating and Planning Commission. The decree
provided for fairly rigorous state control over the self-managed enterprises. In
reality the decree was applied sporadically, and the enterprises remained pretty much
on their own. See *Journal Officiel*, No. 50, June 19, 1964, Décret 64–175.

17. *Révolution et Travail*, No. 73, January 20, 1965.

army he was able to turn to the workers in his effort to swing the balance of power in his favor. His need for support arose following the party congress of April 1964.

Algerian politicians had long considered the first congress of the FLN the assembly that would provide solutions to their outstanding problems. Some of the dissident historic leaders hoped that the congress would bring about "national reconciliation," permitting them to return to positions of power. Ben Bella intended to use the meeting to give Algeria an ideological platform and to establish the foundations of a truly revolutionary party. Pending the congress, the president had postponed any radical reform of the FLN, which therefore remained the front of disparate elements it had been since its creation. However, by 1964 the party had its own structure, while during the revolution it had been merged with the National Liberation Army.

The FLN had a pyramidal organization. Under the Political Bureau were 17 federations, corresponding to the administrative departments.[18] The federations were subdivided into 109 *dairas* (regions), which in turn were divided into 1,112 *kasmas* (districts) at the level of the communes. At the base of the pyramid were the smallest units of the party, several thousand cells each containing a maximum of ten members.[19] By May 1963, the Political Bureau was *de facto* reduced to three members—Ben Bella, Ben Alla, and Mohammedi Saïd—although Khider and Bitat were not officially ousted from it until the congress. The party had its own weekly, *El-Moudjahid*, and fought with the Ministry of Information for control over the daily *Le Peuple*. In addition, the FLN had an active propaganda and information service that produced numerous pamphlets such as *Understanding Self-management*, *Neocolonialism*, *The Cooperative System*, and *Revolution and Counterrevolution*. It also had a special bureau to handle relations with the more than twenty liberation movements and political opposition groups that received aid from Algeria.

18. There was one federation for each of the fifteen departments plus one for the city of Algiers and one in France. The latter was called Amicale des Algériens en France (Association of Algerians in France) in compliance with French law, which does not allow foreign political parties to operate in France.

19. After the party congress, the organization of the party was slightly modified: the size of the cells was increased to a maximum of fifty members, the dairas were eliminated, and the number of federations was increased to 100, corresponding to the arrondissements. The coordination of the party at the departmental level became the responsibility of the national commissaries.

The party was supposed to consist of a small corps of "proven militants," but during the first two years of independence it had grown very rapidly and by the time of the congress claimed a membership of 153,000 full members and 619,000 "adherents," aspirant members undergoing indoctrination. Despite the size of its membership, the FLN was practically nonexistent in the smaller villages and hamlets. There were no strict criteria for recruiting members, a situation of which local potentates had taken advantage to accommodate their friends, turning the party into a mosaic of clans.[20] The typical small town party official was a young man dressed in a French-cut suit and Italian pointed shoes, hiding behind dark glasses and posing as an intellectual. Such officials were more interested in playing politics than in stimulating local initiative or mobilizing the people.[21] As a consequence, they were generally not respected by the people and were often at odds with the local administrators, whose activities they usually tried to control.[22] Party officials earned 1,000 dinars ($200) a month, but many were apparently not satisfied with this adequate sum, as a good number were arrested in 1962 and 1963 on charges of embezzlement and corruption. It was well known that many last-minute converts to the FLN cause had found their way into the party just after independence and had entrenched themselves there. There were repeated demands for a purge of the party, but prior to the congress Ben Bella never felt strong enough politically to carry one out.

Ben Bella began to prepare for the congress in compliance with the agreement he had reached with Colonel Mohand ou el-Hadj in November 1963. A fifty-two-man preparatory committee was formed on November 16. It was selected by the Political Bureau and gave little representation to Ben Bella's declared opponents, although it included four deputies who had voted against the constitution in August 1963.[23]

20. There was a corps of party inspectors, but the inspectors served primarily as liaison agents between the Political Bureau and the federations, and did not exercise much control over the qualifications of party officials.

21. About the only projects local party officials carried out were occasional day-long tree-planting campaigns, which were usually initiated by the party in Algiers.

22. Algerian leaders too had a very poor opinion of the party. Ferhat Abbas claimed that 80 per cent of the federations and dairas were unpopular and that the officials were mostly "voracious budget-eaters and profiteers." Ben Bella said that the party under Khider was composed of "scum." Boumediene, after the June 19 *coup d'état*, defined the majority of party officials as "adventurers, traffikers, courtisans, and opportunists."

23. The preparatory committee was composed of eleven ministers, eight top officials of the FLN, eight leaders of the national organizations, eighteen deputies,

The eight-man secretariat responsible for drawing up Algeria's new ideological platform was composed almost entirely of Ben Bellists.[24] On March 26, the government announced those who would be invited to attend the congress: ministers, members of the Political Bureau and of the preparatory committee, top party officials and ANP officers, former wilaya commanders, leaders of the national organizations, members of the wartime CNRA and GPRA, deputies and ambassadors, and one elected delegate for every two hundred party members. It appeared that Ben Bella was attempting to meet the demands of Ait Ahmed, Khider, and Boudiaf for a congress aimed at reconciliation of the country's leaders. But the president denied that national unity was the objective of the congress: "If we want to define more precisely our socialist goals, we cannot go back to a solution of national unity."[25] The army, however, took the opposite view, and shortly before the congress its monthly magazine *El-Djeich* stated that the congress "must be held under the sign of clarification and national unity."[26]

The difference in viewpoints between the Ben Bella and Boumediene factions went even deeper, as was revealed during the meetings of the preparatory committee, when a split developed between the two groups. The party's future ideological platform had been drawn up almost entirely by Mohamed Harbi and Abdelaziz Zerdani, two of Ben Bella's most leftist advisors, and had a strong Marxist orientation that deeply antagonized Boumediene and his allies. However, the army faction had no intellectuals capable of drawing up an alternative document, and all it could do was to press for modifications in the original text. The result was a greater emphasis on Algeria's Arabo-Islamic

----

three high-ranking government officials, one army officer, and three other members without any official position. For a complete list, see the French review *Maghreb*, No. 1, January-February 1964, p. 24. The weight of the army was much greater than the presence of a single officer suggested, since Boumediene and five of his principal allies—Ahmed Kaid, Abdelaziz Bouteflika, Chief Belkacem, Ali Mendjli, and Ahmed Medeghri—were also members of the committee. Ben Bella's opponents publicly contested the representativeness of the committee.

24. The eight members of the secretariat were: Hadj Ben Alla, a member of the Political Bureau; Abdelmadjid Bennaceur, an official of the FLN youth organization; Captain Bouhara Abderrazak, an officer of the Seventh Military Region; Nourredine Hassani, an official of the student union; Omar Benmahjoub, a top party official; Salah Louanchi, deputy and former editor of *Al-Chaab*; Abdelaziz Zerdani, deputy and former editor of *Le Peuple*; and Mohamed Harbi, editor of *Révolution Africaine*. Only Captain Abderrazak was not a known Ben Bellist.

25. Ben Bella's speech of March 25, 1964.

26. *El-Djeich*, No. 11, April 1964.

heritage and a somewhat more neutral stance in the section on international affairs, but even with these changes the document remained
much too Marxist to please the army. The clash within the preparatory
committee marked the beginning of a feud that was to end in the
coup d'état of June 19, 1965.

Three weeks before the congress began, the proposed ideological
charter was published in the press, and subsequently meetings were
held throughout the country to explain it to the public. By that time, it
was clear that the congress could not bring about reconciliation among
the wartime leaders: Abbas, Boudiaf, Khider, Bitat, and Ait Ahmed
had declared they would not attend. Only Belkacem Krim and a few
other members of the wartime Provisional Government, though not
former President Benyoucef Ben Khedda, accepted the invitation.[27] All
the same, the 1,991 delegates who gathered in the Ibn Khaldun Audi-
torium in Algiers on April 16 were a very mixed group of old-time
enemies and new-found allies. The elected delegates, less than 800,
were in the minority, while Colonel Boumediene's army stood out with
its 250 delegates. However, the machinery of the congress was in the
hands of Ben Bellists, and Bachir Boumaza, minister of national economy, was serving as president.

Except for Ben Bella's opening address, the congress was held behind
closed doors. In his speech, Ben Bella underlined once again that the
time had come to make a clear choice for socialism and weed out of
the party all opponents of this course. The aim of the congress, he
declared, was not to reopen the "dossiers of the revolution" or to argue
about who was responsible for the post-independence crisis or who had
led the country to victory. He also made a pointed effort to destroy the
myth of the historic leaders:

> There are no historic leaders except the ones who gave their lives for
> independence. . . . The only historic ones are those who today work by
> the sweat of their brow in anonymity to rebuild the country. . . . There
> is only one hero, the people.[28]

The FLN, he asserted, had to be reorganized into a "homogeneous party

27. Former members of the GPRA who attended the congress were: M'hammed
Yazid, Ben Bella's special envoy and president of the National Assembly's foreign
affairs committee; Saad Dahlab, ambassador to Morocco; and Lakhdar Ben Tobbal
and Mohamed Boussouf, neither of whom had played an active role in politics after
independence.

28. Ben Bella's speech was incorporated into the Algiers Charter. See Front de
Libération Nationale, *La Charte d'Alger* (Algiers, 1964), pp. 129–167. See also
Le Peuple, April 17, 1964.

drawing its strength from a membership composed essentially of workers and peasants." The contradictions that had plagued the party since its creation having thus been eliminated, the FLN would finally become the "motor of the revolution." The new ideological charter, he stated, would provide clear guidelines for the reorganization of the party and a blueprint for the socialist revolution.

The Algiers Charter, as the FLN ideological platform came to be called, was the most complete analysis of the social and economic situation in Algeria yet to be undertaken and the most far-ranging program the FLN had ever produced. The charter began with a brief history of the nationalist movement, focusing particularly on the conflicts that had divided the leadership of the FLN and influenced the party's policies during the war. Echoing the Tripoli Program, the document accused the wartime leaders of "having continually postponed the moment when the irreversible choices concerning the nature of society after independence would be made."[29] The charter made it clear that Algeria had definitely opted for a socialist society. It denied that Islam was an obstacle to socialism, claiming that the Algerian people had always viewed their religion as a doctrine preaching the "end of the exploitation of man by man" rather than as a "doctrine of resignation."[30]

Analyzing the socio-economic structures of Algerian society, the charter noted that "imperialist domination" had prevented the development of a bourgeoisie and favored the formation of a large proletariat. After 132 years of colonialism, the bourgeoise was a class of no more than 50,000, but its effective force in the "dynamics of the social struggle" was determined not only by its numeric and economic importance, but also by its "ideological, cultural, and political influence."[31] However, continued the charter, the most serious threat to Algeria's socialism was the formation of a "bureaucratic bourgeoisie" rooted in the apparatus of the administration and economy. This bourgeoisie had grown stronger as a result of the continued existence of the former colonial administration in independent Algeria:

> The administrative and economic bureaucracy can become considerably more dangerous for the socialist and democratic revolution than any other social force in the country because it plays an economic role within the structure of the colonial administration.[32]

29. *La Charte d'Alger*, p. 31.
30. *Ibid.*, p. 35.
31. *Ibid.*, p. 39.
32. *Ibid.*, p. 40.

Despite the opposition of the bourgeoisie, there had been "a continuous development of the people's national revolution into a socialist revolution" manifested in the creation of a self-management system. The charter declared that self-management was the expression of "the will of the country's working class to emerge on the politico-economic scene and to establish itself as the leading force."[33]

This analysis of post-independence politics was only partly correct. Undoubtedly there was in Algeria a bourgeois class opposed to socialism, and undoubtedly most Algerian bureaucrats had bourgeois aspirations. But it did not follow that these bureaucrats supported a system of free enterprise. In fact, they mostly favored state capitalism, because this was the system that afforded them the greatest power. However, for Ben Bella's Trotskyite advisors, who meant by socialism direct management of the economy by the workers, the advocates of state capitalism were as much enemies of socialism as the bourgeois.

The greatest error the writers of the charter made was to analyze Algerian politics in terms of class struggle. The political life of Algeria was not dominated by the dialectic between a socialist government representing the peasants and the workers and a bourgeoisie determined to sabotage the revolution. The dialectic that dominated Algerian politics took place between one clan and another, between the allies of Ben Bella and those of Ait Ahmed, between a rallied Mohand ou el-Hadj and the diehards of the FFS, between the Marxists in Ben Bella's entourage and the conservatives in the army, between the wilaya leaders and the French-trained officers in the ANP, between the farm workers and the bureaucrats of the ONRA. The charter implicitly acknowledged the fact that Algeria did not yet have a clearly socialist leadership by warning that the choice of a single-party system did not always lead to the formation of a socialist party representing the peasants and workers:

> The choice of a single party must be made with clarity and precision, eliminating all ambiguities concerning [the party's] goals, its composition, and its functioning. Otherwise there is a considerable risk that [the single-party system] will sooner or later lead to a petit bourgeois dictatorship, or to the formation of a bureaucratic class that uses the state apparatus as an instrument to satisfy its personal interests, or finally to a regime of personal dictatorship that reduces the party to a

33. *Ibid.*, p. 41.

simple political police. . . . The union of all political tendencies, which was an indispensable instrument of the armed struggle, must be reconsidered in light of the objectives and perspectives of the socialist revolution. Such a union is now outdated. . . . The new problems [of independence] have brought about irreconcilable internal contradictions.[34]

Here the analysis was much to the point, but it was not likely to induce the delegates at the congress to approve a massive purge of the party, since many of their number would have been among the victims. Certainly the delegates had no intention of voting themselves out of power. The purge could only have been carried out by Ben Bella and the small group of convinced socialists that surrounded him, but the consequences would have been grave. The dissolution of the front would have given free rein to the rivalry between the innumerable factions of which the party was composed, strengthening the clannish spirit, encouraging regionalism, and undoubtedly provoking new rebellions in the country. The behavior of Ait Ahmed, and of Major Si Larbi before him, was a clear warning of the danger Ben Bella faced. Ben Bella could have dissolved the front only if he had been able rapidly to organize a new force, a sort of Algerian Red Guard, to carry out his purge and be the nucleus of the new party, and only if the army had agreed to support him in this endeavor. But Colonel Boumediene made it clear at the congress that the army was not prepared to plunge Algeria into another civil war. He warned the congress that it was not the moment to provoke a new upheaval and appealed once again for national unity. Boumediene had no choice but to urge unity because his army was still racked with internal divisions. This was made clear even at the congress. Colonel Chaabani launched a violent attack against Boumediene for the second-rate positions that had been given to former guerrilla commanders like himself.

The party therefore remained what it always had been—a front in name and composition. The congress elected Ben Bella secretary-general of the party[35] and then voted for a 103-member Central Committee composed of many factions: wilaya leaders, army officers, Marxist theorists, Kabyle deputies of uncertain allegiance, party and UGTA

---

34. *Ibid.*, p. 105.
35. Technically, before the congress Ben Bella had been secretary-general of the Political Bureau, although he was always referred to as secretary-general of the party.

officials at odds with one another, and regional potentates.[36] However, the dissident historic leaders, moderates like Ferhat Abbas and traditionalists like Minister of Religious Affairs Teufik el-Madani, were excluded from the Central Committee. The new seventeen-man Political Bureau that Ben Bella proposed to the Central Committee for approval consisted of representatives of the Ben Bella and Boumediene clans and the wilaya leaders. Ben Bella had been forced by the army to exclude from the Political Bureau the principal authors of the charter, Mohamed Harbi and Abdelaziz Zerdani. Ben Bella and his allies had just nine seats, a slim one-man majority, but they did not face a united bloc, since the other eight posts were equally divided between the former wilaya leaders and the Boumediene faction.[37] Ben Bella's strength thus rested on the antagonism between the wilaya leaders and Boumediene.

The Algiers Charter was approved unanimously without any modifications in the text, although it was well known that many delegates, particularly those from the army, opposed its ideological orientation. In approving the charter, the congress established that the system of self-management would be progressively applied to the entire economy and to local government as well. It also committed the government to carrying out an agrarian reform; developing a heavy industry; nationalizing all private banks, insurance companies, and mines; establishing state control over foreign commerce and over the petroleum industry; and scientifically planning the country's future economic development. In the area of international politics, the congress resolved that Algeria's

36. The Central Committee was composed of eighty full members and twenty-three substitute members; the latter participated in the debates but did not have the right to vote. The wilaya leaders were given an unusually large representation. Among those included were Colonel Si Larbi; Colonel Saout el-Arab; Colonel Si Othmane; Colonel Si Hassan, former commander of Wilaya Four; Colonel Amar Ouamrane, a former commander of Wilaya Three; Major Hadj Lakhdar, a former officer in Wilaya Four; Colonel Mohand ou el-Hadj; Colonel Tahar Zbiri; and Colonel Mohamed Chaabani.

37. The Ben Bella clan was represented by Ben Bella; Hadj Ben Alla, president of the National Assembly; Mohammedi Saïd, second vice-president of the Cabinet; Ali Mahsas, minister of agriculture; Mohamed Nekkache, minister of public health and social affairs; Bachir Boumaza, minister of national economy; Omar Benmahjoub, a high party official; Ait el-Hocine, president of the Amicale des Algériens en France; and Hocine Zahouane, head of the FLN Federation of Algiers. The Boumediene clan was represented by Boumediene; Ali Mendjli, vice-president of the National Assembly; Abdelaziz Bouteflika, minister of foreign affairs; and Ahmed Medeghri, minister of the interior. The former wilaya leaders in the Political Bureau were Colonel Tahar Zbiri, Colonel Mohamed Chaabani, Colonel Si Hassan, and Colonel Mohand ou el-Hadj.

major objective was the intensification of the "anti-imperialist struggle" through the unification of all revolutionary forces in Africa and the Arab world, and that aiding the liberation movements was a "sacred duty." However, it also approved a statement that coexistence among countries with different economic and social systems was "desirable."[38]

The Algiers Charter did very little to dispel the confusion that characterized relations between the party and the administration. Although its authors recognized that the lack of a clear definition of these relations had raised innumerable difficulties in the past, the charter merely quoted the vague statements contained in the Tripoli Program. It repeated the program's pronouncements that the party "inspires and controls" the activity of the government and that the majority of party officials should not hold posts in the administration in order to avoid a merger of the two structures. However, it differed from the program in insisting that the head of government "must also be at the head of the party."[39] The charter also reemphasized that the FLN was in charge of the political education of the army, a very provocative statement considering the fact that Colonel Boumediene had always refused to accept any interference from the party and had set up instead an independent political commissariat.

The congress ended with the voting of a set of resolutions that represented a compromise between the Marxist and conservative positions. The first resolution expressed "the will of the Algerian people and of their party to carry out their policies at home and abroad under the two banners of socialism and the attachment to Algeria's Arabo-Islamic personality."[40] Another resolution insisted on the need to promote the "arabization of Algeria" by accelerating the teaching of Arabic in the schools, reviving Islamic culture, and establishing closer ties with the Arab world. Algeria's foreign policy was defined as one of "nonalignment," an expression not contained in the charter itself; however, the same resolution included an appeal for strengthening cooperation with

38. The charter described the evolution of world events in the following manner: "Two trends dominate international relations: (1) the progress of the socialist and democratic forces, symbolized by the accentuation of the anti-imperialist struggle, the accession of new states to independence, the economic development of the socialist countries, and the intensification of the struggle of the democratic movements; and (2) the constant shrinking of the sphere of influence of imperialism." *La Charte d'Alger*, p. 46.
39. *Ibid.*, p. 114.
40. *Ibid.*, p. 168.

those countries that could help Algeria free itself from "imperialism"—
a clear overture to the Communist bloc.

As the congress was taking place, Henri Alleg, codirector of the Communist daily *Alger Républicain*, offered to make his paper "an organ of
the party." Ben Bella accepted the offer and then allowed the daily to
remain virtually an independent newspaper.[41] Thus after eighteen
months of patient efforts, the PCA's policy of seeking cooperation with
the regime paid off. There was no formal merger of the PCA with the
FLN, nor was the ban on the Communist party revoked, but in Ben
Bella's entourage the influence of the Communist leaders noticeably
increased. The congress also opened the way for a new entente between
Ben Bella and the Communist-dominated student union, and between
him and the leftist UGTA leaders who had been ousted from power in
January 1963.

Although it did not fulfill his hope of establishing a basis for a homogeneous socialist party, the congress had extremely important consequences for Ben Bella. First, it completed the process of legitimizing
his seizure of power, strengthening his hand against the opposition;
second, it completed the split between him and the army; and third, it
prepared the way for an alliance with the leftist groups outside the
FLN, which heartily approved the orientation of the Algiers Charter.
The congress initiated a race between Ben Bella and Boumediene, the
former attempting to strengthen the leftist organizations in the hope
that this would strengthen him against the army, the latter trying to
resolve the conflict between the wilaya leaders and the new officers of
the ANP in the hope of unifying the army against Ben Bella.

41. Around the time of the congress, there was considerable pressure put on Ben
Bella by the army to ban *Alger Républicain*. Alleg's offer to make his paper an organ
of the party was not only a new offer of cooperation with Ben Bella, but also a
maneuver to save the paper.

chapter seven
the new forces

It is not the person of the sultan, nor the eloquence of his speeches, nor his appearance, nor his physical prowess, nor his vast knowledge, nor the elegance of his writing, nor the depth of his mind that are useful to his subjects, but the ties between him and them.[1]

Ibn Khaldun

The party congress had hardly come to an end when Ben Bella left Algeria on a twenty-four-day tour of the Soviet Union and other Eastern bloc countries. While party leaders traveled throughout the country on the latest "campaign" explaining the significance of the party congress and the Algiers Charter, Ben Bella visited one Communist capital after another, reaping medals, prizes, and applause. He returned to Algiers on May 17 to find that the Front of Socialist Forces was bolder and more belligerent than ever before, extending its terrorist activities into the city and even to his very doorstep.[2] He also found that some of those he had included in the Central Committee and Political Bureau in the hope of gaining their support were in fact siding more and more openly with the opposition. Ben Bella no longer sought to negotiate a compromise. As we have seen, on June 8 he summoned the Central Committee to its first meeting and had it approve a series of measures designed to check the "counterrevolution," among them the creation of a "people's militia" and the confiscation of properties belonging to those abetting the opposition. At the same time, Ben Bella moved to strengthen the FLN. On June 22, he appealed to all wartime FLN militants who had dropped out of the party to rejoin immediately,

1. Ibn Khaldoun, *La Muqaddima*, p. 105.
2. The attack on Ben Bella's private residence took place on May 31. In the days following, there were several bomb explosions in Algiers, notably one at the port on June 10, in which two persons were killed and several injured.

and in early July he ousted a number of Central Committee members and high-ranking government officials.[3] Neither the purge nor the recruitment of new party members put an end to the factionalism inside the FLN, however, and Ben Bella was driven to seek new allies outside the party.

The takeover of the abandoned French farms and factories in 1962, the March Decrees, and the nationalizations of 1963 had given many Algerians a vested interest in the socialist revolution and had attracted many others who hoped socialism would bring an improvement in their lot. Still others favored socialism for ideological reasons. These groups— the industrial workers of the socialist and even of the private sector, the peasants on the state farms, the leftist intellectuals, and the students— were emerging as new political forces in the country and were trying to find a place on a political scene dominated by wartime leaders. Ben Bella had repeatedly promised to give power to the workers and a leading political role to the revolutionary intellectuals and students. His words were part of the rhetoric of a revolutionary leader, but the more radical members of the national organizations, particularly those of the labor and student unions, felt sufficiently encouraged by his promises to organize themselves and attempt to assert their influence in politics.

None of the national organizations had had much influence in national politics during the first two years of independence, not even the labor union, which had rapidly been subjected to party control. Founded during the revolution and based outside the country until independence, the national organizations had only really begun to function after the end of the war, when their leaders returned to Algeria. The process of organization proved long and arduous. Difficulties created by divisions among the leaders of each organization and by the general apathy of the people were compounded by the interference of the FLN, which sought to establish its control over all national organizations.

The women's association, the Union Nationale des Femmes Algériennes (UNFA), was particularly ineffectual and slow in organizing. The women were essentially interested in only one issue, their emancipation, and emancipation was what socialism and Ben Bella meant to

3. For the complete text of the Central Committee's resolutions, see *Alger Républicain* or *Le Peuple*, June 12, 1964. For more details on the purge, see Chapter Five, p. 102.

them. They attended Ben Bella's rallies in surprisingly large numbers, showing that they were ready to be mobilized in the struggle for their rights. But UNFA's leaders never succeeded in channeling this militancy toward constructive goals. Outside of Algiers and the other big cities, UNFA hardly existed. In early 1965, its leaders admitted that the union had only a "few thousand" members and still had no formal organization.[4] It was not until November 1966 that UNFA held its constituent congress, having had half a dozen different executive committees in four years. The union's single triumph was a demonstration on March 8, 1965, International Women's Day, in which ten thousand Algerian women of all ages and social conditions marched defiantly through the streets of downtown Algiers before the eyes of stunned and unbelieving Algerian men. UNFA leaders tried to capitalize on the success of this demonstration to launch the union on a larger scale, but the *coup d'état* of June 1965 interrupted their efforts. Consequently, UNFA never became an important pressure group, even failing to make public issues of the problems that interested women the most, such as a modern family code and a program of birth control. The failure of the union was only partly due to the women's own incapacity to organize; the total lack of encouragement from either party or government officials also greatly hampered the organization of UNFA.

The Jeunesse du Front de Libération Nationale (JFLN) was created in Algiers during the summer of 1962 through the initiative of a small group of party youths apparently acting on their own. The JFLN remained a minor organization until the FLN congress in April 1964, at which time it was decided to expand the youth organization into a nationwide movement. In early 1965, at the peak of its strength, the JFLN had perhaps 50,000 members, with federations established in every department. Having held a pre-congress in September 1964, it was preparing to hold a national congress when the *coup d'état* practically put an end to its activities.

The JFLN's aim was to involve in the socialist revolution the mass of Algerian young people, who comprise over 50 per cent of the population. Its main activity was the organization of volunteer work projects and summer camps where semiliterate teenagers engaged in tasks ranging from tree planting to village reconstruction and received some instruction and much ideological indoctrination. These camps, defined

4. See Zhor Zerrari, "Les Femmes Algériennes Sous le Signe du 8 Mars," *Démocratie Nouvelle*, June 1965, pp. 158–160.

as "schools of socialism," were only moderately successful because of the chronic lack of organization, funds, and counsellors to run them. During the summer of 1964, for example, the party had hoped to enroll about two thousand youths in a number of "work brigades" in such camps, but finally was able to take only five hundred.[5] Despite all its shortcomings and failures in the field, the JFLN formed some of the most unquestioning and enthusiastic supporters of the Ben Bella regime, some of the few who two years after his downfall still talked openly of his time in power as the golden age. However, the JFLN remained too poorly organized to provide the president with much more than cheering audiences at his rallies.

The national organizations to which Ben Bella turned for support after the party congress were the labor and student unions, both of which were potentially troublesome allies. The two unions were for a period of time under the control of leaders installed by the FLN, but in both the more militant members eventually wrested control of the organization away from the incumbent executive committee and sought to make the union independent of the party. Numerically, neither union was very strong. The UGTA, which was believed to have a membership of around 200,000 at the time of its congress in January 1963, had subsequently lost many members because of the undynamic policies of its new leaders. The student union, with 2,500 members in mid-1964, admitted it had a nucleus of only about 300 militants. Another group to which Ben Bella looked for support was the Algerian Communist party, which had a membership of about 5,500.

Ben Bella's attitude toward these organizations had always been highly ambiguous. He had outlawed the PCA and imposed a party-controlled executive committee on the UGTA. By 1964, he was also engaged in organizing a group of party-affiliated students to take over the student union from inside and oust the pro-Communist leadership that had been in power since mid-1963. Ben Bella justified his actions

---

5. During the summer of 1963, only one camp was organized, at Oued Fodda near El-Asnam, where some 250 youths worked planting trees. In the summer of 1964, there were six camps, among them one at Les Ouahdias in the Kabylia, which became an international camp largely financed by the Communist-sponsored International Union of Students. The project of the international camp was to rebuild an entire village destroyed by the war. Several hundred Soviet and Eastern European youths worked there in 1964 and 1965. The Soviets hoped to use the new village as a showcase at the ninth World Youth Festival, scheduled to be held in Algiers in July 1965. Nine work camps were planned for the summer of 1965, but the entire volunteer aid program collapsed after the *coup d'état*.

by invoking the imperatives of the one-party system and denied that his were oppressive measures aimed at restricting the role of the working classes and the students. Yet in fact, this is exactly what they were. After the party congress, however, Ben Bella's position became too delicate to permit him to waste time and effort on trying to dominate national organizations that basically shared his objectives. The decision to take a firm stand against the opposition was making him increasingly more dependent on the army, which considered his policies too radical. At this point, he could not permit the progressive forces, his most natural allies, to turn into a left-wing opposition and take from him the initiative of the socialist revolution. Therefore, he began to revise his policy toward them.

Ben Bella had already made overtures of peace to the PCA at the party congress, accepting Henri Alleg's offer to make *Alger Républicain* an "organ of the FLN" and thereby implicitly acknowledging that collaboration between the FLN and the PCA was possible. However, Ben Bella had not abandoned the idea that the FLN should remain Algeria's only party and that it should control all the national organizations. Having learned from his experiences of the previous years that he could not achieve his objectives by imposing an unpopular leadership, he sought more subtle ways of dealing with the national organizations, accepting less than total domination if he could be assured of their cooperation and support.

The student union, the Union Nationale des Etudiants Algériens (UNEA), had always posed a delicate problem for Ben Bella. For a year after independence, three different party-appointed groups had tried to impose themselves on the union, which was so faction-ridden that it had been unable to elect an executive committee at its congress in September 1962. One after another, the party-imposed committees discredited themselves, and at UNEA's fifth congress in August 1963 a group of pro-Communist students under the leadership of Houari Mouffok took over the union.[6] From then on, UNEA supported Ben Bella's policies with enthusiasm, even exhorting him to accelerate the pace of the Revolution, but stubbornly rejected all interference by the FLN in union affairs. The students who had taken over UNEA were

6. Mouffok studied in East Germany during the revolution and did not return to Algeria until the end of 1962. It was never established whether he was a card-carrying member of the Algerian Communist party, but it was well known he had close ties with the leaders of the PCA.

for the most part the beneficiaries of special "social promotion" measures taken by Ben Bella—young men who had interrupted their studies
because of the war and had subsequently been admitted into the university without a *baccalauréat*. Although they maintained a pretense of
being revolutionaries, these students tended to regard themselves as
an elite and proved unwilling to respond to Ben Bella's call to go out
into the countryside to "lead the peasants."[7]

The politically active students, like most of Algeria's intellectuals,
were better at talking politics in cafés and organizing demonstrations
than at carrying out concrete projects. Student leaders like Mouffok and
Nourredine Zenine preferred to play a conspicuous role in national
politics by assisting at various congresses and touring the country to
give lectures on the March Decrees and the Algiers Charter. They
organized numerous demonstrations over issues of foreign policy, in
support of Cuba or against the United States' policies in the Congo, for
example, but their revolutionary ardor cooled considerably when a
sustained effort was asked of them. In the summer of 1963, only 350 out
of 3,000 students at the University of Algiers volunteered to work in
hospitals, reforestation brigades, village reconstruction projects, or in
the nationwide Cuban-style literacy campaign. Ben Bella's proposal
that all students work in government offices during the summer months
met with so much opposition from UNEA that it was quietly dropped.

The student union established close ties with the Eastern bloc student
and youth movements, showing a pro-Communist and anti-Western
bias that even Ben Bella sometimes found excessive.[8] Ben Bella also
feared that the students would interfere with his diplomacy by organizing demonstrations at the wrong time, which did happen on several
occasions,[9] or would denounce his political acrobatics at home. There-

7. In a speech at opening day ceremonies at the University of Algiers on December
17, 1962, Ben Bella told the students: "A heavy responsibility lies on the students'
shoulders. The Tripoli Program calls for the union of the peasants and the intellectuals. I am convinced that the university will give us an avant-garde. The students
have to understand that they must lead the peasants. They must go into the interior
and participate in the reconstruction campaign just as the students in Cuba go help
pick coffee [*sic*]."

8. At its fifth congress in August 1963, UNEA voted to withdraw from the Pro-
Western International Student Conference. At its sixth congress in August 1964, it
voted to become a full member of the Communist-sponsored International Union of
Students, eventually becoming a member of its executive committee.

9. Ben Bella intervened in person in March 1963 to break up a demonstration of
students protesting the explosion of an atomic bomb at the French testing site in the
Algerian Sahara. In November 1964, when American planes were used to help rescue

fore, he decided to organize a party section of university students in order to infiltrate UNEA and take over its leadership.[10] His ultimate goal was to set up a party-run youth council to supervise and coordinate the activities of the four youth movements: UNEA, the JFLN, the Algerian Moslem Scouts, and the National Union of High School Students.[11] But at the sixth congress of UNEA in August 1964, the student party members failed to wrest the leadership from the pro-Communist faction.[12] Ben Bella then decided that his personal intervention was necessary, and in mid-November he met with the two sides to hammer out an acceptable compromise. The result of this meeting was that while Mouffok remained president and Zenine vice-president, the student members of the FLN gained some key posts in the leadership of UNEA, in particular the posts of secretary-general and vice-president in charge of foreign relations.[13] Mouffok accepted this shuffle gracefully, declaring that it was UNEA's "contribution" to the unification of the youth movements. In this manner, Ben Bella partially achieved his aim without alienating the militant students by blatantly imposing his will. However, he never succeeded in setting up a youth council under the party's supervision.

By far the most powerful and troublesome of the national organizations was the Union Générale des Travailleurs Algériens, the labor federation. In early 1964, through the initiative of its most radical officials, the UGTA had begun to stir from the torpor into which it had sunk immediately after its first congress. By June, the federation was in

---

white hostages being held by Congolese rebels in Stanleyville, he delivered a violent speech against the United States but also asked the students not to demonstrate in front of the American Embassy.

10. The party students began to organize in 1963. By late 1964, they numbered about 150 according to Mohamed Berdi, coordinator of the student FLN section. See the interview with Berdi in the JFLN magazine *Jeunesse*, November 13, 1964.

11. The Algerian Moslem Scouts had been a cover organization for nationalist activity before independence, when Moslems were forbidden to form political associations. After independence, it kept out of politics but nonetheless wanted to remain free of party control. Ben Bella finally had to impose his own leadership in 1965.

12. In elections for the thirty-one-man executive committee of UNEA, the pro-Communist group won seventeen seats and the party students fourteen. With this slim majority, the pro-Communist faction was able to control the executive committee, and Mouffok and Zenine remained president and vice-president respectively.

13. The meeting took place November 16–17, 1964. Mohamed Berdi, coordinator of the party student section, became vice-president, and Abdelaziz Bouchaib, head of the section's "vigilance committee," was named secretary-general. In addition, party students took over the posts in charge of the union's relations with North African student groups and with UNEA sections in the Arab world.

the midst of a major drive to reorganize and expand, which was partly a movement of rebellion against the party-appointed executive headed by Rabah Djermane.

The government and the UGTA leaders did not have a very clear conception of the union's role in socialist Algeria. Nor did the militant union members, who had for the most part been trained before independence in the Communist-dominated Confédération Générale du Travail (CGT) and whose only experience with unionism had been in capitalist French Algeria. In theory both the UGTA and the government rejected Western-style unionism and advocated "managerial syndicalism"; by this they meant that the union's role was to help prepare the workers to take over the management of the economy. In practice there was no agreement about the function of the UGTA. The guiding principle of Secretary-General Djermane apparently was to obey party orders and keep the UGTA from causing trouble for the government.[14] Ben Bella had repeatedly declared that the union should help the management committees combat their disorganization and inefficiency and that it should put pressure on private management to train and promote Algerians in order to make feasible the eventual nationalization of all private industries. In reality government officials had not welcomed the interference of the UGTA in the socialist sector under any pretext; consequently, Djermane had done little to organize the workers of the socialist sector.

Government officials had even tried to restrain the UGTA's activities in the private sector, fearing that constant strikes and harrassment might cause the remaining companies, already hard pressed by the post-independence depression, to close down.[15] Unemployment had grown steadily after independence, and production had dropped off

14. Significantly, the only "revolutionary" decision taken by Djermane was to withdraw the UGTA's affiliation from the pro-Western International Confederation of Free Trade Unions (ICFTU) in July 1963. The decision was justified by the executive committee on the grounds that Algeria was a nonaligned country and therefore the UGTA should not belong to a pro-Western organization. Actually, the withdrawal was largely a response to the ICFTU's protest over the interference of the FLN at the UGTA's first congress. The ICFTU had been the first international labor organization to recognize the UGTA after its foundation in 1956, and had given it substantial aid during the war of independence.

15. Bachir Boumaza, then minister of labor, declared in this regard: "Nothing in the existing laws deprives the workers of the right to strike. The only question is whether [strikes] are useful or not. Strikes have nefarious consequences for employment and slow down the process of economic development. The workers have the possibility of expressing their opinion through other means." See Alger Républicain, June 4, 1963.

sharply. By the end of 1963, even Ben Bella thought it wise to avoid further nationalization for some time. Nonetheless, in the private sector there were numerous strikes led by militant local officials whom the national UGTA leadership was unable to control. These strikes were ostensibly aimed at gaining higher salaries and better working conditions, but in many cases the real object of the work stoppages was to convince the French owners to abandon their enterprises. Ben Bella repeatedly warned the workers against forcing "nationalization" at a pace that could only lead the economy into greater chaos. At a seminar of union officials in November 1963, he stated the government's position clearly:

> . . . we do not want one or another company committee, which thinks that its enterprise should be nationalized, to force the workers into a series of strikes until the government is obliged to nationalize the company. Every nationalization must be decided in the interest of our economy. [Hasty nationalizations] risk causing failures from which the enemies of our revolution at home and abroad would profit. . . . We want to go very fast, as fast as you want to go, but we have to consolidate our economy . . . so that production does not drop off sharply.[16]

Ben Bella's warnings did not stop the strikes, and a number of enterprises did indeed close down. There were indications that the strikes were deliberately provoked by local union officials not only to force nationalization, but also to protest the party's takeover of the UGTA's national executive and to promote a more militant line for the union. Significantly, the number of strikes increased sharply after the UGTA congress in January 1963 and then tapered off in the second half of 1964, when local union officials began to revive the federation.[17] In June 1964, the UGTA started to organize new trade unions. During the next six months, railroad workers, dockers, post office workers, flour mill workers, bakers, petroleum industry employees, municipal workers, state electricity and gas company employees, construction workers, carpenters, and finally state-farm workers held congresses. These congresses injected new vitality into the UGTA; union membership increased sharply, and the movement became steadily more militant.

16. Ben Bella's speech of November 18, 1963.
17. For a detailed study of labor-management strife, see Francois Weiss, "Les Conflits du Travail en Algérie dans le Secteur Privé non Agricole," *Revue Algérienne des Sciences Juridiques, Politiques, et Economiques*, No. 1, March 1966, pp. 17–67, and No. 2, June 1966, pp. 299–345. Weiss's study covers the period from January 1963 through July 1964.

Faced with this new militancy, Ben Bella decided to yield to the workers' demands in part rather than to attempt shackling the federation once again. On August 3, 1964, he signed a decree that, much to the distress of the owners, officially gave the company committees control over all training programs and promotions in private companies. In October, addressing the first congress of the petroleum industry workers, who were pressing for greater participation in the management of the private oil companies, Ben Bella declared:

> I share entirely the aspiration of your federation to promote managerial syndicalism through which the workers will participate more and more actively in the management of certain services of the enterprise.[18]

He also endorsed for the first time the workers' right to strike to back up their "legitimate demands." His speech showed a noticeable change in tone from that of the preceding November, in which he had pleaded for moderation. Nothing had changed in the economic situation, however, to warrant his new attitude. The socialist sector was still in chaos, and there was no doubt that additional nationalizations would cause production to drop further. But Ben Bella now had political considerations in mind: he needed the support of the workers and knew that in order to obtain it he had to give tangible proof that he was a true revolutionary and meant to give the workers a role in the management of the economy. There was no sudden reversal in Ben Bella's policy toward the UGTA, since he was essentially reluctant to see the FLN lose its hold over the union. Nonetheless, he kept the party from interfering with the efforts of militant union officials to strengthen the federation. Some of Ben Bella's closest allies were opposed to the revival of the UGTA's independence and militancy, however, and they worked behind his back to weaken the federation.

In December 1964, there was a major clash between labor leaders and officials of the Ministry of Agriculture over the control of the UGTA's new Fédération Nationale des Travailleurs de la Terre (FNTT). The creation of the FNTT was a major step in the expansion of the UGTA, since the farm workers constituted the bulk of the labor force in Algeria.[19] It also raised the problem of relations between

18. Ben Bella's speech of October 1, 1964.
19. Private industry employs about 200,000 workers and the industrial socialist sector 15,000. The state farms employ 220,000 permanent workers and 440,000 seasonal laborers; to this figure of 660,000 must be added the labor force on private Algerian farms, for which no figure is available. The FNTT initially represented only the permanent workers on the state farms.

the union and the state as employer, as almost all of the farm workers were employed on state farms. Although the UGTA was already organizing in the socialist industrial sector, this problem had not really arisen because the Ministry of Industry did not interfere in the management of the nationalized factories in the way that the Ministry of Agriculture did in the management of the farms.

Ben Bella had repeatedly urged the UGTA to add the farm workers to its membership, but the federation's executive, anxious to avoid strife with Minister of Agriculture Ali Mahsas, had not responded. The few union officials who had tried to enlist the workers of the state farms had met with strong resistance from the directors; in several instances, the director even fired workers for their union activities.[20] It was not until July 1964 that the UGTA began making serious plans to organize the farm workers, holding a seminar that month to train union officials especially for that task. Preparations for the constituent congress of the FNTT took a long time, and sixteen preliminary regional congresses were held over a period of three months, from September to December. However, the UGTA was not permitted to organize freely. The Ministry of Agriculture, realizing it could not prevent the formation of the FNTT, tried to stack the organization with its own representatives, claiming that ONRA employees should also be considered farm workers. The UGTA fought as best it could the attempt of the state agency to infiltrate the FNTT. At the Algiers preliminary congress, which was controlled by UGTA officials, the ONRA was accused of "bullying" union representatives, sowing discord among the workers, and preventing the management committees from playing the role the March Decrees had envisaged for them. ONRA officials were warned "to limit themselves to their role of animators and not [to] try to impose themselves as managers of the farms."[21] At some of these preparatory congresses, there were violent clashes between ONRA and UGTA delegates over the right of the former to be there at all.[22]

The issue was not resolved, and when the national congress opened

20. *Révolution et Travail* and *Alger Républicain* exposed several such incidents. See, for example, *Alger Républicain*, October 18, 1964.
21. See *Alger Républicain*, October 26, 1964.
22. One of the most violent arguments took place at the prepatory congress in Constantine, where the UGTA had some of its most militant officials, notably Mouloud Oumeziane, who in March 1965 became the new UGTA secretary-general. The Constantine regional union had been the first one to try to organize the farm workers, beginning back in 1963, when volunteers participating in the "Socialist Sundays" began recruiting them.

in Algiers on December 25, 500 delegates were present instead of the expected 423 because some regions were represented by both a UGTA and an ONRA delegation. The question of which delegation should be seated was deferred to a special commission which, according to the UGTA, never existed. In any case, the ONRA delegates remained at the congress. The UGTA was also forced to accept the creation of a "coordinating committee" made up of one representative each from the UGTA, the ONRA, and the party, and headed by a member of the Political Bureau. This coordinating committee ended by running the congress; the UGTA therefore lost control from the very outset.

Ben Bella opened the congress with a speech in which, sensing the rebellious mood of many delegates, he acknowledged that all was not well with the self-management system and that the system "was not being applied according to the March Decrees and the Algiers Charter." He went on to say that "relations between the members of the management committees and officials of the Ministry of Agriculture are not harmonious. Some of the latter have exceeded their powers. This is one of our shortcomings, and we must correct it."[23] He concluded with a veiled admonition to Minister of Agriculture Mahsas and the ONRA-appointed directors, commenting that, although militants, they too "could make mistakes." But he made no effort to prevent the ONRA from taking over the FNTT and deliberately avoided becoming involved in the struggle.

The FNTT congress followed the same pattern as the congresses of the socialist sector. The delegates were allowed to speak and criticize freely, but the ONRA and the party kept tight control over the commissions charged with drafting the final resolutions and worked behind the scenes to draw up a list of candidates for the executive committee of the FNTT. No distinction was made between farm workers and ONRA employees, and the list of candidates for the executive committee gave ample representation to the ONRA. In a final attempt to preserve the autonomy of the FNTT, union officials forced through an amendment that established that no ONRA official could also hold a post on the FNTT executive. The ONRA candidates countered this move without difficulty. Acting under instructions from Mahsas, they "resigned" on the spot from their jobs, clearing the way for their election. By this maneuver, Ramdane Bouchebouba, the ONRA representative on the coordinating commission running the congress, became the

23. *Le Peuple,* December 26, 1964.

new secretary-general of the FNTT. As a sop to the UGTA, the final resolutions asked once more for the full application of the March Decrees and included a protest against "bureaucratic methods aimed at concentrating the power belonging to the management committees in the hands of state officials."[24]

The seizure of the FNTT's executive by ONRA officials had been masterminded by Ali Mahsas, one of Ben Bella's oldest friends. The minister of agriculture was not opposed to the theory of self-management, but for reasons of personal power he had built the ONRA into an all-encompassing bureaucracy, thereby suppressing the autonomy of the farms. Mahsas was greatly aided in his endeavors by the absence of any organization representing the farm workers, and he did not want the situation changed by the interference of the UGTA. The takeover of the FNTT was therefore extremely important to Mahsas, but it hurt Ben Bella, creating much bitterness among the UGTA officials whose support he was then seeking. At the congress Ben Bella indeed found himself faced with somewhat of a dilemma. He could not intervene in favor of the workers without alienating Mahsas, who was one of his major allies, but he could not back Mahsas without tarnishing his image as champion of the workers and peasants.

The reaction of the UGTA to the outcome of the FNTT congress was at first one of deep dismay, as could be seen in the editorial of *Révolution et Travail* the same week:

> We learned with consternation of the creation of a coordinating committee representing the party, the ONRA, and the UGTA. We wondered in the name of what statute or law the ONRA, an administrative body, put itself on the same level as the UGTA, a national organization.[25]

Less than a month later, however, the UGTA weekly was considerably more optimistic about the trend of events: "In its present state, the FNTT is the result of a compromise that must be appreciated in light of the evolution of relations among the forces confronting one another."[26] The article left no doubt that union officials saw relations between the government and the UGTA evolving in their favor. A short time later, the weekly noted that the ONRA had not taken over the FNTT completely after all and that there was still a nucleus of "so-

24. See *Alger Républicain*, December 29, 1964.
25. *Révolution et Travail*, No. 70, December 31, 1964.
26. *Révolution et Travail*, No. 73, January 20, 1965.

cialist and revolutionary militants" on the executive committee.[27]

The failure of the UGTA to gain control of the FNTT was attributed by the militant wing of the union mainly to the ineffectual leadership of Secretary-General Djermane. In February 1965, the UGTA weekly, which expressed the viewpoint of this wing, stated that the union was undergoing a crisis, pointing to the loss of control over the FNTT and the inability of the national leadership to check a wave of unauthorized strikes that had affected even the socialist sector:

> There is clearly a crisis of confidence, as the workers have demonstrated by their refusal to listen to any authority other than brother Ben Bella, who alone personifies in the eyes of the people our choice of socialism. This crisis of confidence is even more evident [in the workers' attitude] toward the union's central administration, notably toward its leaders, who have been poorly received everywhere and not heeded.[28]

At is turned out, the FNTT congress acted as a sort of catalyst in cementing relations between Ben Bella and the militant wing of the UGTA. Realizing that he had seriously compromised his standing with this wing, Ben Bella finally agreed to its demand to hold a new UGTA congress to elect new leaders. In mid-January, a group of union officials met with Ben Bella to discuss the problems of the UGTA. The president agreed to the formation of a special committee, from which all the incumbent national secretaries were to be excluded, to prepare the second UGTA congress.

The twenty-member preparatory committee worked rapidly, and by January 29, after a series of working sessions in which Ben Bella personally took part, it completed a number of reports on the UGTA's orientation and activities. These reports made it clear that the primary role of the UGTA was that of preparing the workers, through technical training and political education, to assume a managerial role in the economy. Western-style unionism, with its strikes for higher wages and better working conditions, was rejected as unjustified in a socialist country. Indeed, the committee took a particularly firm stand against the principle of striking:

> It is not admissible that some brothers work full time on a volunteer basis while others, less sensitive to the economic problems of the country, go out on strike capriciously. . . . To strike is to give up the battle. To lay down our tools is to lay down the arms for the construction of

27. *Révolution et Travail*, No. 76, February 11, 1965.
28. *Ibid.*

socialism and admit that we are defeated, . . . it is to become the instrument of enemy forces that want to see the bankruptcy of our economy and of our [socialist] policy.[29]

The committee's reports were adopted on February 12 by the UGTA's incumbent national secretariat and were sent on to the congress for discussion.

The second UGTA congress, which opened March 23 with 562 delegates present, was a historical moment in the life of independent Algeria. Ben Bella had done his best to mediate between the old leadership and the new militants who had come to the fore in the previous nine months. In his opening speech to the congress, he called upon the delegates to give the union a new élan but warned them against the "extremism" that would compromise the "normal development" of socialism in Algeria by pushing the revolution "too far and too fast." Yet despite all the careful preparations Ben Bella had made prior to the congress, neither he nor the party controlled the course of events. The incumbent leadership was given a humiliating public trial and was violently denounced by dozens of delegates. All but one of the national secretaries' reports on their activities during the past two years were voted down by large majorities.[30] Secretary-General Rabah Djermane, whom Ben Bella still hoped to keep in power, was given the worst reception of all: he was accused of shirking his duties and of apathy and inaction during his term in office, and his report to the congress was rejected by a vote of 24 to 291, with 234 abstentions. Again and again, delegates asked for a new leadership of "authentic and revolutionary militants" to replace the incumbent one. In a final effort to redeem himself, Djermane publicly acknowledged his failures and accepted the congress's "verdict" that his record had been highly unsatisfactory. But this confession did not save the discredited secretary-

29. See *Alger Républicain*, January 26, 1965. *Alger Républicain* published extracts from a "report on orientation" approved by the committee. These extracts do not appear in the report published in *Révolution et Travail* (No. 78, February 25, 1965) and later adopted at the congress. It is not clear whether the passages quoted by *Alger Républicain* were dropped from the report or were contained in an altogether different document, which the UGTA weekly did not publish.

30. Only the report on education was approved, by a vote of 286 to 0, with 267 abstentions. The report on the union's organization was rejected by an "overwhelming majority." The report on social affairs was defeated 105 to 133, with 315 abstentions. The official report on finances was also rejected, 162 to 215, with 176 abstentions; the delegates approved instead the report of a special finance committee set up at the congress, which termed the management of the union's finances "deplorable." See *Alger Républicain*, March 27, 1965.

general, who symbolized to the delegates the UGTA's sellout to the party, from being ousted.

The climax of the congress was the election of the new fifty-one-man executive committee and the nine national secretaries. For the first time at any congress in Algeria, the proposed list of candidates seemed to reflect the real choice of the delegates. Less than half the incumbent members of the executive committee were presented for reelection.[31] As usual, there was no formal vote, the list being approved by a show of hands and applause, but this time the acclamation was thunderous, showing that the delegates wholeheartedly approved the choice of candidates. Immediately afterwards, the new executive committee withdrew to elect the nine national secretaries. When it reappeared, and Mouloud Oumeziane, a militant leader from Constantine, was proclaimed the new secretary-general, the delegates leaped to their feet, stood applauding on chairs, or pounded tables in exultation.[32] The name of each new secretary was greeted with similar enthusiasm.[33] As the delegates hoped, none of the former leaders were re-elected. The last name had just been read out when Ben Bella made a carefully timed entry intended to show his approval of the workers' choice. His appearance triggered off another wild demonstration in the congress hall, and the tumult only subsided when Oumeziane rose to speak. "Our second congress has taken place under very favorable conditions and in total democracy," he declared. But he immediately assured Ben Bella that the federation would cooperate closely with the party: "A revolutionary union cannot fulfill its mission and become the manager

31. The list of candidates was drawn up by a special sixteen-man nominating committee. Only twenty-three of the fifty-one incumbent members of the executive committee were proposed for re-election, among them all the national secretaries. Djermane, however, withdrew his candidacy.

32. Mouloud Oumeziane, born December 1, 1920, in Constantine, was a laboratory worker at the Constantine Hospital. He was secretary-general of the CGT Hospital Workers Federation from 1945 to 1955. One of the first organizers of the UGTA, he fled the country in 1959 after being condemned by French authorities in absentia, and worked for the UGTA in Casablanca, Morocco, until independence. He then became secretary-general of the regional union in Constantine. He was also an official of the party and after the party congress became the head of the FLN Federation of Constantine. He was thus the perfect candidate for the UGTA and the party. Although not Ben Bella's personal choice, he was on good terms with the president.

33. The new secretaries were: Mouloud Oumeziane, secretary-general; Boualem Bourouiba (ousted at the January 1963 congress), deputy secretary-general; Lahcene Mimouni, foreign relations; Tayeb Djenadi, education and voluntary work projects; Tahar Ouali, industry and socialist sector; Boualem Rebika, agriculture; Rabah Slimane, press and information; Abdelkader Drider, finance and administration; and Mohamed Abib, legislation and social affairs.

of the economy unless guided and inspired by an avant-garde party. That is why the UGTA will never act independently of the FLN."[34] The new secretary-general called for the strengthening of the self-managed sector, more nationalizations, and closer cooperation between the industrial and farm workers.

After Oumeziane, Ben Bella delivered a highly emotional speech in which he thanked the congress for having shown the outside world that in Algeria "democracy is not an empty word" but "an everyday reality." He promised that there would be more congresses in the same spirit and that by the end of 1965 "the socialist sector [would] dominate the private one."[35] Immediately afterwards, Ben Bella and the new leaders of the UGTA, arm in arm, led delegates and party officials in a triumphant five-mile march through downtown Algiers to the chants of "Yaya Ben Bella," "Tshombe Assassin," "Palestine to the Arabs," "African Unity," "Peace in Vietnam," and other similar slogans. It was the first time since Independence Day that Algiers had seen such a spontaneous demonstration of enthusiasm. It was also to be the last time for many months to come.

The second UGTA congress was viewed in many quarters as a watershed of Algeria's socialist revolution. Ben Bella had at last gained the full support and confidence of the militant wing of the UGTA. For its part, the UGTA had elected the leadership it wanted and imposed on the party its terms for cooperation. The Trotskyite publication *Sous le Drapeau du Socialisme* was ecstatic over the outcome of the congress, declaring that the UGTA had finally become "a powerful instrument capable of defending self-management, of countering effectively the growth of bureaucratic forces, of extending the socialist sector, and of exerting pressure on the party and government to accelerate the application of the agrarian reform, the communal reform, and an economic development plan."[36]

The UGTA congress was far more than a victory of one faction over another within the federation and the government. The new autonomy of the UGTA reflected a definite change in the balance of power in

34. See *Alger Républicain*, March 29, 1965.
35. In July 1965, Bachir Boumaza, then minister of information in the Boumediene Cabinet, revealed during a press conference that just before the UGTA congress Ben Bella had ordered him to prepare a decree nationalizing all remaining private enterprises. Ben Bella wanted to announce this nationalization at the congress. Boumaza said that he had refused to prepare the decree; other ministers had sided with him, and Ben Bella finally abandoned the plan.
36. *Sous le Drapeau du Socialisme*, No. 16, April 1965.

Algeria. For the first time, it seemed that the partisans of the socialist revolution were beginning to supplant the generation of Algerian politicians that had been brought to power by the struggle for national liberation. A new political generation was coming to the fore, with its own program and its own conception of a political alliance. The new leaders of the UGTA were dedicated to the application of the Algiers Charter and the March Decrees. They cooperated with Ben Bella because he promised to carry out these programs, but they refused to give him unconditional and unquestioning support as Djermane had done. The president in turn needed the UGTA's backing to counterbalance the growing weight of the army in his regime and therefore ceded to the demands of the militant union leaders for more independence from the FLN.

The resulting alliance between the UGTA and Ben Bella was something new in Algerian politics. The two parties were bound by a commitment to a common political program, not by aleatory personal ties between a few individuals. Ben Bella had become president as a result of a coalition of disparate clans and personalities whose only common interest had been the seizure of power, a coalition destined to crumble because each member sought all the power for himself. Such had been the alliance between Ben Bella and his initial supporters, Khider, Abbas, and Boumediene. Ben Bella had then maintained himself in power by negotiating fleeting alliances with his potential and actual opponents, offering as bribes important posts in his regime. In this manner, he had gained the allegiance of men like Mohand ou el-Hadj and Tahar Zbiri, an allegiance that only lasted until someone else offered them a greater political role. At the same time, Ben Bella had surrounded himself with a host of personal friends and lesser political figures like Hadj Ben Alla, Ali Mahsas, and Bachir Boumaza, men who were interested in a share of power but who were too weak to aspire to Ben Bella's place.

The alliance between Ben Bella and the UGTA was centered around a broad political program, and power was no longer its sole aim. No ties of fealty were involved, no bribes, and no subservience on the part of the UGTA. The objectives of the labor leaders and of Ben Bella were not identical; the UGTA was primarily interested in self-management as an end in itself, while for Ben Bella self-management was primarily a means by which to enhance his popularity and build himself a power base. The aims of the two were not mutually exclusive, however, and indeed could only be attained if Ben Bella and the

UGTA cooperated closely. It was intrinsically a much more stable alliance than any Ben Bella had entered before. Whether this alliance announced the end of that informal system of personal relationships that Mohamed Harbi had once defined as the "parliamentarism of clans"[37] the beginning of an evolution of the political system in Algeria was never confirmed: less than three months after the UGTA congress, the army ousted Ben Bella from power.

37. Editorial in *Révolution Africaine,* No. 63, April 11, 1964.

chapter eight
the anti-imperialist
struggle

The revolution is realized through an international policy based on the principles of national independence and international cooperation as well as through the continuation of the anti-imperialist struggle and the granting of effective support to all movements fighting for the independence or the liberation of their countries.

The Algerian Constitution

Algeria became independent at a time when the small nations of Africa and Asia, many of them recently independent, were striving to assert their influence in an international community dominated by the great powers. The Bandung Conference of 1955 had been the first dramatic illustration of the awakening of African and Asian countries to their potential role in international politics. In the years following, innumerable conferences were held at both the governmental and nongovernmental levels. While these conferences undoubtedly fostered a sense of community among the African and Asian nations, they also showed that there were marked differences between the governments of these nations and thus encouraged the formation of moderate and radical groups.

The great powers followed this activity with interest and concern. Since Vietnam had not yet become the focal point of the Cold War, the newly independent countries attracted the attention of the United States and the Soviet Union far more than they did in the late 1960s. Also, by the time Algeria became independent, Moscow and Peking were beginning to vie openly with one another for friends and allies in Africa. President Charles de Gaulle, endeavoring to raise France once again to the rank of a world power, was also making a special effort to maintain French presence in Africa. Algeria was regarded by all as one of the strategic nations on the African continent because of the prestige it had won during the war for independence and because of the role it promised to play under the leadership of Ahmed Ben Bella.

Ben Bella aspired to become a great revolutionary leader of the Third World. He actively propagandized Algeria's socialism as a model for other countries to follow, and he was in the vanguard of the movement to form a front of African and Asian nations capable of standing up to the "imperialist" powers. In retrospect, it is clear that the Afro-Asian solidarity movement did not have a lasting influence on international politics, but at the time it appeared an important political development, and Ben Bella, as one of its principal promoters, attracted much attention to himself.

In becoming actively involved in Afro-Asian politics, Ben Bella was following a line of action traced by the Provisional Government during the liberation struggle. Beginning with Bandung, FLN representatives were present at every major gathering of African and Asian leaders in order to gain support for their cause. Algeria attended the constituent meeting of the Afro-Asian Peoples' Solidarity Organization (AAPSO) in Cairo in 1957 and the Belgrade Conference of Nonaligned Countries in 1961; it was also a founding member of the radical Casablanca Group.[1] After independence, most Algerian leaders considered it only natural for Algeria to continue its policy of active involvement in Afro-Asian affairs, believing that the country had a special mission to fulfill in the liberation of the remaining African colonies. Ben Bella expressed a point of view shared by many Algerians when he declared before the United Nations General Assembly in 1962 that "the liquidation of colonialism in both its classic and disguised form will be the credo of our political and diplomatic line of action."[2] The choice of a socialist system at home further strengthened Algeria's commitment to the "anti-imperialist struggle" and put the country in the camp of the progressive African states.

Still, Ben Bella put his personal stamp on Algeria's foreign policy,

1. The Casablanca Group was founded at a meeting of five African chiefs of state held in Casablanca, Morocco, January 3–7, 1961, to express support for Congolese Prime Minister Patrice Lumumba in his struggle with President Joseph Kasavubu. The members of the group were Morocco, Egypt, Ghana, Guinea, Mali, and Algeria (GPRA). Except for Morocco, these were the most radical African governments at that time.

2. Ben Bella's speech at the time of Algeria's admission to the United Nations, October 9, 1962.

giving it the moralistic overtones, the emotional drive, and the missionary zeal it was to lose with his downfall. His conception of Algeria's role in the world was at once grandiose and simplistic. As he saw it, the entire Third World was locked in a gigantic struggle with the imperialist Western powers, which sought to enslave the underdeveloped countries in new forms of colonialism. He declared that Algeria was a nonaligned country, but he gave a special moralistic meaning to the term "nonalignment": "We are not aligned with anyone, and we are aligned with all just causes. We are aligned with good and nonaligned with evil."[3] This meant in practice that Algeria was anti-Western not because it was aligned with the Communist bloc in the Cold War, but because it was aligned with the countries of the Third World in the struggle against "colonialism, neocolonialism, and imperialism." He justified his involvement in the internal affairs of other African countries by expounding his own "domino theory":

> My dear brothers, there is no isolated battle in Africa, and I would dare say there is no isolated battle in the world. We know full well that if we do nothing, it will be Congo-Leopoldville that will fall [to the imperialists] today. Congo-Brazzaville tomorrow, Burundi the day after, then Tanzania and Zambia, and why not Conakry, Bamako, and Cairo? And why not Algiers? We know it is the same struggle. . . .[4]

Ben Bella believed that the best bulwark against the intervention of foreign powers was unity among the underdeveloped countries, and he set as a major goal of his foreign policy the development of closer cooperation in North Africa, the Arab world, and Africa. His vision of unity was colored by his hope to see other African countries adopt a socialist system that would be the image of Algeria's:

> With regard to our responsibility toward North African, Arab, and African unity, I must make it clear that Algeria does not envisage a political grouping similar to the Fertile Crescent, but intends [to act] so that the same [socialist] experience that succeeded in our country succeeds in other countries. The independence of some countries that permit [foreign] trusts to take the place of the colonial power is no independence.[5]

3. Ben Bella's speech of April 15, 1965.
4. Ben Bella's speech of November 24, 1964, commenting upon the American-Belgian intervention against the Congolese rebels fighting to overthrow Tshombe.
5. Ben Bella's speech of November 1, 1962. The Fertile Crescent was a union of Iraq, Syria, and Jordan, envisaged by Iraq in the mid-1950s. The creation of this union, which was actually never formed, was favored by the Western powers because it was seen as a bulwark against Communist subversion.

The goals Ben Bella set for his foreign policy were both individually difficult to attain and blatantly contradictory. The African countries were not ready for unity even on the regional level; moreover, by trying to export socialism and sometimes directly promoting subversion of conservative regimes, Ben Bella contributed to the division rather than to the unification of Africa.

There was no limit to Ben Bella's involvement in international affairs. He supported the African liberation movements, providing funds and training guerrillas. He took a position on all major world issues, traveled abroad extensively, hosted many international conferences, and entertained innumerable chiefs of state and foreign dignitaries. Both revolutionary and conservative leaders of the Third World visited Ben Bella's Algeria, among them King Hassan II of Morocco, President Gamal Abdel Nasser of Egypt, President Salah Bitar of Syria, Ernesto "Che" Guevara of Cuba, President Julius Nyerere of Tanzania, President Félix Houphouet-Boigny of the Ivory Coast, President William Tubman of Liberia, Emperor Haile Selassie of Ethiopia, Communist Chinese Premier Chou En-Lai and Foreign Minister Chen Yi, President Sékou Touré of Guinea, President Modibo Keita of Mali, President Osvaldo Dorticos of Cuba, Congolese opposition leader Christophe Gbenye, President Tchoe Yong Gueun of North Korea, President Hamani Diori of Niger, Foreign Minister Subandrio of Indonesia, Prime Minister Mahmoud Muntasser of Libya, and Vice Prime Minister Abdul Razak of Malaysia. United Nations Secretary-General U Thant, Yugoslavian President Marshal Tito, and Soviet Vice-Minister of Foreign Affairs Jacob Malik also visited Algeria. In 1964, Ben Bella spent seventy-four days abroad visiting Communist countries and African capitals, and dedicated as many days to entertaining chiefs of state and foreign delegations in Algiers. In 1965, he devoted the greatest part of his time to the organization of the second Afro-Asian Conference and mobilized most of the country's resources for the construction of a huge conference complex.

Ben Bella's engrossment in foreign affairs was partly a consequence of his regime's internal problems. Foreign policy, the one field in which he had a free hand, increasingly became an escape from the political difficulties he could not solve at home. He blamed his internal problems on the interference of foreign powers, portraying the opposition to his regime as part of an international conspiracy aimed at crushing Algeria's socialist revolution. He claimed, for instance, that the Front of Socialist Forces was backed by the king of Morocco, West Germany, and the CIA; that demonstrations in Oran in January 1964 were due to the machinations of foreign agents;[6] and that Khider was in league with ousted Congolese leader Moise Tshombe and Portugal's President Salazar. In reality there was no evidence of a foreign plot to overthrow Ben Bella. France, which had the greatest interest at stake in the country, had decided to maintain close ties and provide massive aid to Algeria no matter what political system its former colony chose. Many Algerians realized that Ben Bella was blaming on foreign intervention problems that were purely internal and that in spending so much time and money on foreign policy he was pursuing his personal ambitions rather than defending Algeria against foreign plots. In the end, Ben Bella's success as a Third World leader helped to undermine his position at home by affording his critics arguments and giving him a false impression of his own strength.

In the history of Algeria's foreign policy, relations with France stand apart as a separate chapter. France, a Western colonial country striving to maintain an influence in its liberated colonies, was never attacked by Ben Bella as an imperialist and neocolonialist power. The Algerian leader vehemently denounced United States bases in Cuba and Vietnam, but he seldom mentioned French bases in Algeria; he castigated the intervention of the United States in the Congo, but he remained silent when France sent paratroopers to Gabon.[7] Ben Bella, a romantic revolutionary in his vision of a socialist and united Africa, was very much a realist when it came to Algeria's immediate interests, and these lay in good relations with France. Algeria depended almost entirely on French markets to sell its goods, on the French Central Bank to maintain its financial stability, and on thousands of French teachers

6. The demonstrations in Oran on January 6 and 7 were touched off by the termination of an unemployment-relief work project in a slum area of that city. About 2,500 men put out of work demonstrated in front of city hall the first day. The next day, groups of unemployed workers and teenage thugs marched through the city, shouting "We want work," "We want bread," and even "Long live France." Some French flags were waved by the workers. Before ANP troops were finally called in to break up the demonstration, dozens of store windows had been broken and numerous cars battered. Some 300 persons were arrested. This was the largest demonstration of popular discontent under the Ben Bella regime.

7. In February 1964, de Gaulle sent paratroopers to Gabon to reinstate President Leon Mba, who had been ousted in a military *coup d'état.* In November 1964, American planes flew Belgian paratroopers into Stanleyville in order to rescue white hostages being held there by the Congolese rebels.

and technicians to keep its schools and administration operating. Ben Bella knew from the experience of Guinea that the consequences of a sudden rupture with France could be disastrous.

France, for its part, still had sizeable interests in Algeria. Not only were 90,000 Frenchmen still living in the country[8] and numerous companies operating there, but France had also invested ten billion francs ($2 billion) in the Algerian oil and gas fields, and had important bases in the Sahara, including its only atomic testing ground. Moreover, in 1963 Algeria remained the fourth most important market for French products. However, President de Gaulle saw much more than France's material interests at stake in the country: maintaining good relations with Algeria was for him the key to the success of French policy in the Third World. As French Secretary of State for Algerian Affairs Jean de Broglie explained before the French National Assembly:

> Algeria has taken the lead in the assembly of poor nations pitted against the rich [nations]. . . . Certainly in maintaining its policy of cooperation with Algeria, France defends certain interests and tries to counterbalance the tendency of this country to slide toward Communism. But Algeria is also, and above all, the narrow door through which we penetrate into the Third World. A quarrel between France and another North African country is only a bilateral tension. But a dispute with Algeria would go way beyond the bounds of French-Algerian relations and would risk ruining the efforts of our diplomacy throughout the Third World. . . . It is Algeria that opened for us the road to the Middle East and whose support is useful to us in Latin America.[9]

Because of the strategic importance he attributed to Algeria, de Gaulle was willing to accept the nationalization of French properties without reprisals as long as the former colony remained within the French sphere of influence. De Broglie warned the recalcitrant French Senate of the consequences of a nearsighted policy toward Algeria:

> The example of Cuba is worth considering. Look what happened when the United States decided on a policy of reprisals against the revolutionary government, which had undertaken an agrarian reform. They went to the brink of war, but Cuba is henceforth in the Soviet orbit. Let's not commit the same error in Algeria.[10]

8. According to the French Embassy in Algiers, there were 92,086 French citizens in Algeria as of March 1965. Of these, 28,688 were technical assistants and their families, and another 8,199 were working for the French government in one capacity or another. Less than 60,000 French citizens could be considered permanent residents; almost 20,000 were retired elderly persons.

9. See *Le Monde*, November 7, 1964.

10. See *Le Monde*, November 21, 1963.

The transformation of wartime enemies into peacetime allies did not come about without innumerable strains and crises. Indeed, had it not been for de Gaulle's determination, the policy of French-Algerian co-operation outlined in the Evian Peace Agreements would almost certainly have failed. Ben Bella was the first to recognize this:

> Inasmuch as General de Gaulle alone among Frenchmen has been able to make peace with Algeria, it is on him personally that we depend to make Algerian-French cooperation a success.[11]

The Evian Agreements had assured France a privileged position in independent Algeria in return for a sizeable amount of aid. The Algerian nationalists had been forced to guarantee respect of French interests in the Sahara oil fields and protection of all other French properties in the country; in addition, they had been obliged to accept the presence of French bases, in one case for as long as fifteen years after independence.[12] For its part, the French government had pledged to maintain for three years an aid program equal to the one in effect at the time of independence and to provide Algeria with considerable technical assistance.[13]

French aid actually exceeded the provisions of the Evian Agreements, reaching a total of roughly four billion francs ($800 million) during the first three years. In addition, about 23,000 French teachers and technicians were working in Algeria in 1963. Although this aid was crucial to the country in the difficult immediate post-war period, Ben Bella considered the price the French asked for it too high. Respect of French interests was a major barrier to the fulfillment of the socialist revolution, and Ben Bella as a revolutionary leader could not agree to pay indemnities to the expropriated French colons. Moreover, the existence of French bases was felt to be an infringement on Algeria's hard-won national sovereignty.

11. Ben Bella's interview with *Le Monde*, November 7, 1963.
12. The agreements specified that France would have the right to use for five years its atomic testing sites at In-Ekker and Reggane and a missile testing range at Hamaguir. In addition, Algeria was obliged to "rent" to France the naval base at Mers-el-Kébir for a period of fifteen years. The French left their sites in the Sahara in 1967, as scheduled.
13. The French aid program in Algeria during the last year before independence amounted to about one billion francs ($200 million) in technical and financial assistance. Algeria was the principal recipient of French technical assistance for years after its independence. For example, in 1964, out of the 46,121 "technical assistants" France sent abroad, 19,555 were working in Algeria. Of these, almost 15,000 were teachers.

It was the French military presence that provoked the first major crisis in French-Algerian relations. On March 18, 1963, the eve of the first anniversary of the Evian Peace Agreements, the French exploded an atomic bomb at their testing grounds in the Sahara Desert; this became known to the public, much to the embarrassment of the Algerian government. Protesting vigorously, Ben Bella demanded the immediate cessation of French atomic tests in the Sahara and the revision of the military clauses of the Evian Agreements. The French were willing to hold talks, but the agreement reached on May 2 only partially satisfied Algerian demands. The French agreed to speed up the withdrawal of the 100,000 troops then stationed in Algeria but made no concessions concerning their bases.[14] Privately they also promised to maintain complete secrecy about any future tests in order to avoid embarrassing the Algerian government. Ben Bella accepted this settlement and thereafter did his best to ignore the presence of French bases in his country.

While the Algerians backed down over the issue of French bases in order to safeguard French-Algerian cooperation, it was the French who yielded in the conflict involving the takeover of French properties by the Algerian government. A joint French-Algerian commission had been set up in the fall of 1962 to discuss the indemnification of French owners, but the Algerians had deliberately kept it from meeting. When Ben Bella nationalized the last 5,000 French farms in October 1963, the outcry from the pied noir lobby forced the French government to stiffen its position and to demand immediate talks on the problem of all French properties seized since independence. The Algerian government refused to hold talks, maintaining that the takeover of some 200,000 farms, enterprises, and apartments abandoned by the French did not constitute nationalization, since these properties were vacant and consequently fell to the state.[15] With respect to the last 5,000 farms, which had been nationalized while still occupied by their owners, the Algerians declared they would not pay indemnities unless the French paid "war damages" for the destruction of 8,000 Algerian villages. President de Gaulle decided to drop the demand for immediate negotia-

---

14. France agreed to evacuate the 100,000 French troops still in Algeria by the end of 1964 instead of by July 1965, which was the date set by the Evian Agreements.

15. The definition of "vacancy" given by the Algerians differed considerably from that given by French law. For the French, a "vacant" property is one to which nobody claims ownership (*res nullius*); for the Algerians, a "vacant" property is one left unoccupied by the owner for more than two months.

tions.[16] Essentially, he was not prepared to provoke a crisis in order to defend the interests of the pieds noirs, who had ardently opposed his peace policy during the Algerian war.

Relations between the two countries were tried periodically by a number of other issues. The Algerian government refused to pay the debts incurred by the colonial administration, which amounted to six billion francs ($1.2 billion), although it was bound by the Evian Agreements to do so. On the other hand, the French government began in April 1964 to impose restrictions on the immigration of Algerian workers, although the agreements guaranteed the free movement of Algerians between France and Algeria.[17] The question of the sale of Algerian wine on the glutted French market was another source of discord between the two governments. The French colons had made Algeria into a grape-growing country that annually exported about fourteen million hectoliters of wine to France; indeed, wine was Algeria's leading farm export. After Algeria became independent, the French viticulturists formed a strong lobby to exclude Algerian wine from the French market. As a result of this pressure, the French government established a quota system that sharply reduced the importation of Algerian wine, causing a major economic problem for Algeria.[18] However, neither side found in these issues sufficient reason to jeopardize the policy of cooperation. On the contrary, both Ben Bella and de Gaulle were anxious to give French-Algerian cooperation a sounder basis than the controversial Evian Agreements.

After November 1963, Ben Bella's persistent efforts to revise the agreements focused on the clauses concerning the exploitation of the Sahara oil and gas fields. He counted on oil revenues to help balance the budget and provide capital for industrialization. Under the Evian Agreements, the French oil companies maintained the same privileged

16. Although he did not insist that the Algerians negotiate, de Gaulle withheld one-fifth of the aid promised to Algeria for 1964 (about $40 million) in order to indemnify French settlers. This sum, however, represented only a small fraction of the total value of the nationalized properties.

17. After April 1964, the French limited the number of Algerians allowed into France according to the demand for labor. They also imposed other restrictions: before being admitted into France, Algerians had to show proof of employment and present a medical certificate, a return ticket, and 500 francs ($100) in cash.

18. In January 1964, the French and Algerian governments agreed on a system of decreasing quotas that progressively reduced the amount of Algerian wine sold in France from 8.25 million hectoliters in 1965 to 7.08 million in 1967. The French repeatedly failed to live up to the established quotas and in early 1967 completely cut off the importation of wine pending new negotiations.

status as they did before independence, paying royalties far below the average demanded by other oil-producing countries.[19] Except for a 40 per cent interest in one French state company, the Algerian government did not participate in the exploitation of the country's major source of wealth. After twenty months of difficult negotiations, the two governments hammered out a sweeping new agreement that was at once a new oil code and the framework for a "cooperative association" between France and Algeria. The fifteen-year accord, finally signed in July 1965, one month after Ben Bella's overthrow, had several unique aspects: it was the first oil agreement negotiated exclusively between two governments that also decided the fate of private companies; it created a French and an Algerian state oil company that were to cooperate as equal partners in the exploitation of designated oil fields; and it included a two billion franc ($400 million) aid program to help promote the industrialization of Algeria.[20]

The two governments believed they had set an important precedent in oil negotiations. The Algerians especially were exultant, and Foreign Minister Abdelaziz Bouteflika declared that the accord set forth "an original, even revolutionary, conception of relations between two countries with different social systems, levels of economic development, and political orientations."[21] With the accord, Algeria gained direct participation in every phase of the oil industry, a larger role than any other Arab country had at that time. Royalties were also increased considerably, as they were based on fixed prices far higher than the world

19. Under the Evian Agreements, which incorporated the 1957 Sahara Oil Code, Algeria received the equivalent of $40 million in 1962 and $44 million in 1963. This meant a revenue per barrel of oil of only 32 cents compared to an average of 75 cents in other Arab countries and over 90 cents in Venezuela.

20. The Algerian company SONATRACH and the French company SOPEFAL were to cooperate in the exploitation of oil and gas fields within a 70,000-square-mile area in the central Sahara. The French private companies maintained their concessions but were subjected to a new system of taxation. The aid program was to cover a five-year period during which the French promised to make available to Algeria 400 million francs ($80 million) annually for industrial projects to which both governments had to agree. Of this sum, 40 million francs ($8 million) was a grant, and the rest was partly a twenty-year-government loan (160 million francs or $32 million) at 3 per cent interest and partly purchasing credits (200 million francs or $40 million) guaranteed by the French government. The oil accord did not apply to the non-French companies; however, the Algerian government demanded that they accept similar terms. As of mid-1967, none of the non-French companies had concluded a new accord accepting Algerian terms.

21. Bouteflika's speech of July 29, 1965, on the occasion of the signing of the oil agreement. See El-Moudjahid, July 30, 1965.

market price and were independent of its fluctuations.[22] For President de Gaulle, the agreement had a special significance because it institutionalized his personal policy toward Algeria, of which most French politicians disapproved, and because it permitted France to maintain its independence of the Anglo-American oil cartel.[23] The French oil companies were by far the least enthusiastic about the agreement; although they were given better protection against the danger of nationalization, they were forced to give up most of the privileges they had previous enjoyed.

The policy of cooperation with France has been a mixed blessing for Algeria. It has undoubtedly saved the young nation from bankruptcy, but it has also perpetuated Algeria's dependence on France. Because of its "favored nation" status, Algeria has made little effort to diversify its markets or its economy. In 1965, it still sent over 75 per cent of its exports to France and produced sixteen million hectoliters of wine for which it had no internal market and no important foreign market outside France. President de Gaulle's liberal attitude toward the former colony has made it possible for Algeria to pursue a radical foreign policy without paying a heavy price for it; Ben Bella could afford to visit Cuba even if it meant foregoing American aid, and he could sever relations with West Germany even if it meant losing a 70 million DM (about $18 million) loan.[24] However, this radicalism may prove costly in the long run. Algeria has isolated itself from the West, remaining exclusively dependent on French aid. With de Gaulle's resignation, France is likely to prove much less generous. The Communist countries have shown that they are willing to provide arms and technical assistance but not the financial aid Algeria will need for a long time to come.

It was above all in his attitude toward France that Ben Bella demon-

---

22. The fixed prices varied between $2.04 and $2.095 per barrel depending on the port of embarcation. In 1965, the price of Middle Eastern oil varied between $1.60 and $1.80 per barrel. Algeria's oil revenues increased from $80 million in 1965 to $140 million in 1966 and are expected to reach $240 million by 1970.

23. France imported 22 million tons of oil from Algeria in 1966, nearly 40 per cent of its total needs. The price paid by France for Algerian oil is much higher than the world market price, but it is paid in francs instead of dollars. The French government thus saves over $200 million in foreign exchange every year.

24. Algeria broke off diplomatic relations with West Germany on May 13, 1965, following Bonn's recognition of Israel. Numerous other Arab countries severed ties with West Germany at that time for the same reason. West German aid was to be used to reconstruct portions of the port of Annaba, destroyed in an explosion aboard an Egyptian ship loaded with ammunition, and to irrigate a plain in western Algeria.

strated that there was a realistic side to him. There were only a few other instances of his realism: he never established diplomatic ties with East Germany to safeguard promising trade relations with West Germany, and he never called General Franco a "fascist dictator" as he did President Salazar of Portugal because Spain showed interest in purchasing vast amounts of Saharan gas. In his attitude toward the United States and Cuba, however, Ben Bella showed himself to be an uncompromising revolutionary. The United States was for him the symbol of imperialism and Cuba the symbol of freedom. The violence of his attacks on the United States was such that some Western diplomats saw in it a compensation for his silence over France's dominant position in Algeria.

One of the first foreign policy decisions Ben Bella had to make concerned Algeria's relations with the United States and Cuba. In September 1962, both Washington and Havana invited him to make a state visit following his appearance at the United Nations in early October. The question of whether or not the invitations should be accepted was debated at the very first meeting of the Cabinet. It was evident that Washington, which was considering a fairly sizeable aid program to Algeria, would be greatly annoyed if Ben Bella visited Cuba at a time when Cuban-American relations were particularly tense because of the presence of Soviet missiles on the island. However, Ben Bella feared that only to visit Washington would be interpreted as a sign that Algeria had chosen a pro-Western line in its foreign policy. He and the majority of his ministers, anxious to show that Algeria was a socialist country, decided that he should accept both invitations, no matter what the consequences might be. As Ben Bella later dramatically declared: "We will never accept a piece of bread in exchange for the freedom of others, and above all [for] that of Cuba."[25]

After being warmly received by President John F. Kennedy in Washington, Ben Bella flew to Havana on October 16 for a thirty-six-hour visit that was to make a lasting impression on him. Castro won his admiration as no other person did except perhaps Charles de Gaulle. Ben Bella thereafter frequently compared the Algerian to the Cuban Revolution, even defining Algerian socialism as "Castro-style socialism," although it was never clear just what he meant by this. Much was made of Cuban-Algerian solidarity in both countries, but Cuba and Algeria

25. Ben Bella's speech of April 4, 1963.

were too far apart physically to be of more than symbolic importance to one another. Ben Bella and Castro had only one occasion to work together, the projected expansion of the Afro-Asian Peoples' Solidarity Organization to include Cuba and the revolutionary parties of Latin America. The project was to culminate in a tricontinental conference held in Havana. But even on this occasion, the two leaders found themselves in disagreement over which movements to invite and over whether any of the Latin American governments should be asked to attend.[26] The ideological distance that remained between the two countries was indicated by Castro's failure to repay Ben Bella's visit, although he was repeatedly invited. Cubans in Algiers privately explained that Castro hesitated to make the trip because he had some doubts about Ben Bella's socialism.

The most important consequence of Ben Bella's visit to Cuba was the change in the United States' attitude toward Algeria. President Kennedy, who as a senator had spoken out in favor of Algeria's independence, was well disposed toward the new country. At the time of Ben Bella's stay in Washington, it was reported that the United States was considering an initial $60 million aid program, but Ben Bella's trip to Havana at a time when Cuba was the focal point of the Cold War was taken in Washington as a calculated affront. Thereafter, plans for a substantial aid program were dropped, although the United States provided Algeria with close to one million tons of surplus food through the voluntary agencies (CARE, Church World Service, and Catholic Relief Service) during the first four years of Algerian independence.

Algerian-American relations never recovered from this initial setback. Ben Bella made no effort to befriend the United States or to play Washington against Moscow in order to obtain more aid. He violently denounced America's "aggression" against Cuba, its intervention in the Congo and in the Dominican Republic, its support of Israel, and its "crimes" against the people of Vietnam. In most cases, he was giving expression to sentiments held by many Algerians, who tended to equate any conflict opposing the United States and a Third World country with the conflict that had opposed Algeria to France. This was particularly true in the case of Vietnam, which the Algerian press portrayed as a country engaged in a war of national liberation.

26. Castro was deeply disappointed by Ben Bella's decision to establish diplomatic relations with several Latin American countries, notably Brazil and Venezuela, whose governments the Cuban leader considered reactionary.

By early 1964, a State Department report, noting that Algeria maintained close ties with Cuba, the Soviet Union, and Communist China, called it a "danger point" in the Cold War. Ben Bella's triumphal trip to Moscow in May of that year further confirmed Washington in its view. American presence in the country remained marginal, and the only government aid program, a rural development project designed to give temporary work to 60,000 Algerians, was for the most part a failure.[27] By June 1965, Washington had decided to suspend its aid until the Algerian government showed a friendlier attitude toward the United States.

The great powers that caused the most embarrassment to Ben Bella and exerted the most pressure on him were not the Western "imperialist" countries, but two "socialist sisters," the Soviet Union and Communist China. The two countries had initially taken very different stands toward Algeria. The Soviet Union, uncertain about the political orientation of the Ben Bella regime, maintained its distance and was measured in its praise. China, on the contrary, never showed any reserve and hailed Algeria as a "beacon country" whose victory over the French had been "an enormous contribution to the struggle of the Chinese people against imperialism."[28] Even before 1962, the two governments had differed in their policy toward the Algerian nationalists. China had been the first Communist country to give *de jure* recognition to the GPRA, while the Soviet Union, concerned about preserving good relations with France, had waited to recognize Algeria until after the conclusion of the Evian Peace Agreements. In fact, the different positions taken by Moscow and Peking toward the Algerian Revolution were one of the first signs of the rift developing in the Communist camp. It was largely because of the rivalry between them that the Soviet Union and China began to pay greater attention to Algeria in the fall of 1963. Ben Bella, who sought aid for Algeria and recognition for himself, took advantage of the interest shown by the

27. The American program was intended to provide temporary jobs on reforestation, village improvement, and road reconstruction projects. Algerians, working in two-week shifts, were paid half in food supplied by the United States and half in cash provided by Algeria. The program was more costly for Algeria than for the United States, and the Algerian government was unable to provide the necessary funds to make it work properly. No more than 20,000 Algerians were ever at work at any one time.

28. *Renmin Ribao*, July 5, 1962, quoted in *Maghreb*, No. 8, March-April 1965, p. 4.

two Communist powers, although he tried to remain neutral in their dispute.

In September 1963, the Soviet Union finally abandoned its reserve and announced it was extending to Algeria a 90 million ruble ($100 million) loan in purchasing credits. The *rapprochement* between Russia and Algeria was partly brought about by the Algerian government's desire to procure arms for the ill-equipped National People's Army. The Algerians had first requested arms of several Western nations, including France and the United States, but their request had been denied;[29] they then turned to the Soviet Union. In late September, Colonel Boumediene went to Moscow to discuss the purchase of arms and arrange for Soviet assistance in the training of the Algerian army. The humiliating defeat of the ANP in the brief Algerian-Moroccan border war the following month convinced the Algerians of the necessity for a major arms buildup and made them even more anxious to obtain Soviet aid. During the same period, Communist China also began to give more tangible proof of its interest in Algeria, opening in September a month-long industrial exhibition and signing a cultural agreement with the Ben Bella government. In early October, Peking offered Algeria an interest-free loan valued at $50 million, which appeared to be a direct response to the Soviet loan announced the previous month. Thereafter, the competition between China and the Soviet Union for Algeria's support became increasingly evident.

In December 1963, Premier Chou En-Lai visited Algeria on his first tour of the African continent. During his stay, he was given the unusual honor of addressing a meeting of high-ranking party and government officials. In the speech he gave on this occasion, the Chinese premier exhorted the Algerians to remain in the vanguard of the struggle against imperialism, noting that the international situation was "excellent" for the strengthening of revolutionary forces. He declared that Algeria was the symbol of revolution in Africa: "Just as the flag of the Cuban Revolution floats above Latin America, that of the Algerian Revolution has been planted on the African continent."[30] The joint communiqué pub-

29. The French government refused to provide Algeria with heavy arms because of its fears of an adverse public reaction in France following a long war with the Algerian nationalists. However, it did agree to train the gendarmerie, an internal security force under the army's command, setting up a school at Sidi-Bel-Abbès, the old headquarters of the French Foreign Legion, for this purpose. The French army also left behind some equipment, notably trucks and a few AMX light tanks, as it withdrew from the country.

30. See *Maghreb*, No. 1, January–February 1964, p. 16.

lished on December 27, at the end of Chou En-Lai's ten-day visit, stressed that Algeria and China had "identical views" on the necessity to intensify the struggle against "colonialism, neocolonialism, and imperialism." Not by chance, a day later another communiqué concluded the stay in Moscow of a fifty-man Algerian delegation headed by Hadj Ben Alla, president of the National Assembly. This communiqué noted the "identity of views" between Algeria and the Soviet Union on the need for peaceful coexistence and on the importance of the Moscow test ban treaty.

Ben Bella had deliberately timed the two visits to coincide in order to show his impartiality and his desire to cooperate with both China and the Soviet Union. In the two joint communiqués, he had demonstrated that he was sympathetic to both the Chinese and Soviet positions, which for him were not contradictory, since he believed that peaceful coexistence among the great powers was desirable even while the liberation struggle of the Third World continued. However, he was not allowed to maintain his impartiality for long. In the following months, a new factor came to influence relations between Algeria and the two Communist rivals. In April 1964, the foreign ministers of twenty-six African and Asian countries met in Jakarta, Indonesia, and decided that a second conference of African and Asian chiefs of state would be held in early 1965. Some countries proposed that the Soviet Union, which had not attended the first Afro-Asian Conference at Bandung in 1955, should be considered an Asian power and asked to participate. However, no agreement was reached because of China's vehement opposition to the proposal. From that time on, Moscow and Peking undertook intensive campaigns to win the African and Asian governments over to their respective positions. Algeria was especially courted, particularly after it was chosen to host the conference.

The importance Moscow attached to winning Algeria's support was made clear during Ben Bella's visit to the Soviet Union and other Eastern bloc countries in the spring of 1964. On his arrival in Moscow on April 25, Ben Bella was greeted by Premier Nikita Khrushchev as "Comrade President" and was given a rousing welcome by the Soviet people. In the days that followed, he was awarded the Lenin Peace Prize as an "ardent champion of peaceful coexistence," decorated with the gold medal of Hero of the Soviet Union, and invited to review the May Day parade alongside Premier Khrushchev. The Soviet leaders startled Western diplomats in Moscow by talking of Algerian socialism as if it were orthodox Marxist-Leninist socialism. At the end of the twelve-day visit, the Soviet Union announced that it was extending Algeria an additional 115 million ruble ($127.6 million) loan, most of which was to be used for the construction of a 350,000-ton steel mill. In addition, it promised to set up an institute to train Algerian technicians for the petroleum and textile industries, and to provide technical assistance in many other areas.

After Ben Bella's triumphal tour of Soviet bloc countries, the Chinese increased their pressure on him to visit China as well. However, Ben Bella never made the trip or even sent a high-level delegation; nor did the FLN seek to establish direct relations with the Chinese Communist party, as it had done with the Soviet. Indeed, Ben Bella's attitude toward China became noticeably more reserved in early 1964, after the Chinese delegation nearly broke up the March 22–26 meeting of the Afro-Asian Peoples' Solidarity Organization by using it as a platform for propaganda.

There was undoubtedly another factor that encouraged Ben Bella to draw closer to Moscow than to Peking: the Chinese offered little in return for the support they unrelentingly demanded. They sent some agronomists to study the possibility of growing rice and tea in Algeria, and a few doctors, most of them acupuncturers, whose techniques Algerians deeply distrusted. In an effort to counter Soviet military aid, they also signed in February 1965 an agreement to arm the "people's militia," but only a small quantity of uniforms and light arms were ever delivered. The Algerian government was not even able to make use of the $50 million loan, since the three factories to be financed by the loan never got beyond the planning stage. Instead, the Chinese seemed to excel in giving gifts calculated to attract wide publicity. They sent a cargo ship—the Algerian merchant marine's second one—and an entire boatload of crayons and pencils to be distributed in all Algerian schools.

Soviet aid steadily increased, although it was implemented very slowly. One reason for this slowness was that the loans covered the purchase of equipment in Russia but not "local costs"—the costs of building the plants and installing the machinery in Algeria. The Algerian government was chronically short of funds to meet local expenses, while the Soviets took their time in making the necessary studies. The steel mill the Soviets had promised to build remained under discussion for over two years; no other factories had been constructed with Soviet aid by mid-1967.[31] However, the Soviet Union did send 130 teachers to staff the Petroleum and Textile Institute, which opened in September 1964 with an enrollment of 600 students. It also sent 50 high school teachers, 300 doctors and nurses, and hundreds of technicians and agronomists.

The Soviet Union acted much more promptly in providing military assistance. Shipments of Migs, bombers, tanks, heavy artillery, and small arms arrived regularly in Algeria beginning in December 1963. Over 1,000 Algerians were sent to Soviet military academies in 1963–1964, while hundreds of Soviet advisors helped to set up army training schools in Algeria. At the army parade of November 1, 1964, the tenth anniversary of the outbreak of the revolution, Western military experts were amazed by the progress the ANP had made in one year. They estimated at that time that the ANP, thanks to Soviet aid, was already better equipped than the Royal Moroccan Army.

By 1965, Russia had definitely gained a foothold in Algeria, and the Soviet Communist party was beginning to develop close ties with the FLN. Nonetheless, the influence of the Soviet Union remained far less important than that of France. The French exhibited remarkably little concern over the Soviet presence in Algeria and even agreed to cooperate with the Soviets in building the steel mill, a project the Algerians were very anxious to see carried out. President de Gaulle seemed confident that ties between France and Algeria were strong enough to prevent Algeria from entering the Communist orbit. Moreover, French and Soviet interests were not in direct conflict in Algeria, since the Soviets did not aspire to supplant French culture and were not interested in the Algerian oil and gas de Gaulle coveted.

Not all Western governments were as nonchalant as France was about Algeria's relations with Communist countries. There was much speculation, particularly among American diplomats, that Ben Bella was taking the same road toward the Communist camp as Castro had before him. Actually, Ben Bella's foreign policy remained his own until the end. Although he considered the socialist countries Algeria's "nat-

31. While the Soviets have not helped to build any factories, the other Eastern European countries have provided machinery and technical assistance for the construction of the following: tanneries at Bougie (Bulgaria) and Rouiba (Yugoslavia); textile factories at Batna (Bulgaria), Tlelat (Yugoslavia), and Valmy (Yugoslavia); and a fruit juice canning plant at El-Asnam (Yugoslavia). Yugoslavia and Bulgaria have loaned Algeria about $30 million in purchasing credits; Czechoslovakia announced in May 1964 that it was granting a $15 million loan in purchasing credits, but the Algerians have yet to make use of it.

ural allies," he maintained his independence, avoiding being used by either the Soviets or the Chinese.

Ben Bella was attracted to both countries and wanted to maintain good relations with both. He was pulled toward the Soviet Union by the aid it promised Algeria and by the recognition the Soviets gave him personally as a leading African revolutionary. On the other hand, he had great admiration for the success of the Chinese in mobilizing their people, and for a period he testified to his desire to follow their example by wearing a Chinese-style tunic. He was also receptive to the more revolutionary position of the Chinese in international affairs, although he refused to equate an anti-imperialist to an anti-Soviet position, as the Chinese demanded he do. Uninterested in the ideological aspects of the Sino-Soviet dispute, Ben Bella was deeply disturbed by the tensions the conflict was creating in the Afro-Asian community. Like many other leftist African leaders, he finally turned against the Chinese because he realized that they were willing to shatter the Afro-Asian Peoples' Solidarity Organization and doom the second Afro-Asian Conference simply in order to win their personal battle against the Soviets.

Ben Bella described Algeria as a country of "multiple vocations," meaning by this that it was a country destined to play a role in North Africa, Africa, and the Arab world. For him, Algeria, although a Moslem and Arab nation, was closely tied to Black Africa by the common history of the anti-colonial struggle. His interest in African politics stemmed in great part from his conviction that Algeria could and should help the other African colonies to gain their independence. He did not have the same emotional involvement in Arab politics, although he was personally very close to President Gamal Abdel Nasser.

Ben Bella's interest in establishing a place for Algeria in African politics was heightened in early 1963 by plans for the foundation of a Pan-African organization. A conference of all African chiefs of state was to be held in Addis Ababa in late May for this purpose. Ben Bella gave his wholehearted support to the project, disregarding the reservations expressed by some Algerian leftists about a "unity negotiated at the top among leaders who are for the most part reactionary."[32] He was so convinced that the meeting would have positive results that he deliberately provoked the collapse of the radical Casablanca Group in

32. Editorial in *Révolution Africaine*, No. 4, February 23, 1963.

order to eliminate one of the obstacles to African unity.[33] Nevertheless, he went to Addis Ababa not "to vote just any motion," but to make the problem of the liberation of the remaining African colonies the primary issue of the conference.

The impromptu speech Ben Bella gave in Addis Ababa was brief and highly dramatic. He warned the twenty-nine chiefs of state present that the first and most important task of the Organization of African Unity (OAU) was to aid the liberation movements, since there could be no African unity until the entire continent was free: "We must all agree to die a little or even completely for the liberation of the people still under colonial domination, so that African unity will not be an empty word."[34] On his return to Algiers, Ben Bella was highly optimistic about the future of the OAU. Reporting to the National Assembly, he declared:

> The internal contradictions [of Africa], the consequence of a long colonial domination, were overcome at Addis Ababa. Henceforth, the evolution of Africa will be determined once again by an African dialectic. Despite the differences of their political regimes, the independent African countries are facing the reality of their common problems.[35]

Ben Bella was especially pleased by the creation of the African Liberation Committee, the function of which was to coordinate aid from the OAU members to the nationalist movements.[36] One of the principal promoters of this committee, Algeria became one of its most active members, immediately contributing $200,000 to help finance the committee's activities.

However, Ben Bella did not rely principally on the OAU to aid the African nationalists. By September 1963, Algeria was training 1,000 guerrillas from Angola, Mozambique, and South Africa, and giving funds and advice to many liberation movements. One of the earliest

33. Representatives of the Casablanca Group were scheduled to meet in Marrakech, Morocco, on May 9, less than two weeks before the Addis Ababa meeting. Ben Bella was the first to announce that he would not attend and forced the postponement *sine die* of the Marrakech conference. The Algerians were proud of having forced the dissolution of the group, considering it a proof of their attachment to African unity.
34. Ben Bella's speech at Addis Ababa, May 23, 1963.
35. Ben Bella's speech of June 18, 1963.
36. The African Liberation Committee, also known as the Committee of Nine, was based in Dar-Es-Salaam, Tanzania, and composed of representatives from Algeria, the United Arab Republic, Guinea, Tazania, Nigeria, Ethiopia, Congo-Leopoldville, Senegal, and Uganda.

beneficiaries of Algeria's aid and of its experience in guerrilla warfare was the Angolan nationalist party, the Frente Nacional para Libertação da Angola (FNLA) led by Holden Roberto. Even before independence, the ALN had begun to train FNLA commandos in its camps in Tunisia, and the maquis set up by Roberto in northern Angola was patterned after the one in Algeria. After 1962, Ben Bella continued to aid the FNLA and other liberation movements in the Portuguese colonies.

Ben Bella's declared aim was to help to unite the rival nationalist parties in every colony. He was indeed instrumental in reconciling the nationalist leaders of Mozambique and in helping them to launch an insurrection in September 1964. But in most other cases, he ended by siding with one party, generally the more radical, and thus acted to divide the nationalists rather than to reconcile them. In Angola, for example, he switched his support from Roberto's party to the Movimento Popular para Libertação da Angola (MPLA), and in South Africa he backed the African National Congress over the Pan-Africanist Congress.[37]

Algeria's hospitality was extended not only to African liberation parties, but also to exiles and left-wing opposition groups from all over the world. By the end of 1964, there were at least twenty-one such organizations represented in Algiers, many of them subsidized by the Algerian government. Among those who received the most attention were the Vietcong, whose Algiers bureau was for a long time the only bureau outside the Communist world. Not all of the groups represented in Algiers were so well known: there were several obscure organizations of doubtful authenticity such as the Movement for the Autodetermination and Independence of the Canary Islands.

Among the exiles who sought refuge in Algiers were opponents of Tunisian President Habib Bourguiba and Moroccan King Hassan II. The presence of Tunisian exiles in Algeria caused considerable tension between the two countries. In late 1962, six Tunisians allegedly involved in a plot to assassinate the Tunisian president on Christmas Eve escaped to Algeria. The Tunisian government asked for their extradition, and

37. Ben Bella's policy toward the rival Angolan parties was very inconsistent. Just after independence, he supported the more radical MPLA. In the summer of 1963, however, an OAU commission of which Algeria was a member carried out a study on the Angolan nationalist parties and concluded that the FNLA was by far the most effective and therefore should be the only one backed by the OAU. Ben Bella officially went along with the OAU recommendation, but in practice he continued to favor the MPLA.

when Ben Bella refused to comply it severed diplomatic relations with Algeria. With the mediation of the Moroccan king, the two countries agreed to re-establish relations in late May 1963. Ben Bella still did not extradite any of the Tunisian exiles, but he did promise to curb their political activities, a promise he only partially kept.

The prospects for Maghreb unity, about which North African leaders constantly talked, never became very bright. One fundamental problem was the different political orientations of the three Maghreb regimes. King Hassan II was a conservative monarch and Bourguiba a mildly socialist and benevolent dictator. By contrast, Ben Bella stood out as a radical socialist whose policies were a challenge to both Bourguiba and Hassan and an inspiration to their opponents. There was, moreover, a very concrete issue that set the three countries at odds: neither Morocco nor Tunisia was willing to accept the Algerian borders as established by the French. Even before Algeria's independence, the Moroccan and Tunisian governments had made known their claims to parts of the Algerian Sahara that were believed to contain oil and other mineral riches.[38] Morocco in particular was determined to obtain a modification of its border with Algeria and continually pressed Ben Bella to open negotiations. Neither the king's role of mediator in the Tunisian-Algerian crisis nor his visit to Algeria in March 1963 diminished tensions over the border issue. Instead, relations between the countries steadily deteriorated until war broke out in October 1963.

A minor clash along the border, similar to many previous ones, developed into a major conflict because of the difficult internal situation in both countries. In Algeria the Kabyle rebellion had just broken out, and Ben Bella found it expedient to magnify the danger of a Moroccan invasion to distract public attention and rally support. In Morocco the king was under considerable pressure from the expansionist Istiqlal party, and he hoped to profit from Ben Bella's internal problems to obtain some concessions from Algeria. On October 1, two days after the outbreak of the FFS rebellion, Ben Bella announced that Moroccan troops were poised on the border and accused the king of acting in

---

38. Tunisia had actually tried to seize a part of the Algerian territory it claimed during the conflict that had opposed French and Tunisian troops at Bizerte in July 1961. Having failed, the Tunisian government informed the GPRA that it would bring the subject up for discussion after Algeria's independence. The GPRA had reportedly signed a protocol in 1961 pledging to undertake negotiations with Morocco after independence. The Algerians have never denied that such a protocol existed.

connivance with the Kabyle dissidents. While representatives of the two governments held talks, troops were taking up positions on either side of the border, and on October 8 the first battle of the war took place.[39]

Ben Bella claimed that the conflict had been deliberately provoked by "feudal" Morocco with the encouragement of the United States in order to crush Algeria's socialist revolution. Accepting his interpretation of the conflict, Cuba and Egypt rushed arms to the defense of Algeria and the revolution; Egyptian officers and troops actually fought alongside the Algerians.[40] The war dragged on for three weeks, with the ANP losing one battle after another. Finally, with the mediation of President Modibo Keita of Mali and Emperor Haile Selassie of Ethiopia, Ben Bella and King Hassan on October 30 signed a cease-fire agreement in Bamako, Mali, that provided for the withdrawal of troops from the disputed area and the establishment of a demilitarized zone policed by Malian and Ethiopian officers. The accord also called upon the OAU to set up an arbitration committee to settle the border dispute. This ad hoc committee was established in mid-November, but it proved unable to find an acceptable solution and eventually fell into limbo.

The Algerian-Tunisian border dispute, on the other hand, never came to a crisis. Following a meeting with Ben Bella in December 1963, Tunisian President Bourguiba announced that the frontier question was a thing of the past and let it be known that the Algerian president had agreed to negotiate for the joint exploitation of any resources discovered in the contested area.[41] However, no talks were held before Ben Bella was overthrown.

39. It has never been determined which side was responsible for the outbreak of the fighting. The Moroccans said that Algerian troops penetrated sixty miles into Moroccan territory on the morning of October 8, attacking the oasis of Hassi Beida and killing ten Moroccan auxiliary soldiers. The Algerians claimed that Hassi Beida was an oasis in Algerian territory and that Moroccan troops had occupied it on September 26. After the local commander asked the Moroccans to evacuate the oasis on October 5, the Moroccans reinforced their position and then on October 8 began to advance on ANP units. According to French news accounts, the Algerians attacked the Moroccans and took over Hassi Beida, but the French refused to indicate whether they thought the oasis was in Moroccan or Algerian territory. See Le Monde, October 16–18, 1963.

40. After the outbreak of the war, Cuba sent three ships carrying 40 Soviet T-34 tanks, 4 Mig jet fighters, some trucks, and more than 800 tons of light arms, ammunition, and artillery. Egypt sent about 1,000 troops to Algeria; five Egyptian officers were captured by the Moroccans during the war.

41. Bourguiba was quoted as having said: "I don't see any reason to put forth territorial claims. It is no longer a question of that. The problem today is solved, and

Because of the differences between the three countries, the idea of a united Maghreb remained a political myth. Even a formal meeting of the three leaders, of which there had been talk since Algeria's independence, proved impossible. Ben Bella, Bourguiba, and King Hassan II did meet privately twice in Cairo during conferences of the Arab League and the OAU; however, nothing came of these meetings. The only concrete steps made toward Maghreb cooperation were the conclusion of a number of bilateral trade and technical agreements and the formation in November 1964 of a "permanent consultative committee," to which Libya also adhered. The primary purpose of the committee was to coordinate plans for industrial development of the four countries so that useless and costly competition could be avoided, but so far national pride has proven stronger than economic reason.

Ben Bella had only one close ally in the Arab world, Gamal Abdel Nasser of the United Arab Republic. The friendship between Ben Bella and Nasser dated from the Algerian president's long stay in Cairo at the beginning of the Algerian Revolution. The Egyptian leader had been probably the staunchest supporter of the FLN, providing it with arms, funds, and diplomatic support from the very beginning. To show his gratitude, Ben Bella had wanted Nasser to be the first guest of independent Algeria, but the plan had failed because King Hassan finagled an invitation at an earlier date. However, Hassan received merely a cordial reception, while Nasser was given a hero's welcome. Algerians came by the thousands from all over the country to see the *rais*, repeatedly breaking down police lines and halting the motorcade in order to get near him.[42]

The enthusiasm of Algerians for Nasser stood in sharp contrast to their antipathy for Egyptians in general. Algerians, even government officials, found these Arab "brothers" haughty and overbearing and at the same time narrow-minded and ignorant. Egyptian officers who came to help the ANP during the border conflict with Morocco were accused

---

I'm thoroughly satisfied. At a time when we are discussing the joint exploitation of our resources and the gradual integration of our economies, what is the importance of a few kilometers of sand. . . ." *Jeune Afrique*, No. 164, December 30, 1963.

42. Although Nasser was given what was probably the most enthusiastic reception any chief of state received in Algeria, his visit was marred by so many incidents that many Algerians took it as an ill omen. Upon his arrival May 5, two small Algerian patrol boats that had gone out to meet Nasser's yacht capsized, and several seamen were drowned. Two days later, Foreign Minister Mohamed Khemisti, who had been in a coma for several weeks following an assassination attempt, finally died. Nasser ended up participating in the funeral march and then cut short his visit.

of trying to take over command of the war. The 1,000 Egyptian school-teachers working in Algeria were widely ridiculed as "barbers and bakers" who had come to make their fortunes at the expense of the Algerian government. Algerians who visited Egypt found it a backward country compared to their own. Egyptian diplomats in Algiers, on the other hand, were shocked by the lack of sophistication and polish of Algerian officials as well as by their inability to write or speak classical Arabic.

Despite the prejudices that divided their peoples, Nasser and Ben Bella, as socialist leaders among predominantly conservative Arab and African chiefs of state, each found in the other a natural ally. They both aspired to leadership in the Afro-Asian community, but they did not become rivals because Ben Bella was primarily interested in Africa and Nasser in the Arab world. After Nasser's visit to Algeria, the two men met repeatedly in order to coordinate their policies. The importance Ben Bella gave to relations with Nasser was underlined by the fact that he maintained a special bureau of Arab affairs attached to the presidency.[43] The close ties between Nasser and Ben Bella gave rise to wild rumors about Egyptian influence in the Algerian government and about the existence of a Cairo-Algiers axis that aimed to dominate all of North Africa. It was said, for instance, that Ben Bella was considering making Algeria a part of the United Arab Republic or that he and Nasser had secret plans to conquer and divide between them Tunisia and Libya.

In reality the alliance between Cairo and Algiers had a much more limited scope. The two leaders coordinated their policies toward the African liberation movements, deciding together which one to support in countries where there were several, and collaborated in the Afro-Asian Peoples' Solidarity Organization. The most publicized example of cooperation between Ben Bella and Nasser was their joint offensive against Congolese Premier Moise Tshombe. First, they excluded Tshombe from the second meeting of OAU chiefs of state and from the second conference of nonaligned countries, both held in Cairo in the summer of 1964; then later that year, they flew vast quantities of arms to the Congolese rebels fighting to overthrow him.

Ben Bella maintained his independence of Nasser, however, and pointedly avoided becoming entangled in the alliances and disputes of the Middle East. His independence and detachment made it possible

43. The chief of this bureau, Abderrahmane Cherif, became minister attached to the presidency in December 1964.

for him to play the role of mediator in some cases. At the first conference of Arab chiefs of state, Ben Bella was able to reconcile Syria, which was pressing for immediate armed intervention in Israel, and Egypt, which was against any hasty, ill-prepared action. His proposal that the Arab states help the Palestinian refugees organize their own national liberation army to wage guerrilla warfare against Israel was accepted by all parties and was adopted by the conference. Ben Bella also tried to mediate between Saudi Arabia and Egypt in the Yemeni war, but this time he was unsuccessful.

The friendship between Nasser and Ben Bella helped to bring about a temporary *rapprochement* between the East and the West of the Arab world and to make possible the first meeting of all Arab chiefs of state. Nasser's relations with Bourguiba and King Hassan had been strained for years, and both North African leaders had regularly boycotted meetings of the Arab League. However, after Algeria's independence Bourguiba and Hassan realized the necessity for making peace with Nasser so that the Algiers-Cairo alliance would not turn against them. Bourguiba reconciled with Nasser in December 1963 by inviting him to Tunisia for the celebrations marking the French evacuation of the naval base at Bizerte. It was more difficult for Hassan to improve relations with the Egyptian leader, since the latter had actively supported Ben Bella during the Algerian-Moroccan border war. However, when both Ben Bella and Bourguiba accepted Nasser's invitation to the first Arab summit conference in January 1964, King Hassan also decided to attend, realizing that he could not afford to remain isolated in the Arab world.

The Cairo conference was an unprecedented success in Arab politics. All chiefs of state participated, forgetting their differences and quarrels at least for a time. The three North African leaders held their first private meeting on the site of the conference, and Morocco re-established diplomatic relations with the UAR, which it had broken off during the Algerian-Moroccan war. The final communiqué of the conference announced that the Arab leaders had agreed "to put an end to their quarrels, to clear the atmosphere in the Arab world by stopping attacks [on each other] in the press, and to strengthen ties among all the sister Arab countries."[44]

The spirit of the Cairo meeting, like that of Addis Ababa, was short-lived. The only solidarity developing in Africa and the Arab world in

44. See *Maghreb*, No. 2, March–April 1962, p. 5.

the early 1960s was that linking regimes with similar ideological orientations. The controversial issues debated at conferences of the Arab League and of the OAU—whether to sever diplomatic relations with West Germany over its recognition of Israel, for instance, or whether to recognize Tshombe as the legitimate prime minister of the Congo—helped to bring into the open the differences between moderate and radical governments and thus contributed to the formation of blocs.

The OAU began to split within months of its foundation. Ben Bella, despite his initial enthusiasm for the cause of African unity, soon aligned himself with the other revolutionary leaders—Nkrumah, Touré, Keita, Nyerere, and Massemba-Débat. He developed close personal ties with most of these men, overcoming the hostility of the Black Africans towards the Arabs, something Nasser had been unable to do. Ben Bella called these leaders his "brothers" because like him they were committed to socialism, to the liberation of the remaining African colonies, and to the struggle against Western "imperialism." There was, in fact, a tacit alliance between them, which came more into the open after Tshombe returned to power in June 1964 and especially after the Organisation Commune Africaine et Malgache (OCAM) was formed in February 1965 by thirteen moderate French-speaking countries.[45] But Africa's revolutionary leaders never formalized their alliance as the moderates did; even an effort by Ben Bella, Touré, Keita, and Nkrumah to formulate a common policy toward the OCAM and Tshombe was unsuccessful. A meeting of the four in Bamako on March 14 was broken up by the abrupt departure of Nkrumah after an argument between him and Ben Bella, and ended without the publication of a joint communiqué.[46]

If Ben Bella had some influence in other African nations, it was because of his socialist policies at home rather than because of his aggres-

45. The OCAM was formed February 12, 1965, at a meeting of representatives from thirteen countries held in Nouakchott, Mauritania. Among the aims of the OCAM were countering the subversive activities of Ghana, and to a lesser extent of Algeria, in other countries and supporting Tshombe against the Congolese rebels. The members were: Cameroun, Ivory Coast, Congo-Brazzaville, Dahomey, Gabon, Upper Volta, Niger, Madagascar, Mauritania, Central African Republic, Senegal, Tchad, and Togo.

46. It is not clear exactly what took place at this hurriedly called meeting of the four presidents. Ben Bella and Nkrumah reportedly disagreed more over tactics than substance. The latter wanted to maintain a conciliatory attitude toward the OCAM, at least until after the conference of OAU chiefs of state scheduled to take place in Ghana the following October. Ben Bella, engrossed in his campaign to oust Tshombe, favored a hard line.

sive foreign policy. The widespread nationalizations in Algeria provoked both President Bourguiba and King Hassan II into accelerating
the takeover of remaining French lands in their countries. President
Nyerere of Tanzania and President Massemba-Débat of the Congo-
Brazzaville appear to have been sufficiently encouraged by Algeria's
example to follow a more radical course in their countries. Many African nationalists in Algiers also regarded the Algerian experience with
interest.

In contrast, Ben Bella's overt efforts to export the revolution were
highly unsuccessful. In June 1964, twenty Moroccan commandos trained
by the ANP were captured by the Moroccan army as they attempted to
enter Morocco. In an effort to discredit Ben Bella, the king gave much
publicity to the incident. Later the same year, a similar episode strained
relations between Algeria and Niger. A group of guerrillas of the Sawa-
ba opposition party were caught in northern Niger and revealed that
they had been trained in Algerian camps. This incident was one of the
reasons why Niger's President Hamani Diori turned down his invitation to the Afro-Asian Conference in Algiers, remaining adamant in his
refusal despite Ben Bella's personal efforts.[47]

The most striking reverse Ben Bella suffered stemmed from his policy
toward the Congo. Determined to oust Moise Tshombe, whom he defined as a "walking museum of imperialism," Ben Bella offered his
entire support to the "revolutionary Congolese government" led by
Christophe Gbenye. In November 1964, Algeria began to provide the
Congolese rebels with considerable quantities of Soviet arms, flying the
arms to the southern Sudan to be transported overland into the Congo.
However, many of the arms were seized en route by Sudanese dissidents. Gbenye's movement collapsed shortly afterwards, Tshombe remained in power, and the Sudanese government, which Ben Bella had
no intention of subverting, found itself challenged by a well-armed
rebel force. Furthermore, the intervention of Ben Bella and the other
radical leaders in the Congo was one of the principal reasons that
pushed the moderate African governments to form the OCAM, thereby formalizing the split of the OAU. Ironically, just two years earlier,
Ben Bella had forced the dissolution of the radical Casablanca Group
in order to advance the cause of African unity.

47. Ben Bella flew to Tamanrasset and met with Diori on June 10, 1965, in a last
minute attempt to convince the Niger president to attend the conference. He did
not succeed in convincing Diori.

The real measure of Ben Bella's success and failure as a Third World leader was the second conference of Afro-Asian chiefs of state. The choice of Algiers as the location for the meeting was an acknowledgment of Ben Bella's personal prestige; the difficulties Ben Bella encountered in convincing many African leaders to attend were a consequence not only of the divisions in the Afro-Asian world, but also of the failure of his personal diplomacy.

Algeria had been an active member of the Afro-Asian Peoples' Solidarity Organization since its foundation in 1957. AAPSO was by far the most radical organization in the Third World. It represented "peoples" rather than governments, which meant that liberation movements and even opposition parties in independent African and Asian countries could participate as full members. Although its members declared their respect for the "ten principles of peaceful coexistence" enunciated at Bandung in 1955, they were in fact primarily interested in promoting the struggle against Western colonialism and imperialism. For this reason, an effort was being made to include in the organization Cuba and the Latin American revolutionary movements. Because AAPSO's permanent secretariat was based in Cairo, the organization was for a long time largely under Nasser's control.[48] After Algeria's independence, however, Ben Bella became equally influential in the organization.

Despite its name, AAPSO served less to unite the peoples of Africa and Asia than to give a platform to the radical bloc. However, even the solidarity of this bloc was sorely tested by the dispute between China and the Soviet Union, both of which were members of AAPSO. The disruptive role of the two Communist countries was made particularly clear during AAPSO's sixth conference, held in Algiers in March 1964. The dispute between the Chinese and Soviet delegations prevented discussion of the items on the agenda and finally caused the conference to break up in bedlam.

Shortly after this meeting, the foreign ministers of twenty-six African and Asian countries gathered in Jakarta, Indonesia, to discuss Premier Chou En-Lai's proposal for the holding of a second Afro-Asian conference. The ministers agreed that such a conference should take place in 1965, the tenth anniversary of the first conference at Bandung. They

48. Not only was AAPSO's secretariat in Cairo, but the secretary-general, Youssef as-Sibai, was an Egyptian. Soviet influence in AAPSO was much stronger than Chinese influence because the Soviet Union was much closer to Nasser than China was.

also decided it should be held in an African country, leaving it up to the African states to choose the host country. In July 1964, during an OAU meeting in Cairo, the African chiefs of state designated Algiers as the site for the second Afro-Asian Conference.

Ben Bella undertook preparations for the conference with great enthusiasm, mobilizing the country's most skilled diplomats and meeting in person with reluctant chiefs of state. However, many problems proved insuperable. The Chinese made it clear that they would boycott the conference if the Soviet Union were invited, but a majority of countries, including Algeria, favored the presence of the Soviets. President Sukarno of Indonesia, who had been the host of the first Afro-Asian Conference, hinted that he too would not attend the meeting if Malaysia were invited. In Africa nine moderate leaders announced that they definitely would not participate, and it appeared unlikely that either Bourguiba or King Hassan II would come in person. It was obvious that there would not be sixty chiefs of state in Algiers on June 29, as the press had optimistically announced, and there was a definite possibility that the conference would not be held at all.

In 1965, Ben Bella was working against the tide. The enthusiasm for the Afro-Asian solidarity movement was on the wane after ten years of meetings and seminars that had achieved few concrete results while deepening divisions. It was almost symbolic that Ben Bella, who had become one of the most dynamic leaders of the movement, should be ousted on the eve of the second Afro-Asian Conference. The *coup d'état* of June 19 shattered all hopes that the conference would be held. Only China and Indonesia decided to try to save the meeting and immediately recognized the new regime, calculating that Boumediene in return would agree not to invite the Soviet Union and Malaysia. All other revolutionary countries unanimously denounced the *coup* and lost all interest in the conference. The moderate African leaders were only too happy to have a pretext to ask for postponement without appearing to oppose the meeting in principle. After three days of frantic diplomatic maneuvering, the conference was officially postponed until November 5, but it was already obvious to all that there would not be a second Afro-Asian Conference.

chapter nine

the june 19 coup d'état

The armed forces are the powerful shield and sword that protect the revolution from its enemies at home and abroad. The armed forces are either wholeheartedly with the revolution, thus increasing the strength of the party and of all militants, or they are isolated from the revolution, and in this case any effort to build socialism would be vain. Who could stop the army from openly attacking any given regime?[1]

Houari Boumediene

During Ben Bella's time in power, Algeria lived in an atmosphere of constant excitement and expectation. Hardly a month went by without some new campaign being launched, some foreign dignitary visiting the country, or some congress being held. Ben Bella traveled throughout the country exhorting local authorities, haranguing crowds of peasants and workers, promising sweeping changes, and convincing Algerians that socialism was the right choice. But his deeds fell far short of his promises, and his achievements did not measure up to the expectations he aroused. Undoubtedly Ben Bella had given the young country a "revolutionary" image, but he had not created new political and economic structures capable of making that image a reality. He had given Algeria the March Decrees and the Algiers Charter. However, two years after their promulgation, the March Decrees were hardly being applied, and there were many reasons to believe that they never would be. The Algiers Charter seemed to provide Algerian politicians with quotes for their speeches rather than inspiration for their actions.

1. Boumediene's speech of March 21, 1966. Unless otherwise specified, Boumediene's speeches are quoted from an official collection published by the Minister of Information. Most speeches can also be found in the *El-Moudjahid* of the following day.

Ben Bella had also promised rapid industrialization and a sweeping agrarian reform. However, by 1965 there was not even a plan for economic development, and the few plants being built with foreign aid were lagging far behind schedule. Projects for an agrarian reform languished in bureaus of the Ministry of Agriculture. Since the fall of 1962, Ben Bella had periodically promised that municipal elections would soon be held, but they never were. Few of the programs undertaken by the Algerian president were carried through. The purge and reorganization of the party, decided upon by the Central Committee in May 1964, petered out after a few top officials were ousted and a few war veterans were recruited. A national campaign launched in late 1962 to open unemployment-relief work projects for 500,000 Algerians faltered after a few months and was finally abandoned. After three years of fitful actions, unfulfilled promises, and half-applied measures, many Algerians were becoming skeptical about Ben Bella's rule. Nonetheless, Ben Bella was still far from being unpopular in the country, and he would certainly have been re-elected over any opponent in a free election.

Ben Bella's personality and his ambitions undoubtedly had much to do with his failure to carry through the projects he undertook. There was an overly optimistic, even a naive, side to him, and he forgot all too easily that projects and accomplishments were not necessarily the same thing. His ambitions to make his country an inspiration to the Third World as it had been during the revolution led him to be more concerned with the image than with the realities of "socialist" Algeria. He could hold up the March Decrees as a model of "democratic socialism" for other countries to follow even though Mahsas was quietly working to undermine the workers' authority and to turn self-management into state capitalism. He could wear a Chinese-style tunic even though the party failed to mobilize the people for the construction of the new socialist order.

Yet it was mostly the internal instability of the regime that gave Ben Bella's rule a chaotic and precipitous style. Ben Bella's authority was constantly being challenged, and to every challenge he responded with a concession to his opponents or with the announcement of a popular decision. Khider tried to impose himself as the strong man of the regime, and Ben Bella reacted by publishing the March Decrees. Ait Ahmed openly defied Ben Bella in the fall of 1963, and Ben Bella answered by nationalizing all the remaining French lands. The army became a threatening ally, and Ben Bella turned to the UGTA, giving it the autonomy it demanded and even proposing to nationalize all private enterprises. Ben Bella could not stop to plan his course. In order to keep himself in power, he had to respond immediately to every threat, and these political acrobatics could only be accomplished at the expense of a coherent and chartered course of action.

Ben Bella had given the country formal institutions, but he had not allowed these institutions to function as they were intended to. It was not the National Assembly, but Ben Bella and his advisors who wrote the constitution and the March Decrees. It was not the FLN Central Committee and the Political Bureau, but Ben Bella and his aides who drew up the list of candidates for the second National Assembly and made all the major policy decisions. The National Assembly was consequently reduced to a rubber-stamp operation, and the Political Bureau and Central Committee rarely met. Apart from these institutions, there was always what Mohamed Harbi once called a "parallel political life," involving secret negotiations and shifting alliances among individuals and groups that had no official authority. The "parallel political life" became increasingly important as relations among members of the regime deteriorated, compelling Ben Bella to rely upon the leftist groups outside the FLN; however, he never reformed the country's formal institutions to give an official voice to the new forces that were becoming the mainstay of his regime. Ben Bella's position remained extremely unstable because one by one his old allies turned into rivals, and his new allies had no place in his regime. Thus in the spring of 1965, Ben Bella was poorly prepared for a decisive confrontation with the man who had brought him to power.

Mohamed Ben Brahim Boukharouba, better known as Houari Boumediene, was a product of the revolution.[2] A youth of twenty-two when the war of independence began, he was still unknown to most Algerians when he was named head of the ALN General Staff in 1960. He had joined the nationalist movement shortly before the outbreak of the revolution. His first position in the FLN was that of receptionist in the party's office in Cairo. After being trained as a commando in Egypt, in 1955 Boumediene was sent to fight in the maquis of western Algeria. He rapidly became assistant to Abdelhafid Boussouf, the commander of Wilaya Five, and finally replaced him in 1957. Boumediene's rise to

2. See Appendix II for Boumediene's complete biography.

the top ranks of the ALN was due not only to his ability as an organizer, but also to his friendship to Boussouf, who as minister of arms and liaisons had become one of the most powerful figures in the exiled Provisional Government.[3] Boussouf was instrumental in getting Boumediene named chief of the ALN General Staff in 1960. The fact that Boumediene was a relatively uncontroversial figure among jealous officers also made him an ideal choice; however, he soon became highly controversial. In 1961, he refused to obey an order from the GPRA to hand over control of the military forces inside Algeria to the Ministry of the Interior. His differences with the Provisional Government led him to side with Ben Bella during the civil war in 1962. The intervention of the outside army under Boumediene's command was the decisive factor in the outcome of the summer struggle.

Despite his all-important contribution to Ben Bella's victory, Boumediene remained in the background and came to be considered a mysterious figure, perhaps the *éminence grise* of the regime. Little was known about him, not even his correct name or age. Even less was known about his opinions and intentions.[4] Boumediene was almost the perfect antithesis of Ben Bella, as shy and reserved as Ben Bella was expansive and cordial, as ascetic and intense as the other was bon vivant and easygoing. Even the educational backgrounds of the two men were very different, Ben Bella having been educated in French schools and the French army, Boumediene in a medersa in Constantine and for a short time at Al-Azhar University in Cairo.

Boumediene's only known ambition was to make the ANP into a

3. Boussouf was regarded by many observers as the most powerful man in the GPRA. In addition to being minister of arms and liaisons, he was a member of the three-man Interministerial Committee of War, which was the real center of power in the GPRA. This committee was set up in January 1960, and a month later it decided to create a unified General Staff to command the troops stationed in Tunisia and Morocco and the wilaya forces. Boumediene was considered Boussouf's protégé, and there was general surprise among political observers when the two men took different sides during the civil war in 1962. At the end of the civil war, Boussouf retired from politics, although he maintained his contacts with Boumediene.

4. There are many erroneous reports about Boumediene's past. It is said that he received formal military training in Russia, Communist China, or Iraq. Actually, Boumediene left Algeria for the first time in 1952, remained briefly in Tunis, and then went on to Cairo, where he was a student at Al-Azhar University until right before the outbreak of the revolution. His only military training before he returned to fight in Algeria was at a commando camp at El-Helouan in Egypt. One of the reasons why there are so many myths about Boumediene's past is that it is widely believed that he was born in 1925, while his actual birthdate is August 23, 1932. This error has left chroniclers with a seven-year period about which they have no information.

powerful, united army. The task was not easy because he had to reconcile and organize under a single command such different and hostile
forces as the guerrillas commanders, the officers of the outside army,
and the professionals who had been trained in the French army. The
reconversion of the army initially left him little time for politicking.
He was plagued by the rebellions of the wilaya commanders—Si Larbi,
Mohand ou el-Hadj, and Chaabani—and haunted by the memory of
the ANP's humiliating defeat at the hands of the Royal Moroccan Army.
Ben Bella made Boumediene's task more difficult by playing on the
rivalries between the guerrilla commanders and the colonel in order
to weaken the latter's position. For instance, the president appointed
Tahar Zbiri chief of the General Staff after the outbreak of the FFS
rebellion in October 1963 as much in order to undermine Boumediene's
position as to pacify the dissatisfied wilaya leaders. Significantly, the
appointment was made without the consent of Boumediene, who was
negotiating for arms in Moscow at the time.[5] Boumediene claimed that
in December 1963 Ben Bella had sought to convince a high-ranking
officer to organize a putsch against the General Staff and that the rebellion of Chaabani in July 1964 had been deliberately encouraged by the
president.[6] Whether the result of Ben Bella's machinations, as Boumediene argued, or of the colonel's own policies of favoring French-trained
officers over the former guerrilla commanders, which seems more probable, the ANP remained divided.

The alliance between Ben Bella and Boumediene had no reason to
last. In the summer of 1962, the two leaders had a common interest in
the defeat of the GPRA; however, once they had seized power, there
was much more to divide than to unite them. Despite the forced withdrawal of the army from politics immediately after independence,

5. Boumediene maintains that he first learned of the appointment of Zbiri as
chief of staff from his hosts. He declared later: "[Ben Bella] knew perfectly well . . .
that I would have viewed favorably the nomination of brother Tahar . . . [but] he
waited for me to leave in order to make brother Tahar believe that he had been
named against my will. . . . Ben Bella never ceased to describe us [Zbiri and Boume-
diene] to each other as sworn enemies." See Boumediene's interview with the Cairo
newspaper *Al-Ahram*, October 8–10, 1965, reprinted in *Révolution Africaine*, No.
143, October 23, 1965.

6. Boumediene claimed that Ben Bella had incited a Captain Bouanane to carry
out a *coup d'état* against him: "Imagine a prime minister who incites an army officer
to undertake a military *coup d'état*, to arrest the army's top-ranking officers and the
minister of defense of his own government, and to occupy the radio station, roads,
and bridges. Yes, unfortunately, that is what Ben Bella tried to do in late 1963." See
Boumediene's interview with *Al-Ahram*, cited in note 5.

Boumediene himself was far from being apolitical, and since he was vice-president and minister of defense, his opinion could not be totally disregarded. The colonel was essentially much more conservative than Ben Bella. Military man that he was, he appreciated order and organization and abhorred Ben Bella's improvisations. Although he was not opposed to socialism in principle, he favored orderly state control over the anarchistic self-management system.

Boumediene's opposition to Ben Bella's policies was veiled behind a pseudo-religious argument over the compatibility of Islam and Marxist socialism. This issue had been raised by the conservative religious leaders, who contended that socialism was contrary to the teachings of Islam.[7] At first, the argument did not stir much public interest, as most educated Algerians were too steeped in French culture to care about Islamic orthodoxy. The peasants, who were attached to traditional values, had no reason to complain about Ben Bella, who never preached atheism and even encouraged the building of mosques.[8] However, the issue suddenly assumed great importance during the preparations for the party congress, when the Boumediene faction objected to the strongly Marxist orientation of the party's new ideological charter, insisting that Islam be declared the country's fundamental doctrine. Despite the arguments they put forward in support of their position, Boumediene and his allies opposed the principles set forth in the Algiers Charter not because they were contrary to the *hadiths* (sayings) of the Prophet, but because they were inspired by a foreign doctrine brought to Algeria by foreign advisors. What had begun as a crusade for the revival of Islam on the part of a small group of religious leaders was easily turned into an anti-Communist and xenophobic movement on the part of the army. As Boumediene declared after the *coup d'état*:

7. On January 5, 1964, the cultural association Al-Qiyam, which included the ulama and the most conservative elements in Algeria, held a meeting in Algiers that was attended by 3,000 persons. Ostensibly the purpose of the meeting was to protest the continuing influence of French culture in the country and to demand that the government take steps to promote education in Arabic and greater respect for Islamic values. However, the meeting was widely interpreted as an attack on Ben Bella's socialist policies. In an article signed by a group of left-wing intellectuals and published in all government-controlled newspapers, the organizers of the meeting were attacked as "bourgeois and retrograde." The article said: "Dreaming of a theocratic state in the service of certain interests, [those] of a caste and a class, the organizers of this meeting aim ultimately at stopping the march of the new Algeria and at blocking its revolutionary dynamics." See *Le Peuple* or *Alger Républicain*, January 17, 1964.

8. The Ben Bella government undertook to restore 170 mosques and to construct 187 new ones. See *Révolution Africaine*, No. 129, July 17, 1965.

Algerians did not launch a revolution and sacrifice more than a million and a half martyrs in order to make it possible for a group of Trotskyites and opportunists, led by their apostle Raptis, or Pablo, to run Algeria and to proclaim themselves the custodians of the revolutionaries in the name of socialism.[9]

The growing dissension between Boumediene and Ben Bella was not, however, based primarily on ideological differences. Boumediene was above all concerned about Ben Bella's *rapprochement* with the UGTA and the Algerian Communists because he feared that with the help of these new allies the president would eventually oust him. The words Ben Bella once used to describe the rift between himself and Ait Ahmed were equally applicable to his conflict with Boumediene: "We are opposed on some given problems and ideas even though we have perhaps disguised personal antagonisms behind these ideas. . . . But the opposition remains."[10] Essentially, the conflict was one more episode in the struggle among clans that had plagued Algeria since independence.

In mid-1963, the Boumediene clan had complete control of the ANP General Staff and held as many key posts in the government as the Ben Bella clan. But the balance of power was soon upset. In October of that year, Ben Bella began to undermine Boumediene's control over the army by appointing Tahar Zbiri chief of the General Staff. At the party congress, Boumediene and his allies won only four of the seventeen seats on the Political Bureau. In July 1964, Ben Bella forced Ahmed Medeghri, a close associate of Boumediene's, to resign from his post of minister of the interior and took over that ministry himself.[11] In the Cabinet shuffle of December 1964, another of Boumediene's allies, Minister of Tourism Ahmed Kaid, was ousted from the government, and a third, Cherif Belkacem, was demoted from minister of education and information to minister of education. Only Boumediene

9. Boumediene's interview with *Al-Ahram*, cited in note 5. Actually, most of Ben Bella's foreign advisors, including Raptis, had been dismissed by the end of 1964, although many of them found other employment in the administration (Raptis was an advisor in the Ministry of Agriculture). The Bureau for Nongovernmental Aid to Algeria, which Raptis had organized shortly after independence, continued until the *coup d'état* to recruit leftists from all countries to work in Algeria. By the end of 1964, however, the influence of the Trotskyites had become minimal.

10. Ben Bella's interview with the Swiss newspaper *La Suisse*, May 4, 1965.

11. At the beginning of July, Ben Bella transferred control over the prefects from the Ministry of the Interior to the presidency, thus stripping Medeghri of most of his power. Medeghri resigned, as Ben Bella hoped, on July 13, 1964.

and Foreign Minister Bouteflika kept their positions intact.[12] At the same time, Ben Bella greatly consolidated his position by formally assuming the functions of the minister of the interior and the minister of finance and information. He further strengthened his hold over the government by dismissing all *chefs de cabinet* (executive assistants) appointed by the ministers and personally naming a secretary-general in every ministry. This series of moves strongly suggested that Ben Bella aimed at eliminating the Boumediene faction from the government.

By the fall of 1964, Ben Bella had also begun to prepare his "opening to the Left," making concessions to the UGTA and establishing cordial relations with the Algerian and French Communist parties.[13] These steps provoked an increasing amount of criticism from the religious leaders, who found new reasons for accusing Ben Bella of making Algeria into a Communist state. At a consequence, Ben Bella exhibited an unprecedented concern to prove that Islam and socialism were not irreconcilable doctrines, arguing that Islam itself preached a form of socialism. Above all, he sought to reassure Algerians that his socialism was not atheistic Marxism:

> We adopt the Marxist economic analysis because we believe that it is the only one valid for the economic development of our country; but we do not espouse the Marxist ideology because we Algerians are Moslems and Arabs.[14]

12. The Cabinet shuffle was announced on December 2, 1964. The Cabinet was enlarged to eighteen members with the creation of a Ministry of Commerce and a Ministry of Administrative Reform and Civil Service; in addition, there was to be an under-secretary of state for public works. The most surprising appointment made by Ben Bella was that of Safi Boudissa as minister of labor. Boudissa was a noted Islamist and was close to the army, having been a director of the ALN Political Commissariat. Made at a time when Ben Bella was trying to improve his relations with the UGTA, this appointment was evidently a concession to Boumediene. See Appendix I for the complete list of ministers appointed to the new Cabinet.

13. A delegation of the French Communist party, led by Waldeck Rochet and including three members of the Political Bureau, visited Algeria October 14–19, 1964. A long joint communiqué issued at the end of the visit announced that the FLN and the PCA had agreed to strengthen their ties. The visit marked the end of a long period of strained relations between the two parties that had begun with the banning of the PCA in November 1962.

14. Ben Bella's interview with *Révolution et Travail*, No. 73, January 20, 1965. On another occasion, Ben Bella declared: "Islam did not prevent us from liberating ourselves, and in the past two and a half years it did not prevent us from committing the country to a very clear socialist program. . . . I had a long discussion with Khrushchev when he was in power and with Professor Garaudy, the leading Marxist theorist in France and in all of Europe; both agreed that Islam could be a stimulant in Algeria." Ben Bella's interview with *La Suisse*, May 4, 1965.

On another occasion he declared:

> Some evil-minded persons say we are propagandists for Communism, but we tell them that we have come with an Arab and Islamic mission and that our motto is Arabism and Islam. . . . We did not import our socialism from a foreign country; [socialism] is the reflection of the realities of our own country and the ideal for which one and a half million martyrs gave their lives.[15]

Even the Algerian Communists joined in Ben Bella's campaign to convince the public that Algerian socialism was rooted in Islam, seeking to demonstrate that they too were good Moslems. On the anniversary of the death of Cheikh Ben Badis, the founder of the Algerian Association of Reformist Ulama, *Alger Républicain* wrote:

> We celebrate today the twenty-sixth anniversary of the death of Cheikh Ben Badis. Without becoming too symbolic, we must note that this anniversary is even more significant because exactly a year ago the first congress of the FLN met and reaffirmed the same principles Cheikh Ben Badis had defended and spread among Algerians.[16]

During the last few months before the *coup d'état*, both the UGTA and the religious leaders mounted massive demonstrations to intimidate each other with a show of strength. In April, on the occasion of Aid Kebir, the most important Moslem festivity, the religious leaders organized a public ceremony in downtown Algiers that drew one of the largest crowds ever assembled in Algeria since independence. The demonstration was intended by the organizers to be both a protest over the arrest of the grand mufti of Algiers, the city's chief doctor of Islamic law, and a warning to Ben Bella.[17] However, the president blunted the impact of the protest by joining the ceremony and presiding over the rituals alongside the religious leaders. Partly in response to the Aid Kebir demonstration, the UGTA on May 1 organized a huge Labor Day parade over which Ben Bella also presided, this time showing his solidarity with the Left. Ben Bella assured the workers that the revolution was continuing, and he promised them that the majority of the remaining private enterprises would be nationalized before the

---

15. Ben Bella's speech of February 28, 1965.
16. *Alger Républicain*, April 16, 1965.
17. Ben Bella had ordered the arrest of the mufti and several imams in March because they were preaching in the mosques that socialism was contrary to the precepts of Islam. The arrests had stirred up much discontent in conservative circles. As a gesture of good will, Ben Bella had the religious leaders released just before Aid Kebir.

end of the year. Three weeks later, on May 22, the religious leaders turned out another impressive crowd for the funeral of Cheikh Ibrahimi, a well-known ulama. The funeral possession was widely regarded as another warning to Ben Bella, who on this occasion was absent.

Ben Bella was at that time in eastern Algeria, enjoying one of his last triumphal tours. His popularity with the peasants seemed as great as ever. Large crowds greeted him everywhere, and at one point enthusiastic state-farm workers forced the motorcade to make an unscheduled stop and prevailed upon the president to visit their farm. However, Ben Bella's popularity with the peasants was of little help to him when he returned to Algiers to face a complex situation. The Afro-Asian summit conference was approaching rapidly, and there were numerous logistical and political problems to resolve in the few remaining weeks, since the $30 million conference site was still unfinished and many chiefs of state were still hesitant to attend the conference. Furthermore, Algeria and France were in the last stage of delicate negotiations for the new oil agreement, which Ben Bella wanted to see signed before the conference opened.[18] The ministers were divided over whether or not to accept the terms of the long-range accord, and there were reports that Minister of Industry and Energy Bachir Boumaza had threatened to resign in protest. The Cabinet was also at odds over Ben Bella's proposal to merge the Communist-controlled *Alger Républicain* with the government newspaper *Le Peuple*, creating a new daily that would be run almost entirely by the staff of *Alger Républicain*.[19]

On May 25, Ben Bella held a meeting with all of Algeria's ambassadors, called home to discuss strategy for the forthcoming Afro-Asian

18. Ben Bella hoped to sign the agreement and fly to Paris for a meeting with President de Gaulle before the conference opened. He wanted to hold the agreement up to the African and Asian leaders attending the conference as a formula for cooperation without neocolonialist implications between an underdeveloped country and a Western power.

19. Plans for the merger were announced on June 5. The newspaper, to be called *El-Moudjahid*, was to be under the over-all direction of Abderrahmane Benhamida, a member of the FLN Central Committee. The Communists were to have control of day-to-day operations. Boualem Khalifa, director of *Alger Républicain*, was to be codirector with Benhamida, and Abdelhamid Benzine, editor-in-chief of the Communist daily, was to have the same post on the new paper. Henry Alleg, the French Communist codirector of *Alger Républicain*, was to take a high post in the government news agency. The merger was to take place on July 5, the third anniversary of Algeria's independence. On June 21, two days after the *coup d'état*, a newspaper called *El-Moudjahid* appeared, and *Alger Républicain* and *Le Peuple* ceased publication. However, the staff of the new daily was not the one planned by Ben Bella: the Communists were excluded.

Conference. It was a stormy session; several ambassadors walked out after a dispute with Foreign Minister Bouteflika, who in turn was taken to task by Ben Bella for his handling of preparations for the conference. This meeting brought to a head a conflict between Ben Bella and his foreign minister that had been latent for months. The two men had initially gotten along well together because they agreed on the broad goals of Algeria's foreign policy and on the tactics to follow for achieving these goals. However, Bouteflika, who had served under Boumediene on the ALN General Staff, remained a close ally of the colonel, siding with him on most internal policy issues.[20] As the Afro-Asian Conference approached, new tensions arose between Ben Bella and Bouteflika because the president, anxious to assure the success of the conference, had taken over many of his foreign minister's functions. Immediately after the meeting of the ambassadors, Ben Bella asked Bouteflika to resign, but Bouteflika refused.[21] Nevertheless, the president did not abandon the idea of ousting his foreign minister and began to prepare for the inevitable showdown with the Boumediene faction.

Ben Bella first sought to placate his other major opponents and if possible to gain their backing. In early June, he released Ferhat Abbas and six other important opposition figures from confinement in the Sahara Desert.[22] At the same time, his emissaries contacted in Paris representatives of the FFS, the Kabyle opposition group, in order to negotiate a settlement of that conflict. An agreement was soon reached. On June 16, the Algerian newspapers carried on the front page and under banner headlines a communiqué of the outlawed front announcing that the FFS would cease all hostilities as of that day.[23] The recon-

20. Bouteflika and Boumediene had also strongly opposed Ben Bella's plan for ending the border disputes with Tunisia and Morocco by making some territorial concessions. During a meeting with the king of Morocco in May 1965, Ben Bella had reportedly agreed to open negotiations in the near future. His willingness to compromise appeared largely to be due to his desire to see the king participate in the Afro-Asian Conference.

21. In his interview with *Al-Ahram*, cited in note 5, Boumediene claimed that Bouteflika had actually agreed to resign, provided that the Political Bureau or the Central Committee asked him to do so. Ben Bella refused to bring the question before either body, arguing that the constitution gave him the right to name and dismiss his ministers.

22. Released along with Abbas were Amar Bentoumi, former minister of justice; Abderrahmane Farès, a deputy; Boualem Oussedik, a deputy; Major Si Larbi, former commander of the Constantine military region; Si Azzedine, a former wilaya officer who had joined the FFS; and Brahim Mezhoudi, a deputy. They had all been arrested in the summer of 1964.

23. The communiqué said: "Discussions have taken place between the FLN and the FFS. Considering the fact that national unity is the major concern of all Algerians

ciliation was undoubtedly in the mutual interest of the FFS and Ben Bella. For the front it was an opportunity to end its unsuccessful guerrilla war without admitting defeat and to obtain an amnesty for all its members and possibly even a position in the government for Ait Ahmed. For Ben Bella it was a means by which to lessen his dependency on the army and to gain the backing of Ait Ahmed and his supporters against Boumediene, whom they hated. The colonel, in fact, had long feared a reconciliation between Ben Bella and the FFS, knowing that it could only be at his expense. In an effort to prevent such a development, Boumediene himself had reportedly tried to negotiate with Ait Ahmed shortly after the latter's capture in October 1964.[24]

The publicity given by the official press to a communiqué of an outlawed opposition party greatly surprised the public and for the first time raised suspicions that the government was in serious trouble. But Ben Bella denied the existence of a conflict among the country's leaders. "In Algeria," he declared, "there is one socialist revolution, one country, one regime, and one leadership more united than ever, more determined than ever to uncover all plots, whatever their origin, above all, foreign plots."[25] However, the leadership was not as united as Ben Bella pretended. The day after giving this speech, Ben Bella cut short a tour of western Algeria and flew back to the capital, calling a meeting of the Political Bureau for the next day, June 19. He had reportedly been warned by a deputy that something was amiss.

The meeting of the Political Bureau never took place. In the early hours of the morning of June 19, Boumediene's army moved swiftly and efficiently to take over control of the country, arresting Ben Bella in his bed. Boumediene met with little resistance because the men upon whom Ben Bella counted to protect him from a *coup*—Colonel Tahar Zbiri, chief of the General Staff; Major Ahmed Draia, commander of the Compagnie Nationale de Sécurité (CNS); and Major Mahmoud Guennez, commander of the party-controlled people's militia—had joined the plot. It was actually Tahar Zbiri who came to arrest Ben

---

and that the superior interest of Algeria demands that all forces be mobilized in an effort to consolidate the gains of the revolution, an agreement has been reached to put an end to the armed struggle. This decision will go into effect on June 16, 1965."

24. Ait Ahmed made this claim in an interview published in the FFS *Bulletin Intérieur* dated August 8, 1966.

25. Ben Bella's speech of June 17, 1965. In the same speech, Ben Bella also sought to correct the impression that the FFS had been officially recognized as a legal political party or that there had been a formal agreement with it.

Bella.[26] Three of the president's key allies—Mohamed Nekkache, Hadj Ben Alla, and Abderrahmane Cherif—were also arrested. Reportedly, Ben Alla was the only one to put up a struggle; his house was found pockmarked with bullet holes the next day.

Algerians awoke on the morning of June 19 to find the radio playing patriotic songs and military marches instead of the usual programs; but most Algerians went to work that morning without realizing that a *coup* had taken place.[27] It was only around noon that the Algiers radio station broadcast a proclamation from a body calling itself the Conseil de la Révolution (Revolutionary Council), informing the people of what had taken place. The proclamation explained that the army had seized power to save the country from the evils of "personal power" and to organize "a democratic and responsible state." It also enumerated the many crimes and misdeeds committed by Ben Bella since his rise to power:

> After three years of independence, the country is prey to shady maneuvers, to the clash of factions and groups revived in the interest of an old device of governing: divide and rule. The sordid calculations, the political narcissism, and the morbid love of power find their best illustration in the systematic liquidation of the country's cadres and in the criminal attempt to discredit the former guerrillas and resistance fighters. . . .
>
> People of Algeria:
>
> The men who today answer your desperate appeal, convinced that in doing so they are fulfilling your dearest wish, take the responsibility of restoring your usurped freedom and your trampled dignity. It was high time to diagnose the disease, to isolate it, and to denounce it. It was above all necessary to put an end to this dramatic situation. No matter [what] the importance of his mission, no one [man] can claim to incarnate alone Algeria, the revolution, and socialism. . . .
>
> The record speaks for itself:

26. Major Draia played a key role in the arrest of Ben Bella. The sentries at the Villa Joly were under his command, and he was thus able to assign persons whom he could trust to guard Ben Bella's residence that night. Consequently, no one gave the alarm when Zbiri and a group of armed soldiers arrived at the Villa Joly. In addition, the head of Ben Bella's personal bodyguard had betrayed the president, further facilitating entry into the Villa Joly.

27. One reason why many Algerians did not immediately realize that something abnormal was afoot was that there had been many tanks and troops in and about Algiers during the preceding days as part of the scenery for *The Battle of Algiers*, a film that recounted an important episode in the war of independence. Even on June 19, many believed that the tanks in the city were part of the décor for the film.

Boumediene addressing peasants
(Pierre Ferrenbach)

Ahmed Kaid, head of the FLN
(K. Updegraff)

Women voting in the communal elections of February 1967
(Pierre Ferrenbach)

Ben Bella addressing a crowd in a small tow

. Updegraff)

One of the few French farmers to remain in Algeria after independence teaches an
Algerian farmer how to prune vines
(K. Updegraff)

Women of the Kabylia out to greet Ben Bella
(Louis Giminez)

Ben Bella (with girls) and Boumediene on a tour of the country in 1963
(Louis Giminez)

Foreign Minister Abdelaziz Bouteflika
(K. Updegraff)

Crowds in Algiers June 9, 1967, protesting Nasser's decision to agree to a cease-fire with
Israel following the Arab-Israeli war
(Pierre Ferrenbach)

Hocine Ait Ahmed, leader of the 1963–1964 rebellion against Ben Bella (Associated Press)

Mohamed Khider, head of the FLN in 1962 and Ben Bella's principal opponent until Ben Bella ousted him in April 1963 (Associated Press)

Mismanagement of the country's wealth, squandering of public funds, instability, demagoguery, anarchy, lying, and improvisation have been imposed as methods of government. By threats, blackmail, violation of individual liberties, and creating uncertainty about the future, an attempt has been made to reduce some persons to docility, others to fear, silence, and resignation.

Personal power having become a system of government, all national and regional institutions of the party and government find themselves at the mercy of one man, who delegates responsibility as he wishes, who makes and unmakes the governing bodies of the country according to unsound and improvised tactics, and who imposes policies and men according to his mood, whim, and caprice.[28]

The proclamation was signed by Houari Boumediene in the name of the Revolutionary Council, but there was no indication who the other members of the council were, and for good reason: the council was still in the process of being formed. The *coup* had been masterminded by a small clique of politicians and officers—Boumediene, Bouteflika, Kaid, Belkacem, Medeghri, Colonel Zbiri, and Major Draia. But this group, which represented only a part of the army and one of the wilaya clans, could not hope to retain power without facing major opposition, possibly from within the army itself. Furthermore, Boumediene was anxious to avoid giving the impression that the army, which was not popular in the country, had acted alone and that Algeria was headed for a military dictatorship. In order to make the new regime more representative and more popular, Boumediene sought to enlarge the council before announcing its composition.

The plotters had acted before the Revolutionary Council was formed for two reasons. First, they felt compelled to act immediately, fearing that Ben Bella was preparing a move against them. As one of the organizers of the *coup* declared later: "For us, it was a race against time. It was 'his' *coup d'état*, or it was 'ours.' There was no time to hesitate."[29] Second, Boumediene knew that there were many in the Cabinet and Political Bureau who were dissatisfied with Ben Bella's rule but who would not dare to jeopardize their own political future by entering into an adventure of uncertain outcome. For instance, Ben Bella had

28. *Le Peuple*, June 20, 1965.
29. See *Jeune Afrique*, July 4, 1965. It appears that Boumediene had made plans for a *coup d'état* well in advance of June 1965. However, the final decision to act was not made until Boumediene, returning on May 31 from a meeting of the Arab League in Cairo, heard that Ben Bella had demanded that Bouteflika resign from the government.

finally alienated both Ali Mahsas and Bachir Boumaza, members of his "brain trust," by blaming the country's economic difficulties on their mismanagement.[30] Mohand ou el-Hadj was still disgruntled because of the minor role Ben Bella allowed him and other former wilaya leaders to play in the regime. Even left-wing party officials like Hocine Zahouane were discontent because Ben Bella often took major decisions without consulting the Political Bureau. Still, none of these men was personally close to Boumediene, and with the possible exception of Mohand ou el-Hadj, all of them were at the opposite end of the ideological spectrum. It is highly doubtful that any of them regarded a takeover by the army as a desirable alternative to Ben Bella's rule. Boumediene did not dare to confide his plans to persons who, presented with a clear choice between him and Ben Bella, might well have opted for the latter.

Ben Bella had been warned that the Boumediene faction was preparing a move against him, but he did not think that the danger was imminent.[31] He knew that Boumediene was too isolated politically to force a vote of no-confidence through the Central Committee or the Political Bureau, and he thought he had some control over the army through his appointee to the General Staff, Colonel Tahar Zbiri.[32] But Boumediene had slowly won the confidence of Zbiri, convincing him that Ben Bella was deliberately playing the former wilaya leaders against the professional officers in the army in order to weaken the position of both. Personal revenge also played a part in Zbiri's betrayal: he was still smarting over a public insult from Ben Bella a short time before the *coup*. Perhaps the main reason why the president was caught

30. Just a few days before the *coup*, Ben Bella had castigated the two ministers during an extraordinary session of the FLN Central Committee that had been called to discuss the country's worsening economic situation. The session lasted from June 14 to June 16, 1965.

31. Sources close to Ben Bella disclosed after the *coup* that the president had been warned by a deputy that he was in serious trouble. A few days before the *coup*, Ben Bella was also overheard confiding his suspicions about Boumediene to Mohand ou el-Hadj and asking for el-Hadj's support.

32. Members of the Revolutionary Council claimed that they had a majority in the Political Bureau and could have passed a vote of no-confidence against Ben Bella; they said, however, that they had not tried to do so, believing that Ben Bella would not bow even to a majority decision. While it is true that by July 5 ten of the sixteen members of the Political Bureau had sided with Boumediene (the seventeenth, Chaabani, had been executed), it is highly doubtful that a majority would have voted against Ben Bella on June 19. It should also be pointed out that the Political Bureau had no right to take a vote of confidence, since Ben Bella was responsible only to the FLN Congress.

off guard was that he simply could not believe that Boumediene, whatever his intentions, would act on the eve of the Afro-Asian Conference.

While Boumediene was engaged in consultations with representatives of all major political groups, Algeria lived tense days. The *coup* had taken Algerians completely by surprise, and those who were opposed to it did not seem to know what to do. Few wanted to act rashly or endanger their lives before it was known exactly who was in power, but many wished that somebody would organize an opposition and "issue orders." But no orders came because most of Ben Bella's former allies were holding talks with Boumediene in an effort to assess his policies and their own political futures. Only the Communists, who were fully aware of Boumediene's deep antipathy toward them, reacted immediately and organized demonstrations against the army. During the first week after the *coup*, Communists and left-wing students, among them some foreigners, rampaged almost nightly through the streets of the capital, shouting "Long live Ben Bella" and "Boumediene Assassin." The demonstrators were rapidly dispersed each time by gendarmes reinforced by army troops, and they never succeeded in bringing crowds of more than a thousand into the streets. Only in Annaba and Oran did the demonstrations draw larger crowds and assume a violent character, leading to the deaths of perhaps fifty Algerians at the hands of the army.

Although the *coup* was not followed by a general uprising, there was hardly any public show of support for the new regime, and there were no demonstrations in its favor. The position of the Revolutionary Council was too ambiguous for the council to win the approval of more than a few groups. Spokesmen for the council repeatedly stressed that nothing had changed in Algeria except for one man and that the council upheld the principles contained in the March Decrees and the Algiers Charter. One of them declared:

> I warn all those who doubt, all those who have the unjustified hope of seeing us change our present policies and jeopardize the gains of the revolution, I tell them with force and frankness that anybody who sets himself against our present orientation, . . . against the decisions of the [party] congress contained in the Algiers Charter, will be crushed by the revolution.[33]

33. Declaration of Ali Mendjli in *El-Moudjahid*, June 26, 1965.

However, this and similar declarations did not dispell the widely held belief that the new regime would be much more conservative than Ben Bella's in its policies. On this assumption, religious leaders and conservative groups expressed their support of the Revolutionary Council in a flurry of telegrams and messages in the days following the *coup*. A few other groups also indicated their support: the war veterans because they felt they had been neglected by Ben Bella; some party and government officials because they wanted to keep their jobs; doctors and hospital nurses because Ben Bella had wanted to make them civil servants; the Algiers Chamber of Commerce because it hoped some of the small enterprises nationalized under Ben Bella might be given back to their owners; and the Organization of Moslem Scouts because it was bitter over Ben Bella's interference in its affairs.

Also on the assumption that the new regime would be conservative, none of the left-wing groups backed the Revolutionary Council. Yet most of them were slow in deciding upon a line of action, and by the time they came to a decision public indignation at the *coup* had given way to a wait-and-see attitude. As a result, the Left never succeeded in organizing an effective opposition to the Revolutionary Council. The leftist faction of the party, led by Zahouane, Harbi, and other officials of the Algiers Federation, did not immediately declare its opposition but instead held talks with Boumediene to see if there were grounds for cooperation. However, only Abdelaziz Zerdani, who was a wartime friend of Zbiri, finally sided with the Revolutionary Council.[34] Harbi and Zahouane soon passed to the opposition, the former to be arrested within a few days, the latter to organize with leaders of the Algerian Communist party the clandestine Organization de la Résistance Populaire (ORP).

The UGTA was faced with a dilemma. The federation's executive committee did not trust Boumediene, fearing that he would deprive the UGTA of the autonomy it had only recently gained. On the other hand, the UGTA leaders were afraid that if they declared their open opposition to the council the army would arrest them and disband the federation. Following a series of talks with Boumediene, they chose a compromise solution. They avoided any show of hostility toward the

34. Zerdani had been the political commissar of Wilaya One, of which Zbiri was commander-in-chief. After independence, Zerdani remained a close friend and advisor of Zbiri. He passed for a Marxist and is credited with having written the Algiers Charter in collaboration with Harbi. His friendship with Zbiri was apparently stronger than his commitment to an ideology.

regime and did not encourage union members to join the demonstrations. At the same time, they issued a carefully worded resolution in which they declared that the UGTA approved the principles set forth in the proclamation of June 19 but showed great reserve toward the Revolutionary Council itself:

> The executive committee takes note of the commitments made in the June 19 proclamation.
>
> .   .   .   .
>
> It notes, however, that the continued presence on, or the return to, the political scene of opportunists who have been responsible for the violation of our institutions in the past throws doubt on the meaning of the events of June 19. It declares the attachment of the workers to the gains of a ten-year struggle, namely national independence, self-management, and the edification of democratic socialism within the framework of self-management. The workers are ready to unite in a merciless struggle for the defense of these gains and against those who might consider acting in disregard of the profound aspirations of the Algerian people.[35]

The only national organizations that openly declared their opposition to the new regime were UNEA and the JFLN, whose leaders were among the organizers of the demonstrations that followed the *coup d'état*. However, the resistance of the two youth organizations did not last long. Within a few weeks, some of their leaders had fled the country, others had gone into hiding, and still others had been arrested.[36] As a consequence, the party was able to name executive committees favorable to the new regime. UNFA, the women's organization, also failed to channel its followers' marked antipathy for Boumediene into an organized opposition. In the cities some women spontaneously joined in the students' demonstrations or marched in their own small groups through the streets shouting "Long live Ben Bella," but the leadership of UNFA was unable to decide what to do, and for some time the union ceased to function altogether.

The composition of the Revolutionary Council was finally made public on July 5, as Algeria celebrated the third anniversary of its independence in an atmosphere more of mourning than of joy. There were no flags flying except those on government buildings, and there

35. See *El-Moudjahid*, June 28, 1965.
36. Among the UNEA leaders arrested were three vice-presidents, including Nourredine Zenine, one of the most prominent pro-Communist students.

were no parades or rallies. Boumediene did not appear in public, choosing instead to read his Independence Day message to the nation over radio and television. Such was his phobia for personal publicity that his image did not even appear on the television screen, which remained blank while he spoke. Following his speech, the names of the Revolutionary Council's members were announced.

The twenty-six-man council was made up almost entirely of army officers and former wilaya leaders. It included the commanders of the five military regions, four members of the ANP General Staff, the commanders of the gendarmerie and CNS, the assistant director of the Cherchell Military Academy, and six former wilaya leaders no longer serving in the army.[37] The core of the council consisted of Boumediene and five of his associates on the wartime ALN General Staff—Abdelaziz Bouteflika, Cherif Belkacem, Ahmed Kaid, Ahmed Medeghri, and Ali Mendjli. Although they had returned to civilian life after independence, these men were considered "military" because of their close relationship to Boumediene. Ali Mahsas and Bachir Boumaza were the only two "civilians"—men who had not served in the ALN or who were not associated with the ANP. Ten members of the council belonged to the Political Bureau.

Boumediene was officially declared president of the council, and he was also charged with forming a new government. He had reportedly not wanted to be both president of the council and head of government in order to avoid being accused of seeking personal power, the very accusation he had aimed at Ben Bella. However, he had not succeeded in finding a well-known civilian willing to serve as head of

37. The army officers were: Major Abid Said, commander of the First Military Region (Blida); Major Benjedid Chedli, commander of the Second Military Region (Oran); Major Salah Soufi, commander of the Third Military Region (western Sahara); Major Mohamed Abdelghrani Benhamed, commander of the Fourth Military Region (eastern Sahara); Major Abdellah Belhouchet, commander of the Fifth Military Region (Constantine); Major Abderrahmane Bensalem, member of the General Staff; Major Abdelkader Moulay, alias Chabou, member of the General Staff and chef de cabinet of the Ministry of Defense; Colonel Ahmed Boudjenane, alias Abbas, member of the General Staff and director of the Cherchell Military Academy; Colonel Tahar Zbiri, chief of the General Staff; Colonel Ahmed Bencherif, commander of the gendarmerie; Major Ahmed Draia, commander of the CNS; and Major Mohamed Salah Yahiaoui, assistant director of the Cherchell Military Academy. The six former wilaya leaders were: Salah Boubnider, alias Colonel Saout el-Arab; Youcef Khatib, alias Colonel Si Hassan; Colonel Mohand ou el-Hadj; Benhaddou Bouhadjar, alias Colonel Si Othmane; Mohamed Tayebi, alias Major Si Larbi (not the Si Larbi who revolted in February 1963); and Colonel Mohammedi Saïd (sometimes considered a civilian, since he was a minister in the GPRA after 1960). See Appendix II for biographies of the members of the Revolutionary Council.

government. All the politicians contacted, among them Ferhat Abbas, had refused to become the figurehead leader of a regime dominated by the army.[38]

The composition of the council suggested that Boumediene had finally succeeded in reconciling the wilaya leaders and the officers of the ANP. It also suggested that he had won over two of the most prominent figures in the Ben Bella government, Mahsas and Boumaza, and thus that there might be some continuity in the country's socialist policies, as the council promised. In reality there was no reconciliation among these three factions and no certainty about the council's future policies. Boumediene had simply made an effort to give representation to three of the major political groups of the country in the hope of broadening the base of his regime. He expected this coalition to rule as a collegial body, reaching unanimous decisions on all major policy issues. The announcement of the council's makeup answered some of the questions about the new ruling group, but it was still unclear what the council's functions and prospective relations with government and party would be. There were even rumors that the party would be disbanded. Boumediene offered no clarification of these problems, and it is probable that he himself did not know at that time just what his plans were.

After another week of negotiation, Boumediene finally formed a government, which took office on July 12. Besides Boumediene, there were no army officers among the twenty ministers, half of whom had served in the last Ben Bella Cabinet. Boumediene and his allies took over the key posts: the colonel himself was president and minister of defense; Bouteflika remained minister of foreign affairs; Ahmed Medeghri was restored to his old post of minister of the interior; and Ahmed Kaid became minister of finance. Mahsas remained minister of agriculture, while Boumaza was demoted from minister of economy and industry to minister of information. The strength of the Left was seemingly increased by the presence of Abdelaziz Zerdani as the new minister of labor; Boumediene hoped that Zerdani would be his link to the UGTA. The colonel also brought into the government Rabah

38. Another leader contacted by Boumediene was Abdelhafid Boussouf, his former protector in the GPRA. Boussouf, who had retired from politics since Ben Bella's rise to power, came back to Algiers shortly after the *coup*, declaring that he had absolute confidence in the new group in power. There were reports that he had been asked to serve as prime minister, but there was apparently too much opposition to his appointment, and the idea was abandoned.

Bitat, one of the historic nine leaders of the revolution, with the honorific title of minister of state and for the apparent purpose of giving his regime greater respectability. A number of posts in the government went to "technicians," ministers supposed to be apolitical and particularly qualified for their task.[39] In presenting the new government, Boumediene explained the principle of collegiality that was to be the guideline of his regime:

> No one will be allowed to impose his ideas or his will on the others.
>
> . . . .
>
> The ministers will be responsible to the Council of Ministers, which will judge them according to their work, it being understood that each minister must execute the decisions of the higher authorities.
>
> . . . .
>
> The government has decided to substitute democratic centralism and collegiality for personal power; it has decided to put an end to favoritism in the division of responsibilities and tasks.[40]

Boumediene did not specify who the "higher authorities" were, but it was understood he referred to the Revolutionary Council.

On July 20, Boumediene installed a five-man executive secretariat of the FLN, which was to remain in power until a new party congress could be held. The secretariat's "coordinator" was a trusted aide of Boumediene, Cherif Belkacem; the other positions were held by former wilaya leaders, namely Mohand ou el-Hadj, Salah Boubnider (alias Colonel Saout el-Arab), Youcef Khatib (alias Colonel Si Hassan), and Mohamed Tayebi (alias Major Si Larbi), all of them members of the Revolutionary Council.

In his speech, Boumediene declared that under Ben Bella the FLN had failed to play the role of a revolutionary avant-garde party, becoming instead unpopular in the country:

> He tried to make the party into an instrument of his personal policy; he introduced [into the party] arbitrariness, nepotism, clan politics, agitation, and improvisation, leading to the creation of new feudalities, a race for power, and the dilapidation of our country's riches.
>
> He made unpopular, not only the party, but the very idea of a party, by perfidiously blaming it for his own maneuvers, his own failing, and the nefarious consequences of his own errors.[41]

39. For the complete list of ministers, see Appendix I.
40. Boumediene's speech of July 12, 1965.
41. Boumediene's speech of July 20, 1965.

Boumediene still gave no indication of the respective powers of the Executive Secretariat, which replaced the Political Bureau and the Central Committee, and of the Revolutionary Council. He declared that the party was to "elaborate and orient the government's policies in all areas," but this was also understood to be the function of the council.

The installation of the Executive Secretariat completed the reorganization of the country's governing bodies. Boumediene made no effort to legitimize the *coup* through a referendum or elections, claiming that there was no reason to do so because only one man had changed. Actually, he had suspended both the constitution and the National Assembly without announcing it and was apparently prepared to govern indefinitely through the Revolutionary Council and with the backing of the army.

In the meantime, members of the FLN, the PCA, the JFLN, and UNEA had organized an opposition party, the ORP, which circulated its first tract on July 28. Among the best known personalities in the new organization were Hocine Zahouane, a former member of the Political Bureau; Mohamed Harbi, a former advisor to Ben Bella; Bachir Hadj Ali, first secretary of the PCA; Houari Mouffok, president of UNEA; and Boualem Makouf, national secretary of the JFLN. A number of Europeans, mostly members of the French Communist party and the Fourth International, also joined the movement. Boumediene immediately made it clear that he would have no truck with the opposition, as Ben Bella had done. Harbi and Makouf were arrested in mid-August, Hadj Ali, Zahouane, and Mouffok in late September. By the end of that month, there were at least sixty members of the ORP in jail. The government publicized the presence of many French Communists among those arrested in an attempt to discredit the ORP. It claimed that the ORP was entirely in the hands of foreigners who had come to Algeria on the pretext of serving as "technical assistants" but who in reality had come with the aim of insinuating themselves into political positions and imposing their own Communist doctrines on the country. This initial wave of arrests badly weakened the ORP, leaving it without a strong leadership. As a consequence, it never developed into a significant opposition group.

chapter ten

the second cycle

The true meaning of June 19 can be summarized thus: neither leader, nor leadership, nor message, nor prophet.[1]

Houari Boumediene

June 19 began a new cycle in the political life of Algeria. The *coup d'état* brought to power a coalition of clans similar to the one that had imposed itself in the fall of 1962. The factions that made up the Revolutionary Council had little more in common than their desire for power and their hostility toward the former president, just as the clans led by Ben Bella, Khider, Boumediene, and Abbas had in common only their ambition and their animosity toward the GPRA. There was no more consensus on ideological issues and concrete programs within the Revolutionary Council than there had initially been in the Ben Bella regime. Boumediene, like Ben Bella, was confronted with the problem of how to rule when surrounded by ambitious allies defending widely different interests. His approach to this problem, however, was antithetical to that of his predecessor.

Ben Bella had sought to dissolve the coalition formed during the summer civil war, to impose his programs, and to form a new alliance with groups that shared his convictions and backed his socialist policies. Boumediene, on the other hand, sought to maintain the Revolutionary Council such as it was and to elaborate a compromise program acceptable to all his allies. The colonel's intentions were made clear in his repeated pledges to respect the principle of "collegial leadership," which meant that all members of the council would participate with equal weight in the decision-making process. He vehemently denounced Ben Bella's one-man rule, comparing him to Messali Hadj, the national-

1. Boumediene's speech of March 6, 1966.

ist leader against whose "tyranny" the founders of the FLN had revolted. Boumediene's charge that Ben Bella had been a "diabolic dictator" was almost ludicrous, since far from being omnipotent, Ben Bella had always lacked the power to realize any of his policies. Still, it was true that Ben Bella had never accepted, even in theory, the principle of collegiality that had been a guideline of the FLN since its creation. In this sense, Ben Bella was a "deviationist," as Algeria's new leaders claimed.

The differences between Ben Bella and Boumediene were also reflected in the conception each had of which were the dynamic political groups in the country. Although both declared that power should be put in the hands of the "revolutionary forces," Ben Bella was referring to the workers, the peasants, and the leftist intellectuals, while Boumediene meant the *mujahidin*[2]—the veterans of the war of independence—and the army. The colonel accused Ben Bella of having discredited the war veterans and of having denied them posts in the party and administration. One of his primary objectives was to rehabilitate the mujahidin and the army, which he described as the "guardians of the revolution." On the other hand, he was determined to exclude from the government "all professional politicians, self-styled prophets, and historic leaders,"[3] whom he held primarily responsible for Algeria's political instability.

In speech after speech, Boumediene attempted to convince Algerians that the ANP was truly a "people's army," pointing out that its officers and men were peasants who had taken up arms to free their country from colonial domination and not a caste of professional soldiers brought up in military academies. He emphasized that the army's role in independent Algeria was to contribute to the "national campaign for the construction of the new revolutionary and socialist society";[4] yet his overriding concern since independence had in fact been to transform his army of peasants into a professional, modern army. For this purpose he had reduced the size of the ANP from 100,000 to about 50,000 men, slowly weeding out many of the former guerrillas who were uneducated and incapable of mastering the use of modern arms.

2. The Arabic word *mujahid* means "freedom fighter." The French-language press in Algeria refers to the veterans of the war for independence as *"anciens moudjahidine,"* or veteran freedom fighters.

3. Boumediene's interview with the Cairo newspaper *Al-Ahram*, October 8–10, 1965, reprinted in *Révolution Africaine*, No. 143, October 23, 1965.

4. Boumediene's speech of December 4, 1965.

At the same time, he had made a major effort to recruit young Algerians with a high school or university education[5] and had organized numerous army schools.[6] Boumediene had even integrated into the ANP some 250 Algerian officers trained in the French army, many of whom had rallied to the FLN cause only late in the course of the war. Most prominent among these officers were Slimane Hoffman, commander of the tank corps, and Major Abdelkader Moulay, alias Chabou, member of the General Staff and Boumediene's chef de cabinet in the Ministry of Defense.[7] Boumediene also sent some 2,000 officers to military academies in Egypt and the Soviet Union. The cadres of the ANP were therefore divided into three distinct groups: the officers trained in the French army, who did most of the work of the General Staff and appeared to be the closest to Boumediene; the former guerrilla commanders, who headed some of the military regions and were the most active politically; and the young officers trained abroad after independence, who occupied none of the highest posts but formed the bulk of the officer corps.

The ANP attempted to maintain the appearance of a "people's army." Its highest rank was that of colonel, and only four officers held that title.[8] There was no showy display of ribbons and medals on the uniforms of even the highest officers, and the motto of the army was "the gun and the spade." Actually, the ANP contributed little to the building of socialist Algeria. Although it sent representatives to participate in party-sponsored village reconstruction and tree-planting

5. In early 1962, there were about 40,000 soldiers in the ALN outside Algeria and between 6,000 and 8,000 inside. After the conclusion of the Evian Peace Agreements in March of that year, thousands of Algerians joined the ALN, including many who had fought up to that time on the side of the French. By the summer of 1962, the ALN, interior and exterior forces combined, was estimated to number between 100,000 and 120,000 men.

6. The army has set up the following schools: engineers at Hussein Dey; communications at Bouzareah; transport at Beni Messous and Batna; artillery at Telergma; NCO's at Boghari; gendarmes at Sidi-Bel-Abbès; *meharists* (camel corps) at Ouargla; cavalry at Lido; aviation at Chéragas; technicians at El-Harrach; and an interarmy military academy at Cherchell.

7. Other high-level ANP officers in this category are Major Mohamed Zerguini, member of the General Staff; Colonel Ahmed Boudjenane, alias Abbas, head of the Cherchell Military Academy; and Colonel Ahmed Bencherif, commander of the gendarmerie.

8. The four colonels are Boumediene; Zbiri; Boudjenane, alias Abbas; and Bencherif. Other Algerians who were colonels in the wartime ALN still use the title, notably Mohand ou el-Hadj, Saout el-Arab (Salah Boubnider), Si Hassan (Youcef Khatib), and Si Othmane (Benhaddou Bouhadjar).

campaigns, it never undertook on its own any important project. The army was looked upon by most Algerians as a privileged class of well-paid and well-provided men. In a country where the average per-capita income was about 300 dinars ($60) a year, privates received 200 dinars ($40) a month, plus family allowances. The Ministry of Defense was allotted about 500 million dinars ($100 million) in 1965, 15 per cent of the national budget and the second largest share after that of the Ministry of Education. In addition, over a three-year period the ANP had purchased over $200 million worth of heavy arms on long-term credits from the Soviet Union. The army was almost a state within a state, being virtually independent of government control. A sign of the army's special status in the country was its permission to maintain control over at least fifty large French farms and a number of small industrial enterprises that it had seized during the summer of 1962. These enterprises, misleadingly called "cooperatives," were run not by management committees but directly by army officers, although the workers were mostly civilians.

According to the Algiers Charter, the ANP was subject to the control of the FLN, which was to take particular charge of the "political education" of the soldiers. In practice, however, the army rejected all interference from the party and set up its own political commissariat. Before the *coup d'état*, the army magazine *El-Djeich* had followed a political line noticeably different from that of the party publication *Révolution Africaine*, upholding Boumediene's ideals rather than those expounded by the Algiers Charter. The colonel believed in the necessity for a *"retour aux sources,"* a revival of Algeria's Arabo-Islamic culture. As it was implemented, "return to the sources" actually meant the rejection of modern-day foreign ideologies, particularly Marxism. It also means giving power to those who had fought with arms for Algeria's independence.

Boumediene was intensely nationalistic and wanted the socialist revolution to be "specifically Algerian." It was never clear what he meant by this, but those Algerians who had supported Ben Bella feared that there would be no socialist revolution at all under Boumediene, and they particularly feared that the self-management system, modeled after a foreign example and brought to Algeria by foreign advisors, would be abandoned. Indeed, the new regime was almost xenophobic, seeing in every alien a spy and calling upon all Algerians to be aware of foreign subversion.[9] As a result of the government's attitude toward foreigners, many of the left-wing intellectuals who had come to Algeria after independence left for new revolutionary havens like Tanzania and Congo-Brazzaville. Among those who departed were some Frenchmen who had deserted the French army during the Algerian war and subsequently sought refuge in Algeria. Apparently they preferred to serve their prison terms rather than remain in Algeria in the new atmosphere of suspicion and hostility.

There was certainly little in the style of Colonel Boumediene to inspire Algerian or foreign revolutionaries. Boumediene was essentially a reformist and an organizer. He stressed the need for planning and reflection, and was wary of radical change. He abhorred noisy rallies, slogans, and inflammatory speeches, and liked to warn the crowds that hard work and sustained effort were the only means to carry out a revolution. Where Ben Bella had described the tasks to be accomplished as "difficult but exalting," Boumediene made them sound only difficult. He was neither a good speaker nor a pleaser of crowds. For a long time, he insisted on speaking in classical Arabic, which the vast majority of Algerians could hardly understand, and he refused to ingratiate himself with his audiences by saying what they wanted to hear. Boumediene realized that he was unpopular, and this realization did not help to make him feel at ease in public. He never heard the "youyou" of the women or shouts of "Yaya Boumediene," and he was rarely applauded. Aware that most Algerians disapproved of the *coup d'état*, he displayed an almost obsessive concern to justify his action, exposing in speech after speech the errors committed by Ben Bella.

The changes that took place after the overthrow of Ben Bella were not as radical as had been anticipated. Actually, they were so minor that many talked of "Ben Bellism without Ben Bella." Boumediene was by no means a free agent. First, he could not act before the twenty-six members of the Revolutionary Council reached a consensus, and reaching a consensus was an extremely slow process. Second, he did not want to appear anti-socialist for fear of stirring widespread discontent and opposition. Consequently, he never talked of repealing the Algiers

9. The first FLN *Bulletin Intérieur*, distributed to party cadres on June 19, 1966, denounced the "avalanche of foreign publications falling daily upon the country" as "an abuse of confidence and an attack upon our national sovereignty." It also called upon party members "to double their vigilance and thwart by all means the nefarious activities carried out [by foreigners] against our country."

Charter or the March Decrees, although he considered the former to propagandize Marxist ideas and the latter to have created chaos in the economy.

The first noticeable change brought about by the ouster of Ben Bella was one of pace. The summer of 1965, which had begun in the excitement of the Afro-Asian Conference and the *coup d'état*, ended in the most uneventful period Algeria had known since independence. It was a summer without rallies, without campaigns, and without celebrations; even the banners and billboards carrying revolutionary slogans were torn down. The Revolutionary Council decided to make itself as unobtrusive as possible until the country settled down, postponing all discussion of future reforms until after the Afro-Asian Conference scheduled for early November. In its efforts to remain unobtrusive, the new leaders ended by surrounding themselves with secrecy. Boumediene refused to appear in public for over four months, and if the Revolutionary Council met, the public was never informed of what had been decided. Many Algerians joked that the council was not a governing body but a secret society.

Most Algerians resigned themselves soon enough to the overthrow of Ben Bella. There was clearly a lack of enthusiasm for the new leadership, but few had any precise grudge against it. Ben Bella's former partisans' fears of sweeping anti-socialist reforms were somewhat allayed by the council's immobility. The first minor decisions taken by the government helped to relax tensions. In the cafés of the cities, Moslems were again allowed to order alcoholic beverages without fear of being arrested; civil servants were no longer required to attend indoctrination sessions organized by the party; and doctors and medical students no longer faced a period of compulsory civil service.[10] Within weeks of the *coup*, many Algerians who had at first expressed indignation were commenting that perhaps the order and stability promised

10. In October 1964, Ben Bella put the School of Medicine at the University of Algiers directly under the Ministry of Social Affairs, making the 570 medical students into civil servants. The students were supposed to serve in the public health service for two years after completing their studies. The government planned to use them in the hinterland, where there were few doctors. One of the first steps taken by the Boumediene government was to transfer the School of Medicine back to the Ministry of Education, freeing the students from the obligation of serving in the public health service. However, a decree of April 5, 1966, made all doctors who received their degree after that date permanently civil servants, while obliging the ones already practicing to work part time for the state. The decree also affected dentists, pharmacists, and midwives.

by Boumediene were what the country needed. Even the leaders of the ORP, some of whom had been advisors of Ben Bella, admitted in their tracts that the former president had committed many errors, making it clear that they were less interested in his return to power than in the continuation of a socialist policy.[11]

In the first months after the *coup d'état*, the Revolutionary Council devoted little attention to Algeria's internal problems. Instead, it focused its efforts on gaining diplomatic recognition, particularly from the African and Asian countries whose chiefs of state were scheduled to attend the Afro-Asian Conference in Algiers on November 5. Some fifteen delegations led by government ministers visited the capitals of Asia and Africa to convince other governments that the conference should still be held. Boumediene was not personally interested in the meeting, and he even declared at one point that "spending 150 million dinars [$30 million] for a five-day invitation is not revolutionary. . . . This policy of prestige will not be followed any longer."[12] Yet he did not dare unilaterally to cancel the conference because of the loss of prestige this would entail for Algeria. Even in the area of foreign relations, Boumediene found himself a prisoner of Ben Bella's policies. Despite the efforts made by the Algerian government, the foreign ministers of forty-five African and Asian countries, meeting in Algiers in late October, unanimously decided to postpone the conference *sine die*.

The postponement of the conference finally permitted the Revolutionary Council to concentrate its energies on internal problems and, nearly five months after the *coup d'état*, to begin outlining its policies. On November 15, the council embarked upon a marathon debate that continued for two weeks. Despite the length of the discussion, the council's members could not agree on anything more than to continue existing policies. The document published at the end of the meeting proposed remarkably little that could be considered new. The council's

11. The attitude of the ORP toward Ben Bella was extremely ambiguous. For instance, in its first tract of July 28, 1965, it talked about Ben Bella's "weakness and tactical errors" and commented: "It is true that the power was fragile and that the absence of democratic, revolutionary, authentically socialist structures in the party, unions, and administration created a vacuum that one man could not indefinitely fill; it is even true that very often the militants . . . were disconcerted by the administrative methods and scheming of Ben Bella." Yet the tract declared that Ben Bella was the man who expressed "the most profound revolutionary aspirations of the working masses."

12. Boumediene's speech to Algerian journalists, October 20, 1965.

resolutions called for a reorganization of the party and the decentralization of the socialist farm sector; in addition, they promised that municipal elections and the long-awaited agrarian reform would take
place before the end of 1966.[13] The last two reforms had first been
announced by Ben Bella in 1962, and the party had already drawn up
preliminary plans for both. Ben Bella had also promised greater autonomy for the self-managed farms, and the Central Committee had formally voted to implement this reform a few days before the *coup
d'état*.[14] The council even repeated the specific proposals made by the
Central Committee: the creation of a state bank to finance the farms
and industrial enterprises of the socialist sector; a reform of the marketing system; an accelerated program to train badly needed technicians;
and the "enrichment" of the March Decrees. All these measures had
been demanded by the workers at the congresses of the socialist sector.
In effect, the council was picking up where Ben Bella had left off, only
proceeding more cautiously and methodically. Instead of rushing into
action, it decided to set up commissions to study thoroughly the agrarian
reform, the communal reform, the reorganization of the party, and the
enrichment of the March Decrees.

The only significant deviation from Ben Bella's policies that could
be detected from a study of the council's resolutions concerned the
party. The FLN was no longer the highest authority; rather, the council
elaborated policy and "charged" the party with seeing to its execution.
The resolutions did not admit that the FLN had been relegated to a
subordinate role, however, and still defined the party as "the first
institution of the country," responsible for "elaborating and orienting
policies."

The demotion of the FLN was not surprising, since it was known
that many members of the council opposed the existence of a strong
party, fearing that such a party might become a counterforce to the
council and the army. Nonetheless, Boumediene denounced "tenden-
tious criticisms accusing the June 19 movement of working against the
party and wanting to liquidate it,"[15] and he repeatedly stressed the
continuing importance of the FLN as the only organization capable of

13. The resolutions of the Revolutionary Council were published in *El-Moudjahid*,
December 1, 1965.
14. The Central Committee met in extraordinary session June 14–16 to discuss
economic problems. See *Le Peuple*, June 17, 1965, for the resolutions voted by the
committee.
15. Boumediene's speech to party officials, December 9, 1965.

mobilizing the revolutionary forces of the nation. However, he warned that the FLN would again fail in its mission if it were used, as it was under Ben Bella, "for destructive purposes against the militants of the ANP and the mujahidin."[16] Boumediene made it clear that he felt the party should be composed primarily of war veterans, whom he considered the link between two phases of the same revolution. He had already made sure that the party would become a stronghold of war veterans by appointing four former wilaya commanders to the Executive Secretariat.

Giving the war veterans a leading role in the FLN was just one of the steps taken by Boumediene in his general campaign to rehabilitate the war veterans. He also created a Ministry of Mujahidin and a National Council of Mujahidin to defend the interests of this group.[17] In addition, the council designated August 20 as National War Veterans Day, celebrating it in 1965 with great fanfare throughout the country. The new government made a special effort to provide pensions or jobs for the 300,000 who claimed to be veterans or war widows.[18] It even decided to take some farms away from the self-management committees in order to organize cooperatives for the war veterans. Because of the attention they were given, the veterans became the strongest supporters of the Boumediene regime. This was undoubtedly one reason why Boumediene wanted them to become the backbone of the party.

In its resolution of November 30, the council had called upon the party to establish its control over the national organizations. As Boumediene explained to party officials:

> This autonomy [of the national organizations] is contrary to the principle of a single party because in practice it leads to the formation of a multiplicity of parties within the single party, although this multiplicity

16. Ibid.

17. A Ministry of Mujahidin had existed in the first Ben Bella Cabinet but was eliminated in September 1963 when its functions were transferred to the Ministry of Social Affairs. In December 1964, the Ministry of Social Affairs became the Ministry of Health, Mujahidin, and Social Affairs.

18. After independence, some 300,000 Algerians put in claims for pensions as veterans, war widows, or war orphans. In the summer of 1966, the Ministry of Mujahidin undertook to examine all 300,000 claims, since it believed that many were fraudulent. By April 1967, Minister Ben Hamouda reported that 250,000 claims had been examined and 150,000 accepted. See El-Moudjahid, April 3, 1967. In August 1966, the minister announced that about 33,000 veterans had been found jobs: 13,000 were given employment in the administration; 8,000 received licenses for taxis or cafés; 3,500 were settled on the war veterans' cooperatives. The others had been found jobs in the private sector or in state-run enterprises. See El-Moudjahid, August 16, 1966.

appears in the form of political and regional clans or of national organizations.[19]

The FLN Executive Secretariat immediately undertook the task of imposing its leaders and its programs on the national organizations. It was the same policy followed for two years by Ben Bella, and again it met with little success.

Two of the national organizations, the JFLN and UNFA, had practically ceased to exist following the *coup d'état*. Here the party's problem was not overcoming the opposition of the members to an imposed leadership, but recruiting adherents among the youth and the women, the majority of whom remained hostile to Boumediene. Reviving the two organizations proved almost impossible. For example, UNFA leaders conducted with some success a campaign to recruit new members before the union's first congress in November 1966; however, once the congress elected a moderate leadership submissive to the party, the most militant feminists again dropped out of the union. In June 1967, UNFA claimed a membership of 25,000, only 350 of whom came from the city of Algiers; before the *coup d'état*, the Algiers federation of the union had been the largest and most militant.[20] UNFA and the JFLN continued to exist formally, their leaders sending telegrams of support to the Revolutionary Council on appropriate occasions and appearing at public ceremonies. However, neither organization played a significant political role.

Taking over UNEA proved much more difficult. Although many of its old leaders had been arrested or had fled the country, a clandestine committee maintained more control over the key Algiers section than did the national executive appointed by the party in September 1965. Most of the union's sections abroad also refused to recognize the new executive; the Paris section set up an "exterior delegation," which was

19. Boumediene's speech of December 9, 1965.
20. UNFA's first congress took place in Algiers November 19–21, 1966, with 500 delegates participating. The delegates elected a forty-four-member national council, composed for the most part of the same moderate and conservative women whom the FLN had appointed after the *coup d'état*. A few militant members of the council dropped out shortly after the congress. Shortly before the congress was held, Mamia Chentouf, the secretary-general of UNFA, complained in an interview with *Révolution Africaine* that the young women and the women of Algiers had little interest in the union. These were precisely the groups that had most strongly supported Ben Bella. One of UNFA's few accomplishments since the *coup* has been to establish a skeleton organization throughout the country. The union has also become involved in several pilot family planning projects. For more details on UNFA, see *Révolution Africaine*, No. 242, October 2–8, 1967.

accepted as the legitimate leadership of UNEA by the Communist and most of the Arab student unions.[21] The failure of the party to control UNEA was made clear in a series of incidents that occurred in late January 1966. During a rally called to protest the Paris kidnapping of Moroccan opposition leader Mehdi Ben Barka, students began shouting anti-Boumediene slogans. The police quickly broke up the rally and later raided the university campus, arresting thirteen Moroccan and Algerian students. In retaliation, the clandestine leadership of UNEA called for a three-day boycott of classes, which the party-appointed executive was unable to stop. Nearly all the 8,000 students at the University of Algiers went on strike. The Revolutionary Council was extremely embarrassed by this first overt sign of opposition since the *coup d'état*. It blamed the incidents on "foreign agents," expelled ten students from the university, and replaced the leaders of UNEA, who had proven so ineffectual.[22] The appointment of a new executive did nothing to improve relations between the party and the student body. The students continued to demand that UNEA be allowed to hold democratic elections and that their imprisoned leaders, including Mouffok, be released. The party steadfastly refused to yield, and as a consequence the students lost all interest in UNEA, which became a marginal, apolitical organization.

In its relations with the UGTA, the party followed a different tactic. Not daring to impose a new executive committee upon the federation, it tried to force the one in power to submit to its control. The UGTA

21. UNEA's "exterior delegation" was extremely active in the international student world, attending congresses in order to gain the support of other student unions against the Boumediene regime and the party-appointed executive committee. It was greatly aided by a "committee of support and solidarity" created in Paris by twenty-three student unions led by the French, Moroccan, and North African student organizations. The Moscow-sponsored International Union of Students also gave active moral and financial support to the "exterior delegation." UNEA's dissident members successfully kept the party-appointed leadership isolated from the international student community. Even the pro-Western International Student Conference would not recognize UNEA's new executive committee because it had not been elected.

22. On February 19, the party installed a new executive committee led by Laadi Flici, a medical student who had remained in Algeria throughout the war of independence and was violently opposed to the pro-Communist students, most of whom had spent the war years abroad. Flici believed that students as such had no role to play in politics and that the union's primary concern should be to solve the material problems of student life. He never succeeded in creating a nucleus of "militant party students" in UNEA and was in turn dismissed by the party in November 1966. The new executive committee, the third in sixteen months, was even more closely aligned with the party.

leaders resisted all attempts to deprive the union of its autonomy, all the more so because they regarded the Revolutionary Council as a conservative body. In particular, they considered such influential members of the council as Ahmed Kaid, Ahmed Medeghri, and Cherif Belkacem to be opponents of the self-management system, and they noted that Boumediene himself had stated that "we are for self-management but not at any price."[23] After seeing some nationalized restaurants and hotels handed back to their Algerian owners and some of the richest self-managed farms given over to the war veterans, the UGTA wondered precisely what the council meant when it talked of enriching the March Decrees. It was equally disquieting to the workers that the police were allowed to break up several strikes in the fall of 1965. Despite their apprehensions, union leaders shied away from a direct confrontation with the council, knowing full well that the outcome would not be in their favor. Boumediene was at first equally anxious to avoid an open conflict with the UGTA because any move against the federation was bound to be interpreted as a sign that his regime was anti-socialist.

In February 1966, it seemed that relations between Boumediene and the UGTA were on the mend. On February 24, during a meeting held to celebrate the tenth anniversary of the UGTA's foundation, Boumediene called for the "unity of revolutionary forces."[24] Since this was the expression Ben Bella had used to indicate an alliance of workers, peasants, and leftist intellectuals, it seemed at the time that Boumediene was preparing his own "opening to the Left." However, an incident that occurred during the following month again raised considerable doubt about Boumediene's true intentions. Union officials discovered that over twenty large farms, confiscated in 1964 from Algerians accused of collaborating with the French during the war, had been restored to their owners.[25] The UGTA protested vigorously, and Boumediene,

23. Boumediene's speech to Algerian journalists, October 20, 1965.
24. Oumeziane, who had met with Boumediene in mid-February to discuss party-union relations, was equally conciliatory, declaring in his speech that the UGTA was "an integral part" of the FLN.
25. According to the UGTA, twenty-one farms and one olive-canning factory were restored to their owners. The largest of these farms was a 2,000-hectare plantation near El-Asnam belonging to an extremely wealthy Algerian, Abderrahmane Bouthiba. Local UGTA officials told the authors that on March 29 Bouthiba, accompanied by the subprefect of El-Asnam, had appeared at the farm with an order of restitution. The El-Asnam local alerted Secretary-General Oumeziane, who went directly to Boumediene for an explanation. On April 8, all farms were returned to the workers.

fearing a national scandal, ordered that the farms be given back to the workers. Yet the issue of *Révolution et Travail* that had exposed the affair and declared the revolution to be in "mortal danger" was seized, and thereafter the publication was suppressed altogether.[26]

The orders for the restitution of the farms had come from Minister of the Interior Ahmed Medeghri, but it was never clear whether Boumediene had also given his consent. In any case, the UGTA preferred to believe that the president had been unaware of Medeghri's decision and even praised him for his prompt intervention in behalf of the workers. Apparently the federation's leaders still hoped they could convince Boumediene to defend the workers' interests if in return they offered him their support. This was the tactic the UGTA had successfully used on Ben Bella; however, it did not prove effective with Boumediene, who was not seeking new supporters to strengthen his position against his allies, as Ben Bella had sought to do in 1964. Although he had annulled the restitution of the twenty farms under pressure from the federation, the colonel later announced that a special commission was considering the possibility of returning 6,000 other properties to their owners.[27]

Although Boumediene was not willing to make major concessions in order to gain new supporters, he was definitely interested in winning greater acceptance for his regime in the spring of 1966. Emerging from the seclusion in which he had kept himself since the *coup d'état*, he began to take trips through the country and to expose himself to the public. His voyages were definitely not the triumphal tours of Ben Bella. He still preferred giving sober speeches to party officials and civil servants to addressing mass rallies. Whereas Ben Bella had freely mixed with the crowds, extraordinary security measures were taken to protect Boumediene. Before his trip to Constantine on March 6, for example, the police rounded up hundreds of potential troublemakers

26. The party was only too happy to suppress *Révolution et Travail*, which since the *coup* had been virtually an opposition paper, exposing the difficulties the management committees were having with the administration. The UGTA weekly did not appear again regularly until May 1967.

27. In October 1963, the Ben Bella government had begun a campaign to seize properties belonging to Algerian citizens accused of collaborating with the French during the war. Thousands of properties were nationalized over a period of a year. In October 1964, Ben Bella had authorized the restitution of a few hotels, restaurants, and bars nationalized "by error." Boumediene was just continuing the review of claims made by Algerians who considered themselves the victims of unjustified nationalizations. It is significant that the restitutions made by Ben Bella had not provoked a national scandal.

and thoroughly inspected all houses along the route his motorcade was to follow, demanding that all doors and windows be locked on the day of the president's visit. Both in Constantine and Oran he received only a lukewarm reception, with Algerians showing more curiosity about than enthusiasm for their little-known president. His refusal to speak to crowds in either city was apparently motivated by the fear that his appearance might trigger hostile demonstrations.

Indeed, Boumediene's first performances in the public light were hardly successful. The speech he gave on March 8, International Women's Day, was so maladroit that it provoked a walkout. Instead of encouraging the women to pursue their difficult struggle for equality as Ben Bella had done the previous year, he dwelled upon the social problems created by emancipation: "There is a problem of unemployment. When there is a job available, should we give it to a man or a woman? Should we leave the man at home and let the woman work?"[28] Although three-quarters of the women present wore haiks, he stated glibly that "the problem of the veil has never arisen in Algeria" and added that Algerian women had already won equality of rights during the war of independence. Embarrassed party officials finally had to bar the doors to prevent an exodus.

As the first anniversary of the *coup d'état* approached, Boumediene and the other members of the council were acutely aware that they were still not popular in the country. Their problem was not the opposition, which remained inconsequential, but the isolation in which they found themselves. Except for the war veterans, no group was wholeheartedly behind the council; with continual talk of socialism and an agrarian reform, even the bourgeois and the religious leaders were becoming skeptical about the regime. After a year, the attitude of most Algerians was still "Wait and see."

The little the Revolutionary Council had done did not give a clear indication of the regime's intentions or even prove that an era of order and efficiency had begun in Algeria. Commissions had been created to prepare an agrarian reform, a communal reform, a revision of the March Decrees, a new civil code, a fiscal reform, a new investment code, and an economic development plan. None of these commissions had completed its task by the end of May, and some, notably the commission concerned with the revision of the March Decrees, had not yet

28. *El-Moujahid*, March 9, 1966.

held a single meeting. Most of the concrete achievements the council could point to were completions of projects begun under Ben Bella, principally the signing of the new French-Algerian oil agreement in July 1965 and the inauguration in March 1966 of the country's third pipeline, the first owned and operated by the Algerian government.[29] The list of projects undertaken and finished after the *coup d'état* was hardly impressive. It included the complete reorganization of the courts to simplify the French system;[30] the first census of the population since independence;[31] and a third census of the biens vacants.[32] Boumediene had also made some progress in slowing down the "nomadism" of the civil servants, the continuous movement of personnel from one post to another that plagued the administration. He particularly prided himself on having put an end to the "waltz of the prefects" and on having given the prefects greater authority, thus beginning the decentralization of the administration.[33] But he had not succeeded in cutting down administrative costs: the 1966 administrative budget was 150 million dinars ($30 million) higher than the budget of the previous year.

29. Algeria's third trans-Saharan pipeline was the center of a controversy with France in 1964. Initially, French companies were to build, own, and operate the 500-mile line. The Algerian government asked for a 50 per cent share in the ownership, but the French companies offered only a minority share. Algeria then decided to build the pipeline on its own, obtaining for this purpose a $50.4 million loan from British banks and a $19.6 million loan from the Kuwait Development Fund. The pipeline was built by British companies. The initial capacity of the line was ten million tons a year and the potential capacity, twenty-two million tons.

30. Two decrees, dated November 16 and 17, 1965, eliminated many of the specialized courts that were part of the French system, giving greater authority to a reduced number of courts better distributed throughout the country. The lower-level courts were presided over by one instead of three judges, making it possible to have more tribunals in the rural areas. The reform was also supposed to speed up the process of justice. See *Journal Officiel*, No. 96, November 23, 1965, Ordonnances 65–278, 65–279, 65–280, and 65–281.

31. According to the census, the population of Algeria in March 1966 was 12,093,203. One of the most startling findings of the census was that there were 1.5 million abandoned children between the ages of eight and fifteen.

32. The first two censuses had never been completed, and in 1966 the government still did not know the exact number of houses and apartments abandoned by the French. Many occupants had never paid rent, and many had not even been asked to pay. Ben Bella had launched a campaign in early 1965 to persuade tenants to pay their rent, but the campaign had had little success. Boumediene established tighter control, making it necessary for Algerians to show rent receipts before they could obtain any legal document. This proved a much more successful system.

33. There was an important turnover of prefects and subprefects immediately after the *coup d'état*. In July 1965, ten out of the fifteen prefects and many of the one hundred subprefects were fired or transferred to new departments; but thereafter there were relatively few changes. Under Ben Bella the turnover had been fantastic. Some departments, notably Annaba and Oran, had had six or more prefects in thirty-three months.

In order to improve its record before the first anniversary of the *coup d'état*, the Revolutionary Council rushed into action. On May 7, the government suddenly announced the seizure of eleven foreign-owned mines and the formal nationalization of the *biens vacants*, which *de facto* had already been nationalized by Ben Bella. On May 24, Finance Minister Ahmed Kaid announced the creation of the long-awaited state bank that was to finance the socialist sector. Three days later, the government established a state monopoly over the insurance business, forcing the thirteen foreign companies operating in Algeria to close down. On June 2, Boumediene promulgated new civil service statutes, and on June 8, a new penal code. With the exception of the promulgation of the codes, all these measures were hastily taken in order to make more convincing the council's claim that the socialist revolution was continuing. As in Ben Bella's time, the revolution continued primarily at the expense of foreign interests. Even the style was reminiscent of Ben Bella's. Although it was highly unlikely that company officials would put up armed resistance, some of the foreign-owned mines were taken over by the ANP with a display of troops and machine guns, a technique the former president had used when he nationalized the Borgeaud farm in March 1963.

The impact of the nationalizations was greater abroad than at home. The takeover of the mines caused considerable tension in France and Morocco,[34] and the institution of a state monopoly over the insurance business created difficulties with Tunisia, whose state company controlled 40 per cent of the Algerian market. The nationalization of the *biens vacants* provoked France into temporarily suspending its aid program. At home, the measures were acknowledged by perfunctory telegrams of approval from party officials throughout the country but did not arouse much public enthusiasm. Even the UGTA, which had agitated for months in favor of the nationalization of the mines, was only partially satisfied, since the mines were to be managed by the state rather than by the workers.

The Revolutionary Council had acted too late to bridge the growing gap between it and the UGTA. The UGTA executive committee was

34. Most of the mines were owned by French companies. One of them, Gara Djebilet, was located near the Moroccan border in territory claimed by Morocco. The nationalization of Gara Djebilet caused considerable tension in relations between Algeria and Morocco. There was movement of troops on both sides of the border, and on May 20 an incident occurred, causing the death of one Moroccan and wounding four others.

less and less convinced that its policy of qualified support of the council was serving the interests of the federation. It's doubts were clearly shown in a union report of late May:

> Paradoxically, the workers today reproach our organization for not standing up for the demands they consider legitimate; the leaders of the country accuse it of creating problems, of stirring unrest and even opposition. This situation, which puts the federation between the hammer and the anvil, cannot last much longer without serious consequences for the workers and the country. . . . Our only contacts with the Executive Secretariat [of the FLN] since its installation have been the warnings, interdictions, and restrictions communicated to us. We have never been invited to participate in meetings dealing with the fight against unemployment, the training and education of the militants, or the application of self-management in agriculture, industry, commerce, etc. . . . Although our attitude is one of cooperation and support, we meet only with hostility, difficulties, ambushes, maneuvers, and strict surveillance.
>
> .   .   .   .
>
> We frankly believe that the only aim of these actions is to demobilize our organization and create fear among its members. Harrassment by the police is never a solution to political or other problems.[35]

The UGTA had steadily lost members since the change of regimes. In the Algiers local, the largest and most militant, the membership had declined from 42,000 in early 1965 to 28,000 in June 1966. Although no over-all figure was available, the decrease for the entire federation was believed to be at least of the same proportion and probably higher. By attempting to cooperate with the council, Secretary-General Oumeziane had ended by discrediting himself with the left-wing of the UGTA and by splitting the executive committee. The result was that some of the most militant members, including many officials, had joined the clandestine ORP. In late June, some seventy UGTA local officials and members were arrested in Constantine, Annaba, and Algiers in what appeared to be a government move to check the opposition and undermine the UGTA without directly attacking its national leadership. The arrests had the desired effect, for the federation's national secretaries were cowed into submission and did not dare to protest.[36]

35. See *Le Monde*, June 7, 1965. The report was never made public in Algiers, and the issue of *Le Monde* in which it appeared was banned from the country.
36. For a while, there was talk of a general strike, but the federation never went through with it. UGTA leaders were so uncertain of their position that they refused to talk with journalists, to whom they normally turned for publicity when they were

The arrests marked the demise of the UGTA as an important political force in Algerian politics. For a year, the federation had acted as the "conscience of the revolution," publicly denouncing all attempts to jeopardize the self-management system or to return nationalized properties to their former owners. Fear of a public confrontation with the UGTA had been an important factor in keeping the Revolutionary Council from departing significantly from the socialist course set by Ben Bella. By not making a public scandal of the arrests in June, the UGTA leadership showed that it no longer had the courage to fight. Thereafter, the council no longer felt the need to take the union's reaction into account.

Fear of rousing opposition was only one of the reasons why the Revolutionary Council had not deviated from the policies initiated by Ben Bella. A second and more important reason was the existence of divisions among the members of the council. In the speech he gave on the first anniversary of the *coup d'état*, Boumediene declared that with the "historic decision of June 19" the army had put an end to "the politics of bargaining and negotiating among persons and clans." In reality, far from having been eradicated, the "politics of clans" had been institutionalized by the system of collegial leadership. The bargaining and negotiating among clans were now carried out under Boumediene's patient arbitration within the Revolutionary Council as part of the decision-making process. Whereas Ben Bella, by playing one clan against the other, had brought great political instability to the country, Boumediene, by insisting that all factions in the council agree on major decisions, had brought almost complete immobility.

The council had the greatest difficulty in reaching a consensus because of the wide divergence of interests and opinions among its twenty-six members. For example, it could not formulate a coherent policy for the farm sector. The proposal to convert self-managed farms into war veterans' cooperatives was favored by the former guerrilla commanders like Mohand ou el-Hadj and Si Othmane but was strongly opposed by Minister of Agriculture Mahsas because such cooperatives were to be placed under the supervision of the Ministry of Mujahidin. Mahsas also resisted the plan to give greater autonomy to the management committees because such a plan would have loosened his hold

---

in difficulty with the government. They did, however, negotiate with the party for the release of twenty-five union officials, all of whom were eventually freed.

over the socialist farm sector. As for the agrarian reform, to which the council was in theory committed, many members were clearly unenthusiastic about it because they, their relatives, or their supporters, had important holdings. In fact, any nationalization of Algerian property was likely to affect the interest of some council member. For example, it was understood that the proposal for nationalizing Algerian transportation companies was quitely dropped on account of Colonel Tahar Zbiri, whose relatives owned such a business. Another controversial issue was that of administrative decentralization. Boumediene strongly favored a degree of decentralization but maintained that there must be a "single authority" and no "regionalism." The wilaya leaders and the regional military commanders were also for decentralization, which for them meant strengthening their personal hold over their fiefs, not reinforcing the central authority. Minister of Finance Ahmed Kaid, on the contrary, resisted any move to decentralize the administration because he had a distinctively authoritarian conception of power.[37] On this issue, he was strongly supported by Interior Minister Medeghri.

The council tried to compensate for its inability to come to grips with basic policy issues by lavishing much publicity on some of its minor undertakings. For example, it made a great event out of the return to Algeria of the ashes of Emir Abdelkader, the nineteenth century hero of the resistance to the French invasion. The emir was buried in Damascus, where he had died in exile in 1883. The council arranged with the Syrian government for his remains to be transferred back to Algeria on the fourth anniversary of the country's independence. The solemn ceremony of July 5 was presented by the council as a symbol of Algeria's "return to the sources," but many Algerians saw in it an effort to create a national hero to replace Ben Bella. Indeed, this seemed to be at least one of the council's aims, for pictures of the emir were hung in all government offices where Ben Bella's once had hung. Boumediene's portrait was never put on display to underscore the fact that Algeria was no longer ruled by one man.

Another much publicized step was the campaign against "economic crimes," which began in July 1966 with the creation of three special courts charged with applying new laws concerning corruption of civil

37. One example serves to illustrate Ahmed Kaid's authoritarianism. He ordered all tax offices in "socialist Algeria" to post excerpts from a letter of Turgot to Louis XIV in which the minister explained his policy of taxation toward the king's "subjects."

servants, actions detrimental to the economy, and offenses against the self-management system.[38] The courts began their work dramatically in early September by ordering the execution of a French counterfeiter found guilty of smuggling five million francs into Algeria.[39] In the following months, hundreds of Algerians and foreign technical assistants were put on trial, mostly for embezzlement of state funds or smuggling foreign currency out of Algeria. There were numerous arrests of members of management committees for embezzlement but none for violation of the principle of self-management," although it was well known that the March Decrees were constantly being violated.[40]

It was not until the summer of 1966 that the Revolutionary Council began to come to grips with fundamental issues, approving in August "preliminary projects" for the agrarian and the communal reforms. The two projects were published in extenso in the press,[41] and soon afterwards council members and party officials began a month-long campaign to explain the projects and test the public's reaction under the guise of "consulting the masses." The agrarian reform was intended to benefit the peasants who possessed plots of less than seven hectares. Since there would not possibly be enough land to resettle the 600,000 families that fell into this category, the veterans and war widows were to be given priority according to the principle of "the land to those who liberated it." Land was to be taken from any Algerian who derived from his farm an annual income exceeding the top salary paid by the administration, 24,000 dinars ($4,800) a year. The maximum size of private farms thus depended on the quality of the land and the use to which the land could be put. Furthermore, no one could keep land he

38. These laws were part of the new penal code promulgated June 8, 1966. See *Journal Officiel*, June 11, 1966, Ordonnance 66–156.

39. The French counterfeiter Désiré Drai, who was executed September 15, was the seventh person known to have been put to death in Algeria since independence. The other persons executed were five terrorists of the FFS and Colonel Chaabani. Drai's execution struck Algerians as an extremely harsh punishment, all the more so because he had been caught before any of the counterfeit money was circulated.

40. Articles 418–439 of the new penal code dealt with "crimes against the self-managed enterprises." The code took into consideration two types of crimes: the first were economic crimes such as embezzlement of funds or sale of state property; the second were crimes of a political nature such as preventing meetings of the general assemblies or buying the votes of members of a management committee. Crimes of the second type were punishable with prison terms of up to five years and fines of up to 10,000 dinars. As of mid-1967, no trials involving political crimes against the self-management system had been held.

41. For the text of the projects of the two reforms, see *El-Moudjahid*, August 19, 20, 1966.

did not cultivate himself. It was estimated that about 25,000 Algerians owning a total of three million hectares would be affected by the expropriations.[42] The confiscated land remained the property of the state. It was to be used to create self-managed farms or cooperatives whenever possible, and only in the last resort was it to be divided up into individual plots because "individual exploitation of the land is most often unprofitable." The project stressed that the reform would be carried out gradually and flexibly, permitting special "communal councils of the agrarian reform" to take into account local conditions. The expropriated owners were to be indemnified with fifteen-year government bonds.

The proposed agrarian reform was hardly radical, but it naturally stirred up discontent among the landowners. One of the principal complaints voiced in letters to *El-Moudjahid* was that the project did not take into consideration the fact that a farm often supported the entire extended family, perhaps as many as fifteen or twenty persons. The most important consequence of the publication of the project was that many farmers did not sow wheat crops that fall, fearing that their land would be seized before the harvest. In order to avert a shortage of wheat, the government announced that the reform was postponed until after the 1967 harvest. Crops were then planted, but the large farmers stopped making investments in the improvement or upkeep of their property. The opposition of the large landowners was a major reason why the government did not press the issue of land reform in the years that followed. As of early 1969, the reform had still not been put into effect.

The communal reform was presented as the first in a series of sweeping measures aimed at decentralizing the administrative system that Algeria had inherited from the French and at organizing a "revolutionary state." In reality the reform was much less radical than it purported to be. The new communal authorities—a people's assembly elected at large and a communal executive chosen by the assembly—had an administrative rather than a political role. Indeed, the project stressed that the reform was not intended to make the communes into autonomous entities:

42. According to the project of agrarian reform, there are 8,500 Algerians owning one hundred or more hectares of land and 16,000 Algerians owning between fifty and one hundred hectares. In addition, the lands belonging to the religious brotherhoods will be nationalized. The government has made no estimate of the total number of hectares that will be taken over and redistributed to the peasants.

> The aim of decentralization is not to recognize the autonomy of the commune. Ours is a unitarian state. The new commune is in no way a kind of autonomous republic empowered to legislate on certain matters and distinct from the central power. For our country decentralization is a technique to promote the active participation of the commune and of the people in the revolutionary power.[43]

Essentially, the communal authorities acted as agents of the government, executing policies established in Algiers. They could make independent decisions only on local matters such as the improvement of roads and water facilities and the upkeep of public buildings. Previously, every minor project had to be approved in Algiers, a procedure that usually took months. Government officials explained that the reform, by permitting the people's assemblies to settle such questions on their own, would eliminate the long delays that had discouraged local initiative since independence. Yet it was far from clear what the effect of the reform would be in this regard, since the preliminary texts stated that all projects had to be approved by the prefects and executed under the supervision of engineers and technicians provided by the competent ministries in Algiers.

The political power of the commune resided not in the assembly, but in the party kasma. The project stated that the assembly was to "manage and execute," while local party officials were to "orient and control the [action of] the communal authorities." It was the local party kasma that selected candidates for the assemblies, supervised the elections, and carried out the agrarian reform or "any other project with a direct political objective." The Algerian communes appeared to differ significantly from the French communes only in the economic sphere. Supervision of all the self-managed enterprises was in fact to be transferred progressively from the central government to the townships. The communal authorities were also to stimulate economic development by helping to set up new self-managed enterprises or cooperatives.

The debate over the two reforms involved the factions of the Revolutionary Council in a major confrontation. For over a year, Boumediene had maintained unity at the price of immobility; the effort to emerge from this immobility provoked a schism in the council. In late August, Minister of Agriculture Ali Mahsas left for a vacation in Europe and never returned. After weeks of silence, the council announced a reorganization of the Ministry of Agriculture that greatly reduced the

43. *El-Moujahid*, August 19–20, 1966.

ministry's power, and on September 24 it named a new minister of agriculture, still without giving any indication of Mahsas's fate. On October 8, Minister of Information Bachir Boumaza, who had been under police surveillance for several weeks, succeeded in fleeing the country. Boumaza was "dismissed" from the government four days later, and subsequently both he and Mahsas were formally excluded from the FLN. A communiqué of the Revolutionary Council published on October 28 sought to dispel the impression that the expulsion of these men was a symptom of serious discord within the country's ruling body. It explained that Boumaza and Mahsas had been included in the council only to show that Ben Bella alone was held responsible for the errors of the previous regime, and it emphasized that there had never been a "political alliance" between the "dismissed" ministers and the other members of the council.

Mahsas and Boumaza were not the first ministers to leave the government. Mohamed Hadj Smaïn, minister of reconstruction and housing, had been forced to resign in April 1966 and had joined the opposition abroad.[44] However, Boumaza and Mahsas were the first members of the council to be ousted. As former close collaborators of Ben Bella, they were considered the principal exponents of the Left in the regime; consequently, Algerian leftist and Communist diplomats viewed their expulsion as a victory of the council's "anti-socialist" faction composed of Kaid, Medeghri, and Belkacem. American diplomats, who held Boumaza responsible for the violent anti-American tone of the official press, were also convinced at the time that the moderates were prevailing.

It is questionable whether Boumaza and Mahsas had really espoused the ideals of the Left. Prior to the *coup d'état,* Mahsas had made himself highly unpopular with the UGTA by imposing the control of the ONRA over the self-managed farms, and Boumaza had blocked Ben Bella's plan to nationalize all private industry in the spring of 1965. However, both men had been instrumental in forging the economic policies of the Ben Bella regime, and therefore they resisted any radical change in those policies. For example, Mahsas had bitterly opposed the decision to create war veterans' cooperatives at the expense of the self-managed farms. By August 1966, the resettlement of war veterans on the land had become a major project, with 230 cooperatives already functioning and

44. The Ministry of Reconstruction and Housing was eliminated by a decree of April 5, 1966. See *Journal Officiel,* April 12, 1966.

many more being organized.[45] The Ministry of Mujahidin was choosing the best farms, abolishing the management committees and often evicting the workers, though not without meeting stiff resistance. Both Mahsas and Boumaza had also disapproved of the agrarian reform project, which they considered too partial to the landowners' interests.

The expulsion of Mahsas and Boumaza permitted Boumediene to bring more "technicians" into the government. Mohamed Ben Yahia, the new minister of information, Abdennour Ali Yahia, the new minister of agriculture, and Lamine Khene, who replaced Ali Yahia as minister of public works, were all considered to belong in this category. Boumediene had repeatedly stressed that government officials would be selected for their technical competence rather than for political reasons. However, only six of the twenty ministers he had appointed in July 1965—Minister of Justice Mohamed Bedjaoui (a lawyer); Minister of Communications Abdelkader Zaibek (an engineer); Minister of Public Health Tedjini Haddam (a surgeon); Minister of Industry and Energy Belaid Abdesslam (chief negotiator of the French-Algerian oil accord); Minister of Education Ahmed Taleb (a doctor); and Minister of Public Works Ali Yahia (a wartime secretary-general of the UGTA)— were generally regarded as technicians. Actually, the term "technician" was a misnomer: the ministers so described were not all particularly qualified to fill the posts to which they were appointed, although they were better educated and more capable than most others in the Cabinet. What really set these men apart was that they were not identified with any specific clan, nor did they command a fief anywhere in the country. As a consequence, they had no political power of their own, although they were not all apolitical.

Abdesslam, Taleb, Khene, and Ben Yahia represented a new generation of Algerian politicians who came to occupy important positions because of their capacities as administrators rather than because of their war records, as was the case with most of the members of the Council.[46] Although they had participated in the war of liberation, first founding the student union, then serving in high administrative posts in the

45. By mid-November, the number of war veterans' cooperatives had increased to 320, according to Minister of Mujahidin Boualem Benhamouda. See *El-Moudjahid*, November 17, 1966.

46. Other members of this group are Reda Malek, ambassador to France; Ahmed Ghozali, director of the state oil company; Messaoud Ait Chaalal, ambassador to Rome; Abdelmalek Benhabylès, ambassador to Tunis; and Djamal Houhou, head of the French-Algerian Oil Institute. They all began their political careers during the war as officials of the student union.

GPRA, they had kept out of politics immediately after independence to make their re-entry three or four years later.[47] Their importance in the Boumediene government grew steadily because of their efficiency and ability to conceive new policies, qualities rarely found in most members of the council. Abdesslam was particularly influential, since he was given practically a free hand to devise and execute Algeria's oil policy; however, the power of the technicians was limited by the fact that none of them had a voice in the council's deliberations. Critics of the Boumediene regime accused the technicians of being conservative. Certainly they were not Ben Bella-style revolutionaries, but they nonetheless proved to be much more progressive and dynamic than the dilatory Revolutionary Council.

Both Boumaza and Mahsas promptly joined the Organisation Clandestine de la Révolution Algérienne (OCRA), which had been formed in April 1966 by Mohamed Lebjaoui, a former official of the FLN federation in France, and Ait el-Hocine, a former member of the Political Bureau. Hadj Smaïn and Amar Ouzegane, a minister in all three Ben Bella cabinets, had also joined the OCRA, as had Rabah Slimane, a national secretary of the UGTA and the editor of the suppressed *Révolution et Travail*. Although the OCRA had some following among Algerian workers in France, it was more a club of political exiles than a mass organization and had few supporters in Algeria. Moreover, it did not even include all the political exiles. Ait Ahmed, who had escaped from prison on May 1, 1966, and fled Algeria, still operated on his own, trying to revive the nearly extinct Front of Socialist Forces. In Paris Mohamed Boudiaf continued to run the CNDR as a separate opposition movement, periodically writing "open letters to the Algerian people," which were put on sale in Parisian bookstores but were not circulated in Algeria.[48] Mohamed Khider, another dissident historic leader, kept himself in isolation in Madrid, his hopes of being offered a position in the new regime dashed.[49]

47. Abdesslam was secretary-general of the GPRA under Ferhat Abbas; Ben Yahia occupied the same position under Ben Khedda; Khene was a secretary of state in the first GPRA. Only Taleb never served in the GPRA, having been arrested in France in 1957 and kept in prison until the end of the war.

48. The Comité Nationale pour la Défense de la Révolution was the organization set up in July 1964 to coordinate the opposition to Ben Bella. As a front the CNDR was short-lived, but Boudiaf continued to use the name for his own opposition movement.

49. Khider was shot to death in Madrid on January 3, 1967. The Spanish police identified his killer as Youcef Darkmouche, an Algerian jeweler living in Madrid. It was never clear whether Darkmouche, who has not been captured, was acting on

Boumediene had no reason to worry about any of the opposition groups operating abroad or about the ORP, which struggled to survive in Algeria while its leaders remained in prison.[50] Nonetheless, police and military security maintained close surveillance over the activities of the opposition, promptly arresting persons even vaguely suspected of having contacts with the ORP or the OCRA. In the fall of 1966, the government also began to keep a closer watch on all foreign diplomats and to impose restrictions on the movement of foreign correspondents.

For over a year after the *coup d'état*, the crucial problem confronting Boumediene had been strengthening the council's hold over the country by subduing the national organizations, checking the opposition, and gaining some popular support. By the fall of 1966, however, the colonel's crucial problem had become that of strengthening his own hold over the council. His efforts to maintain the unity of the council had proven vain, and two major factions, representing a centralist and a regionalist tendency, had slowly developed. Boumediene and his closest allies—Bouteflika, Belkacem, Kaid, Medeghri, Mendjli, and the professional officers of the General Staff—wanted a strong central authority in order to maintain the effective unity of Algeria and their own control over the administration, the party, and the army. Some of the regional military commanders and the former wilaya leaders pulled in the opposite direction, since they had a regional power base and did not want it to be undermined by the encroachments of the central government. Boumediene was quite openly preoccupied with this conflict. He warned that "every militant must reject the politics of clans . . . and all actions determined by a regional interest."[51] Party Coordinator Cherif Belkacem was even more explicit: "We emphasize today that we reject unity based on the union of a few individuals who consider themselves the representatives of a political force or a regional entity."[52]

---

his own or was an agent of the Algerian government or another opposition group. At the time of his death, Khider still had control of the $12 million in party funds he had taken before going into exile in 1963. The Boumediene regime is still seeking to recover the money.

50. The three principal leaders of the ORP, Hocine Zahouane, Mohamed Harbi, and Bachir Hadj Ali, were still in prison as of September 1967. Most of the sixty members of the ORP rounded up in September 1965 were released in August and September of 1967. It is not known how many political prisoners there are today in Algeria, but the number is probably not very high. Although the police arrest people very easily, they usually release them after a short period.

51. Boumediene's speech of March 21, 1966.

52. Belkacem's speech to party officials in Constantine. See *El-Moudjahid*, March 10, 1966.

Paradoxically, Boumediene had directly contributed to the weakening of the central authority by including in the council the most powerful regional leaders. He had then played into their hands by promoting the decentralization of the administration and by placing four former wilaya commanders at the head of the party. The result was that many regions in the country were controlled by members of the council who ruled more in their own name than in the name of the collegial body to which they belonged. For example, Major Abdellah Belhouchet, commander of the Fifth Military Region, was the foremost authority in the Constantine area; without his permission, neither the prefect nor the party commissary dared to act. The latter was a close friend of Belhouchet and therefore fairly strong, while the prefect, an outsider, was nearly powerless. Major Abid Said, head of the First Military Region, had more influence in the department of Algiers than the party commissary. Nothing could be done in the region of the Aurès Mountains without the consent of Colonel Tahar Zbiri, chief of the ANP General Staff, who had led the guerrilla forces in that area during the revolution.

In nearly all regions, the military commanders had more political power than the civilian authorities. They did not have this power because the Revolutionary Council had entrusted the military to carry out its policies—this was theoretically the task of the party and government. They were powerful because of the respect they commanded as wartime leaders or because as members of the Revolutionary Council their authority took precedence over that of a prefect or a party commissary. There were some regions, the department of Oran, for example, where the military commander did not play an important political role; yet even in these areas, the most prominent figure was usually not a representative of the central government but a local personality.

Boumediene could do little to strengthen his authority without upsetting the equilibrium of the council and of the army. In October 1966, the colonel attempted to remove Major Said from his fief by promoting him to the General Staff—the same tactic Ben Bella used against Chaabani. But when the major refused, Boumediene did not insist, for fear that like Chaabani, Said would go into rebellion. Since Said was linked to other former wilaya officers, in particular to Major Belhouchet and Colonel Zbiri, his rebellion might have provoked an open confrontation between the centralist and regionalist forces.[53] Such a conflict would have been all the more dangerous for Boumediene, since Ben Bella was detained in the First Military Region under the surveillance of Said's troops.[54]

Preparations for the communal elections proved to what extent Boumediene and his allies had lost out to the regionalist forces. The organization of the elections was theoretically the task of the FLN; in practice it was carried out by local leaders because the Executive Secretariat had not succeeded in reorganizing the party. Boumediene and Belkacem, the coordinator of the party, had hoped to make the FLN the centralizing force in the nation, strong enough to overcome the power of local clans. Following the *coup d'état*, the Executive Secretariat had undertaken what was supposed to be a methodical reorganization of the party from top to bottom. The self-styled intellectuals that Ben Bella had appointed as commissaries and heads of the federations were soon replaced, in large part by retired officers of the wartime ALN. But after this was done, the reorganization of the FLN was stalled in the planning stage for an entire year because many members of the council, and even of the Executive Secretariat, opposed the existence of the strongly centralized party that Boumediene envisaged. Not until the fall of 1966, with the approach of the communal elections, did the party launch a crash program to "implant" cells throughout the country; however, the reorganization of the party could not be completed before the election campaign began.

On November 15, the council announced the creation of sixteen "departmental commissions" and a hundred "federal commissions" which were to prepare the lists of candidates for the people's assemblies. Each departmental commission was led by a member of the council, eleven of the sixteen being headed by an army officer. Although an attempt was apparently made to assign each council member to a department other than the one where he was most powerful, the five regional military commanders were left in their own areas; furthermore, both Major Said and Major Belhouchet headed two departmental commissions, a

53. All three men come from eastern Algeria where they fought during the war. Major Said was an assistant to Colonel Zbiri in Wilaya One during the revolution. The three men lead what is known as the Eastern Clan.

54. Ben Bella is believed to be held in a villa near Blida, thirty miles south of Algiers. No one except his mother has been allowed to visit him, and she has only seen him twice.

clear indication of their influence.[55] The departmental and federal
commissions were composed of one or more party officials, the prefect or the subprefect, and one representative each from the ANP,
UGTA, War Veterans Association, JFLN, UNFA, and Moslem Scout
Organization.

The lists of candidates were supposed to be prepared in the following manner: The federal commissions were to screen candidates proposed by the party kasmas and draw up a provisional list, which was
to be double-checked by the departmental commissions and then submitted to the Revolutionary Council for final approval. Candidates were
to be chosen on the basis of their militancy, morality, and participation
in the revolution, and two-thirds of them were supposed to be workers
and peasants. Neither party officials nor army officers were excluded
from running for office, although the latter were obliged to resign from
the army if elected.[56] There were twice as many candidates as seats to
be filled in order to satisfy "a minimal demand of democracy"; however, the communal reform project specified that "the choice offered
to the elector must remain one relative to the candidates, that is to
say individuals, and not [be] a choice between two or more political
tendencies."[57]

In practice candidates were not selected according to uniform criteria. The Communal Code, which established who could run for office,
was not signed by Boumediene until January 18, that is, until after the
lists had been drawn up. The party had its candidates, but so did the
prefects, the army, and even the UGTA. Who won was mostly a matter
of local politics and varied greatly from town to town. The army had
a strong voice in the regions of Algiers and Constantine because Major
Said and Major Belhouchet took an active hand in the preparation of
the lists. In Oran there was a bitter three-way struggle between the
FLN, the prefect, and the UGTA, which the party finally lost despite

55. Major Belhouchet, who led the commissions for the departments of Constantine and Annaba, was assisted by Ahmed Kaid. The latter was apparently assigned to these departments as a counterforce to Belhouchet, for in no other case
did two members of the council preside over a commission. Major Said was put in
charge of the commissions for both the city and department of Algiers.

56. Initially, it was announced that party officials could not run for seats in the
assemblies so that the party kasmas and the people's assemblies would remain two
distinct bodies. However, the Communal Code did not mention party officials among
those who could not run for office. For details see the Communal Code, published
in *El-Moudjahid*, January 22–26, 1967.

57. *El-Moujahid*, August 19–20, 1966.

the fact that the departmental commission was headed by Cherif Belkacem. The prefects and subprefects often had the final word in the rural areas, where the party was particularly weak. In the Kabylia, however, the party seemed to be the strongest. Although no complete study has been performed to determine the backgrounds of the candidates, it appears that the majority of the candidates were local notables —doctors, lawyers, teachers, and merchants—but were not well-known politicians. The list seemed to include a fairly large number of peasants and workers, but it is doubtful whether persons from these groups constituted two-thirds of the candidates as the government had promised. The Algerian press devoted much publicity to the fact that some women were running for election.

Preparations for the elections stretched over a period of three months, during which time the council and the party made a major effort to arouse the interest of Algerians. UGTA officials also campaigned actively, hoping to get their candidates elected and thereby regain some of their lost power. In the Kabylia, where the percentage of abstentions had been high in previous elections, party officials used more than persuasion to attract people to the polls, hinting that those who failed to vote would not be able to obtain food handouts or emigration permits. The list of candidates was published less than two weeks before the elections. Such late publication was of little consequence in the smaller communes, where the candidates were already well known, but it helped to diminish interest in the elections in the cities, where the candidates were mostly unknown civil servants.

On February 5, 1967, municipal elections, first promised by Ben Bella in September 1962, were finally held. Algerians elected 10,158 communal delegates to serve for four-year terms in 675 people's assemblies.[58] The government reported that about 70 per cent of all registered voters cast a ballot, but it never made available complete returns. It was known, however, that there were a large number of blank ballots, particularly in the cities. The partial figures published indicated that only 47 per cent of registered voters in Algiers and only 37 per cent of those in Oran, cast valid votes.

The Revolutionary Council promptly interpreted the turnout as a vote of confidence:

58. The people's assemblies had a minimum of nine members in the smallest communes (under 5,000 inhabitants) and a maximum of seventy-nine members in the largest (the city of Algiers).

By this participation, the great majority of the people have shown they approve and support the course of our socialist revolution. In going to the polls, Algerians have not only chosen the future managers of the new communes, but above all they have concretely demonstrated their attachment to the principles of our revolution and the interest that they bear in the success of our task of national awakening.[59]

Whether the vote was indeed an expression of confidence in the Revolutionary Council is debatable, considering the large number of voters who cast blank ballots. Nonetheless, with the elections the council had taken its first concrete step toward re-establishing legal institutions in the country, and it had begun a badly needed reform of the administration.

Soon after the elections, the new people's assemblies were officially instated and held their first meetings, only to discover that there was little they could do in the immediate future. The 1967 municipal budgets, already voted, did not include any funds for the new functions of the communes. Moreover, the government made it known that the transfer of powers from the various ministries to the communes would take place gradually over a long period of time and that legislation concerning this transfer had yet to be elaborated. In some communes, however, enthusiastic assemblies immediately embarked upon small projects, particularly in the Kabylia where the tradition of local government had always been strong. In one town in the Aurès Mountains, a well was dug and a small reforestation project carried out. In Sidi-Bel-Abbès in western Algeria, the communal authorities opened a new youth center. In a village in the Kabylia, the assembly undertook to enlarge the movie house, fix up the town hall, and buy land for a new school. These projects were financed by the profits of the nationalized movie houses, restaurants, and hotels, over which the townships were given control, and by fees collected from merchants participating in the local weekly markets.

In May 1967, the Revolutionary Council held a seventeen-day meeting, to review its accomplishments of the previous two years.[60] It concluded that its efforts to organize a "strong state" were beginning to bear fruit. Indeed, the council had scored some major successes in the field of organization and administration: Algerians were finally paying

59. Editorial in *Révolution Africaine*, No. 204, February 8, 1967.
60. The council met May 9–26, ostensibly to discuss financial questions and the lagging economic development plan. The final communiqué was published in *El-Moudjahid*, May 27, 1967.

their taxes, electricity bills, and rent to the state; the budget had been balanced in 1966 for the first time since independence; the self-managed enterprises had begun to pay taxes in 1966, also for the first time; the civil service had become more stable; numerous codes had been promulgated; and the country's first three-year plan was beginning to take shape. There had also been an effective crackdown on corruption, economic crimes, prostitution, and racketeering. These measures had gone a long way toward giving Algeria the "serious administration" that Boumediene had repeatedly promised in his speeches immediately following the *coup d'état.*

The council had been unable, however, to come to grips with some key issues. One such issue was the future of self-management. Economically, the system had proven a liability, with only about one-tenth of the 2,300 self-managed farms making a profit, but it could not be abolished without serious political repercussions. The council's policy was thus to compromise: self-management was maintained, but no effort was made to ensure the correct application of the March Decrees. There were no re-elections of management committees and no revival of the workers' councils or the assemblies. The long-promised decentralization of the farm sector was finally begun, but there is no evidence that the management committees actually gained greater autonomy.

The decentralization was announced in October 1966, shortly after the ouster of Mahsas. Boumediene presided over a much publicized ceremony during which the president of a management committee was presented with a checkbook, symbol of the farm's new financial independence. In late February 1967, the ONRA was dissolved, and the self-managed farms were placed under the supervision of departmental offices of agriculture annexed to the prefectures. However, the management committees were not given individual accounts at the new state bank as originally promised, but continued to depend upon agencies attached to the Ministry of Agriculture. Provisioning of the farms and the marketing of their produce also remained tightly controlled by the ministry.[61]

61. The farms continued to be financed through the Caisse Algérienne de Crédit Agricole and provisioned through the Sociétés Agricoles de Prévoyance. Both organizations had previously been part of the ONRA and remained under the Ministry of Agriculture. A new organization, the Union Nationale des Coopératives Agricoles de Commercialisation (UNCAC), was created in December 1960 to market the produce of the state farms. UNCAC, which replaced the CCRA, was also part of the Ministry of Agriculture.

While these minor reforms were being carried out, the number of self-managed farms was steadily reduced through the creation of co-operatives for the war veterans. By the fall of 1967, there were some 400 such cooperatives covering three hundred thousand hectares, about one-seventh of the land initially in the self-managed sector. For all appearances, the government was determined to convert as many self-managed farms into cooperatives as was necessary to satisfy the war veterans, and it had even begun to resettle on the rich farms of the plains former guerrillas from the poverty-stricken mountain areas.

In the industrial sector, the self-managed enterprises continued to receive no assistance from the government, and the office in charge of self-management at the Ministry of Industry was closed down alto-gether. At the same time, Abdesslam worked quietly to establish a number of state companies such as the National Steel Company (Société Nationale de Sidérurgie), the National Textile Company (Société Nationale des Industries Textiles), the National Glassworks Company (Société Nationale des Industries du Verre), and the Al-gerian National Insurance Company (Société Algérienne d'Assurances). The trend toward state capitalism was made unmistakably clear in August 1967, when nine other state companies were created, absorbing many of the self-managed enterprises. The creation of these state companies and a crackdown on union activities in the state sector provoked a strenuous protest from the UGTA and a bitter debate be-tween Labor Minister Zerdani and Industry Minister Adesslam. How-ever, neither Zerdani nor the UGTA succeeded in preventing the slow abandonment of industrial self-management for what *Révolution et Travail* called the "decadent system" of state capitalism.[62]

The most serious failing of the Revolutionary Council was a total disregard for fundamental political problems. For two years, the council ruled without a constitution or a national assembly, exercising both executive and legislative powers. Boumediene was not anxious to give the country formal political institutions. He once said that a country like Algeria, "which has need of order, organization, and discipline after the terrible crises it has traversed, cannot afford the luxury of formal democracy." He also declared that "the communal, agrarian, and fiscal

62. *Révolution et Travail*, No. 122, August 15, 1967. After this issue, the weekly was again suppressed for several months.

reforms, the municipal elections, and the struggle against hunger are much more important for us than a free press and a parliament that would give free rein to quarrels and conflicts."[63]

The lack of political institutions helped to maintain the gap between the government and the people that had been created by the *coup d'état*. Excluded from the process of government, Algerians became indifferent to public affairs. Although even before the *coup d'état* the people were largely excluded from the process of government, Ben Bella was able to make tens of thousands of Algerians feel an interest and a sense of participation in the socialist revolution. Boumediene, on the other hand, lacked charisma. Even though by mid-1967 he had improved his public appearance, speaking the local dialect and occasionally mingling with the crowds, he still could not move his audiences to more than polite applause.

The party and other national organizations continued to be an embarrassing problem for the council. The most militant members of the UGTA and UNEA remained openly hostile to the regime. UGTA Secretary-General Mouloud Oumeziane, once considered a radical, had discredited himself with the Left by trying to cooperate with the party. The party-appointed student leaders still had no control over UNEA, as was made clear in April 1967 when the militant students finally succeeded in reassuming control of the Algiers section.[64] Only the War Veterans Association was stronger and more active than ever before, working in close cooperation with the Ministry of Mujahidin to gain more privileges for its members. As for the party, it was even weaker and less popular than it was under Ben Bella. One of its key problems was its leaders' total lack of ideological drive. The Algiers Charter had not been formally repudiated, but it had certainly been forgotten. The FLN, like the Revolutionary Council, appeared to have neither an ideology nor a program.

63. Boumediene's interview with *Paris-Match*, May 14, 1966.

64. A general meeting of the Algiers section was held on April 15 to elect new leaders of the section, who were to prepare a new UNEA congress. After an all-night struggle between pro- and anti-party students, the latter succeeded in electing their candidates and also voted a motion calling for the liberation of the "revolutionary militants," the leftist student leaders still in prison. The party decided to recognize the new leadership of the Algiers section; nonetheless, on April 29, it ordered the arrest of several of the new leaders. It also prohibited the anti-party students from participating in the Labor Day parade on May 1, 1967.

chapter eleven
the end of internationalism

We are neither against those who preach Arabism, nor against those who expound socialism or communism, nor against the partisans of African unity. . . . But what we cannot tolerate, no matter the price, is interference in our internal affairs.[1]

Houari Boumediene

The *coup d'état* was a severe blow to Algeria's prestige and influence abroad, isolating the country from most of its former allies. The revolutionary leaders of the Third World and the Communist governments as well were almost unanimous in their condemnation of the event. The easy overthrow of Ben Bella made the other radical African leaders acutely aware of the possibility of a military putsch in their own countries. As President Sékou Touré of Guinea declared, "the *coup d'état* [in Algiers] cannot leave us indifferent because our fate is closely tied to that of Algeria."[2] President Kwame Nkrumah was so shaken that he did not allow the news of the *coup* to be made public in Ghana for four days. Nasser's first reaction was to dispatch Field Marshal Abdel Hakim Amer to Algiers with a message for Boumediene, asking him to hand Ben Bella over to the "custody" of the Egyptian government. Boumediene was naturally outraged by Nasser's request and even more so by his underhanded maneuvers to get the Afro-Asian Conference transferred to Cairo. When a bomb exploded at the conference site outside Algiers four days before the conference was scheduled to begin, Boumediene immediately imputed the sabotage to Egyptian agents. Shortly afterwards he decided to dismiss for security

1. Boumediene's speech of March 6, 1966.
2. See *Le Monde*, June 29, 1965.

reasons all Egyptian military advisors and several hundred Egyptian teachers.

The *coup d'état* also drove a wedge between Algeria and Cuba. Fidel Castro considered Boumediene's accession to power the beginning of "military despotism" in Algeria and predicted that Algerians would rise up against the new regime. As an indication of his disapproval, Castro recalled the Cuban ambassador to Algeria. In response, Boumediene ordered closed the office of Prensa Latina, the Cuban press agency, and the office of the Algerian-Cuban Friendship Circle in Algiers. The two countries only narrowly avoided a formal break in diplomatic relations.

The governments of the Eastern bloc countries made it clear by their prolonged silence that they too had little sympathy for the Revolutionary Council, whose anti-Communist penchant was well known. Without even consulting the new Algerian government, they suddenly cancelled the ninth World Youth Festival, which was scheduled to take place in Algiers in late July. Only three socialist countries—Communist China, Indonesia, and Syria—expressed immediate support for the new Algerian regime. Their recognition could not be considered an expression of confidence in Boumediene; rather, China and Indonesia were interested at that point in saving the Afro-Asian Conference, while Syria welcomed the advent of an anti-Nasser regime in Algeria.

The *coup d'état* was greeted most favorably by the Western powers, which tended to assume that Boumediene would be more conservative and thus more pro-Western than his predecessor. United States diplomats in Algiers were openly exultant with the downfall of Ben Bella, while Great Britain extended recognition to the new regime with undue haste. Boumediene, who did not want to be considered less revolutionary than his predecessor, was greatly embarrassed by the reaction of the Western governments to the *coup d'état*. Even more embarrassing for the colonel was a telegram of congratulations from Marshal Nguyen Cao Ky, who had seized power in South Vietnam the same day that Boumediene had in Algeria.

Rebuffed by most African and Communist governments whose recognition he sought and unwilling to accept the support of the major Western powers, Boumediene maintained Algeria's isolation for a long time. Moreover, he showed remarkably little interest in, or even understanding of, international affairs. When in the fall of 1965, a journalist

questioned him about his views on Algeria's foreign policy, Boumediene declined to answer, suggesting that he address his questions to
Foreign Minister Bouteflika. It was Bouteflika who almost singlehandedly designed and carried out Algeria's foreign policy for many
months after the *coup d'état*, doing his best to re-establish normal relations with Algeria's former allies and to restore the country's standing
in the Third World. Alone, however, he could not succeed, and Boumediene himself contributed little.

Boumediene undoubtedly wished to re-establish Algeria's position
in the Third World, but his narrow nationalism, which bordered on
xenophobia, was not an attitude conducive to success. He went through
the motions expected of a revolutionary leader in a very unconvincing
manner. He participated in the African and Arab summit conferences
in the fall of 1965, but he did so without making his presence noticed.
He pledged Algeria's continuing support of the African liberation movements, but it was no secret that the representatives of these movements
were receiving little aid or attention in Algiers. In December 1965, in
accordance with an OAU decision, Algeria severed diplomatic relations
with Great Britain over the latter's failure to crush the white rebellion in Rhodesia; however, Algeria was the last of nine countries to
comply with the decision, giving the impression that the Revolutionary
Council was acting only to maintain appearances.[3] While in January
1966 Boumediene sent a delegation to the Tricontinental Conference in
Havana, it was a low-level delegation that played only a minor role.

Despite his anti-communism, Boumediene made a major effort to
re-establish good relations with the Soviet bloc. He seemed anxious to
end speculation that Algeria had severed ties with the socialist countries and turned toward the West. Moreover, he realized the ANP was
totally dependent on Soviet arms and advisors. Within days of the
coup d'état, he dispatched to Moscow Mohamed Ben Yahia, the former
ambassador to the Soviet Union, to assure Soviet leaders that there was
no change in Algeria's socialist and "anti-imperialist" orientation. Mohamed Kellou, the Algerian ambassador in Prague, was sent to other

3. Foreign Ministers of the OAU countries met on December 3, 1965, in Addis
Ababa and decided that all members of the organization would sever diplomatic
relations with Britain on December 15 unless the British government took effective
steps to put an end to the white rebellion in southern Rhodesia. Only nine countries
finally complied with this decision; Algeria, the last to comply, severed relations on
December 18. Trade relations between Algeria and Britain, the most important
client for Algerian gas, were not affected by the break.

Eastern bloc capitals on a similar mission. It was not until late July that the Soviet government broke its silence, expressing in a message to Boumediene its satisfaction with the Revolutionary Council's desire to maintain "friendly and fraternal ties" with the socialist countries.[4] However, the arrest in August and September of over sixty French and Algerian Communists implicated in ORP activities prevented any rapid *rapprochement* between the Revolutionary Council and the Soviet Union.

Boumediene nonetheless persisted in his efforts to win the acceptance of Soviet leaders, and he finally obtained an invitation to visit Russia in December 1965. Boumediene's state visit of December 14–18, significantly his first, was decidedly not a triumph as Ben Bella's had been. He was not hailed as "Comrade President," bedecked with medals, or acclaimed by large crowds; his was strictly a business trip. He had long discussions with Premier Alexei Kosygin and President Nikolai Podgorny and a seven-hour unpublicized meeting with Party Secretary Leonid Breshnev. Judging from the final communiqué, Boumediene achieved the primary aim of his visit, that of assuring the continuation of Soviet economic and military aid.[5] The Soviets pledged to continue and even expand their aid program, but they did not make any specific commitments. It was clear, however, that not all disagreements between Boumediene and the Soviet leaders had been dispelled. The final communiqué spoke of "similarity" rather than of the customary "identity" of viewpoints between the two governments, and it made no mention of the re-establishment of relations between the Soviet Communist party and the FLN that *de facto* had been broken off with the *coup d'état*.

Relations between the FLN and the Communist parties of Western and Eastern Europe did not substantially improve in the following months. The French Communist party in particular was implacably hostile to the Boumediene regime, largely because of widespread arrests of its members in Algeria. The PCF daily *L'Humanité* continued its campaign for the release of Ben Bella and other political prisoners. Only the Italian and Soviet Communist parties made any attempt to renew contacts with the FLN. In January 1966, an FLN delegation was invited to assist at the eleventh congress of the Italian Communist party, and in late February another delegation went to Moscow for a two-

4. See *Le Monde*, July 23, 1965.
5. The final communiqué was published in *El-Moudjahid*, December 20, 1965.

week "good-will" visit. All in all, nothing came of these contacts. On the contrary, at the time of the twenty-third congress of the Soviet Communist party in March 1966, an incident provoked new tensions between the FLN and the Moscow-aligned Communist parties.

The Soviets invited the FLN to send observers to the congress, and unbeknownst to the Algerian government, they also allowed several members of the Algerian Communist party to attend.[6] When the FLN delegation discovered the presence of PCA members at the opening ceremonies, it immediately walked out of the hall. Adding to the insult, Party Secretary Brezhnev called in his speech for a special ovation in honor of the Algerian Communists, while Soviet party officials pleaded with Cherif Belkacem, leader of the FLN delegation, for the liberation of the imprisoned Algerian and French Communists. The Algerian delegation left Moscow the next day, embittered by the Soviet attempt to force the FLN into recognizing the PCA. This incident effectively put an end to all contacts between the FLN and the Soviet Communist party for over a year.

Relations between the Soviet and Algerian governments, however, were not seriously affected. Awareness of their isolation as well as economic and military considerations kept the Algerians from exaggerating the importance of the incident. For their part, the Soviets made a distinction between party-to-party and government-to-government relations, carefully preserving the latter from the fluctuations of the former. Soviet officials in Algiers let it be known that Moscow had decided to back Boumediene, being convinced that a new *coup d'état* would bring to power an even more conservative and anti-Soviet government. Consequently, the Soviet Union continued slowly to increase its aid program to Algeria.

By late 1966, Western diplomats estimated that there were about 3,000 Soviet doctors, teachers, agronomists, engineers, and military advisors serving in Algeria.[7] The Soviets were particularly active in train-

---

6. According to some reports, the Soviets had not directly invited the Algerian Communists; it was the French Communist party that included the Algerians in its delegation. Faced with the *fait accompli*, however, the Soviets allowed the Algerian Communists to remain.

7. Among the Soviets working in Algeria are: 300 doctors; at least 600 high school teachers and technical instructors; 200 petroleum technicians working for the state oil company, SONATRACH; 96 engineers supervising the construction of twenty-eight small dams throughout the country; and at least 200 agronomists and industrial consultants helping in the socialist sector.

ing skilled workers and technicians. They equipped and staffed one vocational school at El-Harrach (Algiers) that was capable of taking 1,000 trainees, and they promised to set up fifteen other similar schools capable of handling an additional 3,000 students in 1968.[8] Under considerable pressure from Minister of Industry Abdesslam, the Soviets also made a firm commitment in July 1966 to complete construction of their part of the 350,000-ton steel mill at Annaba by 1970.[9] At the same time, they agreed to build a power station (Algeria's largest) at Annaba and a number of smaller industrial plants throughout the country.[10]

The greatest portion of Soviet aid continued to go to the ANP, which had received by late 1966 an estimated $250 million worth of military equipment. Soviet arms, including SAM missiles, Mig-21's, and 155mm self-propelled guns, arrived in such massive quantities that American military experts speculated that Algeria was serving as a depot for arms to be rushed to other parts of Africa or the Arab world in emergencies.[11] This theory was partly confirmed during the Arab-Israeli war in June 1967, when Algeria sent at least fifty aircraft to the UAR to replace some of the Egyptian Migs destroyed in the conflict. Of equal concern to Western diplomats were visits of the Soviet navy to Algeria. Soviet warships and submarines called at the port of Oran in April 1966 and then again in Algiers in November, both times receiving a warm welcome from local Algerian authorities. American diplomats feared that the ultimate objective of the Soviet Union was to gain access to Algerian

8. By an accord of June 18, 1965, the Soviet Union agreed to train a minimum of 4,000 skilled workers in various specialties. Most of the students at El-Harrach are being prepared to serve in the ANP; the fifteen additional vocational schools, supposed to open in April 1968, will train civilians.

9. Belaid Abdesslam, minister of industry and energy, visited the Soviet Union from July 24 to August 5, 1966, in order to discuss Soviet participation in the completion of the steel mill at Annaba, begun by private French companies before independence but later abandoned. The Soviets had serious reservations about the economic soundness of the project, primarily because Algeria uses less than 350,000 tons of steel a year. Their experts estimate the plant would run in the red until at least 1975. The Soviet Union apparently decided to help build the plant for political reasons. According to Abdesslam, the Soviets also agreed to buy some of the finished product. See *El-Moudjahid*, August 10, 1966.

10. On February 14, 1967, twenty-seven different contracts were signed between the Caisse Algérienne de Dévelopment and the Soviet Union. Among the projects were plans for the construction of a thermo-electric plant at Annaba, a distillery to make alcohol from wine, and several plants for the treatment of zinc and lead. The Soviets also agreed to train Algerian technicians and skilled workers to run these plants.

11. See Appendix III for further details on Soviet arms.

ports on a regular basis and perhaps to make use of the naval base at Mers-el-Kébir after the French evacuated it.[12]

By 1966, it was obvious that the Soviets had a long-term interest in Algeria. Without actively trying to displace France, the Soviet Union was establishing a considerable presence, particularly in the military field, where French aid was noticeably lagging. Mindful of their objectives, the Soviets accommodated themselves with remarkable success to a regime hostile to communism and were content to express their disapproval through a suspension in party relations. For its part, the Boumediene government sought to maintain close relations with the Soviet Union for reasons of immediate political expediency, giving little consideration to the long-term consequences that might ensue from taking such a position. The Algerians' primary objective was to extract the maximum amount of aid from the Soviet Union, which regardless of its generous promises proved reluctant to become deeply involved in the Algerian economy. Instead, it sent a considerable quantity of arms and vast numbers of technicians, the least costly or binding forms of aid, although a powerful source of influence. As a consequence of Soviet long-term calculations and Algerian immediate interests, the Soviet presence steadily increased. Despite his anti-Communism, Boumediene has allowed the Soviet Union to play a much more important role in Algeria than it played under the more leftist government of Ben Bella.

Bulgaria and Czechoslovakia, the other Soviet bloc countries granting aid to Algeria, followed Moscow's lead and continued their small aid programs after the *coup d'état*. Although the Algerian government did its best to make use of supplier's credits granted by these countries, it did not make any special effort to develop close cooperation with either Bulgaria or Czechoslovakia.[13] The only Communist country with which the Boumediene regime sought to establish close political ties was Yugoslavia, a country that was accorded great prestige by the Algerians because of its support of the FLN during the war and because of its successful policy of nonalignment. The fact that Ben Bella had

12. The United States' concern over Soviet designs on the Mers-el-Kébir base greatly increased in late 1967, when it became known that France planned to complete evacuation of the base by February 1968. The French had come to consider the base a strategically useless installation.

13. The Czech government, which first announced it was extending Algeria the equivalent of $15 million in industrial credits in May 1965, concluded an agreement in February 1967 whereby it would provide a rolling mill for the steel plant at Annaba. It also provided Algeria with a 10,000 kilowatt radio transmitter. The Czech loan was for ten years at 2.5 per cent interest.

been on excellent terms with Marshal Tito was an additional incentive for Boumediene to establish good relations with Yugoslavia. Significantly, Boumediene, in October 1966, chose to go to Belgrade on his second state visit. He was preceded by an FLN delegation invited by the League of Yugoslav Communists, the only Communist party with which the FLN was able to re-establish cordial relations after the coup d'état.

Boumediene hoped that his visit to Yugoslavia would enhance his standing among the nonaligned countries. More specifically, he hoped that it would earn him an invitation to a conference of nonaligned leaders that was to take place in New Delhi later that year to discuss a solution to the Vietnam war. However, Boumediene failed to achieve his objective because he and Tito found themselves in sharp disagreement over Vietnam. The Yugoslav president maintained that the nonaligned nations should work to bring about a compromise solution, while Boumediene insisted that they should give their total support to the Vietcong. As a consequence, Tito made no effort to have Boumediene invited to the New Delhi meeting.

Boumediene's eagerness to maintain close relations with the Soviet bloc soon caused the United States to change its favorable judgment of his regime. There were a number of other reasons why Washington's initial optimism soon faded: first, there was no letup in the hostile tone of the Algerian press toward American foreign policy and particularly toward "American aggression" in Vietnam; second, as a consequence of the French-Algerian oil agreement of July 1965, American oil companies were slowly being squeezed out of Algeria; third, the new investment code of September 1966, although more liberal than the previous one, could not dispel the impression that there was little future for private foreign capital in Algeria. In addition, the Algerian government ordered the closure of the United States cultural center in Constantine in August 1966, accusing the center of spreading anti-government propaganda.[14]

14. The information center in Constantine was closed August 31 on orders from Boumediene, following an incident that involved the showing of a USIS film in which Ben Bella appeared. The film, which had been taken out of circulation, was accidentally picked up by an American Quaker volunteer and shown to peasants in a mountain village near Skikda. News of the incident reached the president within twenty-four hours, and Boumediene ordered the closure of the center, although he must have realized that the American government was unlikely to make propaganda for Ben Bella on purpose.

By January 1967, relations between the two countries were so strained that United States Ambassador to Algeria John D. Jernegan wrote a letter to the official newspaper *El-Moudjahid* protesting its anti-American bias. In his letter, the ambassador stated that it was his "unhappy impression that the atmosphere in which relations between our two countries are taking place has deteriorated rather than ameliorated in the past few months."[15] The newspaper devoted an editorial to answering Ambassador Jernegan's letter, explaining that it was not because of a systematic anti-American policy that Algeria found itself generally opposed to the United States:

> The position of Algeria . . . is that of total support to peoples currently in the grip of imperialism. It is not Algeria . . . that has chosen that the United States . . . place itself with such fine consistency in precisely the camp with which these peoples . . . find themselves confronted in sacred combat.[16]

Relations between Algeria and the United States continued to deteriorate in the following months. After six months of extremely difficult negotiations for a loan to purchase 200,000 tons of wheat from the United States, Algeria finally refused the loan in early June because of "political pressures" from Washington.[17] A few days later, the Arab-Israeli war broke out, and on June 7 Algeria severed diplomatic relations with the United States and placed all American oil companies under state control. Such actions did not indicate a radical change in Algerian policy but were the logical consequence of the deep-seated antagonism between the two governments.

France, the country with the largest stake in Algeria, was also the country that showed the greatest indifference to the *coup d'état*. President de Gaulle immediately made it clear that his interest in Algeria transcended the man in power; Colonel Boumediene, who wanted to prove that "Algeria's relations with its friends, allies, partners . . . [were] above men and political fluctuations,"[18] was also eager to maintain French-Algerian cooperation unchanged. As a result of this reciprocal attitude, oil negotiations between the two governments continued un-

15. See *El-Moudjahid*, January 22–23, 1967.
16. *El-Moudjahid*, January 24, 1967.
17. The "political pressures" exercised by Washington were demands that Algeria promise to compensate several American citizens whose property had been nationalized in 1962, before the loan was granted.
18. Proclamation of the Revolutionary Council, June 19, 1965.

disturbed. Five weeks after the *coup d'état*, a fifteen-year agreement, which went a long way toward institutionalizing the policy of cooperation, was signed.

The French government initially believed that Boumediene, with his emphasis on careful planning and stability, would be less likely than Ben Bella to provoke periodic crises. However, French-Algerian cooperation saw as many ups and downs as ever. The cooperative association set up by the oil accord for the joint exploitation of the Sahara immediately ran into difficulties. The private French oil companies opposed the association because it was state-controlled; for their part, the Algerians made cooperation more difficult by systematically excluding French personnel from their state oil company, hiring instead American and Russian experts. The French press spoke at one point of an "Algerian-American plot" to chase the French out of the Sahara.[19] There were other problems as well. Interminable negotiations between the Algerian and French governments regarding payment of pre-independence debts and of indemnities for the so-called biens vacants broke down in April 1966. The following month, the Algerian government took over most French mines, formally nationalized all biens vacants, and created a state monopoly on insurance, putting a number of French companies out of business. By the end of 1966, however, the cooperative association had begun to function fairly smoothly, and the two governments had reached a compromise agreement on the issue of pre-independence debts, although not on the question of indemnities.[20]

The new French ambassador to Algeria, Pierre de Leusse, presenting

19. In 1966, the Algerian government was using the services of over a dozen American engineering, managerial, and consulting firms. These included Bechtel; Booz, Allen and Hamilton; Arthur D. Little; and Sherman, Sterling, and Wright. SONATRACH, the Algerian state oil company, hired forty American technicians and formed joint companies in Algeria with Southeastern Drilling Company of Dallas; Varel Manufacturing Company of Dallas, makers of drilling equipment; and Independex, an American geophysical services company. SONATRACH also arranged a $15 million loan from the Bank of America and the Manufacturers Hanover Trust to help cover the cost of a new 500-mile, $70 million pipeline. In May 1966, a conflict arose between Algeria and France over ALFOR, the Algerian-American drilling company. It was at this point that the French press launched an attack on "American infiltration" into the Sahara oil industry. See for example, *Combat*, May 26, 1966.

20. The agreement, signed on December 23, 1966, stipulated that Algeria would pay France 400 million francs ($80 million) over a thirty-year period. This sum represented only partial reimbursement of loans made by the French government to the colonial administration in Algeria prior to independence.

his credentials to President Boumediene in late May 1967, summed up concisely the state of French-Algerian relations: "Between our two countries, men have woven ties so numerous, diverse, and solid that the dialogue has become a permanent institution."[21] Yet French-Algerian cooperation was clearly not bearing all the fruits President de Gaulle hoped for: under Boumediene, Algeria was no longer a door opening on the Third World. Moreover, the Soviet presence in Algeria was growing steadily, and even French diplomats who had previously affected indifference were beginning to voice concern. Soviet assistance had become crucial to the ANP, while French military aid consisted mainly of training and partly equipping the gendarmerie.[22] The number of French technicians and teachers had decreased to about 10,000 in 1967, and the French government was encountering increasing difficulty in recruiting teachers to serve in Algeria. On the other hand, the number of Soviet experts had increased to over 3,000. Some French diplomats admitted that one day there might be as many Soviet as French technicians in Algeria and that France might no longer be the key to Algeria's stability and development.

In 1967, that day still seemed a long way off. With its five-year, two billion franc ($400 million) industrial development program, its annual aid (about 385 million francs or $77 million in 1967), and its key role in the expansion of Algeria's oil industry, France remained undisputably more important to Algeria than the Soviet Union. However, it was clear that the Soviet Union would emerge as the most influential foreign power in the country, should relations between France and Algeria deteriorate for political reasons.

Despite President de Gaulle's efforts to institutionalize his policy toward Algeria in a series of long-term agreements, many Algerian and French officials expected relations between the two countries to become much more vulnerable to crises after he ceased to be in power. The Algerian government was visibly relieved when de Gaulle was re-elected to the presidency in December 1965. As El-Moudjahid wrote at the time, "General de Gaulle remains the most solid guarantee of French-Algerian cooperation."[23] This view seemed to be confirmed during the Arab-

21. See El-Moudjahid, May 27, 1967.
22. In addition, the French maintain an army hospital at Bab el-Oued (Algiers) and provide some advisors for the army engineering corps and the navy. According to French statistics, there were a total of 358 French advisors, doctors, and technicians serving in the Algerian army in 1966. See Le Monde, May 3, 1966.
23. El-Moudjahid, November 29, 1965.

Israeli war in June 1967, when de Gaulle ignored public pressure for France to support Israel and remained firmly neutral in order to preserve France's standing in the Arab world and its access to Algerian oil. It is doubtful that any other French president would have acted as he did or that French-Algerian cooperation would have survived in face of France's support of Israel.

The most significant change in Algerian foreign policy after the overthrow of Ben Bella was the shift in emphasis from Africa to the Arab world. This change was not entirely Boumediene's choice. Although he eschewed any *rapprochement* with the moderate African leaders, he did court the revolutionaries, only to be rebuffed for over a year. The *coup d'état* in Algiers represented what the radical African leaders feared most—the intervention of the military in politics. Boumediene was extremely annoyed by interpretations of his *coup d'état* as the rise to power of a conservative military junta and even more irritated by the parallel frequently drawn between the ouster of Ben Bella and that of Nkrumah. While he agreed that "the fall of Nkrumah has brought about the end of the revolution in Ghana,"[24] he contended that the fall of Ben Bella had on the contrary assured the continuation of Algeria's socialist revolution. However, none of the progressive African leaders accepted his interpretation. President Julius Nyerere of Tanzania resolutely kept his distance, while President Sékou Touré of Guinea declared as late as March 1966 that "the gains of the Algerian Revolution are in danger."[25] Only Malian President Modibo Keita was slightly more cordial toward Boumediene, probably because he needed Algeria's aid to transport across the Sahara arms coming from the Soviet Union. On the whole, there were relatively few contacts between Algeria and the Black African countries before early 1967.

Because of his character and education, Boumediene was more attracted to the Arab world than to Africa. He accused Ben Bella of having tried to suppress Algeria's identity as an Arab nation in order to make himself more acceptable as a Pan-African leader:

> He [Ben Bella] once talked to us in this manner: "We must not act in Africa as Arabs because Arabism is hated there, but only as Moslem Africans leaving aside any idea of Arabism." We reacted violently, de-

24. See Boumediene's speech to party officials in Oran, March 21, 1966.
25. See *Le Monde*, March 2, 1966.

claring that this was an opportunistic policy. We are at once Arabs and Africans, and we must remain deeply attached to our Arabism in the sense of civilization and progress.[26]

Boumediene was not as isolated in the Arab world as he was in Africa, having immediately gained Syria's support. The Syrian leaders had never enjoyed good relations with Ben Bella because Ben Bella was close to Nasser and openly contemptuous of the ruling Syrian Baath party. The Syrians hoped that Boumediene would side with them in their efforts to put an end to Nasser's domination of the socialist Arab states.

Nonetheless, it was almost a year after the *coup d'état* before Algeria and Syria began to establish close ties. In May 1966, Syrian Foreign Minister Ibrahim Makhos visited Algeria, seeking Boumediene's support for a meeting of the socialist Arab leaders. The Algerians were initially cool toward the idea, as they were fearful of dimming their chances for holding the fourth Arab summit conference, which was scheduled to take place in Algiers that September. However, they gladly agreed to develop closer ties with the Syrian government and the Baath party. Several members of the Revolutionary Council and of the FLN Executive Secretariat visited Syria in early July for this purpose. Another FLN delegation went to Damascus in August for ideological discussions with the Baath party. The joint communiqué published at the end of these talks called for a "democratic alliance" of progressive Arab forces, emphasizing that the FLN and Baath party rejected any "strategy preconceived and imposed by any one of the progressive parties."[27] This admonition was clearly addressed to Nasser.

The Syrian-Algerian entente worried the Egyptian leader and provoked him into seeking an understanding with Boumediene, whom he had only grudgingly accepted as Ben Bella's successor. Nasser made his first overture shortly after the Syrian foreign minister's visit to Algeria, inviting an FLN delegation to Cairo in late July 1966 for talks with the Arab Socialist Union, Egypt's only party. Boumediene himself was scheduled to visit Cairo in August, but he postponed the trip after Nasser announced he would not attend the Arab summit meeting, thereby forcing its cancellation.[28]

26. See Boumediene's interview with the Cairo newspaper *Al-Ahram*, October 8–10, 1965, reprinted in *Révolution Africaine*, No. 143, October 23, 1965.
27. See *El-Moudjahid*, September 8, 1966.
28. Nasser, who in 1964 had taken the initiative of calling the first summit meeting of all Arab leaders, had come to the conclusion that the annual gatherings were

The collapse of that conference marked a turning point in the politics of the Arab world because it formalized the split between the moderate and socialist regimes. Algeria, which had hoped to avoid such a split before the conference, was left no choice but to join the alliance developing among the socialist Arab countries. In the following months, there were numerous exchanges of party delegations between Algeria, Syria and Egypt; in December, Boumediene finally visited Cairo where he and Nasser formally made peace. The colonel was still not as close to Nasser as Ben Bella had been. Relations between the two countries were no longer based on the personal friendship between two leaders, but on ties between the FLN and the Arab Socialist Union, which had become much stronger than ever before.

Boumediene found a *rapprochement* with Morocco and Tunisia much more difficult, since his fervent nationalism was a barrier to the solution of the border disputes that strained relations between Algeria and its neighbors. In the proclamation of June 19, the Revolutionary Council had accused Ben Bella of "high treason" because he had shown a willingness to cede parts of the contested territory in order to put an end to the controversies. By moving troops into the disputed area between Algeria and Tunisia within forty-eight hours of the *coup d'état*, Boumediene made it clear that he, on the contrary, would not negotiate Algeria's borders. Worried by Boumediene's intransigence and by the continuing flow of Soviet arms into Algeria, both Morocco and Tunisia began to press Washington for more arms and military assistance, thereby increasing tensions in North Africa.

Bourguiba realized, however, that Tunisia was too small to resort to the use of force, and he continued to seek a diplomatic solution to the dispute. Although there were several minor incidents along the border and Bourguiba repeatedly angered Algerian leaders by making contemptuous remarks about them in public, the two governments continued to work quietly for a settlement. In early 1967, Algeria finally agreed to the creation of a joint military commission to trace the border line through the disputed area. After several months of unpublicized

---

useless. In 1966, Saudi Arabia was promoting an "Islamic Pact" among all Moslem countries. Nasser violently attacked the project, which he regarded as a reactionary scheme aimed at countering the socialist Arab leaders, particularly himself. In a speech given on June 16, 1966, in Cairo, he denounced the "reactionary" leaders of the Arab world for their hypocritical participation in the Arab summit meetings, and in July he announced that he would not participate any longer in the annual conferences.

negotiations, an agreement was finally announced on May 19. Although no details were revealed, it was understood that Tunisia had given up most of her claims but that Algeria had also made some minor concessions.[29]

The obstacles to an entente between Algeria and Morocco were much greater, since the two countries had already fought one war and the arms race under way made another one likely. There continued to be numerous border incidents, the most serious of which occurred in May 1966 after Algeria nationalized the Gara-Djebilet iron mine, located in territory claimed by Morocco. Movement of troops on both sides of the frontier momentarily raised fears that war would again break out.[30] However, on Morocco's request the OAU intervened and revived the ad hoc commission set up in November 1963 to mediate the border dispute. The attempt to find a permanent settlement was again unsuccessful, but a new war was avoided.

In late 1966, another issue arose between Algiers and Rabat, that of the Spanish Sahara, a mineral-rich territory bordering on Morocco, Algeria, and Mauritania. King Hassan renewed his demands that Spain withdraw from the region and relinquish it to Morocco. In November, the Algerian ambassador to the United Nations unexpectedly announced that his government considered the future of the Spanish Sahara of "vital interest" to Algeria.[31] He did not, however, specifically state that his country sought the annexation of the territory. It appeared more likely that the Algerian government intended to use the issue to counter Morocco's claims to parts of the Algerian Sahara.

In his efforts to bring Algeria to the negotiating table, King Hassan

29. The announcement stated only that the two governments had fixed the border line south of the oasis of Bir Roman. The question under dispute was whether Tunisia's southernmost point was milestone 222, where the French had fixed it, or 233, as the Tunisians claimed, citing a Tunisian-Libyan accord of 1910. Milestone 233 was about twenty miles west of 222 and gave Tunisia greater access to the El-Borma oil field, the only one in Tunisia. In late 1966, Algeria had begun to drill for oil in the same area, creating new tensions between the two countries. Presumably the agreement of May 19 gives Tunisia a larger portion of the El-Borma area than it previously had without excluding Algeria from the oil fields.

30. The Moroccan government announced on May 24 that there had been a "serious incident" in the demilitarized zone the previous week. It claimed that the ANP had illegally occupied the oasis of Merkala, near Tindouf, in violation of the cease-fire accord of November 1963. It also said that on May 21 a Moroccan jeep carrying five men to a prearranged meeting with the ANP near Merkala had hit a mine; one officer was killed and the four others seriously wounded. The communique implied that the road had been deliberately mined by the ANP.

31. See *El-Moudjahid*, November 7, 1966.

attempted in early 1967 to mobilize international opinion in support of Morocco. In a speech to the nation on March 3, the king accused Algeria of arming itself for a "violent showdown" while systematically refusing to negotiate a peaceful settlement of the border dispute. He also called upon the United Nations to set up a special commission to supervise the disarmament of Algeria and Morocco.[32] The plea came shortly after the king made a visit to Washington, during which he asked for more military aid with little success. King Hassan failed to enlist international support for his claims. The fundamental weakness of the Moroccan position was that it involved territorial expansion. On the other hand, the Algerian position conformed to the OAU charter, which states that the borders established by the colonial powers should be accepted.

The two countries seemed destined to remain enemies as long as Morocco persisted in her expansionist policy and probably longer because of fundamental ideological differences between the two regimes. Indeed, in 1967, despite the creation in 1966 of numerous "permanent consultative committees" to further cooperation among the four North African countries, the unity of the Maghreb was still a long way off.[33] The distance was perhaps best measured by the fact that the four North African leaders never once got together in the first five years of Algeria's independence, although chiefs of state were frequently meeting elsewhere in Africa during this time to promote regional cooperation.

In early 1967, Colonel Boumediene became noticeably more involved in foreign policy, and Algeria began to emerge from isolation. In mid-February, Boumediene played host to Senegalese President Leopold Senghor, the first chief of state to visit Algeria since the *coup d'état*. On February 24, a delegation led by Salah Boubnider, a member of the FLN Executive Secretariat, and Major Slimane Hoffman, a high-ranking

---

32. See the *New York Times*, March 4, 1967.

33. The first "permanent consultative committee" was created in October 1964 for the purpose of coordinating the economic development plans of the four Maghreb countries and helping Tunisia, Algeria, and Morocco to establish a common policy toward the Common Market. As of 1967, the committee had achieved neither goal. However, its creation did lead to the creation of other permanent committees in the fields of education, telecommunications, commerce, transportation, and tourism. As of 1967, these committees had not succeeded in carrying out their most ambitious projects such as the creation of a customs union and of a North African airline; however, they were able to coordinate railroad transportation, to establish uniform mail and telephone rates, and to create a North African office for the exportation of alfalfa.

officer of the ANP, left on a month-long tour of fifteen African capitals. The main purpose of their trip was to promote a conference of revolutionary African parties in power. Boumediene hoped that such a conference would help to re-establish Algeria's standing as a revolutionary country, but the proposal met with little success and was quietly dropped. Boumediene was nonetheless slowly gaining acceptance among African progressive leaders. In early April, he participated, along with Nasser, Nyerere, Ould Daddah, and a personal representative of Sékou Touré, in a "little summit" meeting held in Cairo. During the same period, the exchange of party and government delegations between Algeria, Syria, and Egypt became more frequent, and in May representatives of the ruling parties of Mali and Guinea visited Algeria.

Algeria's foreign policy was beginning to bear the personal imprint of Boumediene. His approach was not revolutionary or emotional, as Ben Bella's had been, but rather legalistic. He did not encourage subversion of established regimes except to further the cause of national liberation. Characteristically, the meeting of revolutionary African parties that he sought to promote was to be attended by representatives of parties in power and of liberation movements, but not of opposition groups. Boumediene did not try to export the Algerian Revolution or to project himself as a leader of the Third World. Abroad as at home, he scorned "historic leaders" and "men with a sacred mission" who considered themselves the incarnation of revolution and in its name tried to impose themselves upon others. For this reason, he was always closer to the Syrian leaders than to Nasser and showed more interest in bringing together representatives of parties than in uniting leaders of nations. Whereas Ben Bella had personally carried out his foreign policy, Boumediene relied largely upon the FLN Executive Secretariat to establish contacts and maintain ties with the Arab and African countries.

Boumediene's first successful undertaking in foreign policy was the organization of a "seminar of Arab socialists," which was held in Algiers May 22–28, 1967. The purpose of the meeting was to advance the "unity of revolutionary Arab forces." For one week, eighty-three delegates, including some of the best known theorists of Arab socialism, discussed such issues as the various socialist experiences in the Arab world, the liquidation of feudalism, and the struggle against colonialism, neocolonialism, and imperialism. The seminar was the first of its kind; more significantly, it was the first Pan-Arab meeting in many years that

Nasser did not dominate. It was evident that Algeria and Syria were collaborating to keep the UAR from controlling this seminar as well as the organization of future ones: the Algerian ambassador to Cairo, Lakhdar Brahimi, was named secretary-general of a permanent preparatory committee that was to be based in Algiers, and it was decided that the second seminar would take place in Damascus.

The war that broke out between Israel and the Arab nations on June 5, 1967, had momentous consequences for Boumediene. For the first time since the *coup d'état*, the Algerian people appeared to be united with the colonel in a common cause and to accept him as their leader. Boumediene's call to war against the "Zionist hordes" evoked a tremendous response. Tens of thousands of Algerians volunteered to fight against Israel or joined "vigilance committees" set up throughout the country to "defend the socialist revolution against imperialist aggression."[34] The war brought out the fiery Arab nationalist in Boumediene, who abandoned his usual composure to deliver highly emotional and vehemently anti-Western speeches such as Algerians had not heard since the ouster of Ben Bella. The government even allowed the holding of rallies and demonstrations and made no attempt to prevent the sacking of the United States Information Center and the British library in Algiers. Boumediene demonstrated his new confidence on June 19, the second anniversary of the *coup d'état*. On that occasion, he addressed for the first time a mass rally on the Esplanade d'Afrique, where Ben Bella had so often harangued the crowds.

Algeria's actual contribution to the war effort was limited because the battlefield was distant and the war was of short duration. Nonetheless, Algeria contributed more than any other North African country and even more than some of the Middle Eastern states. The first contingent of ANP troops left Algeria on June 5, followed by forty-eight Mig fighters.[35] In addition, the Algerian government donated about 60 million francs ($12 million) to Egypt, Jordan, and Syria shortly after the end of the war. Half of this sum was raised through a special "war budget" financed primarily by a 5 per cent surtax on all personal income taxes and by the sale of war stamps throughout the country. At the

34. See Boumediene's speech of June 5, 1967.
35. Algeria was believed to have sent two companies of light infantry, two companies of motorized infantry, a battery of artillery, and close to 100 Mig fighters. Some 75 T-34 and T-55 tanks were being loaded on ships in Algiers when the war came to an end.

same time, Algeria carried out a diplomatic offensive against the "imperialist powers," accepting without question Egyptian claims that the United States and Britain had given air support to Israel. On June 6, the country severed diplomatic relations with Washington (it had already broken relations with London eighteen months before), suspended the sale of gas and oil to England and the United States, and placed American and British oil companies under state control.[36]

The acceptance of the cease-fire accord by Jordan, Egypt, and finally Syria after only six days of warfare was bitterly denounced by the Algerian press as an act of treason. Boumediene proclaimed on June 10 that Algeria would never accept the cease-fire and called instead for the total mobilization of the Arab nation in preparation for a protracted guerrilla-style war against Israel. The defeat of Nasser initially enhanced Boumediene's position in the Arab world. The humiliation suffered by the Egyptian leader achieved the goal toward which Algeria and Syria had been working for over a year—the end to Nasser's domination of the progressive Arab camp. Boumediene suddenly became the symbol of Arab intransigence, undefeated and determined to continue the struggle. As the self-appointed spokesman of the Arab countries, he flew to Moscow on June 12 to chide Soviet leaders for their lack of support during the war and to press them into taking up the Arab cause at the United Nations. In the weeks following the war, Boumediene remained extremely active, pressing his scheme for a protracted guerrilla-style war. He promptly found an ally in Syrian President Nureddin el-Attassi. At a meeting of the four socialist Arab leaders in Cairo July 10–16, both Boumediene and el-Attassi tried to convince Nasser and President Abdel Rahman Arif of Iraq to adhere to a militant course of action. However, both Nasser and Arif were extremely reluctant to embark upon a new war before the Egyptian army was rebuilt.

Boumediene's position and his active role in Arab politics immediately after the war gave rise to speculation in many quarters that the colonel might take the place of Nasser as the leading exponent of Arab nationalism. This impression was strengthened at the time of the emergency Arab summit conference held in Khartoum from August 29 to September 2 to discuss Arab strategy toward Israel. At that confer-

36. The suspension of oil and gas exports was of little consequence for the United States. American oil companies obtained less than 3 million tons of oil annually from Algeria. Britain suffered somewhat more, since it imported 1.5 billion cubic meters of gas annually from Algeria, or about 10 per cent of its total consumption.

ence, Nasser declared himself ready to seek a negotiated settlement of the Palestinian question. Boumediene, joined only by el-Attassi, refused to attend the conference, declaring that the only solution was "the continuation of the struggle and the liquidation of all imperialist interests in the Arab nation."[37] To stress his point, he announced in the same speech the nationalization of the five American oil-distributing companies operating in Algeria.[38]

By persevering in his intransigence, however, Boumediene ultimately achieved very little. He was unable to sway any Arab leaders, while Nasser demonstrated at Khartoum that even in defeat he still commanded the course of Arab politics. The Algerian president found himself in the embarrassing position of having loudly advocated a policy he was in no position to implement. Located some three thousand miles from the battlefield, Algeria could not singlehandedly wage a guerrilla war against Israel, and even Syria, its one ally, showed a limited willingness to continue the struggle. Boumediene's only solace was the hope that time, and the failure of negotiations with Israel, would eventually swing Arab leaders to his side.

Even at home, Boumediene's policy was not a success. In June, all Algerians, including his left-wing opponents, had eagerly accepted mobilization; by August, however, few believed that Algeria was on the brink of war, and the Left was once again more concerned with internal than with foreign-policy issues. The fact that it approved Boumediene's stand on Israel, for example, did not keep the UGTA from voicing its strong opposition to Industry Minister Abdesslam, who in July and August had created numerous state companies to the further detriment of the self-management system.[39] The ORP, which in the best

37. See Boumediene's speech of August 30, 1967.
38. The five companies were: Esso Standard Algérie; Esso Africa; Esso Saharienne; Mobiloil Nord-Africaine; and Mobiloil Française.
39. In the editorial of its August 15 edition, the UGTA weekly *Révolution et Travail* violently denounced the creation of the state companies. Although it admitted that such companies were sometimes necessary, the editorial continued: "But once the exception becomes a rule, once it is proven that the self-managed enterprises are being progressively stifled and will soon disappear, absorbed by the national [state] companies, is it not our duty to ring the warning bell? Is it not right to struggle against the decadent system being adopted by the national companies, a system that does not favor the moral and material interest of the worker in what he is producing, but on the contrary maintains him in a role of execution, excluded from the management of the enterprise? . . . We are against the absorption of the self-managed enterprises by national companies." *Révolution et Travail*, No. 122, August 15, 1967. In response to this editorial, the government again suspended publication of the weekly. Abdesslam also angered the UGTA by his decision in early

Algerian tradition had called for a "truce" in the face of an external
threat, was again at war with Boumediene, even condemning his uncompromising stand toward Israel on the grounds that it had isolated
Algeria from the Soviet bloc and the progressive Arab regimes. The
5,000 university students called up for a forty-five day military training
course in mid-July soon lost their initial enthusiasm and came to consider the exercise irrelevant to the success of the Palestinian cause and
prejudicial to their studies.[40] More dangerous for Boumediene was the
fact that some of his ministers, in particular the "technicians" upon
whose support he had come to depend, became disenchanted with his
Middle East policy. The public in general began to view continued
mobilization as simply a political maneuver calculated to rally support
for the Revolutionary Council. As a consequence, in the fall of 1967
Boumediene was approximately in the same position he was in before
the outbreak of the Arab-Israeli war: abroad he carried little influence,
and at home he faced the hostility of the Left and the indifference
of the public.

July to fire union representatives in SONATRACH, the state oil company, because
of their agitation for a larger role in management. Apparently Boumediene was in
agreement with Abdesslam on both issues, as he did not intervene.

40. Boumediene had initially talked of military training for workers, peasants,
women, and all youth. Only a training program for students was finally organized. A
decree published in the *Journal Officiel* of July 25, 1967, made it compulsory for all
students aged sixteen to thirty to attend training sessions once a week during the
school year and to serve in the army for several weeks during the summer.

chapter twelve
the Return to
personal power

... politics requires that only one person exercise control. Were various persons, liable to differ among each other, to exercise it, destruction of the whole world could result. "If there were other gods except God in ... [heaven and earth], they would have been destroyed."[1]

Ibn Khaldun

In the fall of 1967, the national unity created by the Arab-Israeli war gave way in the face of mounting tensions between the former wilaya commanders and the Boumediene clan. The conflict between these two groups had been latent ever since the creation of the Revolutionary Council and had been largely responsible for the immobility of the regime. Boumediene had increasingly sought to bypass the opposition of the wilaya leaders by having the Cabinet rather than the council make decisions; in fact, the council had not met since June 1967. This policy of course aroused the resentment of the wilaya leaders, who rightly saw it as an erosion of their influence.

On November 1, Colonel Tahar Zbiri manifested his dissatisfaction by refusing to attend the traditional armed forces parade, and shortly afterwards he began pressing for a meeting of the Revolutionary Council, reportedly with the intent of demanding the resignation of several members of the Boumediene clan from the Cabinet. Boumediene refused to convoke the council, however, fearing that a meeting would be the occasion not only for a confrontation between his supporters and the nine wilaya leaders, but also for a general debate on the merits of his own leadership, something he was anxious to avoid.

After attempts to settle their differences in private failed, both Zbiri

---

1. Ibn Khaldun. *The Muqaddimah*, trans. Franz Rosenthal, (Princeton: Princeton University Press 1967), p. 337.

and Boumediene prepared for a showdown. In order to weaken his opponents, on December 10 Boumediene dismissed the FLN's Executive Secretariat, which included four wilaya commanders, and named one of his closest allies, Finance Minister Kaid, to lead the party. Four days later, Zbiri began marching toward Algiers at the head of a column of dissident units from the First Military Region that were commanded by several of his relatives. Boumediene was not caught off guard.[2] He personally took command of the army, replacing Zbiri as chief of staff,[3] and ordered loyal ANP units, the gendarmerie, and the air force to block the route of the advancing column. After a brief battle near El-Affroun, forty miles southwest of Algiers, Zbiri and his relatives fled into the mountains and the four dissident units rallied. The clash left thirty persons dead and over a hundred wounded.

Zbiri had apparently counted upon the support of Major Abid Said, commander of the First Military Region, and possibly upon popular demonstrations organized by the UGTA in the capital. However, the demonstrations never took place, and Said failed to join the rebellion. Major Said's attitude toward the rebellion never became clear. According to official accounts, he remained loyal to Boumediene and even tried to act as mediator; then, having failed to dissuade Zbiri and being upset by the disloyalty of his own troops, he committed suicide on the morning of December 15. It seems equally possible, however, that Said was compromised in the plot and that he either was killed by loyal officers or committed suicide after betraying Zbiri at the last moment.

In the wake of the rebellion, Minister of Labor Zerdani, a close friend of Zbiri, and Minister of Agriculture Ali Yahia, a wartime secretary-general of the UGTA, disappeared from the capital. The two ministers, known for their close ties to the UGTA and their sympathy for self-management, had handed in their resignations a short time earlier. The wave of arrests of UGTA officials following the abortive *coup*

---

2. Boumediene claimed that on the night of December 14 he was alerted by Major Said, commander of the First Military Region, that a column of tanks was moving from El-Asnam toward Algiers. In any case, Boumediene had been on his guard ever since August, when rumors of a *coup d'état* first began to circulate. He took extra precautions after November 5 when Zbiri barricaded himself in the military camp at Lido, where his brother-in-law commanded a battalion of tanks. See Boumedienne's speech of January 4 in *Révolution Africaine*, No. 255, January 4-10, 1968.

3. The decision to oust Zbiri was actually made on November 5. The decree did not appear in the *Journal Officiel* until December 22, but it was antedated to November 1, the day Zbiri refused to attend the armed forces parade.

was further evidence that leftist elements had been involved in the conspiracy.

The December confrontation resulted in the eclipse of the former wilaya commanders and the severance of the last ties between the Boumediene government and the Left. Its most important consequence, however, was the abandonment of the principle of collegiality, which had been the fundamental tenet of the Boumediene regime. By refusing to convoke the Revolutionary Council, Boumediene made it clear that he no longer intended to abide by majority rule. The fact that the council did not even meet after the ouster of the wilaya commanders was the first indication that for all practical purposes it had been disbanded. Further confirmation came on January 4, when Boumediene gave a three-hour speech to fifteen hundred party, army, and government officials without once using the word "collegiality" or mentioning the Revolutionary Council.

That the demise of the Revolutionary Council provoked no outcry from its remaining members attested to the fact that Boumediene had succeeded in establishing himself as the sole leader of Algeria. In effect, Boumediene had traveled the same road Ben Bella had five years earlier. Once again the reins of power were held by a few persons, just as had been the case under Ben Bella. As the Tunisian weekly *Jeune Afrique* appropriately commented in January 1968:

> Chief of state (not elected), of the party (through the interposition of Ahmed Kaid), and of the goverment, Colonel Boumediene concentrates in his own hands more power than former President Ben Bella.[4]

Actually, the concentration of power under Boumediene was even greater than the above statement indicates. While Ben Bella had many titles, his freedom of action was always severely restricted by the necessity to heed the demands of the Left in order to maintain its support as a countervailing force to the army. Boumediene, on the other hand, no longer faced any major threat from within the army and thus could afford to disregard the demands of his opponents. His new assurance was reflected in the appointments he made in early March to fill the three vacant posts in the Cabinet. He brought back his trusted associate Belkacem, who had been dismissed as coordinator of the FLN when the Executive Secretariat was disbanded, and appointed him minister of finance and of the plan. He gave the Ministry of Agriculture and the

4. *Jeune Afrique*, No. 365, January 7, 1968.

Ministry of Labor to two relatively uninfluential politicians and thus could scarcely be regarded as granting concessions to rival clans.[5]

Though Boumediene's power was far more absolute than Ben Bella's had ever been, he never played the role of leader with as much conviction and relish. Yet he slowly developed his own style of rule, characterized by long, rambling speeches to the cadres of the nation and periodic "business" trips to the interior with the entire Cabinet to demonstrate his concern for the forgotten masses. In isolated provincial capitals like Ouargla, Batna, and Tizi Ouzou, he would hold working sessions of the Cabinet devoted to local problems, at the end of which he would usually announce the allocation of funds for a regional development plan. His week-long tour of the Kabylia in October 1968 was a remarkable success, for he was cheered with surprising warmth in what had long been a stronghold of resistance to the government in Algiers. Always lacking in charisma, he nonetheless learned to talk the language of peasants and workers and seemed to have gained their respect, if not their enthusiasm. Within the Cabinet, Boumediene did not become noticeably more authoritarian in manner, as he preferred reaching a consensus rather to imposing his own will. Yet despite this element of democracy, there was never any doubt that it was Boumediene who held the power or that any serious challenge to his authority would be tolerated. The extreme efficiency of the military police was just one reminder of the true state of affairs.

After the failure of their *coup*, Zbiri and his supporters did not immediately give up their struggle to topple the regime, and they organized a series of attempts on the life of Boumediene and other prominent leaders, apparently hoping to return to power in the ensuing chaos. On January 24 in Algiers, there was an unsuccessful attack on Kaid's life. In late February, another attempt on Kaid's life was foiled when the police arrested seventeen persons said to be involved in a plot to assassinate him and other members of the government.[6] These

5. Mohamed Said Mazouzi, a Kabyle and the prefect of Tizi Ouzou, became minister of labor and social affairs. Mohamed Tayebi, a former member of the FLN Executive Secretariat was named minister of agriculture and agrarian reform. Tayebi had ties both to Boumediene and to the wilaya group with which he often sided. He did not join Zbiri in the attempted *coup* and was apparently rewarded for his faithfulness. He is no longer considered to represent a specific constituency or to be particularly influential.

6. There was always some doubt whether these attacks were carried out by Zbiri's group or by followers of Belkacem Krim, who had formed the Mouvement

arrests, however, did not succeed in breaking up the clandestine organization. On April 25, a group of terrorists dressed in the uniform of the National Security Forces (CNS) opened fire on Boumediene's car as it was passing through downtown Algiers. The car was riddled with bullets, but Boumediene miraculously escaped with only a cut lip. One of the attackers was killed instantly, but the others got away. After a week-long intensive search for the would-be assassins, the military police on May 1 arrested Major Amar Mellah, a former member of the ANP General Staff and a close confidant of Zbiri, and ten others allegedly involved in the conspiracy. These arrests apparently destroyed the terrorist organization, for Zbiri fled to Tunisia in early June, and there were no further incidents. Nonetheless, the government remained on the alert, obviously determined to check the resurgence of any clandestine opposition. During July and August, it arrested hundreds of labor union members, leftist students, and other suspected opponents of the regime. The release of many of those arrested during the summer at the time of the November 1 celebrations and the improvement in the treatment of the three imprisoned ORP leaders were gestures of generosity toward an enemy no longer posing a threat rather than the beginning of an opening to the Left.[7]

With the ouster of the wilaya leaders from the Revolutionary Council and the consolidation of his power, Boumediene was finally free to turn his attention to the most critical problem facing his regime: the lack of organized support and of political institutions. In his speech of January 4, Boumediene admitted that two and a half years after his accession to power, the party was still in a state of chaos. He spoke of regionalism and nepotism undermining its strength and of officials "equipped only with a militant past" failing in their duties. He announced that the government's main objective in the coming year would

---

Démocratique du Renouveau Algérien (MDRA) in Paris in October 1967. The fact Zbiri's group attempted to assassinate Boumediene makes it seem likely that the group was also involved in these earlier incidents.

7. The three leaders, Bachir Hadj Ali, Hocine Zahouane, and Mohamed Harbi, were taken from prison in eastern Algeria and placed under house arrest in villas near Algiers. The ORP, which became the Parti d'Avant-garde Socialiste (PAGS) in the fall of 1967, worked for a reconciliation with the Boumediene regime after the three leaders were released from prison. In December, the PAGS called for the formation of a "democratic and popular front" composed of exiled and imprisoned leaders and members of the Boumediene government. It also noted the "positive evolution" of the country under Boumediene. See Le Monde, December 4, 1967.

be the restructuring of the FLN and proclaimed 1968 "the year of the party."

Boumediene's speech and the appointment of Kaid as party leader marked the beginning of another massive effort to build a coherent, well-organized, and dynamic political body that would have control over all the national organizations and serve as a catalyst for human resources and energies. It was the third time since independence that the task had been undertaken, and the prospects for success were not much greater this time than they had been in the past. The campaign began in February with a series of meetings and conferences held throughout the country to explain the goals and the role of the FLN and to appeal to Algerians to become involved. Subsequently "control commissions" were established at the various levels of the party hierarchy to organize the election of local officials, oversee a campaign to recruit new members, and weed out those who did not qualify as "true militants." Throughout the summer and fall, there was intense activity within the party, with numerous meetings being held to discuss strategy and train cadres, while the press kept up a steady barrage of propaganda. In November, a national school for cadres was established at Boudouaou (Alma) for the purpose of indoctrinating young party workers and forming a solid elite corps.

The results were few. The recruitment phase of the campaign, which got under way in late September after several months delay, showed that Algerians had not been shaken from their distrust of or indifference toward the FLN. This was particularly the case in the big cities. In Algiers itself, only 80 per cent of those who were party members in January 1968 had reapplied for membership by the end of that year.[8] In the departments of Constantine and Oran, two of the most heavily populated regions of the country, the party had received 35,000 and 40,000 applications respectively by mid-November. In the rural areas, however, the response was considerably greater; in the small arrondissement of Miliana, for example, 8,300 applications were registered by mid-November.[9]

The slow progress of the campaign was acknowledged by Kaid in an interview he gave to the party weekly *Révolution Africaine* in early January 1969.[10] Revealing that party officials were just beginning to

8. *El-Moudjahid*, November 9, 1968.
9. *Révolution Africaine*, No. 286, November 8–14, 1968.
10. *Révolution Africaine*, No. 293–294, January 1, 1969.

examine applications for membership, Kaid said that 1969 would also have to be "the year of the party" and indicated that he had sharply revised his grandiose reorganization plan. He spoke of concentrating all efforts that year on the establishment of cells and kasmas, indicating that the organization of the party at the level of the federation (arrondissement) and the department was still only a "theoretical projection." Even more significant was the fact that he no longer mentioned elections for leaders of the cells and kasmas; rather, he indicated that once the selection of members had been completed, party officials in Algiers would proceed to "choose" local leaders.

The problems Kaid encountered in his campaign to revive the FLN were to some extent the same ones that had contributed to the failures of past efforts, namely the lack of competent cadres, the absence of any concrete program, the political apathy of Algerians, and a lingering distrust of the party. Moreover, to these obstacles the Boumediene regime had added one of its own making: for two and a half years, it had pursued a policy of strengthening the administration and government while allowing the FLN steadily to disintegrate. Efforts to reassert the primacy of the FLN inevitably encountered a great deal of resistance from those who had a vested interest in the new status quo. Government and administration officials doggedly resisted any encroachment on the powers they had progressively assumed for themselves. Opposition to the emergence of the FLN as a powerful force began in the Cabinet and ran all the way down the government hierarchy to the people's assemblies. Within the Cabinet, the conflict developed into an open rivalry between Kaid on one side and Minister of the Interior Medeghri and Minister of Industry Abdesslam on the other. The conflict was in part a manifestation of political rivalries among various Cabinet members, but it also involved the more basic problem of the respective powers and functions of party and government. In effect, the ministers were challenging the leadership role ascribed to the FLN in every ideological charter produced since the beginning of the revolution.

The resistance to the assertion of the FLN's authority was also evident at all levels of the civil service. The party press talked at length about the need to "remold the mentality" of civil servants, whom it accused of understanding poorly the notion of *engagement*:

> Among the cadres of the state, for example, certain [persons] maintain
> that one can be engaged in the service of the economic and social revo-

lution without needing to belong to a cell of the FLN. They believe that their submission to directives of a technical and administrative nature is sufficient in and of itself. The theoreticians call that disassociating political from technical roles.[11]

Even in the communes, party officials and members of the people's assemblies found themselves opposed, though the latter had mostly come from the ranks of the FLN. *Révolution Africaine* noted that party members elected to the assemblies developed "a sort of reserve, in certain cases even hostility," toward the FLN.[12]

Although Kaid failed to assert the supremacy of the party over the government, he did manage to establish the party's control over the labor federation, which ever since the *coup d'état* had succeeded in maintaining an uneasy autonomy. Kaid began his offensive against the UGTA even before he launched the campaign to rebuild the party. By the end of January 1968, he had established party-controlled "interregional commissions" in Algiers, Oran, and Constantine to prepare for the third UGTA congress. The role of these commissions was to "renew the structures and sections [of the union] at the base, prepare the documents to be studied, and oversee the material organization of the congress."[13] "Renewing the structures," it soon became clear, meant installing at the head of each local an official chosen by the party. In effect, the FLN was taking over the UGTA from the inside.

As part of its offensive against the UGTA, the FLN during the summer issued a brochure highly critical of the labor movement and circulated it among the workers. The document accused the Federation's leaders of having taken "irresponsible" positions and of having maintained "an unjustified and systematic spirit of resistance" toward the party.[14] It also claimed the UGTA had committed acts of subversion and sabotage with respect to the economy. It was only after gaining control of the federation that the party admitted that the UGTA had not been allowed to play its proper role. The FLN organ *Révolution Africaine* remarked:

> It would be too easy in this operation of reorganization to blame everything on the present leadership of the executive committee. . . . One cannot deny the bad faith of certain administrative authorities who were determined to muzzle representatives of the labor union.[15]

11. *Révolution Africaine*, No. 286, November 8–14, 1968.
12. *Révolution Africaine*, No. 260, February 8–14, 1968.
13. *El-Moujahid*, January 28–29, 1968.
14. *Le Monde*, October 31, 1968.
15. *Révolution Africaine*, No. 286, November 8–14, 1968.

The weekly pointed out that the UGTA representatives in state enterprises did not even have legal protection against being fired because of their union activities.

Internal conditions made it extremely difficult for the federation to counter the party's offensive. Factionalism and personal squabbles were rife among UGTA officials, and membership had fallen from 250,000 to around 150,000. The national leadership had more or less disintegrated by December 1967; only four of the nine national secretaries were still in office. Furthermore, there was a fundamental disagreement among the remaining secretaries over whether or not to submit voluntarily to the party's control. Secretary-General Oumeziane was willing to accept an accomodation with the party, hoping that in return the UGTA would be granted a role in the management of the economy. He agreed to serve as president of the national preparatory commission for the third UGTA congress, working in cooperation with FLN leaders, but he also spoke out for the direct participation of workers in the management of state enterprises. For instance, standing next to Boumediene at Labor Day celebrations in 1968, Oumeziane called for the establishment of workers' councils in the state companies and for a role for UGTA in writing the statutes of these enterprises. But the government made no concessions and moved instead to weaken further the federation by arresting some of its most militant officials during the summer. By the fall of 1968, even Oumeziane was ready to resign.

The *coup de grâce* came during a national conference of party and UGTA leaders held in Algiers October 26-27. At that time, with half of the fifty-one-member executive committee either in jail, hiding, or exile, the remaining four national secretaries resigned from office, declaring that they had "decided unanimously that it was the party's responsibility to find the correct solutions for a rapid redress of the situation and that for this reason they were handing in their mandates."[16] Oumeziane agreed to continue as secretary-general until the third congress, which it was decided would be held in April 1969. Only the Algiers local, which had refused to participate in the conference, remained a stronghold of resistance to the party.

The party's takeover of the UGTA was largely a hollow victory. The slow process of undermining the federation through arrests, an intense propaganda campaign, and infiltration resulted in sapping the organization of all its vitality as well as forfeiting nearly half of its member-

16. *Ibid.*

ship. Just how the FLN, already stymied by its own problems of reorganization, will find the time, cadres, and energy to revitalize an organization much larger than itself remains to be seen. It is probable that the UGTA will remain a shadow of its former self.

Kaid was less successful in his efforts to bring the student union under party control. Like all FLN leaders before him, he tried to organize a party-sponsored student organization to take over UNEA. The Fédération des Etudiants Militants du Parti (FEMP) was created in February, but once again this tactic failed. When Kaid announced in early February that the party was planning elections for student committees at the University of Algiers, UNEA called a boycott of classes that lasted the entire month. The strike was a total success and soon spread to high schools in Algiers and to the University of Oran. On February 6, some two hundred students staged a "sit-in" at the University of Algiers but were ejected from the buildings the same night by the National Security Forces called in by the government. At least thirty students were arrested, including three members of UNEA's national executive committee. Following the clash, the University of Algiers was closed down for the first time since independence.

The strike dragged on through February, with students demanding free elections, the release of their imprisoned colleagues, and the withdrawal of police from university grounds. The situation grew steadily more serious as Algerian professors at the university openly took the side of the students against the party, as did some of the UGTA locals in Algiers.[17] Party leaders did their best to discredit the organizers of the strike, accusing them of belonging to the clandestine opposition and of being in league with "foreign meddlers." The implication was that French professors were encouraging the students, and one French law professor was in fact arrested. The strike finally ended in late February with a partial victory for the students. The FLN gave up its attempt to take over UNEA and the FEMP quietly disappeared. Kaid refused to release the arrested demonstrators, but he did not carry out his threat to suspend a large number of students from the university or to take

17. The teachers union, known as the Fédération des Travailleurs de l'Enseignement et de la Culture (FTEC), twice called for a strike in support of the students but failed to strike either time. Expressions of solidarity with the students also came from railroad workers, dockers, and state gas company employees, although the national leadership of the UGTA expressed its disapproval of the strike under extreme pressure from the party.

away their scholarships. After this episode, the FLN did not renew its effort to bring UNEA under its control. The example of the student rebellion in France, which almost toppled the de Gaulle government in May, made the Boumediene regime extremely wary of arousing the students once again.

Kaid had little difficulty in maintaining the party's control over the two other major national organizations, UNFA and the JFLN, which both remained docile but totally unable to mobilize their respective constituencies. The FLN continued to pay little attention to the women's organization, although it did undertake a major drive to revive and expand the JFLN. There were numerous seminars and conferences throughout 1968 for the purpose of training youth leaders and drawing up concrete programs, yet little materialized beyond the conference rooms. The JFLN remained the shell of an organization, with probably no more than 25,000 members and only vaguely delineated goals.

The effort to revive the JFLN was only one aspect of the Boumediene regime's strategy for mobilizing Algerian youth. Far more significant was its decision in April 1968 to create the National Service, an organization in which every Algerian nineteen years of age or over was to serve two years.[18] Although some of the mobilized youth were to be given military training, the majority were to be assigned to a wide variety of economic and social tasks or put to work in the administration. The government announced that it would begin the service by drafting 118,000 boys and 116,000 girls in 1969, and it established the basic monthly salary at 111 dinars ($22.20) for those living at home and 361 dinars ($72.20) for those away from home.

The Boumediene regime obviously looks upon the National Service as an excellent vehicle for political indoctrination. *Révolution Africaine* describes it as a "school called upon to produce authentic socialists rather than simply a system of voluntary service."[19] The creation of the National Service may be the most revolutionary step yet taken by the Boumediene regime. It will force the youth of the cities out into the countryside to perform concrete tasks and bring those from the backward regions of the country in contact with the modern world. The service may have a great impact on the emancipation of the Algerian

18. The National Service was created by a decree dated April 16, 1968. See the *Journal Officiel*, No. 32, April 19, 1968, Ordonnance 68–82.
19. *Révolution Africaine*, No. 292, December 20–26, 1968. A fairly detailed description of how the service is to work can be found in this issue.

woman, for it will require the girls to leave their homes and veils to work alongside the men as equals.

Once the leadership of Algeria had been reduced to one relatively homogeneous clan, Colonel Boumediene was free to express his views, and it became clearer what his vision was of the organization of the Algerian state and its political institutions. His idea was to have a system of decentralized local government counterbalanced by a single centralized party and a well-established administration. Though dedicated to building a "strong state," Boumediene began in 1968 to show signs of concern about the "paralyzing bureaucracy" of the administration and even called for a "struggle against centralization."[20] He indicated that the communes—the basic "cells" of the new Algerian society—and the communal assemblies ("peoples assemblies") were intended to play a key role in that struggle.

The next step in Boumediene's plan to build institutions is a radical transformation of regional government through the creation of "departmental assemblies." Elections for these assemblies were scheduled to take place in 1967 and then in 1968, but as of early 1969 they still had not been held. This delay will postpone until at least 1970 the election of a new National Assembly, which will complete the construction of the institutional edifice. The slowness in the establishment of political institutions has partly been the consequence of political difficulties within the Revolutionary Council and the Cabinet and partly the result of the problems encountered in the effort to make the communal assemblies effectively functioning bodies. The activity of the communal assemblies during their first year in existence was severely limited by the lack of funds and competent leadership; nonetheless, particularly in northern Algeria, they brought about a noticeable revival of local initiative, stifled since independence under the heavy-handed government of the appointed special delegations. The following accomplishments of communal assemblies in the Department of Constantine were listed by *Révolution Africaine*: 85 water pipes or conduits; 126 wells or watering places; 29 sewer systems; 430 housing units and 8 health centers; and 1,400 hectares planted with fruit trees.[21]

Many of the communes' financial difficulties stemmed from the fact

20. Interview with *Révolution Africaine*, No. 289, November 23–December 4, 1968.
21. *Révolution Africaine*, No. 259, February 1–7, 1968.

that the government was slow in relinquishing control of local industrial enterprises, while at the same time it demanded that the communes repay the debts incurred by the special delegations, the appointed bodies in charge of local government prior to the creation of communal assemblies. A small oasis town like Touggourt, for example, found itself burdened with a debt of one million dinars ($200,000), which prevented it from undertaking more than a few small projects. Particularly in the south, the limitations placed on the activities of the communal assemblies led to disillusionment with the effectiveness of these assemblies as institutions of local government, a state of affairs that was acknowledged even by the party press. Despite these initial, predictable difficulties, the Boumediene regime seemed determined to make the communal assemblies viable institutions. In December 1967, it dispensed 40 million dinars ($8 million) in grants to help them pay off the debts they had inherited. It also began in early 1968 to transfer to the communes control over more of the small industrial enterprises. These steps brought about a considerable improvement in the financial status of at least some of the communes. For instance, the budget of the commune of Algiers increased by 45 per cent in 1968, from 106.5 million dinars ($21.5 million) to 157.9 million dinars ($31.6 million).[22] However, none of the larger and more profitable enterprises were turned over to the communal assemblies, and it seems unlikely that any will be as long as Abdesslam remains minister of industry. Moreover, it is becoming evident that the revenue derived from the few local enterprises and from indirect taxes is insufficient for most communes in depressed areas like the Sahara and that the government will have to institute a system of direct subsidies.

The problems encountered by the communal assemblies prompted the Boumediene government to postpone elections for the departmental assemblies. Nonetheless, in order to give the impression that the government was moving forward in its plan to establish political institutions, provisional "departmental economic and social councils" were set up in January 1968.[23] The councils, which were soon being called assemblies by government officials, were composed of the presidents of the communal assemblies and representatives of the party, UGTA, and the

22. See *Révolution Africaine*, No. 271, April 25–May 1, 1968.
23. The councils were officially created by a decree signed October 19, 1967, but were not set up until the following January. See *Journal Officiel*, No. 89, October 31, 1967, Ordonnance 67–222.

army. Their function was limited to advising local authorities on social and economic matters and to helping draw up regional development plans. Boumediene also declared that they would help to determine the precise role the elected departmental assemblies should play. Although he had initially announced that these councils would be in existence for only one year, they were still functioning in early 1969, and plans for the election of departmental assemblies have remained vague. It may very well be that the councils will remain in place of the assemblies for some time to come.

The process of economic development advanced steadily during 1968 under the guidance of Minister of Industry Abdesslam, who had clearly emerged as the regime's most powerful minister. With Boumediene's full approval, the dynamic Abdesslam continued to form a vast number of state companies in all branches of the economy, giving priority to the development of heavy industry, particularly of the oil and gas industry. The official rationale for this policy was that Algeria must become totally independent of foreign aid and investment capital as quickly as possible. This conviction had its wellspring in the intense, emotional nationalism of the Boumediene regime as well as in the realization that foreign aid is constantly subject to political fluctuations and brings with it unwelcome pressures. It was with considerable pride that Boumediene announced in January 1968 that Algeria had $400 million in foreign reserves and had been able to convert $150 million into gold, "[a step] that will not fail to strengthen our money, build confidence in our country, and reinforce the most complete independence from all external pressures for both our domestic and foreign policy."[24]

The government's first three-year industrial development plan clearly reflected the policy of giving priority to the establishment of heavy industry and the expansion of the state sector. The plan, covering the years 1967 through 1969, called for a total investment of 5.4 billion dinars ($1.08 billion), fully half of which was earmarked for the development of the oil and gas industries and their subsidiaries such as fertilizers and other petrochemicals. Another 1.2 billion dinars ($240 million) was to be spent for the completion of the huge steel mill near Annaba, which began limited operations in early 1969. [25] The objective

24. *Révolution Africaine*, No. 255, January 4–10, 1968.
25. For details of the three-year industrial development plan, see *Révolution Africaine*, No. 256, January 11–17, 1968, pp. 16–18.

of the plan is to create the basic industries necessary for an economic "take-off" by 1972. During the first two years of the three-year plan, however, actual investment ran far behind schedule, mainly because of difficulties encountered in drawing up and launching projects. In 1967, the government managed to invest only 650 million dinars ($130 million) instead of 1.2 billion ($240 million) but in 1968 the investment ratio improved considerably, reaching 1.5 billion dinars ($300 million) out of a projected 1.8 billion dinars ($360 million).

The government has geared itself for an all-out effort in 1969, with plans to invest around $700 million in the industrial sector. It has a list of eighty projects, including cement, textile, sugar, and canning factories and a tractor and diesel motor plant. The amount of capital earmarked for agricultural development during the same three-year period amounts to about one-sixth of that budgeted for industrial projects, remaining at 537.5 million dinars ($107.5 million) annually. Colonel Boumediene has claimed that Algeria itself is providing 94 per cent of the investment capital. While this is definitely an exaggeration, the fact remains that the country is well on its way to becoming economically self-sufficient.

In an effort to eliminate competition with the expanding state sector, the government continued during 1968 to nationalize foreign private industries, while at the same time severely limiting private investment by Algerian nationals.[26] On May 13, the government took over all companies selling oil and gas products, and a week later it nationalized twenty-seven French firms manufacturing such products as construction materials, fertilizers, machinery, electrical supplies, textiles, and foods.[27] On June 14, eighteen other companies, all but one French, were also seized. Other nationalizations of both French and non-French enterprises followed during the summer. A few French concerns, notably the banks, succeeded in avoiding outright nationalization by reaching an agreement with the Algerian government,[28] but this was

26. By July 1968, the investment commission had received 576 projects for new enterprises, representing an investment of 295 million dinars ($59 million). However, it had approved only 78 of these projects, involving an investment of 59 million dinars ($11.8 million). See *Révolution Africaine*, No. 280, July 1–7, 1968.

27. Fourteen foreign companies, twelve of them French, were nationalized on May 13. The Algerian company SONATRACH thereafter had a complete monopoly on the sale of oil and gas products.

28. The government was willing to negotiate an agreement only in those cases where it needed the help of the companies' engineers, technicians, or skilled personnel. Such was the case for three large construction, engineering, and metallurgy

the exception rather than the rule. Many of the companies nationalized were among the largest in the country. By June 1968, of the three hundred French companies operating in 1966 and employing 28,000 workers, sixty-six employing 10,000 workers, had been seized.[29] Altogether, about 80 per cent of the industrial sector had been taken over by the state. While these nationalizations were obviously part of a long-term strategy to eliminate most independent foreign companies in the country, the timing of them was not totally unrelated to internal political developments. The attempted assassination of Boumediene and government fears that UNEA might initiate a rebellion similar to that of the French students undoubtedly precipitated the wave of nationalizations in May and June.

Boumediene made state capitalism the fundamental economic doctrine of Algeria *de facto* but not *de jure*. The myth of self-management as the "principal path" chosen by Algeria in its march toward socialism was kept alive even while the government persistently sought to stifle the development of the system in the industrial sector and made no major effort to assure its success on the farms. In April 1968, the FLN produced a complete and exhaustive study of the self-management system and of the multitude of problems it had encountered since its inception. The report included proposals for reforms in the farm sector but made no mention of the self-managed factories, implying that self-management would eventually be restricted to the farms. Nonetheless, the FLN document exalted self-management as a "system of social, economic, and political organization the ideological content of which constitutes the principal path chosen by Algeria in its march toward socialism . . ."[30] The study included new statistics on the self-managed farm sector, which showed the slow contraction in the number of units and workers. As of April 1968, there were 1953 self-managed farms covering 2.3 million hectares and employing 136,860 full-time workers.[31]

companies, ALTUMEC, SOTRIBAL, and NEYRPIC, which were all bought out by the Algerian National Metallurgy Company.

29. See *Le Monde*, June 16–17, 1968.

30. Front de Libération Nationale, Commission Révolution Agraire, *Principes Directeurs de l'Autogestion*, April 1968, p. 7.

31. *Ibid.*, p. 12. The figure of 1953 included both self-managed farms and war veterans' cooperatives. The reduction in the number of units can only be the result of further consolidation of the farms, a trend that had begun as early as 1963, since the total number of hectares in the self-managed farm sector remains the same. If there were some restitutions of farms to private owners, the number must have been small.

In 1964, on the same land, there had been 2,284 farms with some 220,000 permanent workers.

The FLN study placed part of the blame for the problems presented by the self-management system on the impreciseness of the March Decrees and on the failure to apply them. The result, it said, had been an "anarchistic centralization" of the agricultural sector by the government "in an unconscious and subjective reflex of self-defense."[32] This extreme centralization had "emptied self-management of its political content—the promotion of the workers and all that it entails—and of its economic [content]—the dynamism and profitableness resulting from the autonomy of management."[33] Paradoxically, the very agencies set up to provide the farms with credits, seeds, and fertilizers, and to market their produce had ended by choking the system to death:

> In effect, the ORNA and the other pseudo-cooperative agencies living parasitically off the self-managed sector, took over the management of the enterprises directly instead of lending their technical aid and exercising an indispensable control over the self-managed units, thus withdrawing from the organs of self-management all effective responsibility and all autonomy in the direction of the unit.[34]

The report was particularly critical of the agencies responsible for financing the farms. It condemned what it called "a policy of confusion and improvisation" by these agencies prior to June 1965[35] and the struggle for control of the farms between the Ministry of Agriculture and the new national bank that was instituted after the change of governments.

These agencies were not the sole cause of the problems afflicting the self-managed farms. The FLN report indicted the workers themselves for their reluctance to obey orders, respect hierarchy, or follow the "golden rule of the farm world: work begins at dawn and finishes at dusk."[36] It also noted that constant carelessness and shoddy workmanship had resulted in a "noticeable drop in the quality of Algerian products,"[37] making it difficult for them to compete in foreign markets. The FLN urged an "intensive political preparation" to explain to the workers their duties and responsibilities.

The FLN report proposed a number of reforms in the structure of the

---

32. *Ibid.*, p. 33.
33. *Ibid.*
34. *Ibid.*
35. *Ibid.*, p. 21.
36. *Ibid.*, p. 15.
37. *Ibid.*, p. 19.

supporting agencies and certain modifications in the March Decrees. It suggested that most of these agencies be replaced by cooperatives run by the workers themselves rather than by civil servants "very little interested in the results of [the farms'] management."[38] In order to decentralize the system and assure worker participation, it proposed that these new cooperatives be established in each arrondissement. Noting that the state bank created in 1966 had utterly failed to serve the self-managed farms as anticipated, the report recommended that a special farm bank be established as one step toward ending the financial chaos of the farm sector. As other steps, it suggested the adoption of price and wage guidelines and the strict regulation of the fees charged to the farms by the various agencies. It also recommended that the payroll, which had too often represented 70 per cent of the farm's operating expenses, be reduced to the 40 or 45 per cent considered normal for a well-managed agricultural enterprise.

With respect to the March Decrees, the revisions proposed by the FLN were by no means sweeping, although the report proposed and drew up an entirely new set of decrees. The structures of management (general assembly, workers' council, and management committee) were to be left unchanged except for the elimination of the workers' councils on farms employing fewer than 150 workers. The proposed decrees spelled out in considerable detail the definition of a "permanent" as opposed to a "seasonal" worker, with the intent of ending the chronic overemployment that had rendered the operation of many units unprofitable. They even authorized the government to fix a limit on the number of full-time workers according to its estimate of the needs of each farm. In order to curtail the nepotism that had transformed many farms into family-run operations, the proposed decrees specified that no farm would be allowed to employ as permanent workers more than three persons from the same immediate family and that no management committee would be permitted to include more than one person from the same family. A special section on discipline formally denounced the workers' right to strike in the self-managed sector of the economy.[39]

38. *Ibid.*, p. 17.
39. *Ibid.*, p. 55, Articles 67–79. Article 79 states: "The strike, as a method aimed at improving working conditions, is a means of recourse to be absolutely forbidden. In effect, it constitutes a violation of one of the fundamental principles of the system of self-management, [that] which enjoins the collectivity of workers to manage the unit of production as 'good administrators.' "

Perhaps the most important reform to be proposed was that concerning the system of profit-sharing. The March Decrees had provided for a three-way division of the farm's profits: one-third was to be shared among the workers themselves, another third given over to a national employment fund, and the remainder deposited in a national investment fund. The new decrees proposed a two-way division of the farm's net profits, one-half going to the state and the other half to a "farm fund." The share taken by the state was to be divided equally between the national employment fund and the investment fund. The share returning to the farm was to be divided four ways, with one part of the profits going into a special reserve fund, another part into the regular treasury for day-to-day financing, a third part into an "economic and social investment fund," and the remainder being divided among the workers. The decrees indicated that a worker's share could not exceed 50 per cent of his annual salary and that any surplus had to be deposited in an "interregional equalization fund." The maximum bonus for a non-specialized worker would thus be 1,272 dinars ($254.00).

Despite the emphatic endorsement of the principle of self-management by the FLN, the future of the self-management system still appears very much in doubt. The wave of nationalizations in 1968 affected not only the private foreign companies, but numerous self-managed factories as well. On June 14, four self-managed enterprises were put under state management. In late July, the government seized eleven large companies being run by management committees and turned them over to SONATRACH and two other big state companies. On the other hand, there have been a few encouraging developments. In June 1968, for the first time in four years, the government authorized the sharing of profits among workers on farms running in the black; however, less than a third of the farms, 572 out of 1953, reported a profit.[40] There were also a few reports in the press of the distribution of profits among workers in some of the self-managed factories, which were apparently succeeding despite the lack of aid from the government. In the Algiers region, for example, 42 out of 138 enterprises were reported to have made a combined profit of eight million dinars ($1.6 million) and to have divided among 5,000 workers almost one and a

40. As happened under Ben Bella, the "distribution of profits" amounted to the granting of a standard bonus calculated independently of the profit made by each farm. The bonus amounted to 1,000 dinars ($200.00), but each worker was obliged to give back to the farm fund one-third of this amount.

half million dinars ($229,600);[41] but this was the first such distribution of profits in those factories since independence. The Boumediene government also promised that as soon as the new decrees were approved there would be elections to renew the management committees and workers' councils. However, as of January 1969, the decrees had not been approved.

The major reason for doubt about the future of self-management in Algeria is that the system remains at the center of a political struggle within the government and has yet to become the common commitment of the entire leadership. The technicians, led by Minister of Industry Abdesslam, now have their political futures at stake in the success of state capitalism. Even some of those nominally committed to self-management are so more out of political calculation than ideological conviction. Kaid, for instance, was no outspoken defender of self-management before becoming party leader, but he suddenly became its champion when he saw it as a means of checking the growing power of the technicians and of asserting his own influence.[42] Characteristically, Boumediene has refused to take a clear stand for or against self-management, preferring to remain neutral in a struggle that now involves his closest allies. His statements on self-management always seem to contain a proviso:

> We are for self-management, but a viable self-management that yields a profit, that results in an efficient organization of work and an increase of production. To liberate the worker . . . is a revolutionary principle, but to produce is also a necessity.[43]

However, he has also begun to show an awareness of the fact that state companies can also be run poorly and unprofitably:

> Numerous state companies . . . have lost sight of the mission conferred upon them, namely that of producing an appreciable profit in order to finance their own development and that of the entire national economy. It is time that those responsible for these [state] enterprises break with the habit of deficit management. . . .[44]

Boumediene is apparently discovering that management by the state can be as inefficient and unprofitable as management by the workers.

41. *Révolution Africaine*, No. 255, January 4–10, 1968.
42. Kaid personally directed the work of the party commission responsible for writing the new decrees on self-management.
43. Interview with *Le Monde*, April 4, 1968.
44. From a circular sent by Boumediene to the directors of all state enterprises, reprinted in *Révolution Africaine*, No. 271, April 25–May 1, 1968.

His realization of this fact could lead to a re-evaluation of the respective merits of state capitalism and self-management and could possibly
tip the balance within the government in favor of the latter. Meanwhile,
in Algeria there continues to be a contradictory commitment to two
forms of economic organization diametrically opposed to one another.
Contradiction is also apparent as well in the political sphere, where
forces of centralization and decentralization are pitted against one
another. Many ministers, supported by the highest echelons of the
administration, seek to concentrate power in Algiers, while the people's
assemblies and regional potentates in the party and army work to dif-
fuse that power into hundreds of centers.

chapter thirteen
the resumption
of a third world policy

We should harmonize our efforts with those of all the vital forces in Africa, Asia, and Latin America, and with all the progressive forces in the world combating colonialism, imperialism, and various forms of exploitation and slavery.[1]

Houari Boumediene

Since the Arab-Israeli war of June 1967, the attention of Algerian leaders has shifted from the east to the north because of recurring crises in relations with France that have threatened to tear asunder the carefully woven fabric of French-Algerian cooperation. This slow but perceptible deterioration in relations was cause for considerable concern to Algerian leaders, as was made clear by Foreign Minister Bouteflika's trip to Paris in July 1968 for a series of meetings with President de Gaulle, Prime Minister Couve de Murville, and Foreign Minister Debré. Bouteflika expressed the Algerian viewpoint this way:

> ... although the will to cooperate exists uncontestably at the political level, it is not reflected at the level of actions. There are professions of faith and encouraging declarations, but the problems are left to accumulate and rot, [a situation] that finally undermines the spirit that we would like to see inspire our relations.[2]

The problems to which Bouteflika referred were the same ones that had plagued French-Algerian relations for years, namely the nationalization of private French properties, the entrance of Algerian wine into the French market, and the application of the 1965 oil accords. Intermittent talks between the two governments throughout 1968 failed to

1. Boumediene's speech to the nation on the fifth anniversary of the country's independence. See *El-Moudjahid*, July 5, 1967.
2. Interview with *Le Monde*, July 28–29, 1968.

solve any of these problems except that of the immigration of Algerians into France.

The successive waves of nationalization of foreign private companies beginning in May 1968 affected French companies primarily and could not help but complicate relations between Algeria and France. Though the principle of indemnification was explicitly recognized in the decrees nationalizing French companies, no compensation was actually paid. Negotiations with France over this and other issues began in December 1968 but almost immediately broke down. Partly in retaliation against the nationalizations and partly because of internal economic difficulties, the French government suddenly announced in June that it was limiting the number of Algerians allowed into France to 1,000 a month beginning July 1. This decision provoked a storm of protest in Algeria, where it was denounced as a "serious unilateral measure."[3] Finally, after prolonged discussions, the two governments reached a new agreement on October 26, fixing the number of Algerian immigrants at 35,000 a year for a three-year period.

Another issue that caused Algeria great consternation was the continued refusal of France to allow Algerian wine into the French market as provided for by the 1964 agreement. The problem became more acute after 1967, when for the first time since independence Algeria ran a deficit in its balance of trade with France. The deficit was sizable, amounting to 670 million dinars ($134 million).[4] By early 1968, Algeria had in stock about fourteen million hectoliters of unsold wine worth approximately 600 million dinars ($120 million). Even if the French had respected the agreement, the trade gap would not have been entirely closed, but the Algerians focused on the issue partly because France had failed to live up to its agreement and partly because wine was the principal source of income for the self-managed farms already deeply in debt. The French government, under extreme pressure from a powerful lobby of wine producers, remained adamant in its refusal to let in more than token amounts of Algerian wine during most of 1968. The Algerians calculated that by the end of 1968 France would have imported eleven million hectoliters less than it had pledged to under the 1964 agreement.[5]

3. Commentary on the Algerian state radio on June 18, quoted in *Le Monde*, June 19, 1968.
4. This figure represented the deficit for the first eleven months of 1967. See *Révolution Africaine*, No. 260, February 8–14, 1968.
5. *Ibid.*

The most serious threat to French-Algerian cooperation, however, was the running dispute between the Algerian government and the French oil companies over the implementation of the 1965 oil and gas agreements. The Algerians accused the French of making no efforts at exploration and claimed that as a result no more than ten million tons of oil had been discovered since 1965. They also reproached the French companies for the practice of selling oil to their own subsidiaries at prices sometimes 20 per cent below those of the world market. Since the French companies were required to return to Algeria one-half of the revenue from all oil sales, the Algerian government saw this practice as a maneuver to reduce to a minimum the amount of money brought back into the country for future investments. In September 1968, Algiers decreed that no oil could be sold for less than $1.73 per barrel and then made it clear that it intended to enforce the ruling by temporarily refusing to permit two of the largest companies operating in the Sahara to export oil.[6] "The advantages conceded by Algeria to France have no reason to continue any longer because cooperation cannot be a one-sided affair," commented the official press agency in early December.[7]

Despite tough words and occasionally tough measures, the Algerians continued to make significant concessions to France. For instance, when the French firm TECHNIP lost the bid on a $180 million gas liquefaction plant at Skikda to Italian and American companies, the Algerian government gave it seven months to revise its bid and eventually awarded it the contract; the reason for this show of favoritism was that the French government offered to provide most of the capital for the project.[8] The same ambivalence in Algerian attitudes was apparent in other areas. Notwithstanding its intense nationalism, the Algerian government never pressed the French to evacuate their huge naval base at Mers-El-Kébir. It was President de Gaulle who in September 1967 decided to evacuate the base by February 1968 without even consulting the Algerians,[9] who immediately sought French help in converting the

6. The figure of $1.73 per barrel is close to the average posted price of oil on the world market, though the price actually paid sometimes goes as low as $1.50. The French oil companies were paying royalties on the basis of fixed prices, which varied between $2.04 and $2.09, depending on the port.

7. Commentary of the Algérie Presse Service (APS) on December 7, quoted in Le Monde, December 8–9, 1968.

8. The French government was providing 700 million dinars ($140 million) in loans and purchasing credits as part of the industrial aid program included in the 1965 oil agreements.

9. The French still maintain an air base at Bou-Ser, adjacent to Mers-el-Kébir; they are allowed by the Evian Agreements to keep it until 1977.

base to civilian use and also asked for an increase in miltary aid. In December 1967, an unpublicized military assistance agreement was signed between the two governments, providing for the training of Algerian officers in French military schools and the detachment of French instructors to work within the ANP.[10]

It would be wrong, however, to assume from these examples that there is no substance to Algeria's present threats and demands. The fact remains that France and Algeria look at the policy of cooperation from fundamentally different, and oftentimes antagonistic, viewpoints, particularly as regards the sharing of the Sahara oil and gas wealth. One of the greatest weaknesses of the policy is that to a considerable extent it relies on the French oil companies to realize a grandiose vision in which they have little faith. The Algerians themselves have recognized this:

> Not all the top officials of the French oil and industrial companies rise to the height of the objectives of French-Algerian cooperation; the oil accords are frequently violated by those very persons who were designated by the French partner to carry them out.[11]

In reality getting oil out of the Sahara at the lowest cost and in as great a quantity as possible remains the oil companies' primary objective; helping the Algerians to develop an oil industry that could eventually exclude the French from the Sahara is a task they have undertaken with little taste or enthusiasm.

The future of French-Algerian cooperation seems subject to many contingencies, not the least of which is the demise of President de Gaulle. The attempt to give form and structure to a political conception has not proved as successful as either government hoped for; patience has been tried and disillusionment experienced on both sides. Negotiations over the renewal of the oil accords in 1970 promise to touch off a stormy debate in both countries on the merits of cooperation. Colonel Boumediene has said that "the interests the two countries have in each other

10. The French had already provided the staff and equipment for a school at Cap Matifou, which opened in September 1967. The school is training engineers and technicians for all the Algerian armed forces. Boumediene hopes that this school will eventually eliminate the need to send officers abroad for technical training. Under the agreement of December 1967, there were thirty-four Algerian officers studying at the Saint-Cyr Military Academy and a smaller number at the gendarmerie school at Melun. French instructors also started working within the ANP to train administrative cadres at all levels of the hierarchy and to help write the basic military manual. See *Le Monde*, April 11, 1968.

11. Commentary of the Algérie Presse Service on May 4, quoted in *Le Monde*, May 5–6, 1968.

are very important" and that both have the desire "to respect their reciprocal interests."[12] While these interests are no doubt still considerable, they are not immutable. Nor is President de Gaulle eternal.

As relations between Algeria and France have progressively deteriorated, those between Algeria and the Soviet Union have noticeably improved. There is every indication that the Soviets have taken advantage of the difficulties between Algeria and France to strengthen their own position in Algeria; at the same time, the Algerians have deliberately sought to extract more aid from the Soviet Union and to develop alternative markets for their products. The basic thrust of Algerian policy has been to play the Soviet Union against France without giving up an inch of independence to either power.

After a period of coolness following the Arab-Israeli war, relations between Algeria and the Soviet Union became noticeably warmer in early 1968. A message from the Soviet Communist Party leader Leonid Brezhnev to Boumediene in April called for a "new phase" in the development of relations through "the intensification of cooperation in all domains . . . and the increase of economic and commercial exchanges."[13] In early July, Industry Minister Abdesslam made his second long visit to Moscow and negotiated a major agreement whereby the Soviet Union pledged to buy 35 million hectoliters of wine over a seven-year period beginning in 1969. This means that Algeria will be selling more wine in Soviet than in French markets, although at about one-half the price. The Soviets also agreed to take 500,000 tons of Algerian oil in 1969 and 1970. In addition, they promised to provide technicians to help run the recently nationalized French companies and to undertake a long list of industrial and agricultural projects.[14] In December, the two countries signed an accord to increase their trade from 300 million dinars ($60 million) to 550 million dinars ($110 million) in 1969, with Algeria exporting wine, citrus fruits, cork, iron ore for Soviet machines, wood, sugar, cotton, and consumer goods.[15]

These agreements marked a turn in the nature of Algerian-Soviet relations. Whereas the Soviet presence had previously been primarily confined to the military sphere, it was now expanding significantly into

12. Interview with Le Monde, April 4, 1968.
13. Le Monde, April 26, 1968.
14. For the details of this agreement, see Révolution Africaine, No. 284, July 29–August 4, 1968, and Le Monde, July 24, 1968.
15. See Le Monde, December 31, 1968.

the economic sphere. While Soviet influence has never been commensurate with Soviet presence, it is bound to grow as Soviet aid steadily increases and trade between the two countries expands. One illustration of this influence is the fact that at the time of the Soviet Union's invasion of Czechoslovakia, the Algerian press relied almost exclusively on the Soviet news agency Tass for an explanation of events. Yet the Soviets have not taken over the naval base at Mers-el-Kébir as Western diplomats had long feared. Soviet Defense Minister Andrey Grechko was given a tour of the base during his visit to Algeria in July 1968, but the army organ El Djeich hastened to point out that "Algeria has not rid herself of French bases with the intention of letting another power install itself there."[16] The French were also reported to have gotten assurances from the Algerians that the Soviets would not be allowed to install themselves at the base.[17] Still, ships of the Soviet Mediterranean fleet continue to make periodic calls at Algerian ports. Of more recent concern to the French and other Western governments has been the lengthening of the airstrips at a dozen Algerian military fields, presumably to permit the landing of the largest Soviet aircraft. The speculation was that Algeria had agreed to allow the Soviet air force to use Algerian airfields in times of crisis or as refueling points for Soviet planes flying south into Black Africa. In any case, many Western powers now regard Algeria as a staging area and arms depot for another war in the Middle East.

While Algeria has chosen to rely principally upon France and the Soviet Union for economic and military assistance, it has begun, with some delay, to look for other trading partners and sources of outside capital. In order to make the gas liquefaction plant being built at Skikda a profitable venture, the government has tried to find markets in Spain and Italy and has therefore developed closer ties with both countries, most notably the latter. In November 1967, Algeria entered an arrangemnet with the Ente Minerario Siciliano, a subsidiary of the Italian state oil company ENI, to study jointly methods of delivering large quantities of Algerian gas to Sicily and southern Italy. In February 1968, the government signed another accord with SNAM-Progetti providing for the construction of a gas-distribution system in Algeria, including a gas line from the Sahara to Skikda. The same month, Italian

16. Quoted in Le Monde, July 26, 1968.
17. See Le Monde, December 1–2, 1968.

Foreign Minister Amintore Fanfani visited Algeria and signed an agreement for a $10 million loan.

In search of other outlets for its vast oil and gas supplies, the Algerian government has negotiated small sales to a number of countries, including Yemen, Morocco, Canada, Italy, Denmark, Egypt, Sweden, and West Germany. The last country has become a very promising customer for Algerian oil, signing in January 1968 an accord to obtain 4.5 million tons over a five-year period. Great Britain has remained the major customer for gas; in fact, the desire not to lose the British market was an important factor in the Algerian government's decision to re-establish in April 1968 diplomatic relations severed two and a half years earlier over the Rhodesian problem. One country toward which the Algerian government has made no overture is the United States. With no prospect for aid or trade in sight, Algeria has made no concessions on the issue of the nationalized American oil companies and has shown no interest in re-establishing diplomatic relations as of early 1969.[18]

Since the Arab-Israeli war of June 1967, Algeria's standing in the Arab world and among Third World countries has steadily improved. The intransigent position taken by Boumediene during and immediately after the war at first left Algeria isolated from all Arab governments except that of Syria. But just as Algerian leaders had calculated, it was only a matter of time before the futility of peace efforts was made manifest and the policy of protracted guerrilla war that Boumediene advocated became that of the entire Arab world. On the occasion of the twentieth anniversary of the creation of the state of Israel in May 1968, the Algerian government set forth its own ten-point plan for a resolution of the Palestinian problem, rejecting all political solutions. The plan called upon the people of Palestine to wage the armed struggle themselves and urged "the unification in one real national liberation front of all the forces working for the liberation of Palestine."[19] This, of

18. The Algerian government was apparently waiting for Egypt to re-establish diplomatic relations with the United States. The nationalization of American oil companies is bound to make the renewal of relations between Algeria and the United States more difficult. However, the oil companies, trying to work out a solution on their own, have not asked the State Department to intervene in their behalf.

19. Front de Libération Nationale, *Palestine 20 Years After: F.L.N. Position in 10 Points*, May 1968, pp. 23–24. The ten points contained generic statements rather than specific proposals. They called upon all Arab countries to aid the Palestinians in their struggle, suggested the creation of support committees "everywhere in the world," and advocated a campaign to mobilize world opinion against Israel in order to force the United Nations to rectify "the injustice" committed with the creation of Israel.

course, had been the policy of the Algerian nationalists' offensive against France. With Algerian financial support and aid in training guerrillas, the Palestine Liberation Organization under the leadership of Yasir Arafat had by early 1969 formed that front, and its commando organization Al Fatah had taken the lead in the Arab struggle to "liberate" Palestine. The Algerians have also been counseling Al Fatah on how to conduct a public relations campaign to swing international opinion to their side, and from the declarations of Israeli officials themselves, it appears the PLO has made major gains on that front.[20]

The intransigence of the Algerians toward Israel was one factor leading to the normalization of relations between Algeria and Cuba, strained ever since the overthrow of Ben Bella. Fidel Castro apparently became convinced that Algeria was still in the vanguard of the anti-imperialist struggle, for he finally relented in his hostility toward Boumediene. A delegation from the Cuban Communist party attended Independence Day celebrations in July 1968 and then stayed on for talks with Algerian officials. At the end of the visit, the two countries signed an agreement for cooperation in the fields of sports, health, and culture. The reconciliation between Algeria and Cuba was confirmed by the visit of Foreign Minister Bouteflika to Havana early in November.

There were also signs that Algeria was regaining its position as a center of Third World activities. In October 1967, representatives of seventy-seven underdeveloped countries in Africa, Asia, and Latin America met in Algiers to hammer out what became known as the Algiers Charter of the Economic Rights of the Third World. The charter was used as the common platform of the underdeveloped countries at the United Nations Conference on Trade and Development held in New Delhi in March 1968. In June of the same year, the executive committee of the Pan-African Youth Movement held a meeting in the Algerian capital, and shortly afterwards representatives of the Arab youth organizations convened there to prepare for the ninth World Youth Festival. In mid-July, the OAU Coordinating Committee for the Liberation of Africa, responsible for funneling aid to the guerrilla movements in the remaining colonies, also came to Algiers for a conference, providing Algerian leaders with the opportunity to stress their commitment to that cause. In September, African chiefs of state gathered in Algiers for the annual meeting of the Organization of African Unity. Finally, Algeria was chosen to host an all-African arts festival

20. See, for instance, James Feron, "Israel Fears She is Losing Public-Relations War," the *New York Times*, February 4, 1969.

in July 1969, serving for the first time as a cultural crossroads.

This revival of international activity in Algiers did not mean that the country was again becoming a model to revolutionaries in the way it had been immediately after independence. Even the Algerians recognized that there was "a total absence of the Algerian Revolution on the ideological plane in the international arena."[21] Yet Algeria had not given up its hope of becoming a leader of revolutionary forces on the African continent and in the Third World. This hope was less evident in Boumediene's attitude than in the policies of Bouteflika, the dynamic and ambitious diplomat who has remained foreign minister of Algeria since 1963. It was also apparent in the thinking of Abdesslam, who saw Algeria's oil policy as a model for other underdeveloped countries to follow in their relations with the industrialized nations.

Boumediene's personal influence on Algerian foreign policy has been evident primarily in the country's increased involvement in the affairs of the Arab world. During 1968, the government sought to strengthen its ties with all the Middle East countries and even made an effort to bring about "peaceful coexistence" in the Maghreb.[22] It signed cultural agreements with Iraq, Yemen, Southern Yemen, and Libya, and it reached an accord with the Syrian government whereby SONATRACH took charge of selling Syria's oil abroad and carried out oil exploration in that country. It also provided a $4 million loan to Yemen. In the Maghreb the border conflict with Tunisia was formally resolved,[23] while relations with Morocco improved to the point where Boumediene could make a state visit in January 1969. This shift in emphasis, from Africa to the Arab world, remains the most noticeable change in Algerian foreign policy since the *coup d'état*. Boumediene has an intense desire to restore the Arab personality of his country, which has been

21. This statement was made by Ahmed Kaid in a speech to party officials in July 1968. See *Révolution Africaine*, No. 283, July 22–28, 1968.

22. Speaking of relations among the three Maghreb countries on June 19, 1968, the third anniversary of his accession to power. Boumediene said "We have proclaimed that if peaceful coexistence has been established among the great powers with different social systems, then this coexistence must, a fortiori, be established among brothers, the sons of one and the same people." See *El-Moudjahid*, June 20, 1968, or *Révolution Africaine*, No. 279, June 24–30, 1968.

23. A preliminary agreement had been reached in May 1967. A formal agreement was signed April 16, 1968, in Tunis, delineating the border from Bir Roman to Fort-Saint. By this agreement, Tunisia gave up her claims on Algerian territory south of Fort-Saint to the frontier marker 233. The border accepted by both sides was thus that established by the French in 1929, the one Algeria had always claimed to be legitimate.

depersonalized by 132 years of French colonialism and still strongly attracted to France by a complex of economic and cultural ties. His interest in the Arab world has led him to embrace wholeheartedly the Palestinian cause, thus restoring to Algerian foreign policy some of the crusading spirit it lost with the ouster of Ben Bella.

conclusion
prospects for stability

t hat leaders as different in personality as Ben Bella and Boumediene should end by following the same course toward personal
power is not coincidental and is explained by a fundamental
reality of Algerian politics: the persistence of asabiya. Boumediene,
like Ben Bella, was faced with the existence of numerous political clans,
each primarily seeking to aggrandize its own influence. Although these
clans made dangerous allies, in the absence of functioning political
institutions Boumediene, like Ben Bella, could only rise to power by
securing the support of some of them. Sharing power with these clans,
however, proved impossible; eventually both leaders were confronted
with the choice of eliminating their allies or being eliminated by them.
Ben Bella's efforts to establish an alliance with the new forces based on
ideological grounds were to no avail. The collegial system created by
Boumediene forestalled the moment of choice but did not make it any
less inevitable.

The ouster of Ben Bella proved that concentration of power in the
hands of one man does not necessarily guarantee the longevity of a
regime. The question then arises whether Boumediene will incur the
same fate as his predecessor or whether he will be able to ensure the
stability of his regime by establishing it on a basis other than the
ephemeral loyalty of his allies. It appears that the Boumediene clan
will continue to be challenged by rival factions. Even after the elimination of the Ben Bellists and wilaya commanders, it is possible to distinguish at least three separate factions in the Boumediene regime. The
first faction consists of Boumediene and the former members of the
ALN General Staff—Kaid, Medeghri, Mendjli, Bouteflika, and Belkacem. The second faction includes the French-trained professional
officers of the ANP, notably Major Chabou, Major Bensalem, Major

Hoffman, and Colonel Bencherif. The third faction is made up of the technicians in the Cabinet, namely Abdesslam, Ben Yahia, Khene, and Taleb.

To date, the professional officers, who hold most of the top positions in the ANP, have shown little penchant for becoming directly involved in politics and have been extremely loyal to Boumediene. However, the possibility of a split developing between them and the colonel cannot be excluded. In the past, one factor making for unity between Boumediene and the professionals was the hostility of the wilaya commanders. Now that the wilaya commanders have been eliminated from the government, there is considerably less need for the alliance. Moreover, with the demise of the council as a functioning body, the professional officers are entirely excluded from politics, since they have no positions in the party or government. This situation might well become intolerable to them, and if it did they might well try to oust Boumediene from power. It is undoubtedly this possibility that prompted Boumediene personally to assume the functions of chief of staff after dismissing Zbiri rather than to appoint another officer to that key post. This move may nonetheless be insufficient to protect him from a military *coup* by the professional officers.

The technicians are less menacing rivals, since they have no armed force of their own. However, their influence is steadily growing, as is their inclination for involvement in politics. In the past, there have been clashes between the technicians and members of the Boumediene clan, notably between Abdesslam and Kaid. There is a real possibility that the technicians will one day join the professional officers in a conspiracy against Boumediene, providing the military with the political support it would need. It is also possible that other factions will emerge in the future. One might consist of the young officers trained in the Soviet Union since independence, who may come to resent the monopoly the French-trained officers have on the General Staff. So far, the young officers have shown no political aspirations, but considering the involvement of the army in politics today, there is a distinct possibility that they too will seek a political role.

Boumediene, then, must find a new, more permanent basis of power. He is attempting to do so by establishing formal institutions of government rather than by forming an ideological alliance with new forces. Today Algeria is ruled by a nonelected president, a nonfunctioning Revolutionary Council, and a poorly organized party—a situation the inherent weakness of which Boumediene fully realizes. The emphasis he places in his speeches on the need to organize the party and to establish local and national institutions is partly the rhetoric of nation-building, but it is also the reflection of his preoccupation with the stability of his regime.

Of course, the successful implantation of political institutions might stave off a new *coup d'état* without assuring the continuation of Boumediene's rule. No institution can prevent a new attempt on his life, the outcome of which fate alone will determine. In this sense, there is bound to remain an element of uncertainty in his position. However, the establishment of political institutions would be an essential step toward the country's stability, since institutions alone can provide continuity of government beyond the demise of any one leader. To be sure, the ultimate test of stability is whether a system of government can continue independently of the men who created it, and there is no doubt that Boumediene has not established a system possessing such a degree of durability. At this point, there is a certain order and continuity in the management of the nation's public affairs, but this order would almost certainly be upset by the passing of Boumediene from power.

In Algeria, as in other newly independent countries, the problem of setting up institutions is essentially twofold. First, the system devised must be adapted to the particular characteristics of the country and must possess a certain efficiency. The people's assemblies may well represent the beginning of a workable system because they have the potential for combating the excessive centralization that has paralyzed Algeria since independence and for involving the local population in the solution of their own problems. Moreover, these assemblies resemble the village djemaa, one of the few traditional institutions to have survived the French occupation. Second, the regime must find a way to gain acceptance for the new institutions that are set up and to get both private citizens and politicians to grant their primary allegiance to them. It is of little use to have communal assemblies if the villagers still look to their elders for leadership. Similarly, it is of little benefit to have a national assembly if the chief of state continues to rule by decree. Only if the new institutions acquire legitimacy in the eyes of the Algerians and in turn become the source of legitimation of their leaders' authority will Algeria enjoy a degree of political stability.

Today there are still no institutions in Algeria that command the loyalty of either people or politicians, partly for reasons that are beyond the control of the country's leaders. Since the French occupation in 1830, Algeria has had no political institutions of its own. The French eliminated the pre-existing system of government and imposed their own, which never acquired any real roots in the country because it largely excluded the indigenous population. With independence, the Algerians had no indigenous political infrastructure to build upon. No system of government could claim a legitimacy based on tradition or count on the ready acceptance that comes from being long established. In the sense that all possibilities were open, the situation was, and still is, a revolutionary one. To this basic problem the Boumediene regime has added that of its own lack of legitimacy. Not only did Boumediene come to power in a *coup d'état*, but nothing in his past gave him an inherent "right" to leadership. He was not a traditional ruler or a historic leader, and he did not possess the charisma to make himself readily acclaimed by the people. The problem of creating institutions that will be accorded legitimacy is obviously a thorny one for a leader whose own power has not been legitimated.

The key to the success or failure of the legitimation of Boumediene's regime and the institutions he is endeavoring to create is probably the formation of a strong party. In the socialist framework chosen by Algeria, only a party can involve the people in the political process and thereby create a sense of loyalty to the new institutions. Yet the organization of the FLN has proved to be a Sisyphean task, and the probability that Ahmed Kaid will succeed where his predecessors failed is not great. The main obstacle to the creation of a strong party in Algeria is the legacy of the war of independence. Created during the revolution as a front of nationalist groups, the FLN essentially achieved its purpose with independence. From that point onward, the goals of the various groups in the front were no longer identical. Yet Ben Bella always lacked the power to purge or disband the FLN and form a homogeneous party. The fact that Algeria's only legal party remained a front was a major liability for Ben Bella, since it meant that clans of widely different tendencies had a voice in politics.

The heterogeneous composition of the front made the FLN into an arena of political conflict rather than into an instrument to unify and mobilize the people. The FLN lost its power to attract Algerians. Indeed, the post-war FLN was hardly a party to incite confidence and admiration, composed as it was of bickering leaders and haughty and often corrupt party officials, most of whom displayed an almost total disregard for the material problems of reconstructing a war-ravaged country. Had the FLN helped to resettle the millions of peasants uprooted by the war, for example, it might have maintained its authority in the country. But by remaining aloof from practical tasks, the FLN lost its influence in the communities and primarily attracted opportunists and fledgling politicians who did not command the respect of the people. Boumediene accused Ben Bella of having "made unpopular not only the party itself, but the very idea of a party."[1] While this accusation was essentially true, it must be added that the attitude of the Algerians toward the FLN did not change after the *coup d'état*. This legacy of divisions and unpopularity must be overcome if the FLN is to become a dynamic and homogeneous party.[2]

In order to correct the present shortcomings of the FLN, Boumediene must radically purge the party and recruit new members sincerely committed to a doctrine and a program. At present, the FLN has no doctrine; the Algiers Charter, though not officially repudiated, is clearly not upheld by Boumediene and his allies. Kaid has come to realize the importance of an ideology in building a party. He has complained of the "total absence of ideological debate" within the FLN and warned officials that "a party and a revolution cannot survive an ideological vacuum."[3] In the past, Boumediene has been reluctant to carry out a purge or revise the FLN charter because of his fear of antagonizing the Left and the wilaya leaders in the Executive Secretariat. Now that he has broken with both groups and taken over the party, he is in a position to carry out these necessary reforms. The question remains whether the ideals he expounds will have sufficient appeal to overcome the indifference Algerians feel toward the party.

The ideological themes of the Boumediene regime, certain to become the basis of a new party charter, have so far attracted only war veterans,

1. Boumediene's speech of July 20, 1965.
2. A popular joke illustrates the attitude of Algerians toward the FLN: Ben Bella and Boumediene were riding together in a car in downtown Algiers when they found themselves caught in a traffic jam caused by a donkey. All efforts to pull the animal out of the way having failed, Boumediene intervened. "If you don't get off the road immediately," he said to the donkey, "I'll call in my army and have you executed on the spot." The donkey did not budge. Ben Bella then walked up to the donkey and whispered something into his ear. The animal leaped from the road and ran away. "I told him," Ben Bella explained to his surprised companion, "that I would make him join the FLN if he didn't get out of the way."
3. Kaid's speech to party officials in July 1968. See *Révolution Africaine*, No. 283, July 22–28, 1968.

conservative religious elements, and other traditionalist groups. The stress on a "return to the sources" of Islam and the revolution, and the rejection of foreign ideologies have left most educated Algerians indifferent and have alienated the young people and leftist elements. As a consequence, it is doubtful whether a party expounding only these ideals will bring large numbers of new supporters to the regime. Nor is it likely that the party will either integrate the left-wing groups or become an effective counterforce to them. Paradoxically, it would appear that the only means of creating a dynamic party is to integrate the UGTA and other left-wing groups, which still have a sizable audience in the country. However, the likelihood of such a development taking place seems slight indeed. First, the gap between Boumediene and the Left has remained wide; second, were Boumediene to attempt a *rapprochement* with the Left, he would risk being ousted by the professional officers and technicians.

Political instability in Algeria has so far had a significant effect on the economy. The fortunes of self-management rose and fell with political fluctuations; the *coup d'état* in particular marked the beginning of a slow transformation of the economic system from self-management to state capitalism. It is, of course, a matter open to debate as to which system—self-management, state capitalism, or free enterprise—would best suit Algeria's needs. Few would contest, however, that any one system consistently followed would produce better results than would continuous changes and half-hearted measures.

The system of state capitalism now being established appears to have a fair chance of weathering future political storms without undergoing serious modifications or being discarded. For one thing, state capitalism has strong partisans in the present Cabinet, many more than self-management ever had under Ben Bella. Moreover, it would appear that the technicians, who are the supporters of state capitalism, are less likely to be removed from the government than politicians like Boumaza and Mahsas were. This fact should help to ensure a continuity in economic policies. An additional reason for optimism about the future stability of the Algerian economy is the inherent durability of state capitalism. The system entails the creation of a large centralized bureaucracy whose control over the economy is likely to prove less easily shakable than that of isolated management committees. Finally, so many of the self-managed enterprises have gone bankrupt that the new state companies have a better than even chance of proving more efficient, although it is becoming clearer that not all the recently created state companies are economically sound. The stabilization of the Algerian economy after years of chaos is perhaps the most positive achievement of the Boumediene regime.

Since Algeria attained its independence, its political history has been written almost entirely by those who led the war of liberation—members of the GPRA, the historic leaders, the wilaya commanders, and the General Staff of the ALN. If the clans in power have changed, the elitist character of Algerian politics has not. Only a small civil-military oligarchy has been involved in the political process, while there has been remarkably little participation on the part of the people. Even the mass organizations' power to influence events has depended more on the personal influence of particular leaders than on the number of members in the organizations. The possibility of the Algerian people rising up to impose their will on the ruling oligarchy cannot be altogether dismissed, although it seems remote. There is at least a precedent: the war of national liberation, in which hundreds of thousands of Algerians took part. Algerians know from this experience that a popular revolt can topple much stronger regimes than the one presently in power.

Today there are still many Algerians who are dissatisfied with their lot, which has not significantly improved since independence. Unemployment has grown substantially; the landless peasants are still without land; the cost of living has risen considerably; and the disparity between poor and rich has not noticeably diminished. The discontent of the populace remains unfocused and is seldom translated into political grievances. The dissatisfaction of the Left, however, is much better articulated:

> The failure to carry out the agrarian reform, the quasi-liquidation of self-management in the commercial and industrial sector, the difficulties plaguing the farm sector, and the exclusion of the workers from the management of the economy all contribute to the anxiety of the underprivileged classes. [These classes] suffer all the more painfully from these injustices because they see themselves systematically shunted aside from the political, economic, and social life of the country. Union rights are flouted almost everywhere, and union liberties are constantly violated.[4]

The alienation of the Left presents a constant threat to Boumediene,

---

4. Editorial in *Révolution et Travail*, quoted in *Le Monde*, December 21, 1967.

and the arrest of hundreds of UGTA officials and ORP militants suggests that he is well aware of this. The problem may become more serious in the future because the stratum from which the Left recruits most of its followers, the industrial working class, is growing rapidly as a result of the process of economic development. Moreover, there are hundreds of thousands of Algerians who have worked in France and been exposed to the ideologies of the Communist and socialist labor unions.

"If the UGTA put fifty thousand men into the streets," remarked an Algerian journalist to the authors, "Boumediene would not dare to use the army against them." Although one cannot state categorically that Boumediene would not use the army in such an instance, there is no doubt that he would risk splitting it by doing so. It suffices to recall the numerous rebellions within the ANP since independence, the most recent being that of Colonel Zbiri in December 1967. Although the ANP is now more united than it has been at any time in the past, it is still far from being a professional army with a tradition of aloofness from politics. It is altogether possible that Boumediene would weather a revolt within the army that grew out of a popular uprising, but it is also altogether possible that such an event would bring an end to his rule and permit the rise to power of a leftist coalition, perhaps even bring about the return of Ben Bella.

A left-wing government brought to power in the wake of the popular revolt would not necessarily bring about a radical change in the political system. In fact, the institutions set up by such a government would probably not be significantly different from those Boumediene plans to set up. There would be a single-party system, and elections, whether for a president or for people's assemblies, would be limited to the endorsement of the party candidate or the party list. At best, there would be a choice between two candidates or lists from the same party. However, the workers would undoubtedly have a larger role in the management of the economy, and a greater number of workers, peasants, intellectuals, and youth would probably be attracted to the FLN.

In this book, we have not discussed the prospects for Western-style democracy in Algeria, so irrelevant does such a discussion appear considering the present political climate of the country. Ferhat Abbas is the only politician of national stature who has consistently advocated a multi-party system, and he only finds supporters among the bourgeois, who constitute a group of relatively little political influence. The alternatives for Algeria are not a socialist and a democratic regime, but two socialist regimes, one favoring state capitalism and the other self-management. It seems probable that the latter type of regime would be more popular, but it also seems probable that Algeria will live under the former type for some time to come.

appendixes

algerian executive bodies and cabinets

COMITÉ RÉVOLUTIONNAIRE D'UNITÉ ET D'ACTION (CRUA)
ALGIERS, APRIL, 1954

Hocine Ait Ahmed, Ahmed Ben Bella, Moustafa Ben Boulaid,* Mohamed Larbi Ben M'hidi,* Mohamed Boudiaf, Rabah Bitat, Mourad Didouche,* Mohamed Khider, Belkacem Krim.

COMITÉ DE COORDINATION ET EXÉCUTION (CCE)
CAIRO, SEPTEMBER 5, 1957

Ramdane Abbane,* Ferhat Abbas, Lakhdar Bentobbal, Abdelhafid Boussouf, Mahmoud Cherif, Lamine Debbaghine, Belkacem Krim, Abdelhamid Mehri, Amar Ouamrane.

GOUVERNEMENT PROVISOIRE DE LA RÉPUBLIQUE
ALGÉRIENNE (GPRA)
TUNIS, SEPTEMBER 19, 1958

President: Ferhat Abbas; vice-president in charge of armed forces: Belkacem Krim; vice-president: Ahmed Ben Bella;† ministers of state: Hocine Ait Ahmed,† Rabah Bitat,† Mohamed Boudiaf,† Mohamed Khider;† minister of foreign affairs: Lamine Debbaghine; minister of arms and supplies: Mahmoud Cherif; minister of the interior: Lakhdar Bentobbal; minister of liaisons and communications: Abdelhafid Boussouf; minister of North African affairs: Abdelhamid Mehri; minister of economic affairs and finance: Ahmed Francis; minister of information: M'Hammed Yazid; minister of social affairs: Ben Youccef Ben Khedda; minister of cultural affairs: Teufik El-Madani; secretaries of state: Lamine Khene, Omar Oussedik, Moustafa Stambouli.

At a meeting of the CNRA at Tripoli in January 1960, Krim became minister of foreign affairs while remaining vice-president in charge of armed forces. Also, Krim, Boussouf, and Bentobbal formed the Interministerial Committee of War.

GOUVERNEMENT PROVISOIRE DE LA RÉPUBLIQUE
ALGÉRIENNE (GPRA)
TRIPOLI, AUGUST 27, 1961

President, minister of finance: Ben Youccef Ben Khedda; vice-president, minister of interior: Belkacem Krim; vice-presidents: Ahmed Ben Bella,†

* indicates persons who died during the war.
† indicates persons imprisoned in France at the time.

Mohamed Boudiaf;† ministers of state: Hocine Ait Ahmed,† Lakhdar Bentobbal, Rabah Bitat,† Mohamed Khider,† Mohammedi Saïd; minister of foreign affairs: Saad Dahlab; minister of arms and liaisons: Abdelhafid Boussouf; minister of information: M'hammed Yazid.

The Interministerial Committee of War was eliminated.

FIRST BEN BELLA CABINET
SEPTEMBER 28, 1962

Prime minister: Ahmed Ben Bella; vice-president: Rabah Bitat; minister of defense: Houari Boumediene; minister of foreign affairs: Mohamed Khemisti; minister of finance: Ahmed Francis; minister of agriculture and agrarian reform: Amar Ouzegane; minister of industrialization: Laroussi Khelifa; minister of the interior: Ahmed Medeghri; minister of commerce: Mohamed Khobzi; minister of justice: Amar Bentoumi; minister of reconstruction, public works and transportation: Ahmed Boumendjel; minister of education: Abderrahmane Benhamida; minister of labor and social affairs: Bachir Boumaza; minister of public health: Mohamed Seghir Nekkache; minister of mujahidin: Mohammedi Saïd; minister of information: Mohamed Hadj Hamou; minister of youth, sports, and tourism: Abdelaziz Bouteflika; minister of religious affairs: Teufik El-Madani; under-secretary of state for post and telecommunications: Moussa Hassani.

Ben Bella assumed the functions of minister of foreign affairs after the death of Khemisti on May 7, 1963.

SECOND BEN BELLA CABINET
SEPTEMBER 18, 1963

President: Ahmed Ben Bella; first vice-president and minister of defense: Houari Boumediene; second vice-president: Mohammedi Saïd; third vice-president: Rabah Bitat; minister of state: Amar Ouzegane; minister of the interior: Ahmed Medeghri; minister of foreign affairs: Abdelaziz Bouteflika; minister of national economy: Bachir Boumaza; minister of justice: Mohamed Hadj Smaïn; minister of public works and reconstruction: Ahmed Boumendjel; minister of social affairs: Mohamed Seghir Nekkache; minister of orientation and education: Cherif Belkacem; minister of posts and telecommunications: Abdelkader Zaibek; minister of religious affairs: Teufik El-Madani; minister of tourism: Ahmed Kaid; under-secretary of state for youth and sports: Sadek Batel.

Bitat resigned from the Cabinet on September 19, 1963. Medeghri resigned on July 3, 1964, and Ben Bella assumed the functions of minister of the interior.

THIRD BEN BELLA CABINET
DECEMBER 12, 1964

President: Ahmed Ben Bella; first vice-president and minister of defense: Houari Boumediene; second vice-president: Mohammedi Saïd; minister delegated to the presidency: Abderrahmane Cherif; minister of justice: Mohamed Bedjaoui; minister of industry and energy: Bachir Boumaza; minister of agriculture and agrarian reform: Ali Mahsas; minister of public health, mujahidin, and social affairs: Mohamed Seghir Nekkache; minister of foreign affairs: Abdelaziz Bouteflika; minister of education: Cherif Belkacem; minister of posts and telecommunications, public works and transportation: Abdelkader Zaibeck; minister of reconstruction and housing: Mohamed Hadj Smaïn; minister of commerce: Nourredine Delleci; minister of labor: Safi Boudissa; minister of youth and sports: Sadek Batel; minister of administrative reform and civil service: Said Amrani; minister of tourism; Amar Ouzegane; minister of religious affairs: Tedjini Haddam; under-secretary of state for public works: Ahmed Ghozali.

FIRST BOUMEDIENE CABINET
JULY 12, 1965

President and minister of defense: Houari Boumediene; minister of state: Rabah Bitat; minister of the interior: Ahmed Medeghri; minister of foreign affairs: Abdelaziz Bouteflika; minister of finance: Ahmed Kaid; minister of industry and energy: Belaid Abdesslam; minister of agriculture: Ali Mahsas; minister of commerce: Nourredine Delleci; minister of justice: Mohamed Bedjaoui; minister of education: Ahmed Taleb; minister of public health: Tedjini Haddam; minister of labor and social affairs: Abdelaziz Zerdani; minister of public works: Abdennour Ali Yahia; minister of reconstruction and housing: Mohamed Hadj Smaïn; minister of mujahidin: Boualem Ben Hamouda; minister of youth and sports: Abdelkrim Ben Mahmoud; minister of religious affairs: Larbi Saadouni; minister of posts and telecommunications: Abdelkader Zaibek; minister of information: Bachir Boumaza; minister of tourism: Abdelaziz Maaoui.

Smaïn was dismissed April 5, 1966, and his ministry merged with the Ministry of Public Works. Mahsas was dismissed from his post on September 22, 1966, and Ali Yahia was named to replace him on September 24, 1966. Lamine Khene was named to replace Ali Yahia as minister of public works on September 24, 1966. Boumaza fled Algeria on October 8, 1966. Mohamed Ben Yahia was appointed minister of information on October 24, 1966. Zerdani and Ali Yahia left the Cabinet on December 15, 1967. Mohamed Saïd Mazouzi replaced Zerdani as minister of labor and social affairs and Mohamed Tayebi took over for Ali Yahia as minister of agriculture and agrarian reform on March 7, 1968.

bioqraphies of members of
the revolutionary council

THE BOUMEDIENE CLAN

Houari Boumediene. Born August 23, 1932, in Clauzel, near Guelma in eastern Algeria. His real name is Mohamed Ben Brahim Boukharouba. His father was a small landholder. Boumediene attended both French and Koranic schools in Guelma until the age of fourteen. He then enrolled in the Kettania Medersa, a conservative Moslem school in Constantine. In 1952, he was called up for service in the French army but chose to flee the country rather than serve. He went first to Tunis, then on to Cairo, where he reportedly enrolled at Al-Azhar University. While in Cairo he came in contact with members of the FLN exterior delegation and served as a receptionist in the FLN Cairo office. After the outbreak of the revolution, he dropped his studies and underwent commando training at El-Helouan near Cairo. In early 1955, he went to Morocco and then entered Algeria, joining the maquis in Wilaya Five. He became the military assistant of Abdelhafid Boussouf, commander of Wilaya Five, whom he replaced in October 1957, having attained the rank of colonel. In September 1958, he was named head of the General Staff-West in charge of military operations in Wilayas Four, Five, and Six. In February 1960, he was named head of the unified General Staff of the ALN, probably on Boussouf's recommendation, and set up his headquarters at Gardimaou, Tunisia. In September 1961, he resisted President Ben Khedda's order to disband the General Staff. From then on, he was at odds with the GPRA, and this position led him to join Ben Bella in the summer of 1962. He became minister of defense in September 1962 and a year later first vice-president as well. In April 1964, he was elected to the FLN Political Bureau. After the *coup d'état* of June 19, 1965, he became president of the Revolutionary Council, chief of state, and minister of defense. In December 1967, he added to his other titles that of chief of staff.

Abdelaziz Bouteflika (alias Si Abdelkader el-Mali). Born March 2, 1937, in Oujda on the Moroccan border. His father was the owner of a Turkish bathhouse. He attended French schools in Oujda and then in Tlemcen. He quit school in 1956, when UGEMA, the Algerian nationalist student union, called for a general strike of Algerian students, and joined the maquis in Wilaya Five. He was in the political commissariat of that wilaya and in 1960 was put in charge of opening a new front along the Mali border. He was associ-

ated with the General Staff, and in February 1962 became the contact between the army and Ben Bella, then still in prison in France. He sided with
Boumediene during the summer civil war and became minister of youth,
sports, and tourism in September 1962. In September 1963, he was named
foreign minister and has held that post ever since. He also became a member
of the FLN Political Bureau in April 1964. It was Ben Bella's efforts to remove Bouteflika that triggered the *coup d'état* in June 1965. Bouteflika is
considered to be one of the most astute and ambitious Algerian politicians.
He is supposed to have shaped largely by himself Algeria's foreign policy
after the *coup d'état*.

Cherif Belkacem (alias Si Djamal). Born July 31, 1933, at Beni Mellal,
Morocco, of a bourgeois family. He attended French schools in Morocco and
went on to law school at the University of Rabat. As a student he was
UGEMA's representative in Morocco until he joined the maquis in Wilaya
Five in 1956, becoming head of the Tlemcen sector. At the end of the war,
he was head of the General Staff Command Post-West, and he always remained a close associate of Boumediene's. In September 1962, he was elected
to the National Assembly and was one of the deputies who presented to the
assembly the party-sponsored constitution in August 1963. In September
1963, he was named minister of education and orientation (information),
but in December 1964 he was demoted to minister of education. He became
a member of the FLN Central Committee in April 1964 and was one of the
few outspoken critics of Ben Bella in that body. After the *coup d'état* he was
named coordinator of the FLN Executive Secretariat and remained in that
post until December 1967. He is considered a moderate.

Ahmed Kaid (alias Major Slimane). Born March 17, 1927, near Tiaret of
a bourgeois family. He attended French schools in Tiaret, the French military
school at Hussein-Dey (Algiers), and the School of Education in Algiers. He
belonged for some time to the moderate UDMA nationalist party but joined
the FLN after the outbreak of the war of independence. He was a member
of the General Staff Command Post-West and of the CNRA and finally became assistant chief of staff of the ALN. He sided with the Tlemcen group
during the summer of 1962, and for a time was held prisoner by supporters
of the GPRA in the Constantine region. He was elected to the National Assembly in September 1962. In September 1963, he was named minister of
tourism, but he resigned in December 1964 after Ben Bella accused him of
embezzlement and slapped him in public. He was elected a member of the
FLN Central Committee in April 1964. Immediately after the *coup d'état* he
was the principal spokesman for the Revolutionary Council and in July 1965
was named minister of finance. He held that post until December 1967,
when he was named head of the FLN. He is considered a moderate.

Ahmed Medeghri. Born July 23, 1934, in Oran. He was a teacher at Saïda
when the war broke out. He became assistant to the head of the FLN delegation in Morocco and then joined the ALN. By the end of the war, he was
a major in the General Staff Command Post-West. During the summer of

1962 he served for a short time as prefect of Tlemcen; then in September he was elected to the National Assembly and named minister of the interior. He held that post until forced to resign in July 1964. Medeghri was a member of the FLN Political Bureau. After the *coup* he was again named minister of the interior and still holds that post. He also became acting minister of finance in December 1967. Although not much in the public eye, he is considered a powerful figure in the Cabinet.

Ali Mendjli. Born 1922 at Jemmapes, near Skikda. He belonged to the MTLD nationalist party before joining the FLN in 1954. He fought in the maquis in the eastern Kabylia. By 1958, he was commanding troops along the Tunisian border. In 1959, he became a member of the CNRA and in February 1960, assistant chief of staff at Gardimaou. He represented the ALN at the peace negotiations at Evian. Although close to Boumediene, he has not occupied any prominent posts since independence. He was a deputy and became vice-president of the National Assembly in September 1963. In April 1964, he became a member of the Political Bureau. Since the *coup*, he has held the title of president of the National Assembly, a body that has ceased to function.

THE BEN BELLISTS

Bachir Boumaza. Born November 16, 1927, at Takitount, north of Setif. His father was a small merchant. Working as a carpenter in France, he joined the MTLD and became secretary to its leader, Messali Hadj. He rallied to the FLN early in the war and helped to organize the FLN Federation of France, of which he became the leader. He was arrested in December 1958 but escaped from Frèsnes Prison in October 1961. He was co-author of *La Gangrène*, a book describing the tortures Algerian political prisoners underwent at the hands of the French. He sided with Ben Bella during the struggle for power in the summer of 1962 and was named minister of labor and social affairs in September 1962. A year later, he was made minister of industry, one of the most important posts in the Cabinet, and remained in that position until the *coup*. Boumaza was also a member of the Political Bureau. Considered a Marxist, he was one of Ben Bella's key aides; however, he joined the Boumediene Cabinet after the *coup* and was given the lesser post of minister of information. He soon found himself in disagreement with Boumediene and fled the country in October 1966 to join the OCRA, an opposition party based in Luxembourg. He was expelled from the council in October 1966.

Ali Mahsas. Born November 17, 1923, at Bouzaréah (Algiers). A member of the terrorist Organisation Secrète of the MTLD, he was arrested together with Ben Bella in 1950 for his participation in the holdup of the Oran Post Office in 1948. He escaped from Blida Prison along with Ben Bella in March 1952 and fled to France, where he became an organizer of the FLN Federation. He joined Ben Bella in Cairo in 1954 and worked with him to procure arms for the ALN. After Ben Bella's arrest in 1956, Mahsas fell into disgrace with the leaders of the FLN and fled to West Germany, where he remained in exile until he rejoined Ben Bella at Tlemcen in 1962. In April 1963, he became head of the ONRA and in September 1963 minister of agriculture and agrarian reform. He was also named to the Political Bureau in April 1964. Mahsas was considered one of Ben Bella's closest allies. Nonetheless, he remained minister of agriculture after the *coup*. In August 1966, he fled the country and joined the opposition abroad. He was officially expelled from the Revolutionary Council in October 1966.

THE WILAYA COMMANDERS

Mohand ou el-Hadj. Born March 7, 1912, at Bouzghen in the Kabylia. His real name is Mokrane Belhadj. He was a landowner and a merchant before the war. He joined the maquis in Wilaya Three in November 1955. He became military assistant to the commander of that wilaya in January 1958 and political assistant in January 1959. In April 1959, he became commander of Wilaya Three and remained in the maquis until the end of the war. He was promoted to colonel in March 1960. During the summer of 1962, he sided with the GPRA and fought against Boumediene's troops. Nonetheless, he became a deputy and remained commander of the Kabylia (new Seventh Military Region). In September 1963, he joined the FFS rebellion and was stripped of his command. A month later, he rallied to the government and was named to the Political Bureau in April 1964. He joined Boumediene in the plot against Ben Bella and was made a member of the FLN Executive Secretariat in July 1965. He was ousted from the secretariat in December 1967 and apparently backed Zbiri in the attempted *coup* against Boumediene. Although a well-known figure in the Kabylia, where he is affectionately called "Le Vieux," he is no longer considered to have much political influence.

Salah Boubnider (alias Saout el-Arab [Voice of the Arabs]). Born in 1925 at Oued Zenati, near Constantine. He was a waiter in a Moorish cafe before joining the FLN in late 1954. By early 1958, he was military assistant to the commander of Wilaya Two and became a member of the CNRA in late 1958. He became commander of Wilaya Two in October 1959 and was promoted to colonel in January 1962. During the summer civil war of 1962, he was deposed from his command by pro-Ben Bella troops but was later reinstated as commissar for political and administrative affairs of Wilaya Two. He subsequently left the army and was arrested in the summer of 1963 for subversive activities. After his release in November 1963, he was named Algeria's representative to the United Arab Command in Cairo. He is said to have been involved in organizing the *coup* against Ben Bella. Appointed to the FLN Executive Secretariat, he became the principal rival of Belkacem. He is considered an Arabist and has played an important role in establishing close relations between the FLN and the Syrian Baath party.

Youcef Khatib (alias Si Hassan). Born in 1932 at Orléansville. He was a second-year medical student at the University of Algiers when UGEMA, the nationalist student union, called for a strike of all Algerian students in 1956. He joined the maquis in Wilaya Four, serving as a doctor, and by 1959 was the head of the health service of that wilaya. He was promoted to major in

July 1961 and in July 1962 became commander of Wilaya Four with the rank of colonel. During the summer civil war, he fought against Boumediene's troops and then left the army to finish his studies. Although a member of the National Assembly and later of the FLN Political Bureau, he did not play a prominent political role until the *coup d'état.* In July 1965, he became a member of the FLN Executive Secretariat, continuing at the same time to pursue his medical studies. He was dismissed from the secretariat in December 1967.

Mohamed Tayebi (alias Si Larbi). Born December 17, 1918, at Sidi-Bel-Abbès. He was a merchant before the war began. He fought in Wilaya Five from 1957 to 1959, becoming head of Zone III in that wilaya. In late 1959, he had a nervous breakdown and was given a minor post in the General Staff Command Post-West. In September 1962, he was elected deputy to the National Assembly. Between 1962 and 1965, he served as ambassador to Havana, head of national security, and then ambassador to Brazil. He was also a member of the Central Committee. After the *coup* he became a member of the FLN Executive Secretariat but did not play a prominent role. He was dismissed from that post in December 1967. He should not be confused with the Si Larbi who was commander of the Sixth Military Region (Constantine), whose full name is Ben Redjem Larbi.

Mohammedi Saïd. Born in 1912 in the Kabylia. He worked in Belgium and France and during World War Two served first in the French army and then in the German Army. In 1944, he was parachuted into Tunisia as a German agent. Captured by the French near Tebessa in eastern Algeria, he agreed to serve in the French secret service but was finally condemned to hard labor for life. He was finally freed in 1952. In 1955, he joined the maquis in Wilaya Three, and thanks to his military training rose quickly to become commander of Wilaya Three in August 1956. He was also a member of the CNRA. After a year as commander of Wilaya Three, he went to Cairo for advanced military training. In April 1958, he was named head of the General Staff-East but left that post in December 1959 to become minister of state in the GPRA. At the Tripoli meeting in May 1962, he was named to the Political Bureau. Saïd did not play an important role either before or after the *coup d'état.* He apparently owes his appointments to the desire of both Ben Bella and Boumediene to have a "loyal Kabyle" in the regime. He is noted for his strong religious convictions.

Benhaddou Bouhadjar (alias Si Othmane). Born in 1927 at Aïn Temouchent, near Oran. He was a farm worker before the war. A member of the Organization Secrète of the MTLD, he was arrested for terrorist activities in June 1950 and not released until May 1953. He joined the FLN in November 1954 and rose through the ranks of Wilaya Five to become its commander in September 1960 and a colonel the following month. He remained commander of Wilaya Five until independence. He gave his support to Ben

Bella during the summer civil war. He served for a short time as chief of staff of the ANP after December 1962. In May 1963, he became Ben Bella's military chef de cabinet and in October 1963 head of the FLN Federation of Oran. In April 1964, he was named to the FLN Central Committee while continuing as head of the Oran Federation. After the *coup*, he remained active in the FLN but did not play a prominent role in national politics.

Tahar Zbiri. Born in 1920 at Oued Keberit, near Annaba. At the age of sixteen, he began working at the Ouenza Mine. He participated in the first ALN attacks on November 1, 1954, at Guelma. He was captured and imprisoned in early 1955 but escaped from the prison in Constantine in November of the same year. He fought in Wilayas One and Two and along the Tunisian frontier until September 1958. He was a member of the General Staff Command Post-West until June 1960, when he broke through the Morice Line and returned to Wilaya One, of which he became commander in January 1961. He was promoted to colonel in September 1961. During the summer civil war, he sided with the Tlemcen group. He remained commander of Wilaya One until early 1963. In October 1963, Ben Bella named him chief of staff without consulting Boumediene. However, Zbiri was won over to Boumediene's side and personally arrested Ben Bella on June 19, 1965. He remained chief of staff, although he really never had operational control over the ANP. He was finally stripped of his command in December 1967 after attempting a *coup d'état* against Boumediene. Zbiri was considered to be a leftist and supporter of self-management.

COMMANDERS OF THE MILITARY REGIONS

Abid Said. Born December 10, 1933, at Sedrata in eastern Algeria. After fighting in the maquis in eastern Algeria, in 1960 he became head of military operations for southern Tunisia in the General Staff Command Post-East. In late 1962, he became assistant to Zbiri in the Fifth Military Region and succeeded him as commander with the rank of major in March 1963. During the FFS rebellion in the Kabylia, he was in command of ANP operations against the rebels. In June 1964, he was named head of the First Military Region with headquarters in Blida. After the *coup d'état*, he was reportedly entrusted with guarding Ben Bella. In December 1967, he committed suicide during Zbiri's rebellion. Said was considered the most able field commander in the ANP. He had considerable influence in the army and, after the *coup*, considerable political influence in the Algiers region.

Abdellah Belhouchet. Born June 1, 1924, at M'Daourouch (Sedrata). He was a sergeant in the French army before joining the ALN. He fought in Wilayas One and Two before being transferred to Tunisia. In 1958, he was involved in the "conspiracy of the colonels" against the GPRA and was arrested in January 1959 by the Tunisian army at the request of the ALN. Released from prison in October 1960, he joined Bouteflika in the maquis being organized along the Mali border and subsequently became military commander of that maquis. During the summer civil war, he sided with the

Tlemcen group and later became the first head of the commando school at the Cherchell Military Academy. In 1963, he was head of the FLN Federation for the department of the Saoura but rejoined the ANP during the border war with Morocco. In June 1964, he was named commander of the Fifth Military Region with headquarters in Constantine. He became an extremely powerful political figure in the Constantine region after the *coup.* In December 1967, he was named commander of the First Military Region after Major Said committed suicide. He holds the rank of major.

Benjedid Chedli. Born in 1929 at Sebaa, near Bone. He fought during the war in Wilaya Two along the Tunisian border and attained the rank of major. In February 1963, he replaced Major Si Larbi as commander of the Sixth Military Region (Constantine), and in June 1964 he was named commander of the Second Military Region (Oran), where he has remained to date. He has been a minor political figure and a loyal officer of the ANP.

Salah Yahiaoui. He fought in Wilaya One during the war, attaining the rank of captain. He became a national commissar of the FLN in October 1962 but later returned to the ANP and was named assistant director of the Cherchell Military Academy. In April 1964, he was made a member of the FLN Central Committee. In December 1965, he was put in command of the Third Military Region (Colomb-Bechar).

Mohamed Ben Ahmed Abdelghrani. He fought during the war in Wilaya Five and in 1959 was in charge of sending ALN troops across the Morice Line. He attained the rank of captain in the ALN. In May 1963, he became commander of the First Military Region (Blida) and was proposed by Boumediene for the position of chief of staff. In 1965, he was named head of the newly formed armored battalion stationed at Sidi-Bel-Abbès and in March of that year became head of the Fourth Military Region (Ouargla).

Salah Soufi. Born January 1, 1933, at Sedrata in eastern Algeria. He was a corporal in the French army before joining the FLN and the GPRA in 1958. During the war, he was considered to be extremely anti-Boumediene. At the end of the war, he commanded ALN forces stationed in southern Tunisia. In September 1962, he was elected to the National Assembly and became a member of the Armed Forces Committee. In 1964, he was in charge of relations with the national organizations in the FLN Federation of Annaba. In June 1964, he became commander of the Third Military Region (Colomb-Bechar) and held that post until December 1965. He has no important post in the ANP today.

HIGH-RANKING ARMY OFFICERS

Ahmed Bencherif. Born April 25, 1927, at Djelfa in central Algeria. He was a sergeant in the French army when the war broke out. He attended officers school at Saint Maixemet, France. In 1957, he was a second lieutenant stationed at Cherchell and was attending the Cherchell Military Academy when he was arrested for providing arms to the ALN. In

July 1957, he defected from the French army and joined the ALN in Wilaya Four. In 1958, with the rank of captain, he headed an ALN military school at Khablani in Tunisia. He returned to the maquis in 1959 and in July 1960 became commander of Wilaya Four with the rank of major, and a member of the CNRA. In October 1960, he was captured and condemned to death, but he escaped execution because of the intervention of the International Red Cross. He remained in prison until the signing of the Evian Agreements and then returned to the maquis in Wilaya Six, having been promoted to the rank of colonel. On September 17, 1962, he became head of the gendarmerie, a post he has held ever since. In April 1964, he became a member of the Central Committee. He played a key role in the execution of the *coup d'état*. He is considered a powerful figure in the ANP.

Ahmed Draia (alias Si Ahmed). Born May 10, 1929, at Souk Ahras in eastern Algeria. He joined the ALN early in the war and was involved in the "conspiracy of the colonels" against the GPRA. Arrested by the Tunisian army in 1958, he spent two years in prison. After his liberation he was sent to Mali to help organize a maquis in southwestern Algeria. After independence he commanded ANP forces in that area. In September 1963, he joined the Compagnie Nationale de Sécurité and was made head of security at the presidency in March 1965. In May of the same year, he was named commander of the CNS, a post he still holds today. He is considered close to Boumediene.

Abderrahmane Bensalem (alias Si Abderrahmane). Born in 1923 at Chiebra, near the Tunisian border. As an officer in the French army he fought in Italy and Indochina, earning numerous citations for bravery. He deserted to the ALN in March 1956. By November 1956, he had left Algeria and was political and military chief of ALN troops at Aïn Sraia, Tunisia. In December 1958, as a captain, he was put in charge of ALN operations in northern Tunisia and was stationed at Gardimaou. He strongly supported the ALN General Staff against the GPRA in the summer of 1962. He was elected to the National Assembly and became a member of the Armed Forces Committee. In March 1964, he was named to the General Staff of the ANP and a month later he became a member of the FLN Central Committee. He is still a member of the General Staff and head of the Quartier Général of Algiers. He has had little formal education but is considered an important member of the staff and extremely loyal to Boumediene.

Ahmed Boudjenane (alias Abbas). Born June 1, 1929, at Ouled Ali, near Tlemcen. He was a member of the MTLD and was forced to flee to Morocco in 1948. He studied at the Islamic University of Karaouiyyin in Fes until 1952, when he was thrown out of Morocco and returned to Algeria. In 1954, he joined the FLN and fought during the war in Wilaya Five, becoming commander of Zone II and a captain. He was acting commander of Wilaya Five for a time but was demoted to second lieutenant in 1961 when he refused to go through the Morice Line along the Moroccan border. He sided with the Tlemcen group in the summer of 1962 and became head of the Second Military Region (Oran) in late 1962. He was also active in the FLN Federation of Oran. In March 1964, he was named to the General Staff and also became director of the Cherchell Military Academy. He remained a member of the General Staff and director of the academy until his death in an automobile accident January 17, 1968. He is considered to have had a great deal of influence with Boumediene and to have been one of his closest friends.

Abdelkader Moulay (alias Chabou). Born about 1924 of a rich family of the Oran region. He attended French schools and after obtaining his baccalauréat he went on to the French army cavalry school at Bou Saada. After eighteen years in the French army, he had the rank of major, reportedly the highest rank attained by any Algerian officer in the French army. He was stationed in Germany when he deserted along with several other Algerian officers in 1958. He then joined the ALN in Morocco and remained in the outside army until the end of the war. After independence, he became chef de cabinet of the Ministry of Defense, a position he still holds. In March 1964, he was also named to the General Staff. Although he did not hold the title of chief of staff, he took over many of the responsibilities of that position.

aLGERIan aRmeÒ foRces in 1967

Total Armed Forces: 75,000[*]
Defense Budget: roughly $100 million annually (about 15 per cent of the total administrative budget).

Army (chief of staff: Colonel Tahar Zbiri)[†]
   Total strength: 60,000
   One motorized division and a second division in formation.
   Up to 50 independent infantry battalions
   4 or 5 tank battalions with Soviet T-34 and T-54 tanks and SU-100 self-propelled assault guns; a total of 300 to 350 tanks
   15 artillery batteries
   2 or 3 anti-aircraft batteries
   Armament includes 152mm cannons, 120mm and 160mm mortars, 240mm rocket launchers, and SA-2 surface-to-air missiles.
   The ANP is believed to have at least 300 T-34 and T-54 tanks and SU-100 guns.

Gendarmerie (commander: Colonel Ahmed Bencherif)
   Total strength: 10,000
   Some motorized units using French Panhard armored cars

Air Force (commander: Captain Said Ait Messaoudéne)
   Total strength: 3,500
   About 100 combat planes including MIG-15, MIG-17, and MIG-21 jet fighters; Ilyuchin-28 light bombers[‡]
   About 12 Antonov-12 Antonov-14 turboprop transports
   About 50 Mi-1 and Mi-4 helicopters
   30 to 40 Yak trainers

Navy (commander: Captain Si Ben Moussa)
   Total strength: 1,500
   3 submarine chasers
   1 coastal minesweeper
   8 motor torpedo boats (P-6 class)
   About 6 missile-launching boats (Komar class)

[*] Obligatory military training for all university and high school students was instituted in July 1967; See *Journal Officiel*, No. 60, July 25, 1967, Ordonnance 67-124, July 8, 1967. Students will probably constitute a reserve force.
[†] Replaced by Colonel Boumediene on December 14, 1967.
[‡] The number of combat planes had increased to 200, including 150 MIG's, by late 1968.

Foreign Aid

Nearly all heavy armament in the Algerian armed forces is of Soviet origin. Algeria is estimated to have spent about $250 million for the purchase of Soviet arms, buying them on long-term credits. France has trained and equipped the gendarmerie and has also trained some naval and army officers. Around 2,000 army and air force officers have attended schools in the Soviet Union. Several hundred Algerian officers have gone to Egypt for training and a few to Communist China. England has trained a few naval officers.

Top Officers of the National People's Army

Defense Ministry: Colonel Houari Boumediene, minister of defense, and Major Abdelkader Moulay (alias Chabou), chef de cabinet.

General Staff: Colonel Tahar Zbiri, chief of staff;† Major Chabou; Major Abderrahmane Bensalem; and Colonel Almed Boudjenane (alias Abbas).§ Other top officers: Major Slimane Hoffman, commander of the Tank Corps; Major Zerguini, associated with the General Staff; Major Hachemi, head of the Political Commissariat.

Military Regions: Commanders and Headquarters.

1. Major Abid Said,‖ Blida
2. Major Benjedid Chedli, Oran
3. Major Salah Yahiaoui, Colomb Bechar-Western Sahara
4. Major Mohamed Abdelghrani, Ouargla-Eastern Sahara
5. Major Abdellah Belhouchet, Constantine

Military Schools and Their Locations

Engineers, Hussein Dey (Soviets) and Cap Matifou (French); tank drivers, Batna; pilots, Cheragas and Ouargla; artillery gunners, Telergma; commandos, Skikda; communications operators, Bouzareah; truck drivers, Beni Messous; NCO's, Boghari; gendarmes, Sidi-Bel-Abbes; meharists, Ouargla; cavalry, Lido; cadets, Kolea; officers, Cherchell; political commissars, Algiers; anti-aircraft and missile experts, Reghaia; naval cadets, Algiers; mechanics, carpenters, and technicians, El-Harrach.

---

† Replaced by Coloniel Boumediene on December 14, 1967.

§ Killed in an automobile accident January 17, 1968.

‖ Committed suicide December 14, 1967. He was replaced by Belhouchet on December 18. Belhouchet in turn was replaced by Abdelghrani, who was installed as commander of the Fifth Military Region December 29, 1967.

selected bibliography

selected bibliography

Most of the material for this book was collected from firsthand sources in Algeria: interviews, conversations, and pamphlets and mimeographed papers not available in libraries. Little of the material is taken from books or printed material available to outsiders. The works listed here mainly provided background information. The books have been divided into two categories: the first includes historical works generally well documented, although sometimes biased; the second includes works of a clearly partisan nature, interesting for the point of view expressed rather than for the information contained therein.

HISTORICAL BOOKS

Barbour, Nevill, ed. *A Survey of North West Africa.* London: Oxford University Press, 1962.

Bedjaoui, Mohammed. *La Révolution Algérienne et le Droit.* Brussels: Association Internationale des Juristes Démocrats, 1961.

Behr, Edward. *The Algerian Problem.* London: Hodder and Stoughton, 1961.

Berque, Jacques. *Le Maghreb entre Deux Guerres.* Paris: Editions du Seuil, 1962.

Bourdieu, Pierre. *The Algerians.* Boston: Beacon Press, 1962. Original French ed., *Sociologie de l'Algérie.* Paris: Presses Universitaires de France, 1958.

Clark, Michael. *Algeria in Turmoil.* New York: Praeger, 1959.

D'Arcy, François, Annie Krieger, and Alain Marill. *Essais sur l'Economie de l'Algérie Nouvelle.* Paris: Presses Universitaires de France, 1965.

Duchemin, Jacques. *Histoire du F.L.N.* Paris: la Table Ronde, 1962.

Favrod, Charles-Henri. *La Révolution Algérienne.* Paris. Plon, 1959.

Gallagher, Charles F. *The United States and North Africa.* Cambridge, Mass.: Harvard University Press, 1963.

Gendarme, René. *L'Economie de l'Algérie.* Paris: Armand Colin, 1959.

Gillespie, Joan. *Algeria: Rebellion and Revolution.* London: Ernest Benn, 1960.

Gordon, David C. *North Africa's French Legacy.* Cambridge, Mass.: Harvard University Press, 1962.

———. *The Passing of French Algeria.* London: Oxford University Press, 1966.

Humbaraci, Arslan. *Algeria: A Revolution that Failed.* New York: Praeger, 1966.

Ibn Khaldoun. *La Muquaddima.* Extracts translated by Georges Labica. Algiers: Hachette, 1965.

——. *The Muqaddimah.* 3 vols. Translated by Franz Rosenthal. Princeton: Princeton University Press, 1967.

Julien, Charles-André. *Histoire de l'Afrique de Nord: De la Conquète Arabe à 1830.* 2d ed. Paris: Payot, 1956.

——. *L'Afrique du Nord en Marche.* 2d. ed. Paris: Juillard, 1953.

Kraft, Michael. *The Struggle for Algeria.* New York: Doubleday, 1961.

Lacoste, Yves. *Ibn Khaldoun.* Paris: Maspero, 1966.

——. André Nouschi, and André Prenant. *L'Algérie Passé et Présent.* Paris: Editions Sociales, 1960.

Launay, Michel. *Paysans Algériens.* Paris: Editions du Seuil, 1963.

Le Tourneau, Roger. *Evolution Politique de l'Afrique du Nord Musulmane.* Paris: Armand Colin, 1962.

Mandouze, André. *La Révolution Algérienne par les Textes.* Paris: Maspero, 1961.

Opperman, Thomas. *Le Problème Algérien.* Paris: Maspero, 1961. Original German ed., *Die Algerische Frage.* Stuttgart: Kohlammer Verlag, 1959.

Teillac, Jean. *Autogestion en Algérie.* Paris: Peyronnet, 1965.

PARTISAN BOOKS

Abbas, Ferhat. *Le Jeune Algérien.* Paris: Jeune Parque, 1931.

——. *La Nuit Coloniale.* Paris. Juillard, 1962.

Ait Ahmed, Hocine. *La Guerre et l'Après-Guerre.* Paris: Editions de Minuit, 1964.

Alleg, Henri. *La Question.* Paris: Editions de Minuit, 1958.

Arab, Bessaoud Mohamed. *Heureux les Martyrs Qui n'ont Rien Vu.* Colombes: By the Author, 1963.

——. *F.F.S.: Espoir et Trahison.* Colombes: By the Author, 1966.

Bennabi, Malek. *Perspectives Algériennes.* Algiers: Editions En-Nahda, 1964.

——. *Memoires d'un Temoin du Siècle.* Algiers: Editions Nationales Algériennes, 1965.

Boudiaf, Mohamed. *Où va l'Algérie?.* Paris: Librairie de l'Etoile, 1964.

Bourges, Hervé. *L'Algérie à l'Epreuve du Pouvoir.* Paris: Editions Grasset, 1967.

Camus, Albert. *Actuelles, III: Chronique Algérienne 1939–1958.* Paris: Gallimard, 1958.

Cercle Taleb-Moumié. *Fidel Castro ou Tschombé? La Voie Algérienne vers le Socialisme.* Paris: Maspero, 1962.

Chaliand, Gérard. *L'Algérie est-elle Socialiste?* Paris: Maspero, 1964.

Fanon, Frantz. *L'An V de la Révolution Algérienne.* Paris: Maspero, 1960.

——. *The Wretched of the Earth.* Translated by Constance Farrington. New York: Grove Press, 1966. Original French ed., *Les Damnés de la Terre.* Paris: Maspero, 1961.

Feraoun, Mouloud. *Journal 1955–1962.* Paris: Editions du Seuil, 1962.

Hadj Ali, Bachir. *Qu-est-ce que c'est qu'un Révolutionnaire Algérien en 1963?* Paris: Editions Sociales, 1963.

——. *L'Arbitraire.* Paris: Editions de Minuit, 1966.

Keramane, Hafid. *La Pacification*. Lausanne: La Cité, 1960.
Khaldi, Abdelaziz. *Le Problème Algérien*. Algiers: Editions En-Nahda, 1946.
Khelifa, Laroussi. *Manuel du Militant Algérien*. Lausanne: La Cité, 1962.
Lacheraf, Mostefa. *L'Algérie: Nation et Société*. Paris: Maspero, 1965.
Lentin, Albert-Paul. *Le Dernier Quart d'Heure*. Paris: Juillard, 1963.
Merle, Robert. *Ahmed Ben Bella*. Paris: Gallimard, 1965.
M'Rabet, Fadela. *La Femme Algérienne*. Paris: Maspero, 1965.
Nora, Pierre. *Les Français d'Algérie*. Paris: Juillard, 1961.
Ouzegane, Amar. *Le Meilleur Combat*. Paris: Juillard, 1962.
Sahli, Mohamed. *Décoloniser l'Histoire*. Paris: Maspero, 1965.
Taleb, Ahmed. *Lettres de Prison: 1957–1961*. Algiers: Editions Nationales Algériennes, 1966.
Tillion, Germaine. *France and Algeria: Complementary Enemies*. New York: Alfred Knopf, 1961. Original French ed., *Les Ennemies Complémentaires*. Paris: Editions de Minuit, 1960.
A Travers les Wilayas d'Algérie. Tunis: Front de Libération Nationale, 1960.
Yacef, Saadi. *Souvenirs de la Bataille d'Alger*. Paris: Juillard, 1962.

ALGERIAN NEWSPAPERS AND PERIODICALS

Unless otherwise indicated, the periodicals listed below are in French.

Government Dailies

There has been one morning French-language daily in Algiers since independence. It was called *Al-Chaab* from September 1962 to February 1963. It became *Le Peuple* in March 1963 and continued under that name until June 1965. Since then it has been called *El-Moudjahid*.

There is just one Arabic-language daily in the entire country, *Al-Chaab*. It has been published in Algiers since September 1962. *Al-Chaab* is mostly, but not entirely, a translation of the French-language newspaper.

An afternoon daily, *Alger Ce-Soir*, was published in Algiers from April 1964 until September 1965.

A morning daily, *An-Nasr*, has been published in Constantine since September 1963. In Oran a morning daily called *La République* has appeared since March 1963.

Other Dailies

The Algerian Communist party published a daily called *Alger Républicain* from July 1962 to June 1965. After April 1964, the Communist daily was supposedly an FLN publication, but in fact it remained independent until it was banned in June 1965.

FLN Publications

The French-language magazine *El-Moudjahid* was first published in early 1956 and appeared irregularly until July 1956 when it became a weekly. It was published in Tunis until the end of the war and then in Algiers until July 1964 when it was discontinued. It was replaced by *Révolution Africaine*, which was founded in February 1963. This weekly was for a time semi-independent, but it gradually came under party control and was finally proclaimed the official organ of the FLN in October 1965.

Since independence the FLN has also published an Arabic-language weekly called *El-Moudjahid*. This is not a translation of the French-language weekly but a separate publication.

The JFLN, the party youth organization, published a number of short-lived magazines. The first of these was *Jeunesse Algérienne*, which appeared only once in April 1963. It was followed by *Le Jeune Algérien*, which was published from November 1963 to February 1964. A new publication, *Jeunesse Sport*, appeared from June 1964 to September 1964. At the latter date, it became *Jeunesse* and was published under that name until June 1965. Since then the JFLN has had no publication.

Publications of Other National Organizations

The UGTA published *L'Ouvrier Algérien* irregularly from August 1962 to November 1962. In February 1963, it started a new publication, the weekly *Révolution et Travail*. This weekly was banned in March 1966 and did not reappear until April 1967. It was then published as a semiweekly until August 1967, when it was again banned for several months.

UNEA, the student union, published irregularly a magazine called *Révolution à l'Université* from November 1962 to November 1963. A new edition of the same magazine appeared from December 1963 to August 1964. A new magazine, *Révolution et Université*, has appeared very irregularly since May 1966.

The ANP Political Commissariat has published a monthly magazine called *El-Djeich* since 1963. The magazine is written for the general public rather than just for members of the armed forces.

Other Algerian Periodicals

Acualité et Documents, a bimonthly publication of the Ministry of Information. It reprints official speeches and publishes the most important decrees of the government.

L'Algérie Agricole, a monthly publication of the Ministry of Agriculture and Agrarian Reform, contains statistics and studies on the farm sector. It began to appear in 1963.

Bulletin Mensuel de Statistique Générale, a monthly publication of the Office of Economic Studies in the Ministry of Industry.

Humanisme Musulman, a publication of the religious association Al-Qiyam Al-Islamiyyah. It began to appear in January 1965 as a monthly but soon became a semimonthly.

Information Rapide, a monthly bulletin published by the Secrétariat Social d'Alger, an organization run by the French Pères Blancs. The Secrétariat Social also publishes sociological and economic studies on Algeria.

Journal Officiel de la République Algérienne Démocratique et Populaire, the official journal of laws, decrees, ordinances, and other official acts of the Algerian government. It has appeared several times a week since September 1962.

Office des Nouvelles Algériennes, an independent weekly bulletin of economic studies. It contains some of the few available statistics on the Algerian economy.

Revue Algérienne des Sciences Juridiques, Politiques, et Economiques, a quarterly publication of the Faculty of Law and Economics at the University of Algiers. It began to appear in January 1964.

Revue Algérienne du Travail, the quarterly publication of the Ministry of Labor and Social Affairs. The first issue appeared in January 1967.

Revue de Presse, a review of the North African and Middle Eastern press published monthly in Algiers by the Pères Blancs.

FOREIGN PERIODICALS

Annuaire de l'Afrique du Nord, published by the Centre des Recherches sur l'Afrique Méditerranéenne, Editions du Centre Nationale de la Recherche Scientifique, Paris.

Jeune Afrique, an independent Tunisian weekly published in Rome, Italy.

Le Monde, an independent daily published in Paris. It offers the best coverage of North African affairs of any foreign daily.

Maghreb, a semimonthly publication of the Foundation Nationale des Sciences Politiques, Paris.

Maghreb Digest, published by the University of Southern California, Los Angeles. Originally a monthly review of the North African press, it became a quarterly in January 1967.

DOCUMENTS

Chambre de Commerce et d'Industrie d'Alger. *Situation Economique de l'Algérie 1964,* Algiers, 1965.

Front de Libération Nationale. *La Charte d'Alger.* Algiers, 1964.

––––. *Projet de Programme pour la Réalisation de la Révolution Démocratique Populaire* (Tripoli Program). Algiers, 1962.

Journal Officiel de la République Francaise. *Algérie: Accord de Cessez-le-feu, Déclarations Gouvernementales du 19 Mars 1962.* Décret No. 62–43, March 1962.

Ministère de l'Economie National. *Revue du Plan et des Etudes Economiques: Situation Economique en 1963.* No. 1. April 1964. No other issue of the review appeared.

Ministère de l'Information. *Algerie An II: 1962–1964.* Annaba, 1964.

––––. *L'Autogestion en Algérie.* Annaba, 1966.

————. *Une Année de Révolution Socialiste.* Algiers, 1963.

————. *Discours du Président Ben Bella: September 28, 1962 to December 12, 1962.* Algiers, 1963.

————. *Discours du Président Ben Bella: January 5, 1963 to March 30, 1964.* Annaba, 1964.

————. *Discours du Président Boumediene: June 19, 1965 to April 22, 1966.* Algiers, 1966.

————. *Documents sur l'Autogestion.* Algiers, 1963.

————. *Documents sur l'Autogestion.* Algiers, 1964.

————. *Le Secteur Socialiste Industriel.* Annaba, n.d.

Présidence de la République Algérienne. *Traités et Conventions de l'Algérie: Accords Algéro-Francais.* Algiers, 1963.

Secrétariat d'Etat Chargé des Affaires Algériennes. *Accord entre la République Française et la République Algérienne Démocratique et Populaire Concernant le Règlement de Questions Touchant les Hydracarbures et le Développement Industriel de l'Algérie.* Paris, 1965.

Service de la Statistique Générale de la Délégation Générale en Algérie. *Tableau de l'Economie Algérienne: 1960.* Algiers, n.d. This study contains the latest accurate figures concerning the Algerian economy.

Union Générale des Travailleurs Algériens. *Deuxième Congrès UGTA: Ensemble des Textes Adoptés.* Algiers, 1965.

index

index

Abbas, Ferhat, 13, 14 n., 19, 24, 70, 78, 102, 118, 184, 193
Abdelghrani, Mohamed Ben Ahmed: biography, 302
Abdelkader, Emir, 28, 214
Abdesslam, Belaid, 219, 220, 228, 249, 257, 264, 276, 280
Administration: structure, 41 n., 83 ff., 210, 262; civil service, 83 ff., 120, 211, 257 f.; purge, 85; cost, 85 f., 210; decentralization, 214, 262 ff., 271. *See also* Communes
African Liberation Committee, 163 n., 279
African liberation movements, 163 f., 168, 232
African opposition groups, 164, 171, 246
African unity, 146, 162 f.
Afro-Asian Conference, 159, 172 f., 202
Afro-Asian People's Solidarity Organization (AAPSO), 145, 156, 160, 168, 172
Agrarian reform, 122, 203, 214, 215 f.
Agriculture, 39 ff., 216; land ownership, 40 n., 216 n. *See also* Socialist sector
Ait Ahmed, Hocine, 16, 18, 19, 73, 79, 81, 88, 94 ff., 101, 104, 118, 185, 220
Al-Fatah, 279
Algerian Communist Party, 89 ff., 124, 129, 180, 182, 189, 233
Algerian Moslem Boy Scouts, 131, 190
Algerian press, 90 f., 124, 183
Algerian Socialism, 67 f., 70 f., 81 ff., 107 f., 119 f., 142 f., 146, 175 f., 181 f., 197. *See also* Self-management
Algiers, 33 f.
Ali Yahia, Abdennour, 219, 252
Alleg, Henri, 89, 91, 124, 183 n.
Arab-Israeli War, 235, 247 ff.
Arab Socialist Union, 242, 243
Arab summit conferences, 169, 242, 248
Arif, Abdel Rahman, 248
Armaments. *See* Armée Nationale Populaire
Armée de Liberation Nationale (ALN):

general staff, 15, 16 n., 19; strength, 15; reconversion, 22 f., 24, 178
Armée Nationale Populaire (ANP): 24, 121, 197 ff., 305 f.; mutinies, 92 f., 97, 100, 103, 178 n., 252; and FLN, 117 ff., 121, 123, 199, 203, 222; political commissariat, 123, 199; arms, 158, 161, 235, 240, 305 f.; cadres, 161, 178, 198, 235, 240, 275, 301 ff., 305 f.; farms, 199
Asabiya, 5 ff., 282

Baath Party, 242
Bandung Conference, 159
Bank: central, 85; state, 109, 110, 113, 203, 267, 268
Bedjaoui, Mohamed, 219
Belhouchet, Abdellah, 15 n., 222, 223; biography, 301
Belkacem, Cherif, 180, 187, 192, 194, 207, 234, 253; biography, 297
Ben Alla, Hadj, 18, 106, 159, 186
Ben Badis, Cheikh 'Abd el-Hamid, 47
Ben Bella, Ahmed: in civil war, 16, 18, 19, 23; and National Assembly, 24, 72 f.; and UGTA, 57 f., 124, 134, 137 ff., 182; conflict with Khider, 58, 74 ff.; and FLN, 58, 73 f., 75 f., 118 f.; style of rule, 59, 63, 81 ff., 107, 142, 174 f.; conflict with Boumediene, 77 n., 80, 117 f., 122, 124, 176 ff.; conflict with Abbas, 78 f.; as President, 79 f., 175 f.; power of, 80 ff., 175 f., 197, 253; and FFS, 96 ff., 100 f., 104 f., 184 f.; popularity of, 106, 114, 175, 183; and UNEA, 124, 129; trip to USSR, 125, 159 f.; foreign policy, 145 ff., 161 f., 170 f., 172 f.; ouster, 185 ff., 223. *See also* Opposition
Bencherif, Ahmed: biography, 302
Ben Khedda, Benyoucef, 14 n., 17 n., 18, 19, 20, 80, 118
Ben M'hidi, Larbi, 14 n.
Bensalem Abderrahmane: biography, 303

DATE DUE

5/26			
GAYLORD			PRINTED IN U.S.A.